WONDERBOOK

Design by Jeremy Zerfoss,
Jeff VanderMeer, & John Coulthart

WONDERBOOK·
AN ILLUSTRATED
GUIDE TO CREATING
IMAGINATIVE FICTION
JEFF VANDERMEER

ART BY JEREMY ZERFOSS

(AND MANY OTHERS)

Abrams Image – New York

Editor: David Cashion
Designers: Jeremy Zerfoss, Jeff VanderMeer, John Coulthart
Production Manager: Erin Vandeveer

Library of Congress Control Number: 2013936041

ISBN: 978-1-4197-0442-0

Printed and bound in China
10 9 8 7 6 5 4 3 2 1

Abrams Image books are available at special discounts when purchased in quantity for premiums and promotions as well as fundraising or educational use. Special editions can also be created to specification. For details, contact specialsales@abramsbooks.com or the address below.

THE ART OF BOOKS SINCE 1949
115 West 18th Street
New York, NY 10011
www.abramsbooks.com

TABLE OF CONTENTS

Chapter 4: Narrative Design

Chapter 5: Characterization

Chapter 6: Worldbuilding

Chapter 7: Revision

Essays: "Thoughts on Revision" by Lev Grossman (p. 265), "Finding My Way" by Karen Joy Fowler (p. 275)

Spotlight on: Peter Straub (p. 258)

Writing Challenge: Transformation by Increments (p. 260)

Acknowledgments & Credits

Art by Myrtle Von Damitz III

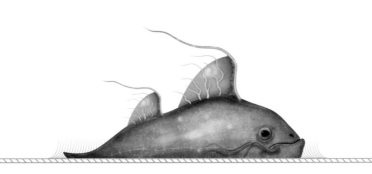

Welcome to Wonderbook. *Before you begin, check your supplies. Make sure you have plenty of water, food, and at least some mountaineering equipment. Get lots of sleep. Always carry pen and paper with you; you never know when that electronic device will give up the ghost. Remember, too, that knowledge of the languages of strange talking animals is a plus when going on a real adventure. So study up. And always—always—keep your wits about you. Now, strengthen your resolve . . . Ready? You're about to plunge into the middle of . . . everything.*

INTRODUCTION

As the painting opposite this page, "The Backyard," suggests, even the most mundane moments of our existence can be inhabited by hidden complexity and with wonder. Some of my favorite books on creative writing acknowledge that fiction is one way of making sense of a complex, often mysterious world, and that stories exist in every part of that world. The best of these books celebrate creativity but remain grounded in useful advice. They are practical, but they also elicit delight in the reader.

Which brings me to the book you hold in your hands. *Wonderbook* functions as a general guide to the art and craft of fiction first and foremost, but it is also meant to be a kind of cabinet of curiosities that stimulates your imagination. This book reflects my belief that an organic approach to writing should be coupled with systematic practice and testing to improve your fiction. You will also find that in *Wonderbook* I have eschewed workshop jargon and solutions that are too easy—*practical* solutions are another thing altogether. You should be able to pick up the basics of fiction writing from *Wonderbook* but also find that it challenges you from time to time with more advanced material. *Wonderbook* is also largely

THE HISTORY OF SCIENCE FICTION

OBSERVATION

EXPLORATION

TECHNOLOGY

ADVENT
DOMIN

1900   1920

"METAMORPHOSIS"
FRANZ KAFKA

GARRETT P. SERVISS:
"EDISON'S CONQUEST OF MARS"

"A ROMANCE IN MANY DIMENSIONS"
FLATLAND
EDWIN ABBOTT

WM. MORRIS
"NEWS FROM NOWHERE"

THEODOR HERZL
"OLD NEW LAND"
INSPIRES UTOPIAN
COMMUNITIES

JACK LONDON:
STAR ROVER

"WE", YEVGEN
ZAMYATI

E.M. FORSTER:
"THE MACHINE STOPS"

"LOOKING BACKWARD"
ED BELLAMY
"A CRYSTAL AGE"
W.H. HUDSON

· ISLAND OF DR. MOREAU
· WAR OF THE WORLDS
H.G. WELLS
THE TIME MACHINE
· FIRST MEN IN THE MOON
· THE SLEEPER AWAKES
· THE INVISIBLE MAN

THE
THIN

THEODOR HERTZKA
"FREILAND"

"THE COMING RACE"
E. BULWER-LYTTON

VICTOR HUGO
"THE LEGEND OF
THE CENTURIES"

EREWHON
SAMUEL BUTLER

MARK TWAIN:
CT. YANKEE IN KING ARTHUR'S COURT
"ON TWO PLANETS"
KURD LASSWITZ

GARRETT P. SERVISS:
"A COLUMBUS
OF SPACE"

"R.U.R
UNIVER
KAR

"VOYAC
DA

"LA PLURALITÉ DES MONDE
'HABITÉS' - C. FLAMMARION"

"AFTER LONDON" - R. JEFFERIES

"JOURNEY IN OTHER WORLDS"- J.J. ASTOR

"STAR DU PSI DE CASSIOPEIA"
C.I. DEFONTENAY

"ACROSS THE ZODIAC" - P. GREG
"Le Moet de la Terre" - J-H ROSY-AINÉ

"WHEN WAR CAME"-SAKI

WORLD
WAR
I
COMES

MURRAY
LEINSTER

· FUTURE WAR NOVELS ·
"BATTLE OF DORKING-GT. CHESNEY
"THE 20TH CENTURY WAR"- A. ROBIA
"YELLOW DANGER"- M.P. SHIEL
"THE PURPLE CLOUD"

"RUNAW

"THE GREAT WAR IN ENGLAND IN 1877"
"INVASION OF 1910" - W. LE QUEUX

HUGO
RA

ARTHUR CONAN DOYLE:
"THE LOST WORLD"

L.P. SENAREN:
FRANK READE
STEAM H

EDGAR RICE BURR

TARZAN

EDWARD ELLIS
"STEAM MAN OF THE
PRAIRIES"

JOURNEY TO THE CENTER OF THE EARTH
FROM THE EARTH TO THE MOON
TWENTY THOUSAND LEAGUES UNDER THE SEA
AROUND THE WORLD IN 80 DAYS
OFF ON A COMET

"THE BRICK MOON"
ROBERT WM. COLE:
THE STRUGGLE FOR EMPIRE"

FILM

TRIP TO
THE MOON
GEORGES
MELIES

JULES VERNE

EDWARD EVERETT HALE

EDGAR
WALLACE

KING KONG

"SANDERS O
THE RIVE

SCIENCE ADVENTURE

H. RIDER HAGGARD:
"KING SOLOMON'S MINE"
"SHE"

L. FRANK BAUM
WIZARD OF OZ BOO

LORD D

FANTASY ADVENTURE

WILKIE COLLINS:
"THE MOONSTONE"

ROBERT LOUIS STEVENSON:
"DR. JEKYLL + MR. HYDE"

BRAM STOKER:
"DRACULA"

WM H
"HOU

LEGEND

OVID: METAMORPHOSES

ARABIAN NIGHTS

ATLANTIS

NEW WORLD
EXPLORATION

PRE-
SCIENTIFIC
IMAGINATION

OLEM

EPLER

MOONE

GERAC
MOON

RLD"

"ROBINSON"
CRUSOE
DANIEL DEFOE
CONSOLIDATOR
WORLD IN THE
MOON"

VOYAGES ET
ADVENTURES
de J. MASSE

LUDVIG
HOLBERG
UNDERGROUND
TRAVELS OF
NIELS KLIM

SCIENCE

ALICE IN
WONDERLAND

FANTASY ADVENTURE

ETA HOFFMANN
"DIE AUTOMATE"

FANTASY ADVENTURE

S. LE FANU:
"THROUGH A GLASS DARKLY"
"UNCLE SILAS"

ARTHUR MACHEN
"THREE IMPOSTO

OCCURRENCE AT OWL CREEK BRIDGE"

1900

J.M., M. RYMER: VARNEY THE VAMPIRE
STRING OF PEARLS (FEAST + BLOOD)
(SWEENEY TODD)

OSCAR WILDE
"DORIAN GRAY"

AMBROSE BIERCE:

SHERLOCK HOLMES

ELS"

"HARRINGTON:
"COMMON WEALTH
OF OCEANA"

SAMUEL MADDEN:
"MEMOIRS OF THE 20TH
CENTURY"

EPLER: FAUST

GOETHE: FAUST

L.S. MERCIER:
"L'AN 2440"

COUSIN de GRAINVILLE:
"LE DERNIER
HOMME"

ENGLISH
ROMANTIC POETS
S. COLERIDGE:
"RIME OF THE ANCIENT MARINER"
LORD BYRON
(MODEL FOR THE
BYRONIC HERO)
PERCY B. SHELLEY
Prometheus Unbound

THOMAS LOVE PEACOCK
"MELINCOURT"

DR. POLIDORI:
"THE VAMPYRE"

VICTOR HUGO
"THE HUNCHBACK
OF NOTRE DAME

E. BRONTE:
"WUTHERING HEIGHTS"
C. BRONTE:

JANE
EYRE:

"THE FALL OF THE HOUSE OF USHER"
THE PIT AND THE PENDULUM

WESTERNS (BUNKHOUSE GOTHIC)

RAFAEL SABAT
"SCARAMO
"CAPTA

ANN RADCLIFFE
"THE MYSTERIES OF UDOLPHO"
"THE ITALIAN"

"THE PRIVATE
MEMOIRS CONFESSIONS
OF A JUSTIFIED SINNER"
JAMES HOGG

"THE MODERN SHORT STORY"

"AUGUSTE DUPIN"

DETECTIVE STORY

HOWARD PYLE
ROBIN HOOD
KING ARTHUR

ROMANTIC
MOVEMENT

WILLIAM BECKFORD
"VATHEK"

THE GOTHIC NOVEL

THOM. de QUINCEY:
"CONFESSIONS OF AN
OPIUM EATER"

EDGAR ALLAN POE

ON:

S OF
SIAN"

HORACE
WALPOLE:
"CASTLE OF OTRANTO"

MATTHEW LEWIS:
"THE MONK"

"THE CASTLE SPECTRE"

REGINA MARIA ROCHE
"CLERMONT"

CHAS. BROCKDEN BROWN
"WIELAND"

JAN POTOCKI:
"THE MANUSCRIPT FOUND
IN SARAGOSA"

GRIMMS' FAIRY TALES

IN THE
GOTHIC
TRADITION

J. FENIMORE COOPER
NATHANIEL HAWTHORNE
HERMAN MELVILLE
WILLIAM FAULKNER
JOHN STEINBECK
TENNESSEE WILLIAMS

1950

FOLK
CULTURE

SUPERSTITION

SIR WALTER SCOTT · HISTORICAL ROMANCE
"IVANHOE"

ALEXANDRE DUMAS:
THREE MUSKETEERS
COUNT OF MONTE CRISTO

1800

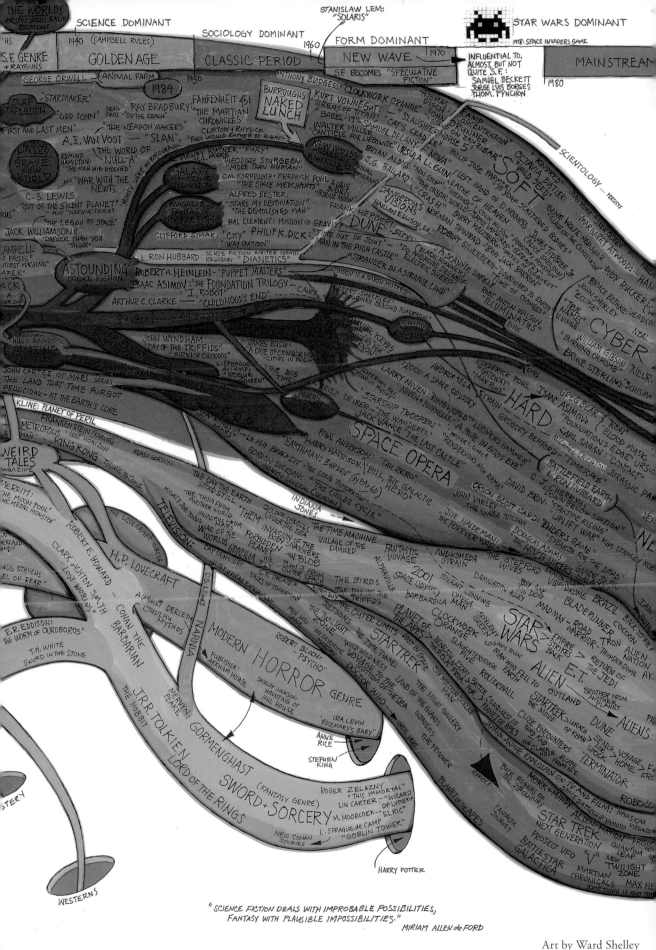

"SCIENCE FICTION DEALS WITH IMPROBABLE POSSIBILITIES,
FANTASY WITH PLAUSIBLE IMPOSSIBILITIES."
MIRIAM ALLEN de FORD

Art by Ward Shelley

nondenominational, in the sense that its approach to teaching technique has universal applications across both so-called "literary" and "commercial" fiction. Whether you want to write a heroic fantasy trilogy spanning centuries or a novel exploring a single day in the life of a lonely man—or, perhaps, something in between—you will find *Wonderbook* of use.

UNIQUE FEATURES

Wonderbook differs from most writing books in two distinct ways. First, images often replace or enhance instructional text. Although more than thirty artists have contributed their work, all of the diagrams were created by Jeremy Zerfoss from my sketches and concepts. This book may provide more instructional illustrations and other visual stimuli—both functional and decorative—than any other writing book to date. Images cannot always substitute for text, but they can be of tremendous use in helping to convey key concepts or in breaking down the complex into simple

"Fishhands" (2010) by Scott Eagle.

parts. My hope is that the results also engage your creativity.

Second, although of use to beginner and intermediate writers working in any genre, *Wonderbook*'s default setting is fantasy rather than realism. Most general writing guides operate from a default of realistic fiction, while books on writing the fantastical often feel divorced from a whole spectrum of other species of storytelling. If you think of yourself as someone who writes fantasy, horror, science fiction, magic realism, or in any absurdist or surrealist mode, I hope that *Wonderbook* makes you feel as if you've come home. If you don't write in those modes, I think you'll discover a fresh way of looking at familiar subjects (as well as get a solid grounding in those basics I mentioned). You will probably also find that—in thought, theory, and execution—there is not much of a divide between "realistic" and "fantastical" fiction. Certainly, you find "imaginative" work across the entire spectrum of approaches to storytelling.

My own beginnings were in the literary mainstream but I soon found that my fiction tended to be more fantastical. I would give my fiction to friends and they would find surreal what I thought was quite realistic. My influences were from all modes of writing, and I came by my dual citizenship honestly. Then, too, my earliest experiences of the real world were, because of my family's travels, evidence of the ways in which the marvelous and the wonderfully strange permeate reality.

Whether it was encountering by flashlight a huge crown-of-thorns starfish on a reef off a Fijian island at night or, sick with asthma, watching with astonishment as two emerald-and-ruby hummingbirds mated on the wing outside our Cuzco hotel window, I had the sense that we lived in a place that required some deeper explanation, some chronicling that went beyond a faithful nonfiction account. Storytelling came out of my need to reconcile these experiences, and I chose fantasy in part because we moved through so many places that only by the combining of fragments of each could I find a true home. And only in fiction could I find a way to express the complexity and beauty—and sometimes horror—of the world.

ORGANIZATION AND APPROACH

Although you can use it piecemeal, *Wonderbook* should be read from beginning to end for the most immersive experience. It is organized to first ground you in thoughts about inspiration and information on the elements of story—after which you will embark upon several different storytelling adventures. Chapters 3 through 6 present different entry points into fiction. Most writers are compelled to write after having come up with an interesting *beginning and/or ending* or, depending on how their brains work, after thinking about the story's *plot and structure, characters,* or *setting*. Throughout, I use "short story" and "novel" somewhat interchangeably in discussing technique, but I do try to emphasize one or the other where a topic or subtopic seems more applicable to a particular form. Much writing advice can be applied across both stories and novels, however, even if it manifests differently in each.

The approach used in each chapter varies somewhat to suit the subject matter. For example, Chapter 3 relies the most heavily on my own work. By dissecting a novel I wrote, I can show you the full range of choices available when writing the typical beginning, without having to rely on hypotheticals or trying to guess the rationale behind another writer's decisions. In the chapter on characterization, I tend to rely much more heavily on the dozens of interviews I conducted with some of my favorite writers for this book, interweaving their opinions with my own. The chapter on worldbuilding has fewer instructional diagrams and more examples in art and photographs of types of settings—the captions do much more heavy lifting. Tips on revision are intrinsic to the text of most chapters, but Chapter 7, Revision, directly addresses the subject and, again, uses the experiences of other writers. Consistency in this regard, or the rooting out of a sliver or two of inevitable repetition, is less important to me than providing what I hope is the best advice in the best context.

Such considerations do not apply, however, to the Workshop Appendix that follows the main chapters. The Workshop Appendix is unpredictable, volatile, and may well take you to some very strange places. It's meant more for dipping into

Writer and teacher Matthew Cheney served as my consultant on the text. Several sections are much richer as the result of discussions we had while I wrote this book.

GUIDES TO HELP
YOU ALONG THE WAY

Wonderbook provides a variety of guides that educate, illuminate, and entertain: Myster Odd, the Little Aliens, the Devil's Advocate, the All-Seeing Pen-Eye, and the Webinator.

MYSTER ODD: "Think of me as that eccentric aunt or uncle who always makes a spectacular entrance at family gatherings and can never quite tell you what line of work they're in. But when you really listen, you find that they have interesting anecdotes and information to share. I'll be there to show you something useful. Flamboyantly. Mysteriously. Oh, and my gun? It's a water pistol."

LITTLE ALIENS: "We're the practical ones. Although sometimes we might just be taking a break and goofing off, most of the time we help explain the nuts and bolts of a concept or a term. We also help Myster Odd when old beak-head is trying to convey something really complex. We've come from a far-away planet to help, so make sure you pay attention—or you might wake up tied down like Gulliver."

THE DEVIL'S ADVOCATE: "I'm really just a different type of little worker alien. I'm the annoying one who offers a counterpoint to some information set out in a diagram or illustration. I help you hold two opposing ideas in your head at the same time, as well."

ALL-SEEING PEN-EYE: "I came with the little worker aliens, but unlike them, I serve one very specific purpose. Whenever I notice that your attention is flagging or that you're in need of extra stimuli, I suddenly jump out with a writing challenge related to the text you're reading.

WEBINATOR: "Some think of me as the most ordinary of the *Wonderbook* guides, but I perform a very valuable function. I pop up anytime you can find more content about a subject or writer at the *Wonderbook* website. You can use the site in conjunction with the book to enhance your experience. I may be small, but I hold multitudes."

than reading straight through. Therein you will find complex writing exercises that will work you hard, along with additional perspectives on fiction from experts in live-action roleplaying and gaming, and an interview on craft with George R. R. Martin. Have fun—and don't get lost. Or do. Sometimes getting lost is the best part.

In addition to the main text, you will find supplemental special features that add depth to the chapters.

- Sidebar essays by other writers, including Neil Gaiman, Ursula K. Le Guin, and Lev Grossman. These essays are meant to provide additional information or to expand upon some subject in the main text. Most of these guest essays are original to *Wonderbook* and can be identified by their green frame.
- Sidebar features by me. These short essays provide further context, and are distinguished from those by other writers not just by the lack of a byline but also because they feature a blue, not green, frame.
- "Spotlight On" features. These short pieces consist of an extended quote from a single writer or other creator to convey something interesting about a very specific topic.
- "Writing Challenges" tied to specific images. These mini-exercises allow you to practice some aspect of the subject under discussion. Some are practical, but others are deliberately esoteric to help stretch your imagination. The writing challenges supplement the more complex Writing Exercises section in the Workshop Appendix.

In the margin you will find:

- Blue text that defines terms or makes additional observations.
- Captions that identify images but sometimes also instruct.
- References to additional content online at Wonderbooknow.com.

You will also find a rather major disruption in the margins—in the form of a dragon. Disruption dragons feature ideas or thoughts by several excellent writers (all of whom I recommend highly to readers). These dragons either call into question something in the main text or expand on a point made in the main text. They are a kind of insurgency within *Wonderbook*, reminding us that engagement with what we read is more important than memorization of information.

WONDERBOOKNOW.COM

Additional materials related to the craft of writing exist at Wonderbooknow.com. The web icon used throughout the book references specific materials available there, but does not describe everything you can find on the site. One major supplement to this text is an editorial roundtable, wherein several respected fiction

I am a disruption dragon. My goal is to make you think about some aspect of the text. I delight in shaking things up a bit. But is that really a good idea? You'll have to decide for yourself. Me, I'm conflicted. — **Sincerely, The Disruption Dragon**

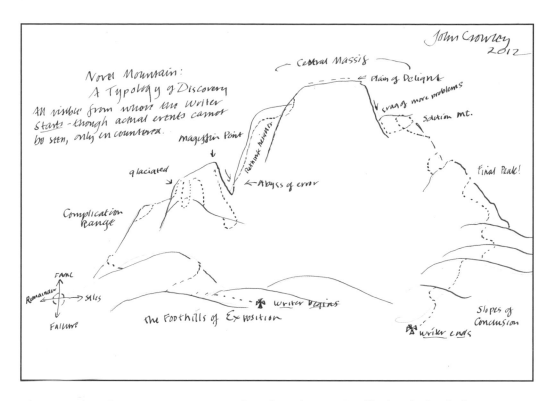

The map of "Novel Mountain" is labeled with the following handwritten text:

John Crowley 2012

Novel Mountain:
A Typology of Discovery
All visible from where the Writer
starts - though actual events cannot
be seen, only encountered.

— Central Massif —

Plain of Delight
crags of more problems
Solution Mt.

Magician Point
Rethink Heights
Abyss of error

glaciated

Final Peak!

Complication Range

FAME
Remainder — — Sales
Failure
Writer begins
the Foothills of Exposition

Slopes of Conclusion

Writer ends

editors read and critique a promising but flawed story. You'll also find a links section to additional resources supporting the writing workshop section of the appendix, the full text of the interviews from which I pulled quotes for this book, and much more. Everything on the site applies to the craft, or art, of writing. You can find more posts on craft—along with advice on careers and negotiating the modern publishing landscape—at Booklifenow.com, which supports my previous book, *Booklife: Strategies and Survival Tips for the 21st-Century Writer*.

The Journey

Writing can be a difficult profession, and it requires a certain amount of mental toughness, as John Crowley's sketch may suggest. There are many rewards, but setbacks also await you. Some of it you will just have to experience; some of it you can forestall with the right guides. A useful guide can take a few years off of your learning curve, as well. I hope that *Wonderbook* proves a faithful and honest companion throughout your long journey of becoming and remaining a writer. Where it is not true to your vision, you must follow your own path.

May your fiction bring you pleasure, fulfillment, and every good thing you desire. May you have fun, too. Lots of it.

FOLLOWING PAGE
"Shelves of Ideas for the Journey" (2010) by Scott Eagle.

Creative play and the imagination are at the core of a writer's life. How we nurture the imagination affects all aspects of what we write, and how we write it. As Jung said, "The dynamic principle of fantasy is play, which belongs also to the child, and as such it appears to be inconsistent with the principle of serious work. But without this playing with fantasy no creative work has ever yet come to birth."

CHAPTER 1: INSPIRATION AND THE CREATIVE LIFE

THE MOST MIRACULOUS aspect of creativity is the ability to conjure up images, characters, and narrative out of seemingly nothing: to be inspired and for that inspiration to lead to words on a page. This very process is, to my mind, fantastical at its core. Almost anything can feed the imagination with the raw material necessary for transformation into narrative. An image of a hummingbird on the wing, a typographical error in a newspaper article, a fragment of overheard speech, a memorable line in a novel. My wife once bit into a type of fruit she had not eaten since childhood, and a memory welled up of the fruit trees in her grandmother's backyard. Until that moment, she had not remembered those trees in many years, and all at once the stories about her grandmother spilled out, that one bite having unlocked a treasure trove of personal history.

"Inspiration" is often inadequately defined as the initial spark or sparks that lead to a story. In fact, the word describes a *continuing process* that occurs throughout the development of a particular piece of fiction—an ongoing series of revelations put together by your subconscious and conscious minds working in tandem. These revelations often take the form of connections between elements of the story. Examples include a crucial shift in the story because of a change in the relationship between two characters, a revelation about the setting, or even just the realization that one scene isn't needed but another must be written. The fact that the woman with a gun at the story's beginning is actually a friend of your penguin protagonist, and they're not strangers to this place but coming home.

For some writers, these additional moments of "eureka" may never match the impact of those initial moments when the story first opened up to them—even though that spark can become a kind of sustained chain reaction. Indeed, writers usually find it easier to talk about technique, perspiration, and the *long slog* rather than inspiration. And maybe there's some truth to that approach. A lot of your days

Samuel Delany's workspace as documented by Kyle Cassidy (April 2009).

are spent slogging through the forced march necessary to complete a work of fiction. You can't be inspired every day, just like you can't be madly, deeply, insanely in love every day. But how such moments manifest as you move through the world and the world moves through you defines the core of your creativity.

In this chapter, you will find a series of views and perspectives on inspiration and the imagination that should be of use in encouraging a healthy, productive creative life. As you read, remember that we pull apart the act of inspiration and the act of writing only to talk about how they work. Further, because this chapter speaks to aspects of your core identity as a writer, these ideas come with a warning: When it comes to your uniqueness and personal creativity, discard what doesn't resonate with you and use only what makes sense.

THE IMPORTANCE OF IMAGINATIVE PLAY

Carol Bly's wonderful creative writing book *The Passionate, Accurate Story* includes this hypothetical situation: One night at dinner, a girl announces to her father and mother that a group of bears has moved in next door. In one scenario, the father says (and I paraphrase), "Bears? Don't be ridiculous," and tells his daughter to be more serious. In the other scenario, the father says, "Bears, huh? How many bears? Do you know their names? Do they have any hobbies? What do they wear?" And his daughter, with delight, tells him. Encouragement of the concept that bears have moved in next door highlights the role of creative play in fostering and strengthening the imagination—and thus practice at storytelling. It also emphasizes how creative play functions as communication. Even though I know she's just words on a page, I feel bad for the daughter whose father can't see that she's making an effort to talk to him, to build something together. (Therein lies a story, too.)

Bears figured prominently in our own household when my stepdaughter was growing up, invoked through the trickster aspect of our relationship. I had been feeding her lines of what one can only call tall tales or creative hogwash. For example, she would find a letter under her pillow from the "frog fairy," not the tooth fairy, with a couple of Chinese coins enclosed. The letter apologized for a lack of U.S. currency and explained that the exchange rate for teeth wasn't favorable right now.

Bly's book also delves deeply into more practical subjects like the ethics of characters, and how this should govern their actions.

"The Three Psychedelic Bears" by Jeremy Zerfoss.

FOLLOWING PAGES
"The Muse" by Rikki Ducornet.

THE MUSE always has wings

...AND NESTS IN FIRE!

I think our species is wired to tell stories, just as we are wired to be curious, loving, playful. We tumble into the world with this extraordinary thing: a creative imagination. And it is erotic — inspirited by the breath of life. In other words, the impulse to create, is like the impulse to breathe. (Did you know that people who have been shut down often have trouble breathing?)

The imagination is often distrusted and feared — as much as it is misunderstood. Perhaps because it mirrors the world's mutability. It is supremely restless. It does not accept things as they "are." It is impatient with received ideas. In this way it is subversive. When the child asks "why" (the first great ✸ COSMOGONIC QUESTION ✸) and the parent says "Because I say so." that child has been betrayed. Perhaps we all carry a thorn from Kaspar Hauser's stolen crown. Perhaps we have all been betrayed somehow. Somehow compromised. Writing is a place to reclaim the initial impulse, to ask all the questions, to EXPLORE THE MYSTERIES OF BEING and BECOMING. Writing is a great adventure.

The fact that the adventure is often lonely doesn't mean it is narcissistic — a common (and lethal!) misunderstanding. The beautiful paradox of art is that what is a private journey is released to the world where it enters into the fabric of other lives.

At least, this is how I see it. Which means I am not interested in writing a book that has already been written. I want my book to teach me how to see the world differently. I want it to ask me vital questions, questions I never dreamed of asking. A novel is a great excuse to investigate things one knows all too little about. Sometimes a book will stimulate a series of VIBRANT DREAMS. Sometimes a book will be ENGENDERED BY A DREAM: My first novel was precipitated by a dream of such power it sustained me for ten years and enabled me to write four novels in that time. CHARACTERS have a WAY of INTRUDING and demanding their OWN BOOK! When that happens, you are IN LUCK! YOU ARE IN GOOD HANDS!

I have no "SYSTEM" other than never taking the easy way out, not writing a book that bores me — Not for an INSTANT!; above all: WRITING A book I WANT to READ! Taking the path that has not been taken, seeing each book as A RIDDLE TO BE SOLVED, A RIDDLE and A REVELATION!

My WATCHWORDS ARE, HAVE ALWAYS been and will always be:

RIGOR + IMAGINATION

Rikki Ducornet

Finally, she decided to get back at me. She knew that I, an agnostic, was trying to learn more about her mother's Jewish faith. So during our first holiday season together she told me all about the glory that was the "Hanukkah Bear," and I wound up reciting these "facts" to the rabbi at my wife's synagogue—only to find out, much to everyone's amusement, that she had "punked" me. I wasn't mad at all; instead, I was impressed by the quality of her imagination. This imagination manifested in many other wonderful ways. When she pointed at a ferret while at a park and said, "long mouse," I didn't know if she was joking or finding the best description for an animal unknown to her, but I knew that detail would one day make it into a story.

We also teamed up for acts of creation. Once, when she had friends over, I asked her to "remember to find the iguana and feed him." We had no iguana, but that

"Ghost Iguana" by Ivica Stevanovic.

didn't stop Erin from picking up on the hint and looking for the iguana all over the house, much to the wide-eyed consternation of her friends. Later, I pretended a ghost of the now-dead iguana haunted us—a logical progression of its story arc, we thought, and no big deal, but somewhat problematic for other people. That ghost iguana, that Hanukkah Bear, stuck in my head for more than a decade; these characters led later to a novella entitled *Komodo* and to a galaxy-spanning science-fiction epic entitled *The Journals of Doctor Mormeck* that features huge, undead bears and a species of large, intelligent, dimension-hopping lizards.

When unburdened by the need to put words on a page, the imagination often appears as a form of love and sharing: playful, generous, and transformative. The best fiction is often driven by this invisible engine, which hums and purrs and sighs.

It's this flicker, or flutter, at the heart of good stories that animates them, and this movement—ever different, ever unpredictable—that makes each story unique. The more we allow it into our lives, the better, and the less we treat it just as a pack of lies, the more we're enriched. In a very real sense, too, the history of the world could be seen as an ongoing battle between good and bad imaginations—and the existence we have created on Earth is both sad and uplifting as a result. Your imagination and your stories exist within this wider context, and sometimes you'll find you need to break free of other people's imaginations to allow your own uniqueness to shine through.

Perhaps because the power and influence of the imagination is greater than we often think, our attitude toward it has sometimes been ambivalent. To take just one example from the world's cultures, during the Middle Ages in Europe the imagination was often associated with the senses and thus thought to be one of the links between human beings and animals. The Catholic Church believed the imagination was merely a mechanism for memorizing and internalizing the divine words of scripture—a lower mental activity. Representations of fantastical beasts tended to be in the context of Heaven and Hell as shown in illuminated manuscripts. The rise of the Grotesques—ribald Boschian images typically created by silversmiths and goldsmiths—may have added a greater sense of play and a corresponding lessened religious subtext at times, but they did little to lift the imagination out of the (blissful) gutter.

Not until the Renaissance did the imagination become linked to the intellect, in part through what were known as *contes philosophiques* (philosophical stories). Based on the works of Francis Bacon and Johannes Kepler, these stories used fantasy to explain the Copernican universe. They usually took the form of an imaginary voyage or a dream story and allowed otherwise inexplicable travel through the solar system or deep into the Earth. Kepler's *Somnium*, for example, is a treatise on planetary motion disguised as a fantastical story about a witch's son transported by demons to the Moon.

Different forces are at work today with regard to the imagination. Modern ideals of functionality and the trend toward seamless design in our technology have taken the very human striving for perfection and given us the illusion of having attained it (which, ironically, seems very dehumanizing). In this environment, some writers second-guess their instincts and devalue the sense of play that infuses creative endeavors: "This antique Tiffany lamp must provide light right now, *even before I screw in the lightbulb and plug it in*, or it's worthless." At best the imagination can be seen as heat lightning with no real

weight or effect, instead of *the source*. At worst, it's dismissed as frivolous and a waste of time, with no real-world applications.

To some extent, I understand the reasons for this attitude. Creative play speaks to an aspect of the imagination that defies easy measurement. It brings yet another level of uncertainty to an endeavor already saturated with the subjective. That truth can make writers and readers alike uncomfortable. The world wants to believe in technique and craft, in practice and hard work as the primary ingredients of success. Related to this idea is the cautionary tale about two writers. One had a brilliant imagination and the other a slightly lesser imagination, but Lesser had more tenacity and drive than Greater, so Greater failed while Lesser went on to a substantial career. There's rarely much follow-up discussion about Greater (and what might have been lost) after that point, except a kind of lingering subtext of pity for the one who couldn't quite handle it . . . perhaps because we fear being that person. Or perhaps because we sometimes look across the room at the looming shadow of our imagination curling back on us, and we realize we cannot control the at times uncomfortable things it can bring us. (The world is filled with people who have too much imagination solely because the people around them have too little.)

Inherent in this idea of "play" being immature and frivolous is the idea that, just like business processes, all creative processes should be efficient, timely, linear, organized, and easily summarized. *If it's not clearly a means to an end, it must be a waste of time.* In the worst creative writing books, this method is expressed in **seven-point plot outlines** and other easy shortcuts rather than as exercises to help encourage the organic development of your own approach. This kind of codification sometimes reflects a fear of the *uncertainty* of the imagination and the need to have a set of rules in place through which to understand the universe.

It's also a push back against the idea that a Hanukkah bear or ghost iguana might ever have creative value. *Bears should just be bears. Iguanas should be real.* An iguana is not a plot outline. Except, it *is* the beginning of a plot outline, because the creative process can begin anywhere and look like anything. The structure of a story can grow as easily from the way the residue at the bottom of a coffee cup resembles a continent as it can from reading a newspaper story about a heroic act. The most important thing is allowing the subconscious mind to engage in the kind of play that leads to making the connections necessary to create narrative.

ABOVE
John Coulthart's interpretation of Alice in Wonderland (2010).

OPPOSITE
Illuminated monsters in the margins of the *Luttrell Psalter*, British Library collection (circa 1325–1335).

A simple try-fail structure for the main character across three acts that has become a paint-by-numbers approach.

THE FANTASTICAL AND THE IMAGINATION

In considering the worth of "fantasy" and "science fiction"—modes of fiction still perceived as valuing concepts and settings over characters—this sense of imagination being "frivolous" is allied to society's ideas of what is "serious" versus what is "entertainment." Fantastical writers like Ursula K. Le Guin, Jorge Luis Borges, and Italo Calvino might be inextricably intertwining *play* with their exploration of complex *intellectual* ideas, but this aspect is often ignored in reviews, perhaps because it is considered irrelevant to the "point" of good fiction. Instead of being essential, core, *inseparable from*.

The word "frivolous" lurks in the subtext of such opinions, along with the assumption that flights of fantasy have no moorings to reality, a tether believed by some to be essential. Yet completely un-utilitarian fantastical "documents" like the famed *Codex Seraphinianus* (created by Luigi Serafini in the 1970s), the mysterious fifteenth-century Voynich Manuscript, or writer-artist Richard A. Kirk's "Iconoclast" imaginings have a marvelous intrinsic value no matter what we can actually glean from them. Lewis Carroll's *Alice in Wonderland* may or may not include some interesting life lessons, but that is beside the point of the mathematical precision of its frivolity. As the award-winning Australian writer Lisa L. Hannett points out, "'frivolous' reading is as important as creative play. Reading for fun, reading to feed your imagination, reading to revel in the childlike wonder of being elsewhere."

Whether accepted by the mainstream like *Alice* or kept on the fringes like *The Codex*, these creations are among the greatest examples of pure imaginative play in fantasy. The *Codex*'s encyclopedia of images and text of an imaginary world, written using an invented language, has no practical value at all. The Voynich Manuscript, also written in a language no one has been able to decipher, contains botanical and astrological sections that are clearly fantastical no matter what the actual purpose of the document. It, too, exists for its own sake. Kirk's "Iconoclast" series has perhaps a more practical point to make, but just barely. It posits a strange alternate universe in which language is expressed through complex images. As a result, even the most basic communications take weeks; but since the participants "speak" in different styles, understanding is rudimentary at best and wars break out over inadequately expressed paintings. All of these ultimate expressions of the imagination share one thing in common, however. By existing at the outer edges of practicality, they expand the range of the possible for the rest of us.

But this idea of the fantastical imagination being *unmoored from reality* causes issues, too. It spreads the lie that fantasy has no causality, and it implicates the imagination in this crime. The subtext is that in fantasy fiction the sense of play that surrounds the fantastical

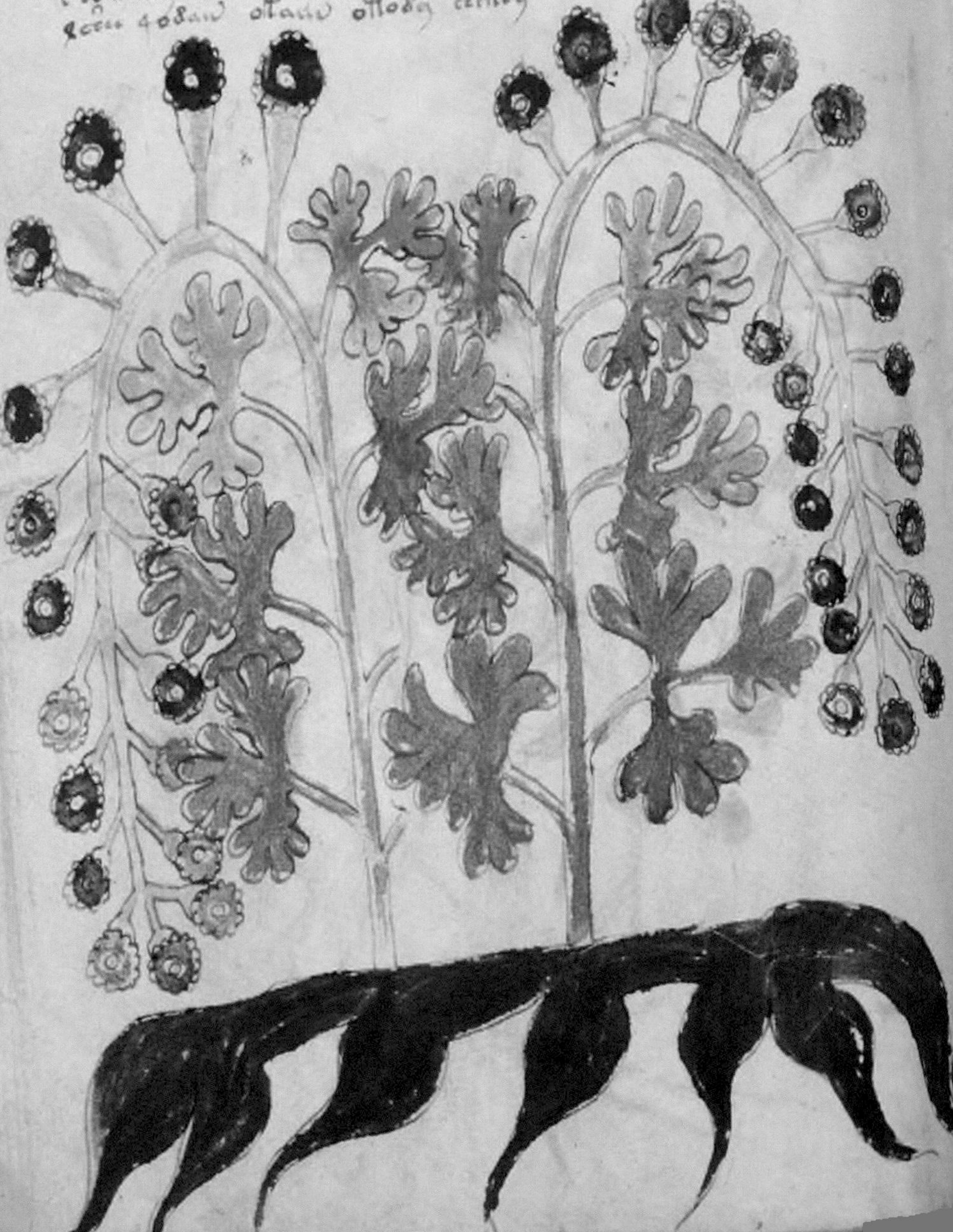

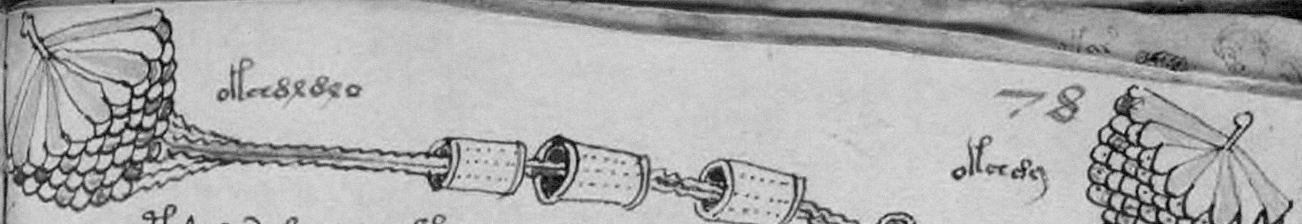

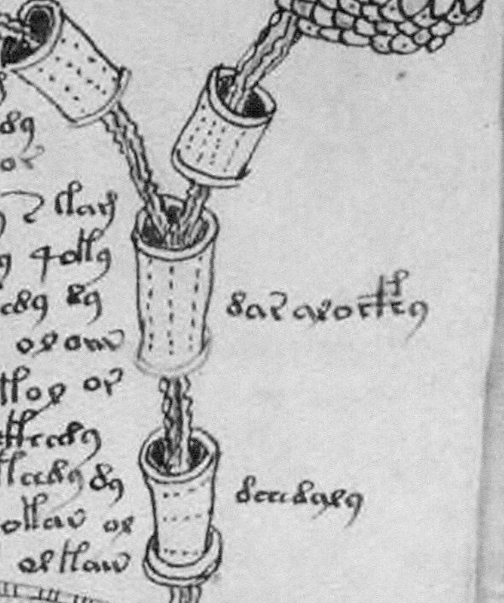

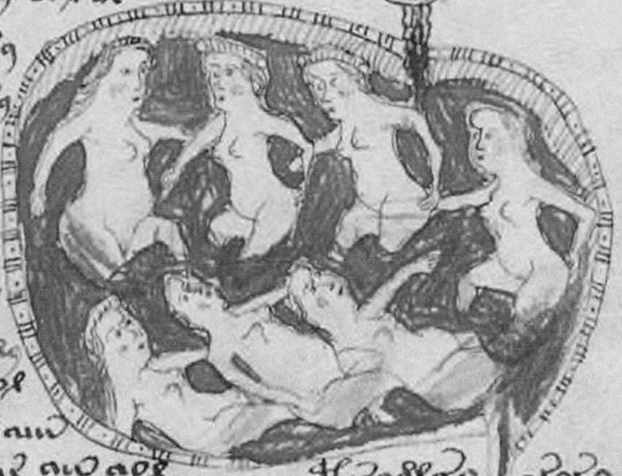

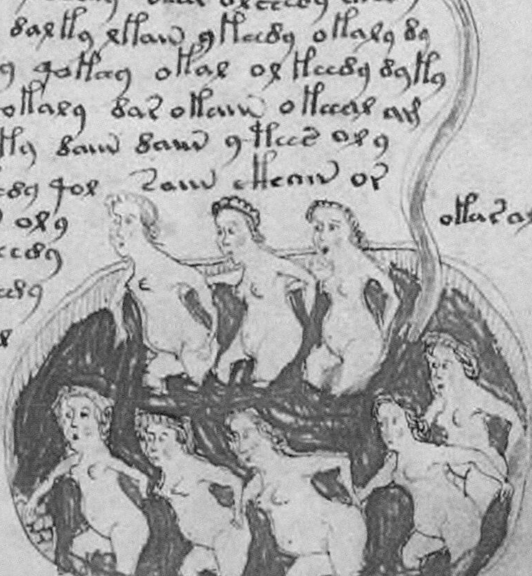

and leads directly to creation needs less shaping somehow—the attempt to convey an ordinary reality is more complex and messier—as if the ghost iguana needs no real transformation, just fleshing out. And yet the imagination isn't just responsible for—to take some random examples—talking alligators, a man as big as a county, a flying woman, or superheroes. It also can take credit for the alligator knowing the plot better than anyone and the flying woman having an admirer who ties her to the Earth, for knowing why the man as big as a county is weeping and that the superhero is going to have to get a job to pay the bills.

Even the issue of what is imaginative or fantastical can be misunderstood, especially by those who are overinvested in the tribalism of genre. Does it really matter if the imaginative impulse results in the "fantastical" in the sense of "containing an explicit fantastical event"? No. For one thing, "imaginative" writing occurs across every possible genre and subgenre. And for a certain kind of writer, a sense of fantastical play will always exist on the page.

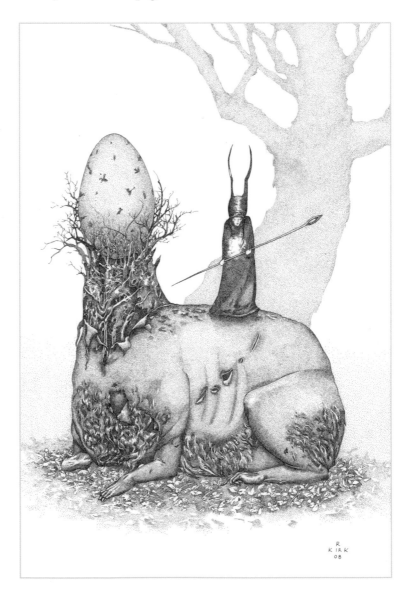

PREVIOUS PAGES
Pages from the Voynich Manuscript (circa 1404–1438).

RIGHT
An image from Richard A. Kirk's "Iconoclast" series: translating language into art (2008).

When I asked one of our greatest writers, Haruki Murakami, about the surreal aspects of his work, he said: "It's not that I'm trying to introduce into the story surrealistic things and situations that I became aware of. I'm just trying to portray things that are real to me, myself, a little more realistically. However, the harder I try to realistically portray real things, the more the things that appear in my work have a tendency to become unreal. To put it another way, by viewing it through an unreal lens, the world looks more real."

This is often what we really mean by the *voice* of the writer. *Talking bears have moved in next door.* Does the reality matter more than the quality of the metaphor? Perhaps not. Consider Mark Helprin's *A Winter's Tale* and his World War I novel, *A Soldier of the Great War*. *A Winter's Tale* includes a winged horse and other fantastical flourishes. *A Soldier of the Great War* contains no fantastical elements, but through its descriptions, its voice, through Helprin's animating imagination, this novel takes on a fantastical aspect. Rikki Ducornet can write the lyrically phantasmagorical *Phosphor in Dreamland* as well as the intense, fiercely realistic story collection *The Word "Desire"* . . . and yet they exist in the same country, perhaps even come from the same area of that country. This is the power of one type of unusual imagination.

Imaginative Outputs

A few key attributes help to define and support your imagination. These traits exist in different proportions in different writers and affect every aspect of writing, but they first manifest in the arena of inspiration.

> **Curiosity.** Nothing is more essential to a writer than sustaining an inquisitive nature—being actively interested in the world and the people in it. Curiosity reflects a willingness to be disappointed in a search for knowledge. Curiosity sends out a series of queries that exist for their own sake, and curiosity gathers back into itself anything that it finds, transforming what's found in the process. Truly curious people try to see everything as freshly as a child with an adult's mind. This gathering of information—of textures, of anecdotes, of smells, of histories—should be nonjudgmental and find pleasure in seemingly disparate, often contradictory elements. From the fusion of these elements comes an essential aspect of creativity. Curiosity is in a sense allied with qualities such as cleverness and with random collection—like a pack rat that accumulates buttons and bottle caps and scraps of paper without caring about the source of such items. Just because you're busy or you're convinced your daily environment no longer holds any surprises, don't forget to be curious about the world around you.

> **Receptivity.** Openness and empathy spring from being receptive to the world and the people in it, not just being curious about them. Receptivity means letting in more than just information. Eliminating barriers to other people's emotions, predicaments, tragedies, and other aspects of the human condition is crucial to

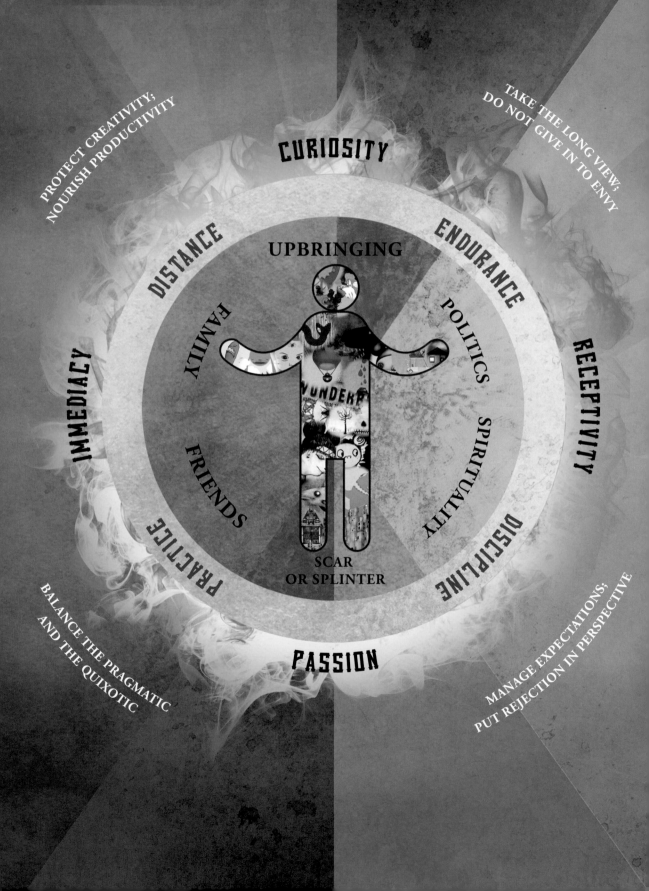

a writer, even when it hurts or makes you uncomfortable. As much as possible, allow yourself to be a raw nerve end that internalizes whatever is experienced in life. When you allow this, you not only create fertile soil for stories, novels, and nonfiction, you also build a better understanding of your fellow human beings. Putting up walls to avoid being hurt may temporarily solve problems in your life, but it may also shut you off from one potent source of your personal creativity. Your imagination needs curiosity and receptivity as fuel for both its serious and deeply unserious aspects. Being available to social media 24/7 does not count as receptivity; it's just fragmentation.

PASSION. Cynics find it hard to be passionate about anything, and therefore passion is linked to retaining your idealism, which is in turn linked to retaining your openness. If you are not passionate about what you write—if you don't care— no amount of effort can revive your work. It will remain inert, waiting for an infusion of new life. Passion is the blood that fills the veins of your creative self. It provides for the circulatory system that allows your imagination to breathe. What is obsession but curiosity and passion taken to an extreme? But in the discipline of writing as opposed to "real life," obsession is an essential part of creating an enduring work of art. (In a dysfunctional situation, first you lose your curiosity, which turns off your receptivity, and that short-circuits your passion.)

IMMEDIACY. Your imagination thrives best when you live in the moment and fully experience everything that is going on around you. Even a fantasy writer— especially a fantasy writer—requires stimuli from the surrounding world. Anything has the potential to be transformed or to provide the grace note of believability that makes a story a success or a failure. Being distracted from your environment is a direct hindrance to your imagination— it blocks receptivity, it redirects passion, and it ultimately channels your curiosity down well-worn and uninteresting paths. "Live in the moment" may be a cliché, but it is increasingly important to remind writers in the age of social media that you must be fully engaged to be a good writer.

These qualities do not exist in a vacuum. They are tempered, or given form and purpose, by other elements, foremost among them discipline and endurance. Without discipline, which translates in writing into focus and good work habits, your imagination can atrophy. Discipline balances the imagination by grounding the writer in pragmatism and structure. Discipline is learning craft, practicing craft, and, on the micro level, isolating the particular problems you need your imagination to solve.

Endurance, meanwhile, is toughness or *persistence* manifesting over time—the perfect writer in motion rather than inert, the potential for work expressed through work. Imagination and discipline create endurance—and long careers—by continually replenishing creativity, giving it form and reinforcing the writer's identity *as writer*.

Taken together, these attributes represent a continually refreshing and renewing cycle that feeds and nourishes your imagination. They are also qualities that will probably make you a more grounded and contented human being.

WEB

TIPS ON
DISCIPLINE

THE SCAR OR THE SPLINTER

Another influence on creative behavior requires some additional explanation: the Scar. The contradiction in the Scar, the ghost of a wound, is that everything I have been setting out in this chapter has been about joy, openness, and generosity. So "Scar" is a strong word in that context, perhaps too strong, and I sometimes also call it the "Splinter." It is not the severity of the Scar or Splinter that helps define the depth of a person's creativity, but the way in which you use it. What's important is that some initial irritant, some kind of *galvanizing and enduring impulse*, combines with the need to communicate, to tell stories . . . leading to inspiration, then that first story, and all that follows after.

The Scar or Splinter is often the memory of a loss, a disappointment, a perceived great wrong that continues to create an agitation, an irritation, or at times an agony. In retreating to the Scar, it is only natural that the writer experiences emotions of sadness, regret, and loneliness—all of which feed into the writing. Negative emotions are also a key part of what inspires and drives most writers to write.

Although I love to tell stories, I am convinced I became a writer because of my parents' long, combative divorce when I was a child—made more horrifying by the contradiction between that ugliness and the beauty of Fiji, the island paradise where we lived. My particular Scar helped teach me to seek distance from events, to try to be on the outside looking in, to observe. In becoming a writer I channeled that distancing into art, rather than solely into alienation from friends and family. I had an outlet for those feelings and a practical application for that stance.

That is my Scar. But the Scar varies from writer to writer, can be greater or lesser, can be more or less personal. For new writer Jennifer Hsyu, her Scar is her "complicated, intercultural, and intergenerational relationship" with her mother. "I love her more than anything, but she is a classic domineering Chinese mother, and when I'm around her I regress into the rebellious teenage American daughter. The language barrier doesn't help either; there's anger and frustration and a love that is unconditional but often mutually born of loss (of understanding)." In her early stories, Hsyu was more "occupied with learning the craft than imbuing my stories with my point of view, but after one workshop she "went home for an extended visit, and I went with my mother to visit my grandmother, who suffers from dementia and lives in a nursing home and is the carbon print from which my mother came." Hsyu's devastating series of visits to the nursing home became a magic realism short story that combined "wishful thinking and painful reality." It was really awful to write, Hsyu said, because "it was hard to re-live those moments over and over again, searching for details and nuances of my mental and physical environment, and trying to maintain a respectable distance from my 'character.'" But she also had "never felt such a connection with the words on the page, because they came from somewhere within. Somewhere painful, of course—but genuine, and true."

This is a direct, specific example of a wound or Scar manifesting as fiction. But to some degree, too, despite its personal aspect, my Scar is just another entry point into writing, a way into channeling the seriousness and depth of a character by recalling my own anger and sadness. Whenever I am moody and sit down to write, I am in a sense transforming something from my own life, the memory of the Scar hovering over me, and the writing is a way of drawing out the poison of memories. Even if it's not why I stayed a writer.

Philip K. Dick Award finalist Karin Lowachee calls this all a form of method writing. "My writing of heavier subject matter—while not exact to my own experience—is pulled from those darker aspects of my life or personality, and the emotional truths are what I attempted to get on paper, and thus: method writing. An actor once said that acting to him was 'finding truths in imaginary circumstances,' and I think that applies equally to writers. Writers, to me, are very similar to actors in how they engage with their process and with the ultimate work. It's just that actors output through motion and speech, and writers output through the written word."

This idea can take many other forms, too. Lisa L. Hannett notes that "real-life yearning can work in the same way. Not necessarily romantic yearning, though that might be part of it, but the memory of unrequited desire, or the presence of as-yet-unfulfilled desire, or possibly the knowledge of never-to-be-fulfilled desire, which can be as creatively stimulating as the Scar. You *wish*, you *want*, you Yearn—these emotions can be channeled into your fiction, transformed; they, too, need to be communicated."

Word Beast by Molly Crabapple (2010).

INPUTS FOR INSPIRATION

As noted, your imagination feeds on almost anything, like the most greedy of omnivores, and anything can become narrative. The act of becoming a writer—of committing to learning the craft or art of writing—is largely about providing structure to what your imagination creates and is an ongoing process of attaining an elusive mastery (there is always another door). But generating these initial sparks is one of the few parts of writing that becomes easier as you gain more experience—as long

42

A masquerade party. Our hero overwhelmed
Shown as innocent
tho' not for long
Everyone is better at this than him—
Grotesque, leering.

From the collection of Myrtle Von Damitz III, a note card by Cassandra N. Railsea (1970). A scene sketch for Railsea's novel *The Incredible Sex Life of Boggie Crisper* (1971).

as you don't suppress the impulse. Which is to say, if you reward your imagination by writing down your ideas and exploring them, even the slightest little fragment, your imagination will reward you with a more or less continuous stream of ideas. If you turn off or blunt the enthusiasm of your subconscious for engaging in creative play, the stream can dry up.

Over the years, I have learned to always keep pen and paper with me—even on the nightstand—so if I wake up in the middle of the night, there's as little time as possible between the idea and the recording of the idea. I sometimes type into a cell phone, but cell phone batteries can die and a cell phone can reset, wiping out notes, so I prefer pen and paper. I also don't wait on ceremony or politeness if I am with people and some idea comes to me—I just break off the conversation and scribble what needs scribbling. If you do observe the social niceties, you may well lose something important. Images, characters, fragments of dialogue are all incredibly vulnerable to erosion by your environment. I once wrote most of a long novel titled *Shriek: An Afterword* just by organizing scraps of paper that represented stray moments of inspiration; it never would have happened if I hadn't rigorously recorded every thought that came to me. The idea of doing so came from Vladimir Nabokov, who liked writing on note cards; he would put one thought or snippet of a scene on each card, and then he was able to organize them later into the book's order.

In terms of general categories of influence, here are just a few to make you think about where inspiration comes from:

- Family situations, anecdotes, or histories
- Work experience
- Travel
- Religion
- History/research
- Overheard conversations
- Friends
- Environment (including nature/the wilderness)
- Hobbies
- Other novels and stories
- Social or political issues
- Interest in a particular genre
- Science
- Newspaper and magazine articles
- Images (photographs, TV, movies)
- **Dreams**

How you process these influences tends to fall into one of the following categories:

- Direct observation and transference into your story (for example, the real detail that becomes the identical detail about one of your characters)
- In reaction to (for example, reading a science-fiction story and thinking you could do that concept better)
- Transformation (for example, a misheard fragment of conversation that lends itself to fantastical interpretation: "she's flying through the gates" becomes a flying woman)

As fodder, but be aware that dream logic usually isn't story logic. Dreams can be inspirational, but you usually can't transcribe them and come up with a story that makes sense to anyone but yourself.

Depending on the type of story or novel you're working on, you may find that almost anything in your environment will attach itself to the initial spark or inspiration, creating a series of secondary and tertiary sparks. When I wrote my multigenerational fantasy saga, *Shriek*, nothing in my environment was safe from being consumed by the novel. Everything from the particular tone of a woman's laugh to a newspaper headline immediately found a place in my narrative. At one point, I was writing during a concert, at a table in the back, and the way in which the lyrics of the band got into my head was written into a chapter in which the narrator, wandering, happens upon an impromptu concert.

To give another example, the writer Kali Wallace, whose fiction has appeared in *The Magazine of Fantasy & Science Fiction*, among other periodicals, recently completed a novel about a modern teenager living in Ohio. She has "pulled in and used pieces of information I've collected in notes and scribbles from, among many other things, early medieval monastery rumors as described in a popular science book about the Little Ice Age, weird traditions in nineteenth-century European morgues, ancient Islamic mythology, and a single random factoid I learned from a *Criminal Minds* episode." Wallace stresses that the book "isn't *about* any of these things, not even remotely, and I was not reading/watching/thinking about any of those topics with this story in mind, but of course that's exactly the point." She was reading about the Little Ice Age "because climatology interests me as a scientific topic, and at some point I scribbled down a note about what monks in England in the fourteenth century observed when the climate abruptly changed and it rained for five years straight, just because I thought it was weird and interesting." A few years later, Wallace figured out that this "one detail is exactly what I needed to add the right layer of history and depth to the modern fantasy world I was creating, in a story that has absolutely nothing to do with climate change and atmospheric physics."

The somewhat frightening and heady truth is that when you are in a certain mode of waking dream, of deep and sustained thought about your story, your mind can transform anything *into your current project* and make it work. But on a higher level, knowing what entry points into writing most appeal to you can help you channel inspiration. Here are just five such entry points:

WRITE WHAT INTERESTS YOU. The received wisdom in many books and online articles is to write what you know. The problem with this advice is that what you know may not interest you, just as what you're talented at may not interest you as a career. A writer often has to be a kind of benevolent liar, to convince the reader he or she is an expert in the absence of real expertise. You can always find out what you do not know, but you can't fake that spark of curiosity that comes from being *interested* in something. Writing what interests you engages more than your imagination—it ensures that you can reconcile your writing and nonwriting lives. Besides, sometimes the mind needs to come at things sideways.

If you write what interests you, you may find a way to write your way toward the things you know. The great fantasist Angela Carter, for example, wrote about her experiences in Japan at one point in her career and then later, after studying fairy tales, published the feminist collection *The Bloody Chamber*.

WRITE WHAT'S PERSONAL. If you feel compelled to write what you know, let what you know be personal. There's great cathartic power, and thus ample room for inspiration, in taking the events of your life (and, frankly, the lives of people close to you) and finding ways to fictionalize them. Writing what's personal is different from writing what you know because it emphasizes your stake in the fiction. The personal doesn't have to be weighty to spark fiction. Charles Yu's *How to Live Safely in a Science Fictional Universe* includes a lot of smaller-scale personal details that helped inspire the larger, totally made-up story: "For instance, my father really is an engineer, and he has a very entrepreneurial spirit and is one of the most intellectually curious people I know. And my mother is a Buddhist, and she really

How to Live Safely in a Science Fictional Universe

a novel by Charles Yu

Admittedly, the larger canvas of a novel usually can capture more elements without losing focus.

The hardcover jacket design for the North American edition of Charles Yu's first novel (2010).

FAMILY ENVIRONMENT

PERSONAL EXPERIENCE

RELIGION

RESEARCH

LUCK/CHANCE

OTHER TEXTS

dark lighthouse
seen from afar

a certain phrase in
the novel *The Night Circus*

photo of mother
as a teenager

baby's shoe stuck
in a chain-link fence

hesitation in clerk's voice
while saying "Is that all?"

being shouted at by a drunk
in a subway station

the texture of a wall
in Morocco

irritated by fantasy elements
in Harry Potter

imagining pet lizard
as size of a dragon

fascinated with angels
as described in holy books

friend looks like shambling
undead creature in morning

burying the family dog turned
into an all-night adventure

father's old pipe hides
a piece of microfiche

RECEPTIVITY   IMAGINATION   EMPATHY
CREATIVE PLAY   LISTENING   VISUALIZATION

* Wonderbook's visualization
of the average writer

Scott Eagle's "Icarus Elck" (2013), inspired in part by Pieter Bruegel's Elck (1558) and the lines accompanying Bruegel's art, which read in part, "Everyone seeks himself in all things / Throughout the entire world; he is already damned; / How then can someone become lost / If everyone now always seeks himself?"

does worry a lot." However, recognize that confessional or deeply personal writing often requires time to gestate—that trying to write about events that you're still too close to may block inspiration. John Chu, whose work appears in publications such as the *Boston Review* and *Asimov's Science Fiction* magazine, notes that he couldn't engage with the material in his very personal story "Restore the Heart into Love" until "six years after my mom's death. Even then, I literally could not write the story unless I pulled a 'Hey, look, a spaceship!' every other scene."

WRITE WHAT'S UNCOMFORTABLE. Subjects that interest you on a personal or nonpersonal level may also trouble you. Either you shy away from a subject or an approach because you can't believe anything worthwhile can be written from that perspective, or because in writing about the subject you will reveal something you don't want to reveal to the world. The problem, then, is not with inspiration, but with your perception of audience. Here's the good news: You don't need to share what you write with *anyone*. Emily Dickinson didn't share much of anything while alive, and she's become immortal. If you are drawn to write what's

Studying the creative processes of people in different media can be of use to you as a writer. The change in perspective can help you view inspiration in a new light. The attempt to translate that process to writing can also be fruitful. Here are artist Scott Eagle's thoughts on creating "Icarus Elck":

"For me, painting, or any type of making, is like having a teenage child, or being in a car wreck. If at that moment, someone stopped me and asked me to explain what was going on, or 'What does that mean?' the answer would quite simply be, 'If I survive this ordeal, I will let you know.' The name Elck alludes to Pieter Bruegel the Elder's drawings by the same name and means Everyman. The Bruegel print centers on the idea that each of us looks everywhere and projects ourselves onto all things in the vain attempt to find ourselves. The image of the man with a candle was found in a book of clip art. My personal associations for the man are:

he seems to be searching for something; Max Ernst's collages; the alchemical pilgrim; Goethe's *Faust*. For me, this image represents the first step of the wanderer's journey toward a confrontation with the unknown and hopefully a sublimation of the antagonist through the realization of 'I am that.' The Icarus Elck series was a way for me to begin to confront the main antagonist in my work—the tornado. To greatly over-simplify, the tornado has come to represent the things I cannot control or predict. To confront the unpredictable both conceptually and through process, I decided to print archival digital images on top of painting, drawings, and prints on paper. The paper was either found or given to me, then repeatedly distressed through physical abuse, automatic drawing techniques, and collaborations with others. I then printed the digital image on top of this distressed paper, painting, collage, to form completely new and unique juxtapositions of forms and textures." ❧

uncomfortable, it may help to recognize that you are allowed to write *for yourself*, and that any decisions about seeking publication are separate from that first, fundamental decision (and freedom). Denying your attraction to the uncomfortable may result in thwarting inspiration. A good example of drawing strength from this mode of inspiration can be found in Caitlín R. Kiernan's recent novels, including *The Drowning Girl*, which has difficult autobiographical elements. Such fictions aren't just personal; they draw on elements of the writer's life that might be considered the most uncomfortable to give over to an audience.

WRITE WHAT'S RANDOM. Some writers require chaos to find inspiration. You might be someone who needs a jolt to the system—who needs to tell yourself, on seeing a duck wearing a sun hat, being led on a leash by a child, "I need to write about that duck, that hat, that child." You don't require anything more than surprise and the unexpected moment for inspiration. That sudden shock—that introduction of chaos into the world—serves as the catalyst back into writing what's interesting, personal, or uncomfortable.

WRITE FROM EXTERNAL OR SELF-GENERATED PROMPTS. Some writers require order in the form of writing prompts to find inspiration. What are writing prompts? Self-imposed mechanical suggestions or suggestions from editors or other gatekeepers. For example, choosing a random photograph and building a story around it. In terms of external prompts, the

Molly Crabapple's visual adaptation of Salvador Dalí's "My Struggle," originally commissioned for the blog Brain Pickings (2012).

WRITING CHALLENGE

If suddenly confronted by an image like this from Jugend *magazine (c. 1900), could you create a story about it? Write one right now.*

amazing, award-winning Jeffrey Ford, collected in *The Oxford Book of American Short Stories*, often works best when he receives a request to write a story for a theme anthology. Perhaps he gains some essential element from the constraint of being told to "write about this," which challenges his storytelling chops. Sometimes, too, just being in a setting with a constraint helps fuel creativity. In one of the workshops run by me and my wife, Finnish writer Leena Likitalo wrote a prompt story entitled "The Watcher" that, virtually unchanged, was published in *Weird Tales*. Movements like Surrealism, and approaches to writing like the Oulipo school, provide ample opportunities to write from external prompts.

Each of these approaches is connected and can serve as an entry point to the others, like a honeycomb of interconnected tunnels. The mental trick for you is to consider how each entry point affects your ability to be inspired to write. Once beyond the initial spark, you'll find that you'll probably interweave inspiration from multiple entry points but that the way you perceive those possibilities has changed from indifferent or negative to positive. Over time, you may need to change your initial approach, however, because lack of inspiration often means your subconscious mind is bored—it needs a challenge.

You may also need to tweak the received wisdom of needing "distance" to write about something personal—you may find you need distance no matter what your initial inspiration. If research on a subject was your initial spark, you may, for example, need time to internalize what you've learned before you can write about it. Inherent in a concept like distance is that you must be receptive—internalizing the world, but also be *removed* from your subject matter to write about it effectively. You must be observant and aware but also allow some part of your brain to process stimuli in a writerly way.

As Pulitzer Prize winner Junot Díaz told me: "I've never been able to write directly about things that happen to me: I need to deform them in ways to make them strange to me, I need to change them enough so that I can 'play'—invent freely.

SURREALIST
GAMES AND
OULIPO WRITING
EXERCISES

"Cognitive Transformation" by Ben Tolman (2004).

My art begins when I stop trying to be faithful to my life—if I'm playing the court stenographer, then there isn't going to be room for play, and if there is no room for play the work sits on the page lifeless. It's during the play that I come up with all the weird connections, when my subtle structures come to life, when what's best about the book starts to unfold."

Distance also includes the need for the writer to disengage to pursue the narrative forming in their heads. Karin Lowachee, for example, notes that she "daydreams a lot. Whether it's when I do menial tasks or sit on a subway or jog on a treadmill, I find this essential to do—and not necessarily to work out specific details of an idea or a story, but to allow myself to sink into the feel or the tone of an idea or a novel, to let my mind live in the world I'm trying to create, following incoherent threads of possibilities or just going over random conversations my characters might have, or situations without conversation. I go for walks in the summer that allow me to do something repetitive while letting my brain kite off. A naturopath doctor once told me that not all meditation requires sitting still and staring at a wall, that some people find peace through 'walking meditation.' It was an epiphany for me, and I realized that it was essential to my process."

It's important to remember, too, that personal inspiration can come from a shared cultural identity. Finnish writer Johanna Sinisalo, author of *Troll* among others, says that she "lived a substantial part of my life practically in the woods, and to a Finn the wild nature is never something to be afraid of—it's a source of nutrition, and adventure, a place of tranquility. A lot of my works are about the relationship between humankind and environment." Be aware of the general approaches you use to create a story; nurturing them is important not only to the quality of your writing but also to your peace of mind.

WEB

NATURE AND FICTION

What Is/What If: The Beauty of Mystery by Karen Lord

Karen Lord is a writer and research consultant in Barbados. Her first novel, Redemption in Indigo, *was nominated for the World Fantasy Award and won the Frank Collymore Literary Award, the William F. Crawford Award, and the Mythopoetic Award for Adult Literature. Lord's second novel,* The Best of All Possible Worlds, *was published by Del Rey in 2013.*

I am a writer—at least, that's what it says on my passport. It is a word that encompasses hobby, craft, vocation, and even drudgery. I find it a very broad career, especially when I turn from writing up research reports according to the expected professional format to plotting a minor character's development and significance within the larger story arc. Ultimately, whatever the style or the purpose, fiction or nonfiction, I work with words and get them to say what I want them to say. Sometimes I want them to communicate facts, other times I wish to convey truths, and occasionally I want to share the beauty of Mystery, which is no less poetic than the beauty of Truth.

There is both truth and mystery in the act of writing. It is true that writing is a skill like any other to be learned and practiced and improved on, and there are books, articles, and clichés that present as many rules and guidelines on style and story craft as any author could desire. But it is also a mystery—not a puzzle to be solved, nor merely a process to be analyzed and applied, but a mystery that cannot be explained, only tried and experienced. For writing a report, "write what you know" is simple, practical, and useful advice, but for writing fiction that directive is insufficient. It is possible to make facts into fiction—for example, directly translating a life event or a scientific discovery into a plot point—but writers also celebrate the ability to tell tales about things beyond their ken.

Fiction is both process and mystery, knowledge and imagination. It lies somewhere on a spectrum that begins with poetry and ends with statistics. It is art. It takes the forms and shapes of the real world and re-views them with new perception: the shade, texture, and weight of the subconscious and the unreal.

Various stories can be told using only what you know. Jane Austen wrote what she knew from her own life and the lives around her: a music box of a world with familiar society characters dancing to a familiar wedding burden. An intimate knowledge and a small stage can provide enough material for a story. A sufficiently self-aware and observant writer should be able to convincingly depict love, loss, family, childhood, growing up, growing old—in other words, the experience of becoming and being a human among other humans. It is the literary equivalent of a still life: the portrayal of everyday things in a familiar setting.

Knowledge traces the outline, but adding unusual texture and color to that outline creates the variation that makes fiction more than mere retelling. Breaking into the unexpected and the unknown transforms a photo-realist image into the dreamy blur of an impressionist painting, or the edged, off-kilter planes of a Cubist sketch. This is art's paradox: Images unseeable from the vantage point of so-called "real life" may be more evocative of the real than the real itself. Similarly, art that uses the medium of the printed page requires more than unvarnished facts to illuminate truths.

Mary Shelley wrote what she did not know, what could not be known at that moment in history. She took the hypothesis of galvanism and the process of dissection, then added speculation, drama, and fear. It was no mere vivification of a lifeless human body, no tame laboratory filled with bored student

assistants, but a lone genius assembling limbs and organs left over from dissections and re-enchanting them with the primeval force of raw lightning. She revisited Austen's familiar tale of courting, the search for a helpmeet in the manner approved by society, and converted it into the tragedy of a Creature who should never have been made and a Bride who would never be wed.

Was Shelley truly writing the unknown? She was pregnant at the time of writing and had already suffered through the death of a child. She had the experience of being a Victor Frankenstein, assembling a Creature and being somehow a part of whatever miracle put life and soul into the gathered flesh, blood, and bone. But she had also witnessed the reverse, when life and soul depart and cannot be recalled—neither by lightning nor desperation. She was unmarried, shunned by a conservative society, attached to a man whose behavior proved he was not made for monogamy. She would have understood the longing for a spouse and a family, and the destruction of that hope. She fractured what she had known and scattered the small pieces until the picture no longer resembled her life. Then she took those fragments of experience and reassembled them into a newly imagined creation.

Shelley's method contained multitudes of knowledge, and she used that knowledge to push hard at the secure boundaries of the norm. The reader is kept engaged by the tension that comes from the resulting uncertainty, the breaking of rules, and the realization that the author is quite willing to leave you—not at the altar, which would still be within expectations, but stranded on an ice floe at the edge of the known world.

I may be showing a bias toward speculative fiction by pitting Frankenstein against Mr. Darcy, but I believe I can partly defend my choice. Throughout history, every human society has examined its dreams and nightmares through the filter of *what-if*, both playful nonsense and grim paranoia. Grappling with the unknowable has produced fairy tales and scriptures and even literature. Of course not every author uses the speculative as part of their writer's tool kit. The unknowable need not be supernatural; it can be either realist or fantastical. What is key is

that it should have a level of communion with the known. A fictional character can represent a life drawn differently, a parallel-universe self diverted by time or crisis or a different choice of career. That character's story can be entirely rooted in observed reality. It is perfectly valid and no less transformational that a character should become a father or a prisoner rather than a wizard or a beetle.

Making up a story can feel like a sort of intense method acting, playing not just a single role but several, learning worlds and ways beyond the common round. Visiting locations and interviewing people can provide marvelous content, but some of us will never have the resources for that level of immersion. Some of us will have lives that are relatively innocent of parenting, incarceration, magic, and six-legged scuttling no matter how much research we try to put in. Experts and novices alike will encounter a moment when they must make the leap of imagination and filter the facts they have, few or many, through their character's temperament, the demands of plot, and the story's setting. Whether mundane or magical, characters are icons of souls, plots are stylized sketches of the randomness of life, and settings are often dim imagination or dimmer memory. These thin representations somehow imbue what they represent with deeper meaning. That artist's trick, creating the illusion of three dimensions using only shades, lines, and angles on a flat canvas, also belongs to writers.

Fiction is the playground of your what-ifs, where questions get more mileage than certainties, and exploration is not only allowed but essential. By challenging yourself to write what you don't know, you become both student and teacher, employing research, thought experiments, observational studies, and sheer luck to craft a work that is layered, textured, and true. Sometimes it works just the way you want it to. Sometimes it escapes your conscious control. It is a mystery of content and process, and it is beautiful. ❧

RELEVANT WORKS

Holmes, Richard. *The Age of Wonder: How the Romantic Generation Discovered the Beauty and Terror of Science.* New York: Pantheon Books, 2009.

Shields, Carol. *Jane Austen*. New York: Viking, 2001.

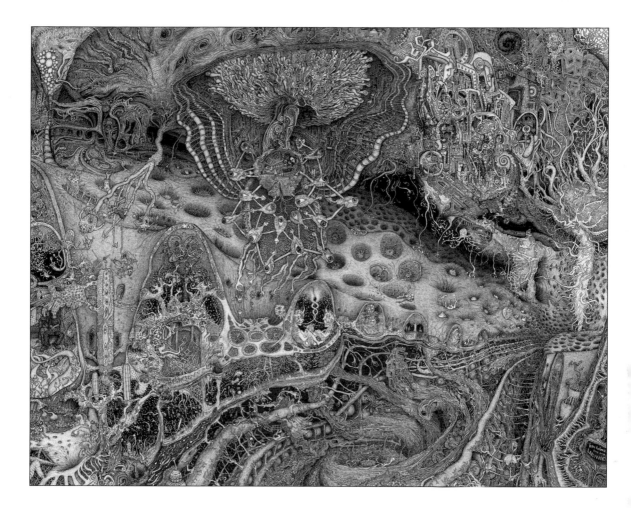

THE STRANGENESS OF THE IMAGINATION

Often exhilarating and a delight, the imagination is also deeply strange, perverse, disturbing, and, at times, frightening. Yet we shouldn't shy away from the darker parts of our creativity. If the beautiful things your imagination conjures up are valid and useful, so, too, is the ugly, inexplicable, untamed material.

When you commit to opening yourself up to your imagination, to the thoughts and ideas that come to you, and using them in your fiction, you are in a sense *surrendering* to the idea of inspiration—all of it, not just the fun parts. You may find yourself in the grip of powerful forces. Your conscious mind may even try to censor these ideas, but if you do, you run the risk of limiting your mind's capacity for the alien, the sinister, and the cruel.

The most direct result of my imagination manifesting in a disturbing way led to a story, "The Transformation of Martin Lake." A few years after going through a traumatic emotional period, a shadowy figure began to appear in my dreams. In these dreams, I would walk up to a house and extend my arm through a hole in the screen door. The figure would open the main door, hold my hand, palm up, and then plunge a knife into the middle of my palm. And keep cutting at it while I just stood there and let the figure do it. It's the most intense nightmare I've ever had—

"Novus Natura" by Ben Tolman (2006).

with a clinical vividness to the violence—and after a while I couldn't take it anymore. I had to do something about it, so I wrote the scene into "The Transformation of Martin Lake," where it became one of the central images of the story. Once I worked the images into "Martin Lake," which went on to win the World Fantasy Award, I stopped having the nightmare.

Direct embedding of something from the subconscious into narrative is one thing. But most of the time, your subconscious provides just the prompt or the beginning and then expects the writer to fill out the implications. My novel *Annihilation* was inspired by a dream in which I was walking down the spiral staircase of a submerged tower, descending into the ground below. The darkness was lit by some unknown means. Soon, I noticed words written in English on the curling stone wall, at about the height where an adult human could have written them. But the words weren't written with ink or spray paint. They were written in living tissue of some kind. As I walked farther down, I realized that the words were slightly swaying, and that they were getting *fresher*. I understood with a shiver of dread that whatever or whoever was responsible for the words *was still down below me, and still writing*. I went deeper into the tunnel and eventually saw a light beckoning from beyond the next curve of the staircase. I was about to encounter the source of the writing . . . and that's when I woke up, jotted some notes, and ran to the computer.

In a sense, my subconscious mind was handing off the idea to my conscious mind—or you could say that my conscious mind had told my subconscious: "No, no—don't tell me anything more. I'll take it from here." And my subconscious was trusting that I **wouldn't balk from following up**, no matter how strange the context.

But the point at which you experience this emotion can vary—an epiphany can be time delayed. In my 2009 novel, *Finch*, there is a revolutionary character given the moniker of the Lady in Blue. I first encountered the real lady in blue on a trip to England, back in 1996. She was busking in the Underground, with a CD for sale. I came upon her unexpectedly, and in the gloom of the corridor, on our way to catch a train, the sound of her singing was ethereal. I hesitated, meaning to stop to buy her CD, but we were in a rush, so I didn't, and my mind was left with questions: "What was the CD like, and was it as good as her singing? Was she a well-known singer just busking on a lark? What is her name?"

Four years later, getting onto a tram in Boston, something about the tram reminded me of the train in the Underground station, and that reminded me of the Lady in Blue, and suddenly my subconscious mind had delivered up to me a detailed history for her. I spent a good half hour on that tram writing down what had appeared spontaneously in my mind. Before I knew it, the Lady in Blue was a rebel leader in my fantastical city of Ambergris, and I knew everything about her childhood and her adult years. Would any of that have occurred if we had stopped and bought the London Lady in Blue's CD, and thus known her name and her background? I don't think so.

This time delay as your mind worries at the problem can also encompass more radical transformations. Remember the two encounters from my childhood I mentioned in the Introduction—the crown-of-thorns starfish in Fiji and the hummingbird hovering outside of my hotel window in Peru? I have never stopped thinking about

The novel's setting turned out to be a transformed version of a trail I've hiked for fifteen years. If my subconscious wanted to explore the irrational and bizarre, some part of me was also wise enough to surround the strange with something both real and personal.

how to make sense of these events, but along the way they have come together at least once, in a story entitled "Ghost Dancing with Manco Tupac." Late in the story, the Quichua guide leading an old conquistador-like character through the Andes has a vision. In the early-morning light, "the Conquistador's horse stepping gingerly among the ill-matched stones of the old Inca highway," the guide sees that "a flock of jet-black hummingbirds encircled the Conquistador's head like his Christian god's crown of thorns." As I wrote those words in the rough draft, it ignited the dual memories from my childhood as my subconscious provided one small, elegant answer by combining the two images.

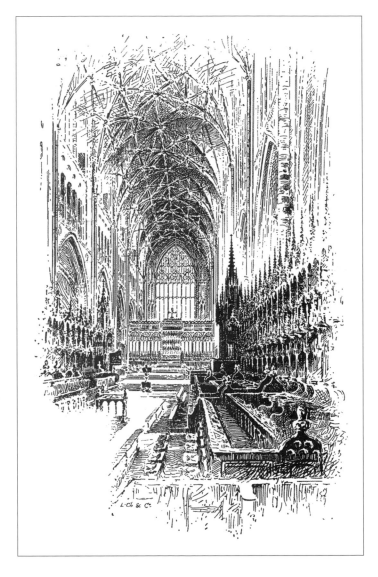

From the book *York Minster* (1897, London), art by Alexander Ansted.

Distance from something has no bearing on the power of memory to transform and stimulate creativity. As writer Vandana Singh notes, "One story that I'm working on, for instance, picked up without warning a scene from my childhood, a vivid one, of walking home from the bus-stop after school, and seeing my little sister playing with a friend and a dog under a gulmohur tree in full flower. I didn't realize then what I know now, that the reason I've remembered that image all these years had something to do with my sudden awareness of the passing of time. And that's relevant to the story, but I had no warning it was going to be appropriated until a few seconds before I actually wrote that scene."

Sometimes, too, that rush of transformative inspiration can save a piece of fiction already in progress—like my far-future novel *Veniss Underground*, which was foundering. When my protagonist came to an underground organ bank to rescue his lover, I couldn't visualize the place. For some reason, without visualizing the organ bank, I couldn't visualize the rest of the novel, and I had to abandon it for several months. Then my wife and I visited the York Minster cathedral in England. As soon as we entered the church—a place older than Westminster in London—and I traced the path of the columns up to the stunningly high ceiling, the little hairs on my arms lifted, and I shivered. The columns, looking like multiple tubes tied together, were utterly alien to me. I'd seen nothing like them. My scalp was tingling. I could feel something rising up inside of me. The organ bank was becoming a reality right in front of my eyes.

But it wasn't until I walked around a corner and saw steps leading down to a door and a window set into the wall, wooden bars across it, that the back of my head exploded and I found myself hardly able to breathe. I could clearly see my main character walking around the corner as I had . . . and being confronted by a scene out of Dante's *Inferno* in that room with the little steps leading down to it. In my vision, that room stretched out and opened up into a much larger space filled with body parts in various stages of decay. As I saw this spreading out before me, so, too, the rest of

the cathedral changed, until the columns became conduits for blood and the sculptures of saints on the columns were bodies set into the columns and the design on the ceiling of the cathedral was instead a series of floating cameras. I stood there scribbling away for long minutes, writing down what was being written into me. I couldn't keep up with the images and ideas cutting into my head. I had to find more paper. I had to keep writing. It was all spilling out. It was all becoming real.

If you're lucky, you have five or six experiences like this during your career. I can't describe it as anything other than a phantasmagorical vision that overtook me. Anything I put down on paper could only be a shadow, an echo, a ghost of what I had experienced in the flesh. But, on a grand scale, it does remind you why you write: for those small and also profound moments of sudden knowledge that occur when you are *written*. In my case, that half hour in the York cathedral got me past the point of most resistance. A lot of hard work remained ahead of me, but I could see my way to the end.

What you produce during blind inspiration is not necessarily superior to what you produce during the slow slog. Everyone knows the deep disappointment of being unable to make the vision on the paper match the vision in one's head. But if you're not in love some of the time, how do you continue—especially if being in love some of the time leads to practical results? And, as the 1960s cult writer Cassandra Railsea once said, "Even expressing angst and frustration and despair in fiction are forms of pleasure seeking, because they speak to catharsis, or at the very least externalizing pain."

York Minster transformed for the cover of the Polish edition of *Veniss Underground*; art by Tomasz Maronski (2009).

☞ ☞ ☞

WRITER'S BLOCK
BY MATTHEW CHENEY

Matthew Cheney's work has been published by English Journal, One Story, Web Conjunctions, Strange Horizons, Failbetter.com, Ideomancer, Pindeldyboz, Rain Taxi, Locus, The Internet Review of Science Fiction, *and* SF Site, *among others, and he is the former series editor for* Best American Fantasy. *He teaches English, Women's Studies, and Communications & Media Studies at Plymouth State University.*

ONCE UPON A time, I thought writers' blocks were the wooden blocks with letters on them that I played with as a little kid. Though I later learned this was not what people meant by the term, I think it is useful still to think of writer's block that way. Imagine writer's block as a wall built with writers' blocks. It looks sturdy and impregnable if you've got your nose up against it, but it can be toppled over if you're willing to give it a push and then play around with the chaos. Here are some thoughts on writer's block with that in mind.

1. Writer's block can be as much a matter of perception as reality. Theodore Sturgeon complained frequently about writer's block, and yet he wrote, among other things, enough short stories to fill thirteen books. What might have happened if Sturgeon one day encountered *New Yorker* writer Joseph Mitchell at a café? Mitchell wrote a book, *Joe Gould's Secret,* that was itself about a man struck with writer's block, and then, from the book's publication in 1965 until his death in 1996, Mitchell showed up at his office at *The New Yorker* every day and didn't write a thing.

2. Or consider Tillie Olsen. A very fine short story writer, Olsen's major work is a slim book of four stories, *Tell Me a Riddle.* She also published a fragment of a novel she'd begun when she was nineteen, *Yonnondio,* and a book of nonfiction, *Silences,* about all the forces that cause writers—particularly writers who are female and/or poor—not to be able to write or publish. Olsen herself became as famous for not writing as for what she had written. She became a cherished symbol of the social inequalities that rob some writers of the time and money necessary for concentration. *Tell Me a Riddle* garnered extraordinary praise, and it would have been difficult for even the greatest of writers to live up to the expectations Olsen's readers built up for her over the years. (See also: Ralph Ellison and Harper Lee.) Her mythic power as a writer was strengthened by not writing.

3. Expectation can destroy artists of all kinds. It's a cousin to ambition, but ambition is a different thing (a distant cousin): the desire to be better than everybody else, the desire to match your skills against the best in history, the desire to make aesthetic objects of utter perfection—for all its perils (arrogance, ruined friendships and families, self-hatred), ambition can fuel writers toward great accomplishment. Expectations are more burdensome. Expectations put the wrong kind of voices in our heads. The voices of ambition say,

"Let's try to be great!" The voices of expectation say, "You must be great. Or else you are nothing."

4. In an essay on Theodore Sturgeon in *Starboard Wine*, Samuel R. Delany proposes that a defining difference between science fiction writers and more self-consciously "literary" writers is a difference in their attitudes toward revision. For various reasons, Delany maintains, it is not in the SF writer's best interests to appear to labor too hard over any particular piece of work, but for the writer who wants to attain literary (and academic) respectability, the exact opposite is true. While any writer trying to make a living off of their work would be better off being fast and prolific than not, there is more acceptance and encouragement of fast, prolific writing in the genrefied fields than in the marketplace of literary respectability. Joyce Carol Oates has published hundreds of short stories and more than fifty novels, a feat that is questioned in interviews and looked askance at in reviews, with nearly every reviewer who dislikes her work raising the question of whether she writes too much and too quickly. Such questions rarely arise for writers who are not perpetual candidates for the most prestigious literary awards; indeed, as George R. R. Martin can attest, many readers clamor not for a writer to be patient and careful, but rather to write faster.

5. Researching examples of writer's block, I wondered why most of the examples I found came from the more hallowed realms of the distinctly Literary. Certainly, writers of all types will acknowledge occasional struggles, especially with individual pieces of work, but my unscientific survey of interviews and biographies failed to find many genre writers of repute whose struggles with writer's block were as public as those of writers who have achieved some literary canonicity. Partly, this may result from genre writers being less biographied and interviewed (indeed, biographies and interviews in such venues as *The Paris Review* do much of the work of creating canonicity), but I suspect that Delany is right to see a difference between the types of perceptions that benefit genrefied and

literaried writers. If we remove the commercial liabilities of writer's block for anyone who seeks to make money from their work, there remains the fact that, at least during the last one hundred years or so, it has been nearly impossible for genre writers to sustain a reputation with a small body of work, and nearly impossible for literary writers to avoid skepticism and contempt with a large body of work.

6. I rarely suffer writer's block because I don't have many expectations for my writing, and among those expectations I don't have is that most of my writing will be in one particular genre or another. I've written in every genre imaginable, even ones I have no talent for, such as journalism. (Journalists have to talk to people on the telephone. I don't like telephones. Neither did Thoreau. Also, journalists have to deal with fact-checkers, and I think fact-checkers are as annoying as telephones and careers.) Perhaps this is why I love Gertrude Stein's book *How to Write*, which is utterly different from all other writing guides—it is its own genre, and every genre, and none. Its oddness appeals to mine. It doesn't tell you how to write a best-selling novel in three months or how to get an agent or how to write poetry that rhymes. Instead, it contains paragraphs such as this: "There were three kinds of sentences are there. Do sentences follow the three. There are three kinds of sentences. Are there three kinds of sentences that follow the three." Also, my single favorite piece of writing advice: "Forget grammar and think about potatoes."

7. "What do you do about deadlines?" you say to me. I'm glad you asked that question, because I was just wondering it myself. For instance, I've been given a deadline for these words that I'm writing right now. That deadline is not pressing, but it's within a couple of weeks, and the next few weeks of my life are rather busy, so if I'm going to get this done, I'd better get it done now. But how can I write something about writer's block? Aside from the paradox of writing about not writing, there's also a big and practical problem: I don't

really have anything useful to say. It's not like I'm somebody you've heard of. Somebody you care about. And look at these sentences! Drivel. Anybody could write better sentences than these. They don't say anything. The words are simplistic and stupid. There are no ideas. I'm not communicating anything. If I ever manage to finish writing this, it will be rejected, so why do I even bother? It's just drivel. Pure drivel.

8. The greatest gift any writing instructor ever gave me was the lesson offered by the teacher of a course called Advanced Expository Writing at New York University. He required us to read *The Celestine Prophecy* because he ardently believed we needed to know what bad writing is. And he was right. It was inspiring. No matter how hard I try, I will never be able to write as badly as James Redfield. I will also never sell as many copies of a book as he did with that one. But nonetheless. This isn't about sales. This is about me worrying that I'm not Shakespeare or Joyce or Gertrude Stein or another writer of gobsmacking talent, such as Georg Büchner, who, by the time he died, had written two of the greatest plays of all time (*Danton's Death* and *Woyzeck*), a breathtakingly original work of fiction (*Lenz*), an amusing satirical comedy (*Leonce and Lena*), a radical political pamphlet ("The Hessian Courier"), and a pathbreaking scientific treatise on the nervous system of a common river fish. Büchner died at age twenty-three. He and I share a birthday. Whenever I am tempted to say to myself, "By the time he was my age, Büchner had been dead for fourteen years," I instead look at whatever I am writing and say to myself, "This isn't quite as bad as *The Celestine Prophecy.*"

9. One of the most important expectations to give up as quickly as possible is the expectation of being original. You will not be original. The last person to be original was Gilgamesh. He didn't have a career or fact-checkers or a telephone, so he was far less burdened than anyone who came later. You should be grateful to him. It's a terrible burden, originality.

"People do manage to be original, though," you say to me. Maybe. But why put that burden on yourself? Do you think you'll ever get anything written if you keep holding yourself to a high standard of originality? Sure, it's possible. What do I know? I'm not omniscient. I don't even know who you are. Maybe you're Gilgamesh.

10. You can always write something. Literally. Something. Something. Something. Something. Something. Something. Gertrude Stein. Something. Something. Gertrude Something. Gertrude Gertrude. Stein Something. Something. Something. Goose.

11. But maybe there's nothing wrong with not writing. "So you're saying I should shut up?" you say to me. No, I'm sorry, that was rude. Writer's block feels horrible, I know, even if you're creating art. In my early twenties, after becoming disillusioned with the sort of writing I thought would make me rich and famous and loved, I stopped being able to write anything except bad poetry and shallow academic papers. For a year. I hid out in backwaters and tried to sweep up the shattered shards of my expectations, ambitions, desires, and dreams. It was one of the lowest periods of my life. I could sense that there were words somewhere in me, sentences that I needed to form, structures I needed to fill, but everything I actually wrote looked awkward, stilted, pretentious, incoherent, childish, stupid, weak, vapid. For a while, I didn't write anything, not even bad poetry or shallow academic papers, because to look at the vapid, weak, stupid, childish, incoherent, pretentious, stilted, awkward junk I'd written made me hate myself. I wanted to run around the corner and see the world blow up. I hated my inadequacies, my failure. Writing made it all so obvious, put it there on paper, let it stare at me in hateful, bitter ink. I couldn't bear it anymore. I stopped writing. I shut up. It's the closest I've yet come to feeling dead.

12. With time, I found words again. With time, I stopped hating all the words I found. With time, I

learned to stop expecting to write in one particular way, one genre or style or mode. I stopped caring about whether I created art or not-art. Some people can stick to one type of writing and be perfectly happy. I'm not one of them. Once I knew that, and once I stopped trying to pigeonhole myself for the sake of a career and originality and beating Georg Büchner, I didn't suffer any significant writer's block again. The lesson I take from that experience is that the way to beat writer's block is to get to know yourself better as a writer, and once you know yourself, accept yourself. You're not Shakespeare or Joyce or Gertrude Stein or Theodore Sturgeon or Joseph Mitchell or Tillie Olsen or Fran Lebowitz or James Redfield. For better or worse, you're you.

13. One of the most original of American writers, David Markson, wrote a series of novels composed of glimpses of ordinary, mortal life scattered in amid blocks of facts and quotes, most of them about writers and artists. One of those books is called *Reader's Block*. Some of its many short paragraphs include: "René Descartes was born in a hayfield," "Christina Rossetti almost certainly died a virgin," and "It remains a scandal to philosophy that there is as yet no satisfactory proof of an external world, Kant said." Early on in the book, we see this paragraph: "What is a novel in any case?" It's a guiding question for the rest of the book, a question that gives force to the form. It's a good question to ask about whatever genre you think you're writing in. ("What is this x in any case?") It may be that your assumptions about the genre (x = linear narrative), your expectations for it (x = well-rounded characters), are holding you back, blocking you. Maybe you need to mix up your equations and add more in any case. Why shouldn't you write a novel like a poem, a short story like an essay, a memo like a song? Why not try?

14. I have a folder on my computer named "Failed Attempts." I created it at least ten years and a few computers ago, expecting I could go back to a failed attempt sometime later and give it another shot, or at least grab some shreds and use them in something new. I've never done that, though, never resurrected a failed attempt. I might as well have thrown them all away. But I'm glad I didn't throw them away and instead filled that folder. It relieves any feeling of guilt I have for abandoning a piece of writing once it begins to feel like it's failing. I do so happily now. I drop it into the Failed Attempts folder and, liberated, start something else, something new, something different. I tell myself that we're taking a bit of a break from each other. I can always go back to it. I can always pull it out of the Failed Attempts folder if I need to. Failure doesn't have to be permanent. Think of the symmetric property of equality in algebra: X = Failed Attempt also means Failed Attempt = X.

15. "You didn't really answer my question about deadlines," you say to me. Didn't I? I'm sorry. I got distracted. Distraction, actually, is a key to overcoming writer's block. You need to misdirect yourself. You have a map in your head, and you think that's the direction you're traveling in, so you go down the road that the map tells you to go down, and in the middle of the road is an infinitely high wall that wasn't on the map. You can bang your feet and fists and head against the wall for eternity, but the wall is stronger than you. What you need to do is get rid of the map and get off the road. You need to get yourself lost, at least for a little while. (Go around a corner, watch a world blow up.)

16. Or, you could think about potatoes. ❧

The Strahov
Theological Hall
in Prague, Czech
Republic (photo by
Jorge Royan)

Some elements, then, that lead to inspiration and story, that shape and protect your imagination, are deeply allied with your subconscious. But you can train yourself to enter these built-in states by creating the conditions and environment optimal to conjuring up inspiration. Creating conditions and an environment in which it is *harder* to channel inspiration and creativity is one way to induce writer's block.

Sometimes, too, your conscious mind has to let your subconscious mind know the plan. In much of what I am documenting here, I am trying to give you permission to engage in a set of behaviors common to most writers. I want you to recognize that any or all of these impulses or *states of being* you exhibit are normal, that the very attributes that may make your friends or family at times find you strange or unengaged are part of the process. Our imaginations never really sleep if we protect and feed them properly, although they may need to hibernate from time to time.

If there is anything I hope you take away from this chapter, it would be the following:

- Beware of advice from people who say you have too much imagination. There is no such thing as too much imagination.
- Don't self-censor sudden flashes of inspiration because they strike your conscious mind as "stupid," "frivolous," "strange," or "unsettling." Even if you don't use the material, you are telling your subconscious that you want to believe that bears moved in next door.
- Remain open to possibilities for creative play with others, and understand that you are exercising the muscle of your imagination when you engage in creative play. You are also enabling others to do the same.
- Don't become impatient with the amount of time it takes for a story or novel

to come alive in your mind before you start writing. Thoughtfully considering what you write is an essential part of the process.

- Be open to including autobiographical elements in fantasy—it will often salvage what might otherwise be inert on the page.
- Be fiercely protective of your imagination, and nurture it.

Still, there are limits, and not all minds are built for the kind of creativity that fiction requires, in part because the point of the imagination at times is to fabricate, to in a sense *lie*, and by lying make the lie—that which does not exist—the truth.

Kali Wallace tells the story of having had a very smart friend in college, a neurology researcher who writes nonfiction, who claimed "with absolute certainty to have no imagination." Wallace recalls that "we had a great many conversations in which both of us would be utterly baffled and bemused by how the other person's brain works. She wanted to learn how to tease out imaginative thoughts from her brain, but I had absolutely no idea how to help her do that. Making things up comes so naturally to me I didn't even really understand how the world looked from her point of view."

∽ ∽ ∽

The imagination is infinite—it can encompass all you want it to encompass, if you let it. Everything we see around us, whether functional or decorative, once existed in someone's imagination. Every building, every fixture, every chair, every table, every vase, every road, every toaster. In fact, the world we live in is largely a manifestation of many individual and collective imaginations applied to the task of altering preexisting reality. So the question becomes, *How can you position yourself to dream well?*

Your fiction is part of a complex ecosystem, and within that ecosystem, it is an organism with many complex parts. Understanding the Elements of Narrative, including the Greater and Lesser Mysteries, should be in the service of also understanding how they work together. Once you have even a little mastery of these elements, that monstrous penguin you just created that walks on water and belches fire will have three eyes by design rather than by accident. It also might just find a reader or two . . . .

Chapter 2:
The Ecosystem of Story

ESCARTES WAS WRONG: The world is more like a living creature than a machine—and so, too, are stories. In our context, in fact, stories are animals that would be the pride of any medieval bestiary. Like living creatures, stories come in a bewildering number of adaptations and mutations. Even within the constraint of written words, incredible variety occurs due to the near-infinite number of possible combinations. Anyone who tells you there are only a dozen types of stories should be viewed with as much suspicion as someone who tells you "all animals are the same." A penguin is not a hamster; nor is a prawn a sea cucumber, an elephant a squid, an anteater a dragon.

Still, each of these story-creatures conforms to certain unities of shape, habit, and function. Stories eat, drink, sneeze, run around, and hunt for food like any animal. They experience life through five or more senses. They often have a head, a torso, and, hopefully, a tail— or, if you must, a beginning, middle, and end. They have a particular style, depending on the texture of their prose-skin. Their musculature, bones, and internal organs, while not visible to the reader's eye, work together in perfect union to create movement, thought, action, reaction, and any number of other functions. And, like some animals, a great story watches the reader through some uncanny animating impulse that goes beyond any blueprint or technical precision on the page.

Just as the elements of a story or novel can be viewed as the parts of a fantastical creature, so, too, can stories be viewed as part of a complex, codependent ecosystem of narrative—perhaps even a little bit like Robert Connett's vision for "Night Trawler," reproduced in this chapter. Fiction ranges from megafauna—like novels—all the way down to practically microscopic life forms like flash fiction. The different sizes of these life forms in no way reflects the quality or importance of each; a good short story, lithe and swift and intelligent, can be more intricate and more involving than the most sprawling novel that clomps through the underbrush or pushes leviathan-like through the sea. From the reader's point of view, the best examples all share that *frisson* of discovery and mystery, some sense of life beyond the page. If you were to disappear into that landscape, you'd find yourself not backstage looking at ladders and props, but in *another world*.

To grow as a fiction writer, you absolutely must engage in some dissection of stories, your own and the work of others. But you also have to be a kind of *zoologist* or *naturalist* of narrative. Observations of a living organism require a different approach, one that doesn't so much catalogue separate parts as seek to understand how everything works together. (It's also worth noting that no amount of searching through entrails will ever replicate or truly explicate the actual experience of reading a good story or novel.)

The paradox is that, by its very nature, any writing book must at least begin by addressing many of those elements in isolation and often be definitional in nature, artificially freezing in place what exists in a larger, shifting context. The purpose is to establish the basic foundation for the exploration found in the later chapters. There you will discover these elements set into motion or working in complex ways, and be reminded once again that the metaphor of stories being *alive* is both powerful and useful.

Narrative Life Forms

NOVEL

NOVELLA

NOVELETTE

SHORT STORY

FLASH FICTION

POEM

NOVEL: The megafauna of the literary world, the novel ranges from about 55,000 words to 250,000 words, although some are larger. In a few painful cases, publishers have insisted on long novels being broken into two or more shorter novels. This can result in permanent skeletal and muscular damage. Other novels may be "padded" by the author, resulting in unnecessary scenes and sections; this negatively affects the novel across its circulatory, respiratory, and organ systems. A novel allows for digressions that may seem like tangents but support theme or characterization in interesting ways. Novels can also entertain the idea of, for example, entire chapters on whaling practices (*Moby Dick*) or using many viewpoint characters. These options don't just lengthen the text but widen and deepen narrative in ways different from the short story and the novella. The novel shown in this panel is "in progress," with some parts of the structure not yet in place; nor is every passenger-character on board.

NOVELLA: Perhaps the purest form of life in the literary world, the novella ranges from about 11,000 words to 55,000 words (some call the length from 11,000 to 17,000 a "novelette"). The novella combines attributes of the novel and the short story. The best novellas allow for ample expansion of character arcs, with room for extended exploration of theme and situation—with less chance of extraneous scenes. A novella can entertain more viewpoint characters but often keeps its main focus on one person. Like the short story, the novella depends on a certain precision of language. Here, you can see a rare night-time shot of a novella in motion, as it is being read, accompanied by a few nocturnal flash fictions.

SHORT STORY: Combining dexterity and depth, the short story ranges in length from about 1,500 words to 10,000 words; anything shorter is likely to be labeled "flash fiction." Contrary to popular belief, the short story can be just as profound as any novel, the compression of idea, characterization, and structure all working to create a memorable experience for the reader. The best stories can travel a century or more and come back to the present, all within the span of a single paragraph or page. Stories rarely feature more than two viewpoint characters, and usually just one. This focus can make the short story seem more personal, as can the need for every sentence to count; in a skillful short story, no detail is without some purpose beyond the decorative. The short story pictured here has already found an eager reader, who is so devoted to the story that he won't let go of it. ❦

THE ELEMENTS

What are the main elements of narrative? Because they can be identified as separate and present in the typical story, seven components qualify—even if the ways they interact with one another are myriad and thus unpredictable. These elements are the cells, the blood, the organs necessary for story life.

CHARACTERIZATION. The methods by which the primary and secondary people (or aliens or talking animals or raging monsters) in a story are made to seem real or interesting. These methods include the choice of point of view, use of exposition, and all of the other elements of story. Chapter 5 examines characterization in detail.

POINT OF VIEW. The use of first person ("I"), second person ("you"), third person ("she"), limited omniscient, or omniscient approaches to portray the main characters and possibly minor characters as well.

SETTING. The physical environments in which the story takes place. Chapter 6 explores setting, or "worldbuilding" in detail.

EVENTS/SITUATIONS. What actually happens in the story, sometimes known as *plot* when describing a *sequence* of events—and often expressed through *scenes*. Events and situations are given significance and emphasis through *structure*. The organization of fiction is covered in detail by Chapter 4.

DIALOGUE. The conversations and snippets of speech that convey what the characters are saying to one another and that help to dramatize scenes. Indeed, use of dialogue often distinguishes a scene from summary (pure exposition).

DESCRIPTION. The details that "set the scene" and, in conjunction with dialogue, make a scene seem real and in-the-moment. Description can also be said to create a tone. A subset of description, exposition, is used for a specific purpose. It relates needed information by telling it directly to the reader rather than showing (or dramatizing) it. Read Kim Stanley Robinson's essay on Exposition later in this chapter.

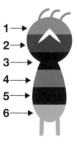

STYLE. This slippery term more or less means the way the story is told; i.e., the patterns of words, phrases, and sentences through which the writer achieves certain effects. Some writers would group it with the Greater and Lesser Mysteries described later in this chapter.

A Closer Look at Some of the Elements

Those elements that commonly form the inspiration for story—narrative design (events/plot/structure), characterization, and worldbuilding (setting)—are explored in subsequent chapters. Here, let's take a closer look at elements found in most stories but that can be considered "layers" or "things deployed in the text": point of view, dialogue, description, and style.

Point of View

Who tells your story and how close you get to their perspective depends in part on **point of view**. In some stories, the reader may feel as if they're perched on the character's shoulder, or inside that person's head. In others, the reader feels more remote. That distance, or lack of distance, is key to other elements of the story, including the style and what details you convey.

In *First Person,* "I" is the narrator. First person sounds natural—we all function as first-person narrators every day—and is an easy way to give the reader access to the narrator's thoughts. If the narrator is not the main character, however, it is also an easy way to obscure the main character's thoughts. As critically acclaimed writer Nick Mamatas points out, "Using Dr. Watson as the narrator of the Sherlock Holmes stories allows Arthur Conan Doyle to keep some distance from his famous detective." For this reason, too, every first-person narrator is unreliable to a degree, a fact that you can use to your advantage in creating suspense or surprise.

First person can be very complex: "Remember that we all create narratives about other people," Mamatas says. "When Nick Carraway describes the Gatsby's death in forensic detail—'He stopped at the garage for a pneumatic mattress that had amused his guests during the summer, and the chauffeur helped him pump it up.'—he's not a witness. He pieced it together from talking to the chauffeur, the butler, and the gardener. But he describes it as fact, because that's just something Nick would do, given his obsession with Gatsby. The only true limit of a first-person narrator is determined by the character's personality." Just take care to know the difference between when a first-person narrator is conveying something interesting and when they're rambling.

In *Second Person,* "You" is the narrator. Essentially, the reader is in the brain of the narrator, experiencing life as that person does. Second-person narration may be rarely used, but it can provide immediacy and a sense of seeing things more intensely. However, as Mamatas notes, "Many readers also reject being told who they are. When reading a sentence like 'You are a child soldier, AK-47 in hand. You are standing over the corpse of your mother;' some readers react by thinking, *No, I am not!*" The best second-person stories also give the reader a little room to ease into the narration. Mamatas cites the example of *Bright Lights, Big City* by Jay McInerney, which begins, "You are not the kind of guy who would be at a place like this at this time of the morning." By telling us who we are not, "the author has the chance to win us over by describing a debauched evening and early morning in a nightclub."

Third Person takes two main forms: omniscient and limited, but with subjective and objective forms of each. In *omniscient third-person* stories, the narrator is a godlike

Much of the information in this section is adapted from writer Nick Mamatas' very useful lecture on point of view.

Matthew Cheney on "Who Speaks"

voice with perfect knowledge of the characters and setting. Thus, there can be no real secrets kept, without the reader feeling cheated. Omniscient narrators, though they know everything, tend to be a bit distant from their characters. On the plus side, an omniscient narrator's knowledge is not limited to the characters. As Mamatas says, "Asides about the inner workings of submarines, the fate of the unborn children of characters, etc., are all acceptable, but can be tricky for an author to pull off—will readers remain interested throughout the course of the lecture? Also, omniscient narrators are often subjective narrators, and readers sometimes confuse their opinions with those of the author. So make sure your own opinions are sophisticated ones . . . "

In *limited third person*, the narration follows a single individual. What the writer can describe is limited by what the individual character perceives or experiences. This is the most common narrative choice in commercial fiction. But because the technique is heavily influenced by film and television, it can be problematic. "Often, writers and readers talk of a character being 'off-screen' instead of 'off-page,'" Mamatas says. "Or of a protagonist being followed around 'by a camera' instead of by an observer who makes choices about what to detail and what to edit out. But the camera metaphor can be misleading, as there is more to limited points of view than what the camera sees, and the camera can also be used in ways which violate the idea of limited point of view."

Many times, too, a point of view will choose *you* in a sense. You will sit down to write a rough draft, and you'll just *know* what character to follow and whether you want to use first, second, or third person. When Haruki Murakami attempted third person early in his career, he felt "embarrassed," as he explained in an interview with Hideo Furukawa. "I couldn't get past the feeling that writing in the third person was like playing God— you're on top, your characters way below" while first person "just felt so natural."

But if you get stuck or the finished piece just doesn't quite work, experimenting with a change in point of view can help rejuvenate the story and present you with new possibilities. Once, for my novel *Veniss Underground*, I couldn't figure out how to write about a character. I tried first and third person. Only when I settled on second person did the character come to life.

Veniss Underground
VERSIONS

DIALOGUE

Speech in fiction may feel casual or "unstaged" from the reader's point of view, but regardless of this effect, the purpose of dialogue is focused and specific. In addition to being the primary impetus for why a scene feels in-the-moment and "like" real life—providing a sense of immediacy—dialogue in a scene can perform one or more of the following functions:

- Convey a mood
- Reveal character traits or motivation
- Provide information
- Move the plot forward and/or increase its pace
- Create or reflect conflict, tension, or understanding between characters
- Foreshadow what is to come

Point of View: "Subjective Versus Objective" and "Roving" by Nick Mamatas

Nick Mamatas is the author of several novels, including Bullettime, *which involves three separate first-person points of view (from the same person in different universes!) plus a third-person present, and* Sensation *(a first-person plural POV via the sensory organs of a collectively intelligent species of spider). His other books and stories are as weird.*

Point of view is itself a matter of fashion and sensibility—that is, point of view and how it works in fiction depends partially on your point of view. Ideas about point of view have changed during the life span of the novel. Limited third-person and first-person points of view are more popular today than omniscient third person, for example. But if you've read many nineteenth-century novels, you've experienced the voice of omniscient narrators. These stories not only explored the interior lives and external conflicts of the characters, but also the social worlds they inhabited. Collective opinions, class distinctions, dollops of history, and technical information abound. There's no need for a character to be contemplating the basics of Utilitarianism or the price of gold for the omniscient narrator to stop the story and helpfully explain philosophy or economics to the reader. Anything at all could be said—as long as it was appropriate to the story and suited the sentiments of the time.

In modern times, there's less interest in omniscience, because there is less of a need to construct a social world for readers to identify with. We no longer read novels to learn "how we live now"; some might say that society is fractured, while others contend that now novelists write for classes other than a narrow middle one. We don't all aspire to a good marriage and a manor house anymore. But we still have an abiding interest in seeing through other people's eyes. And two concepts—the subjective versus the objective and deployment of roving narrators—help to add complexity or complication to fiction.

Objective versus Subjective Narration

Objective narration means that the observing narrator has no opinions and does not editorialize—for example, "The Killers" by Ernest Hemingway. You might call this a "camera's eye view," but I prefer to think of a disinterested human observer. Thinking in overly cinematic terms can lead to bizarre shifts to details like the buttons on someone's shirt, or roving from one character to another. A camera lens can zoom in anywhere but probably shouldn't. When a camera takes off into the recesses of a human ear, or spirals upward toward the moon, it means something profound for the story being told on the screen. Shifts of attention on the page have to be as meaningful.

Sometimes objective point of view is called "dramatic"—that is, it is the point of view of the *audience* watching a drama unfold in the theater. The viewer can see anything on the proscenium stage but can see nothing beyond it about the world, or

nothing too deeply within it—say, what characters are actually thinking as opposed to how they are behaving.

Note that objective narration is very stringent: A single subjective statement by an otherwise objective narrator can make the narration subjective. A subjective narrator can make any number of objective statements, however.

Subjective narration allows for the reader to see the inner thoughts of characters, sometimes but not necessarily presented as dialogue. These thoughts and feelings can also be simply described, limning the narration. If a character wakes up to a day of gray skies, that's objective. If the same character wakes up to a day of bleak and hideous bullshit, that's subjective. To be subjective, information must not be apprehendable simply by observing the scene. Also, another note: If a character's thoughts match his or her actions exactly, the thoughts aren't very interesting and are probably not necessary to share.

As with omniscient narration, if we get to read a character's mind, we get to read it for the entire scene. The narrator cannot simply ignore a character's secret plans. Subjective narration also influences the rhetorical idiom of the narration. *Sam woke up one shitty Monday morning* is an example of subjectivity. Once editorializing emerges, the narrative is subjective. (Note that in "The Killers," there is little to no such editorializing.)

Subjectivity goes beyond the camera. Of course, subjective narrators can make objective statements, but subjectivity colors everything. Not only can we hear a character's thoughts—and indeed, we often *must* hear the most dramatically important thoughts—we see the world as they see it, through their minds, and not just over their shoulders.

ROVING POINT OF VIEW

Having a third-person narrator shift from one character to another is called "roving." (Switching from third person to, say, first person, or second, is best called "alternating" points of view.) Thanks to the influence of TV and movies, many beginning writers like to rove too much. Remember that point of view is a way of signaling to the reader which character or characters are the most important. We don't need to follow everyone, or to hear the innermost thoughts of all characters.

The current fashion is to rove from one point of view to another only between scenes or chapters. "Head-hopping" between characters within a single scene is often frowned upon by editors and, to a lesser extent, by readers. However, there are exceptions. In romance fiction, it is not unusual for the first encounter between the heroine and hero to switch point of view—we read her reaction to him, and his to her, to create a sense of "love at first sight" or destiny.

Roving points of view can be effective, but be careful not to "head-hop" for no good reason. The movie camera has inoculated some readers against roving point of view, but that's because we almost never enter the heads of two characters on screen at the same time. But the camera-eye view seems so intimate that when it comes time to create a similar effect on the page, many writers make the error of telling us every random jejune thought that comes to the mind of the characters in the scene. In film, the point of view may seem to change as shots and reaction shots are shown in quick succession, but in fact, the film's scenic point of view is objective, not roving.

To rove properly, think of the dramatic impact of the scene. A sudden shift to another character's point of view within the same scene can work, but likely not more than once or twice a novel, and that character had better be thinking or experiencing something profound. A change of point of view within a scene is like a "jump cut" in a film; a very powerful technique that is best used sparingly.

However, the opposite can also work—when two characters are experiencing or observing or thinking very nearly the same thing, a shift within a scene from one to another can also work. The classic example of the "meet cute" in a romance novel—a scene in which the female protagonist catches a glance at the male lead and falls in love at first sight, and then the scene is virtually replayed from the male point of view—works because of the near-identical emotions being experienced by both characters. Point of view is ultimately about information, and the most important information a writer can give a reader is information with emotional weight. ❧

- Remind readers of things they may have forgotten
- Reveal the complexity of character relationships

Theoretically, no two characters should speak in the exact same way, and even two characters who do speak in a similar fashion might express themselves differently depending on the context. The dragon hunter who says, "Oh shit!" when cornered by the beast is very different from the ones who say, "Don't kill me—I'll give you gold," or, "Holy crap. I'm an idiot"—or a fourth who says **nothing coherent at all**, but is instead overtaken by a memory of her last good draught of beer sipped at a nearby tavern. Some people even unconsciously mimic the speech patterns of whomever they're talking to.

Sometimes insight into character and dialogue means being silent.

If you're stuck on what someone might say, try to triangulate what you know about the character with the emotional context or conflict of the situation and what they've said up to that point (and how they've said it). Also think less about "Here I need the talking penguin to say 'You know nothing about feathers or my life, you bastard!'" and more about "What would naturally develop out of the drama of this scene?"

Dialogue is meant to emulate real speech, not reproduce it. Replicating real speech results in chaos and boredom for the most part— just read a transcript of any cocktail party. Your approach should try to approximate how people really sound, but edited, and usually without um's, ahem's, and coughs. Remember, too, that most real people don't speak using perfect grammar. Words are left out. Interruptions occur—and so do misunderstandings. People say one thing but mean another. They say things they don't truly believe because they want to impress or because they want to appear to be other than who they really are. Regional differences affect dialogue, too. I use "jeeze louise" as a curse because part of my family is from Chicago (and Lutheran), but to my wife, Ann, raised in Miami, "jeeze louise" might as well be Portuguese.

Some general rules about uses of dialogue, all of which have been broken at one time or another:

- People generally don't have conversations about basic information they already know *and* the person they're talking to knows too. "I am a penguin, Bob, and as you know because you too are a penguin, penguins are covered in feathers, although in this case, feathers are almost like fur." Pushing information that you think the reader needs into dialogue may be a "tell" that you are having trouble with your story. If one character does lecture another, it should reveal something about that character's personality, level of stress, or other factor. Otherwise, it's not **dramatically interesting**. In some forms of science fiction, a scientist will convey information to a layperson in dialogue—"I've brought you here today to discuss the penguin-seeking death ray developed by Dr. Psychopath"—but even then there may be a much more elegant solution by using summary instead.

Obvious exceptions include mystery fiction where readers expect explanations through conversations.

- Use of a regional dialect can be a stumbling block for the reader. A compelling reason to use dialect that arises out of the needs of characterization or culture is certainly legitimate. But otherwise just describe the person's general speech patterns before they first speak and/or use a few repeating idiosyncrasies as anchors to convey the difference. Otherwise, too, if you are not intimately

DIALOGUE IN ACTION

conversant with the dialect in question, there are few more obvious ways for writers to embarrass themselves on the page.

- Some writers use dialogue tags like "he said excitedly" or "the penguin exclaimed boisterously." In most cases, such tags aren't necessary and can actively interfere with the reader's enjoyment of the text. At worst, such tags are insulting to the reader. Good dialogue, aided by references to a character's demeanor or mannerisms, should convey the tone and emotion of what is being said. In a few cases, such as use of sarcasm, dialogue may be ambiguous enough to require a tag. "You're so cultured," Dr. Maim said sardonically to the talking penguin. "Why, if I didn't know any better, I'd think you were actually Danger Duck in disguise," the talking penguin mumbled in irritation.

Overuse or bad deployment of dialogue usually takes one of two forms: **where is everything?** and **overstaying your welcome**. "Where is everything?" refers to encountering pages and pages of dialogue without any anchors of description or other context. Although some writers prefer to write sections of dialogue without exposition, readers may require **some sort of reminder** of setting and the characters before very long.

"Overstaying your welcome" refers to having put too much dialogue on the page. Doing so means that these parts of your scene may seem to drift, formless, and thus slow the pacing of the story without any reward for the reader. In such cases, you should ask yourself:

- Are there exchanges within this conversation that I can cut without harming the scene? (When you cut some exchanges, you may find no evidence that the deleted material ever existed.)
- Did I start the conversation too early or end it too late?
- Are there sections of dialogue that would be better conveyed through summary?

Please also recognize that no good ever came from *not* putting dialogue between quotation marks, or use of some other easily noticed way of differentiating dialogue from non-dialogue. Just as readers need paragraph breaks, so too they need quotation marks to anchor them—without which irritation and confusion result. Dr. Maim, you brought me flowers, the penguin said. Are they poisoned? . . . *See?* I'm still convinced that the relative obscurity of the brilliant American writer Edward Whittemore is due to his refusal to use quotation marks.

When in doubt, keep these words from writer Stephen Graham Jones in mind: "The reader doesn't want to hear how stupidly real people talk. No, the reader wants people to talk in poetry, like on the television show *Deadwood*. What the reader wants also is just the meat of the conversation, and sometimes for that meat to be pressed until it bleeds. The job of the writer is just to dip into that blood, keep on writing."

DESCRIPTION

Dialogue can make a character come alive, and move a story forward. But one of the main reasons that your characters, places, and situations seem three-dimensional and real is description. Whether you tell us what your main character is wearing or only

Unless you're a master of dialogue like Elmore Leonard.

purr
purr
purr

As this artist rendering demonstrates, writers who are sloppy in their description of characters may elicit reactions of indignation and horror from readers. Try to make readers purr instead.

that she has a perpetually arched eyebrow, your use of description helps to define how the reader perceives each moment in your story or novel. Some writers, depending on their style, rely heavily on rich passages of description and others use mostly dialogue with little grace notes of description. Any approach can work, if it's inherent to your personal voice and style. But while I wouldn't want to constrain your personal choices, you can make things easier or harder for yourself, and clearer or less clear for the reader. Keeping at least some of the following points in mind should be of use.

- **Specific and significant detail is the key to good description.** In a world conquered by pop culture and LOLCats, part of being original is making sure to use specific details that are not once- or twice-removed from reality. This requires you to be a keen observer of your environment, and to collect details that you can then use in your fiction to good effect. If you receive most of your external stimuli from television, movies, and video games, you may be stunting your ability to write good description. Avoiding clichéd expression can be very difficult; exercises like sitting in a park and trying to word-sketch the people around you can help. You should also learn to give the reader not just a specific detail, but a *significant* detail, where necessary. In other words, it might be evocative to describe that stunning sunset, but how does that moment illuminate character or situation? Perhaps the sunset is significant to the talking penguin as he sits at the seaside bar looking out at the horizon. Perhaps the next day he has to do something difficult and unpleasant, and the fading of the light reminds him soon it will be time. Not every detail has to do that much work—you're allowed an evocative sunset for its own sake—but look for those kinds of opportunities.
- **Use all five senses to enrich your descriptive powers.** The best writers don't just give readers what can be heard and seen, but also what can be smelled, tasted, and touched. Although certain modes of modern fiction have moved away from creating an immersive experience, it is still important to vary the

kinds of details you give readers. If you want to convey a convincing illusion of reality, then we need not just the look of panic from your character, and the words, "I don't know where the talking penguin is, honest," but the grain of the wood scratching the speaker's hand as he clutches the dock railing tight and, through the open sliding glass doors beyond, the faint sour smell of a room too-lived in, and the taste on your character's tongue from where he just swallowed something bitter a minute before. Note how this sample description is integrated into the situation, not imposed over the top of it or to the side of it. Employing all five senses does not mean slowing down the pacing to add paragraphs of description (although it can as necessary). It does not mean larding your story with unnecessary verbiage, a common misunderstanding that makes leery some beginning writers who prefer sparse description.

- **Describe people, settings, and things in the right progressions.** Jumbled descriptions can be very jarring for readers, as the brain doesn't know how to process what's being read. As Samuel R. Delany and others have noted, people read one line at a time and, on a micro level, one or two words at a time. So if you jump around, it can cause confusion. Describing a person's shirt and then their eyes followed by their feet and then their belt is less useful than describing their eyes, their shirt, their belt, and then their feet. Make sure that your descriptions follow some logical progression, making exceptions for the most critical details. For example, if someone approaches your main character and that person is bleeding profusely from the arm, it is unlikely that your character will first notice that they're wearing a colorful scarf. Conversely, if they're just fine but wearing a red neon scarf, that detail may eclipse all else about them.

- **When describing people's actions, do not divorce body from mind.** Your mind is not separate from your body; you do not sit perched in a cranial cage atop your meat-self and operate controls to move your arms or legs. Thought and action are instantaneous to our consciousness. So writing "She turned her eyes to the window and saw the bird" is less accurate than writing "She looked out the window and saw the bird." And, as the award-winning Margo Lanagan pointed out about even this example, "I generally would try to dispense with the looking action altogether: 'A bird landed in the acacia outside the window and cleaned its beak against a branch.'" In the worst cases, this robotic crane-operator approach can be laughable: "He had his hand pat her shoulder and then swiveled his eyes to look at her in the face." (A related mistake is having eyes rather than one's gaze "wander around the room," which can be especially confusing in surreal and fantastical fiction.) Exceptions include outliers, like situations where a character may be injured and is moving a limb by a force of will.

- **Use figurative language appropriately.** Figurative language largely refers to the use of similes and metaphors in your fiction. A simile compares one thing with another thing of a different kind and generally uses "like" or "as." A metaphor applies a word or phrase to an object or action to which it is not literally applicable. Here's an example of a simile: "Her hair was as white as snow." Here's an example of a metaphor: "Again, I suffered a conversation with my acquaintance the toad." (Unless, of course, you're writing a fantasy novel in which toads talk.)

But a description also tells us how the character experiences the world. Therefore, if your character really is distanced from his/her own body or surroundings, this would actually work. — **Karin Tidbeck**

Thoughts on Exposition by Kim Stanley Robinson

Kim Stanley Robinson is a winner of the Hugo, Nebula, and Locus Awards. He is the author of twenty books, including the bestselling Mars trilogy and the critically acclaimed 2312, Forty Signs of Rain, The Years of Rice and Salt, *and* Antarctica. *Robinson has been named a "Hero of the Environment" by* Time *magazine. He lives in California.*

EXPOSITION IS HALF of a binary term used mostly in writing workshops and associated reading communities. Its other half is variously called plot, dramatization, or simply fiction itself. Exposition is therefore all the other kinds of writing that appear in a story—descriptive or analytical, summarizing or generalizing—and it is clearly the bad half of the binary, the thing to avoid. If it has to be done at all, it should be snipped into bits and distributed through the text so the story won't be interrupted. If you don't do it that way you are amateurish, and your text will be full of *expository lumps* that should be taken to the *info-dump.* Another way to say this is *show don't tell,* because plot always shows while exposition always tells.

None of this makes much sense. The good/bad encoded in the binary is wrongly applied, because writing is always telling stories, it's a function of being caught in time; whether the protagonist of the story is a person or a rock, whether the story is narrated or exposed, there is an equal chance of it being interesting. And the advice "show don't tell" is a zombie idea, killed forty years ago by the publication in English of Gabriel Garcia Marquez's *One Hundred Years of Solitude,* yet still sadly wandering the literary landscape, confusing people.

Still, there remains something here to discuss, some things to clear up. Granting there is sometimes a mode called exposition, I like it, and I will take my expository lumps and defend them. Indeed, I'm tempted to declare the binary has it exactly

backward, that what is boring in fiction tends to be the hackneyed plots with all their tired old stage business, while the interesting stuff usually lies in what is called the exposition, meaning the writing about whatever is not us.

But that, too, would be wrong. Because there is no denying we are addicted to the human stuff; we read fiction for its characters and what they do and say, and to find out *what happens next.* We read fiction's dramatized scenes to enter a flow state in which we seem to be living other people's lives, and anything that interferes with that can quickly get irritating.

So exposition, if it is going to add to this fictional experience, has to be careful. Ezra Pound once remarked that poetry should be at least as well-written as prose; similarly, exposition should be at least as well-written as a story's dramatized scenes— and perhaps (as I think Pound also meant to imply, a little sardonically, about poetry and prose) it should want to be even better. Done well, exposition becomes a huge part of the pleasure of fiction, containing much of its specificity, texture, richness, depth. This should come as no surprise, because, after all our narcissisms are exhausted, the world still smacks us in the face like the rocket in the Man in the Moon's eye. The not-us is the permanent and inescapable Other; and writing about the Other is what we invented literature to do.

Modes of writing go in and out of fashion. Nineteenth-century fiction contained more exposition than twentieth-century fiction. Often a prominent narrator would comment on the action, detail settings or histories, direct the reader's responses, ruminate philosophically, judge characters, report the weather, or in many other ways generalize. One of modernism's reactions against all this was to remove the narrator as a character and present stories without comment, as if by way of a "camera eye" (plus its audio recorder). This narrative stance meant that many kinds of exposition could not be done at all, and the usual work of fiction in this mode was made up of a string of dramatized scenes, which readers interpreted by following subtle or not-so-subtle cues. This was the moment when Percy Lubbock advocated "show don't tell" (in *The Craft of Fiction*, 1921). Hemingway's popularity might have helped spread the mode, Dashiell Hammett possibly helped it along; in science fiction, Robert Heinlein famously dismissed all the old-fashioned exposition of the *Encyclopedia Galactica* with his sentence "The door dilated."

For a while after that, "camera eye" and its dramatized scenes dominated. Then *One Hundred Years of Solitude*, a novel with no dialogue or fully dramatized scenes, a tale told by a teller, was published and celebrated. "Show don't tell" completely failed to account for its greatness, and there was a paradigm breakdown in that failure, and now we live in more open-minded times. Fiction still contains many dramatized scenes, but narrative methods have gotten a lot more flexible and various. Some writers have flourished using expository forms as frameworks, including Calvino, Lem, Ballard, Borges, Russ, Le Guin, Guy Davenport, Cortazar, and Coover. Stories have appeared in the forms of indexes, scientific reports, prefaces, glossaries, tarot readings, abstracts, constitutions, Post-it notes, encyclopedia entries, book reviews, racing cards, you name it.

All wonderful. Of course, a story's exposition still needs to be done well if it is to fulfill its purpose. This is mainly a matter of writing well, which in any mode is always the issue. It's true that there are some techniques for deploying exposition in a fictional text, but these are very simple and obvious. If the story depends on an idea, which is so often true in science fiction, then exposing the idea will be the work of the story, and exposition and plot become the same thing. It's also always okay to have one character explain something to another. This needn't be an "As you know, Doctor" embarrassment, because in reality we teach each other things all the time, sometimes crucial things; so moments like these are simultaneously exposition, characterization, and plot. This happens so often that again the binary collapses. And it's much the same in scenes where a character is thinking about what to do next; the indirect style makes the narrator very free, and information of all kinds gets conveyed in a slurry of modes.

It does seem clear to me that exposition gets both easier and more interesting (like almost everything else in a story) when the story has a narrator who is not the writer but rather a character, also. If this narrator confidently takes the reader by the hand and says, implicitly or explicitly, "I know best what you need to know to understand and feel this story," the reader will accept any mode the narrator cares to use, trusting that it will pay off, that, in fact, it is the story.

Of course, the camera eye can still be very effective, and creates its own particular effects. And one can still split a story's exposition into info-bursts tucked into the flow of the action. It can make the narrator look a little ADD at times, but that's okay, too.

The opposite strategy, however, I like more, because it is more of an opening up: One can create a narrator who loves exposition and revels in it, even to the point of italicizing it, which serves to mark distinctly the different modes being employed, while also suggesting that there is nothing to hide, that all modes are equally worthy. And really it can go beyond that, because the italicized sections, being rarer, look like they must be something special, perhaps the parts of the story most compressed and poetic. As, hopefully, they are.

Am I advocating a return to the *Encyclopedia Galactica*? Yes. Its entries were always (at least potentially) bits of Stapledonian prose poetry, soaring like phoenixes out of their stories. Face it: Sometimes the world is more interesting than we are. Even if the interest is always human interest. ❧

Similes and metaphors are highly unstable—susceptible not just to the appropriateness of the core comparison you make, but the tone and texture of those comparisons. For example, although "Her hair was as white as snow" is a cliché, "Her hair was as white as milk" sounds wrong because the texture of milk doesn't match the texture of hair. Yes, both are white, but they still have to have more tactile points of commonality. In this example, you could conceivably write "Her wet hair was as white as milk," with "wet" changing the texture to something more suitable, but it's still a stretch and doesn't really work. Similarly, describing a helicopter as looking like an airborne tadpole might make some sense in terms of shape (sans propellers) but a tadpole is squishy and a helicopter is hard. Comparing a helicopter to a hummingbird might be closer, if the reader equates a helicopter's movement with that of a hummingbird and views the metallic colors of the bird as comparable to the metallic texture of a helicopter. If you are tone-deaf to the uses of figurative language, you will discover this early on and should perhaps limit how you deploy them.

A couple additional pitfalls bear mentioning. First and foremost, make sure that you are comparing different things. If you write "The panther leapt like a big cat," you are really saying "The big cat leapt like a big cat," which is a waste of the reader's time. In addition, remember that metaphors and similes tend to catch the reader's attention more than the words around them. So you usually create added emphasis by using them (unless your work is nothing but figurative language). Don't use them just to bolster description or you will wind up making the most mundane actions, ones you want to occur more or less invisibly to the reader, carry unwanted added significance. The result may be to **render the important part invisible.**

> "Pass the butter," she said, looking like a beagle being eaten by an obese raven. "I'm leaving you," he replied.

For more on figurative language, I highly recommend Mark Doty's *The Art of Description*, perhaps the finest book of its type I have ever read. Within its pages you will find some wonderful ideas about figurative language, like the need for it to have a quality of resistance, show us something new, potentially juxtapose the natural and the artificial, and much more.

- *Study poetry for interesting approaches to description.* Poetry truly does contain a richness of approaches to description and, in particular, figurative language. While the compression found in poetry, the weight of words, is not as applicable to most fiction, the lessons you can learn from studying poetry will expand your own range of technique in this area. Take, for example, these great lines from Alex Lemon's poem "Other Good," taken from the collection *Mosquito*: "Anesthesia dumb, scalpel-paste/Rawing my tongue, I found/Myself starfished In sky/Spinning days . . . " How beautifully these lines capture the sensation of disorientation, and in such clear, precise, and yet gritty language!

- *Keep in mind the (irrational) power of some types of description.* Images can have great power, and subtextual weight. Our subconscious minds are often able to bring onto the page very strange and arresting images that resonate and have an almost dream-like significance. As Michael Moorcock wrote in his essay "Exotic Landscape," the work of visionaries "may not be judged by normal criteria but by the power of their imagery and by what extent their writing evokes that power, whether trying to convey wildness, strangeness, or charm; whether like Melville, Ballard, Patrick White, or Alejo Carpentier they transform their images into intense personal metaphor, or, like Bunyan, give us simple allegory." Moorcock was writing about setting, but the point applies to imagery generally. If you find that you have written an image that seems inexplicable or illogical but still seems to generate energy, that seems luminous or to have hidden significance, be careful not to change that moment too much, or to cut it just because it doesn't seem entirely functional in your narrative.

STYLE

As noted, style in fiction is the arrangement of words in a story by the writer. If the writer is said to have a distinctive style, it is because the writer's voice has found expression in a unique way that resonates with the reader. Style is the means by which the writer's subject matter, passions, and interests reach their fullest expression on the page. Most writers fall not just between Ernest Hemingway and Angela Carter, but also between Chagall and Picasso in terms of style. What do I mean? Chagall always painted more or less in the same style, with small variations of tone and subject matter, and became iconic doing so. Picasso, on the other hand, mastered many styles and expressed them all through his painting.

Most writers are neither as sparse as Hemingway nor as lush as Carter in terms of style, nor as single minded as Chagall or as varied as Picasso. Instead, a certain range exists, emanating from a base style, depending on the demands of a particular story or novel. Complicating the issue are elements like the use of first-person narrators with their own distinctive way of saying things and third- or second-person narratives that create a need to, in a sense, replicate another approach to style: that of the main character.

Within that context, then, here are a few general points about style that should provide food for thought, or for enraged food fights. Either reaction is desirable; your indifference is not.

- *Each and every story must be told in the style best suited for it*, whether simple and unadorned or convoluted and ornate. The wider your range, the more types of stories and types of characters you can animate. Therefore, as you develop as a writer, think about what constitutes your "base style" and find ways to alter it by context or through mechanically making changes to allow it to achieve different effects.
- *Inasmuch as a story has depth (or depth perception), it achieves this quality* not just through insight about the human condition, society, or an individual character, but also through expression of its central passion or focus *via a style that has depth*, one that can "multitask," to use a horrible word. Skillful writing isn't just about "telling a good story," because you can't tell a good story if your style works against you. Every sentence or paragraph can perform many complex functions simultaneously, and in ways unique to each individual writer. Complexity does not necessarily mean writing lush prose; many great styles that create complex, nuanced, layered effects are invisible.

THREE DRAGONS IN
THREE STYLES

Scott Eagle cover painting for *City of Saints and Madmen* (2001) by Jeff VanderMeer.

- *Some writers' styles cannot multitask, or cannot lithely pivot* as might be needed, but instead can only grandly and with ponderous weight turn like a flaming funeral barge or a baroque, jewel-encrusted mechanical elephant. This quality—which can itself be a strength—is, again, not necessarily a function of the sparse or ornate aspect of a style but more a function of tone, context, and how the parts of a scene work together. Don't be mad that you're a flaming funeral barge rather than a schooner skimming the waves: Own your barge-hood, and make of your style all that it can be.

- *Artists and writers are somewhat similar with regard to style,* although they have different goals and different ideas of what constitutes "story." Crudely speaking, an artist creates a painting by using colors applied via brushstrokes. The size, shape, and texture of these marks on the canvas are dictated by the type of brush, the type of paint, and the individual approach to where and how they create the brushstrokes. How they mix and layer the paint also affects the result. The resulting image may seem to exist independent of those myriad decisions, but it has no such autonomy. The individual decisions that find expression through a writer's style may not enter into a reader's thoughts about why they liked or disliked a story, even though, were that person to view a painting, they might think about the use of charcoal rather than watercolor, oil as opposed to acrylics, and the different effects achieved by the short, stippling brushstrokes in the middle versus the long, wide strokes at the edges. Yet the process for a writer is, to some extent, the same.

WRITING CHALLENGE

The artist Scott Eagle used many different approaches to "style" in creating the piece of art above. The cut-apart work of masters like Bruegel forms a collage of a city. A photograph of irregular stones resembles a street. He also painted parts of the image, including the flames in the background. Eagle then painted over the collaged parts taken from other paintings to make the light fall consistently. The result has cohesion and an oddly consistent texture despite the disparate elements he brought together.

For this exercise, choose a subject (for example, mushrooms or dive bars) and gather materials related to that subject from at least four different text sources written in diverse styles and/or points of view, including essays and short stories. Identify the parts of each that could be used to create a two- to three-paragraph passage of description. Then collage those parts together without changing the words. Keeping as many of the original words as is feasible, rewrite the passage to smooth out any "klang" in tone, mood, or texture. Finally, rewrite the passage again so it reflects not just your style but also the point of view of a character (who may bring their own style to the description).

APPROACHES TO STYLE

EXAMPLES

"He walked out to the main road, turned, limped toward the main gates. A man was dead, murdered, or perhaps very much alive. Borchert was playing with him, and perhaps the others were as well. The night was cool, cloudless. Where was this place? He turned and looked back, saw the building he was staying in, the only light being that of his own room."—BRIAN EVENSON, "THE BROTHERHOOD OF MUTILATION"

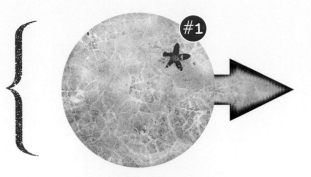

"Amy Fremont got up from the rocking chair, and came across the porch. She was a tall woman, thin, a smiling vacancy in her eyes. About a year ago, Anthony had gotten mad at her, because she'd told him he shouldn't have turned the cat into a cat-rug. Although he had always obeyed her more than anyone else, which was hardly at all, this time he'd snapped at her. With his mind. And that had been the end of Amy Fremont's bright eyes, and the end of Amy Fremont as everyone had known her."—"IT'S A *GOOD* LIFE," JEROME BIXBY

"A moment I float beneath her, a starry shadow. Distant canyons where spectral lightning flashes: neurons firing as I tap into the heart of the poet, the dark core where desire and horror fuse and Morgan turns ever and again to stare out a bus window. The darkness clears. I taste for an instant the metal bile that signals the beginning of therapy, and then I'm gone."—ELIZABETH HAND, "THE BOY IN THE TREE"

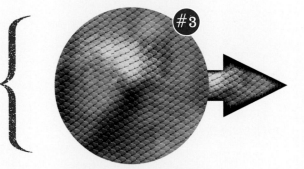

"Stilt-legs scissoring, snip-snap! the bird gods dance. Old craneycrows, a skulk of powers. How they strut and ogle with their long eyes, knowing. How they serpentine their necks. And stalking, how they flirt their tails, insouciant as Groucho. Fugue and counter-fugue, the music jigs and sneaks. On tiptoe, solemnly, they hop and flap; they whirl and whet their long curved clever bills."—GREER GILMAN, "DOWN THE WALL"

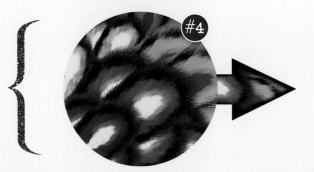

Devil's Advocate
- almost any style can seem lush or invisible in the right context
- any style can achieve many different effects

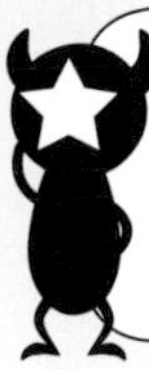

Representative Writers

(many may deploy a range of styles across their fiction)

#1 Minimal / Stark

Sparse, understated prose that often relies on inference and suggestion. Use of detail is minimal but may be more powerful in isolation. Descriptions are rare and take on significance common to poetry. Poor execution leaves no purchase for the reader and induces boredom and sometimes contempt. Characterization relies in part on what's not said, or not expressed.

- Samuel Beckett
- Raymond Carver
- Brian Evenson
- Ernest Hemingway
- Amy Hempel

TRANSITIONAL → *Carol Emshwiller*

#2 Invisible / "Normal"

The "baseline" approach common to much fiction, especially in commercial modes, picks its spots with balance in scene/summary and judicious use of sensory detail. Immersive reading is usually the goal. Few long sentences. Poor execution induces a reaction of "mediocrity."

- Octavia Butler
- Daphne Du Maurier
- Joe Haldeman
- Mary Doria Russell
- Karin Tidbeck
- Kurt Vonnegut

TRANSITIONAL → *Karen Joy Fowler*

#3 Muscular / Conspicuous

Sentence structures tend to be more complex and summary/half scene is employed in a more layered way, with time perhaps more easily manipulated as a result. Character POVs may be differentiated as much by style as content. Ample use of extended metaphor and sensory detail. Poor execution induces a reaction of "too clever" or "lost the thread."

- Martin Amis
- Michael Cisco
- Elizabeth Hand
- Ursula K. Le Guin
- Kelly Link
- Joyce Carol Oates
- Ben Okri

#4 Lush / Ornate

TRANSITIONAL → *China Miéville*

Word play, extended (sometimes raucous) metaphors, and self-conscious approaches may occur, with longer sentences and descriptive passages likely. The paragraphs exist to advance story and showcase the words. Characterization can occur through stylistic exaggeration. Poetic meter may be present. Reverie and hyperbole become more foregrounded. Poor execution induces a sense of thickness, "encrustedness," and a lack of emotional resonance.

- K. J. Bishop
- Angela Carter
- Robert Coover
- Rikki Ducornet
- Jamaica Kincaid
- Tanith Lee
- Mervyn Peake
- Salman Rushdie
- Catherynne M. Valente

Some people believe that style is merely an overlay, rather than intrinsic to the skin, the flesh and blood, of a story. In part this is because although we can talk about style as a separate element, like dialogue, it functions in a different way. An element like dialogue forms a discrete, finite series of units within a story: It exists in certain places and not in other places. Style, however, *permeates*. It *inhabits*. It exists at the particle level of this creature we call fiction. If you are a writer as sensitive to uses of language as Greer Gilman, it doesn't exist just in sentence and syllable—it exists in each meaning and derivation of every word from the beginning of written history. Thus, as you read, the words form additional layers of association that constitute a very unique style.

Put another way: Style is not story. If it were, then, as writer Matthew Cheney has observed, fiction in translation would convey no true sense of what happens in a story, or even any idea of the tone and texture of the author's original style. But as surely as each element of plot or character or structure deployed throughout your fiction affects your story, so, too, does style, on a very personal and microscopic level. Give three talented writers with unique voices the exact same events to write about, in the same order, and, by virtue of their style, those stories will seem very different. The particles known as words *accumulate*, each sentence building up or changing, in ways both minute and potentially earthshaking, our perception of characters, the mood, and events. Through the weight of each decision, many instinctual, what we write is different than it could have been—ghost phrases and sentences spinning off by what we discard, creating millions of pocket universes filled with layers of other versions of story. And by this same process we make our mark as to how we differ from *that* writer, and *that other* writer, and even that talking penguin trying to write over in the corner above the noise and drama of this instructional text.

THE GREATER AND LESSER MYSTERIES

Allied with the seven elements are other components that factor into the creation of narrative. For various reasons, these cannot be termed "elements" because they are not, strictly speaking, as quantifiable, or they exist at a different hierarchical level. Hopefully, this brief discussion will help clear up any confusion about, for example, form versus structure, or what voice means in relation to tone.

VOICE. This term, like style, can be slippery, but it basically refers to some quality of the writer's style and worldview that comes through in every piece of fiction, no matter how the writer's style varies from story to story. Many writers talk of "finding their voice" as they develop, and this generally means that they have achieved enough mastery over the elements of story and assimilated their core influences to the extent that their innate uniqueness now comes across in more concentrated form on the page. Writers can be encouraged in ways that allow them to more easily find a unique voice, but in general finding one's voice is a private process of discovery and exploration, and it matures in ways that cannot be quantified.

TONE. The tone of fiction refers to the atmosphere created and the mood evoked. The tone can fluctuate greatly within a story, depending on the effects required to make individual scenes a success. Examples of tone include serious, playful, terrifying, exciting, creepy, and sad. Tone is created not just by word choice, but also through the rhythms and lengths of the sentences, the images evoked, and the descriptions. The tone is at the service of the style, which must be flexible enough to allow for the necessary changes in tone throughout the narrative. Stories trying to achieve a single effect must display at least some agility in this area; to avoid devolving into *monotone* during longer narratives, suppleness and variety are even more important. Control of tone can be useful in other ways. An inappropriate tone can be used as a counterpoint to the events depicted in a story. Sometimes this results in humor. Other times, it can help make fresh some aspect of the human condition to which many have become indifferent due to overexposure.

Vladimir Nabokov's use of the language of the vacation brochure to describe internment camps in *Bend Sinister* makes it impossible for the reader not to engage with the horror of such places.

STRUCTURE. This term refers to what you could call the arrangement, pattern, or design of the story, as you will learn in Chapter 4. We are preconditioned to think of structure in terms of plot, but structure is about how things happen and when as much as about *what* happens.

THEME. When we talk about a story's subtext or what the story means beyond the events described on the page, generally we are zeroing in on *theme*. Theme is a tricky subject, because even if a writer decides to write a story about social injustice or love or death, what occurs on the page is usually much more complex and not reducible to slogans or abstract ideas. Thus, to talk about the "theme" of a story is to erase or render invisible many of the narrative's other attributes. The other reason theme is less useful to the fiction writer than other inhabitants of the fiction ecosystem is that theme tends to occur organically in a writer's work, in their rough drafts, in a way somewhat akin to *voice*. Like voice, it can recur regardless of conscious thought. Having a general idea of what theme means, along with examples, is helpful, but too much self-conscious examination of theme while writing can freeze a writer or render the writer pompous or didactic. However, figuring out what themes you've been exploring can be of use during revision. It can help you decide what things to emphasize or deemphasize, as long as theme is considered only in the context of many other concerns.

FORM. As distinguished from plot or structure, *form* can refer to the shape created by a story's structure *or* refer to the type of narrative you are creating, whether a novel, novella, short story, or poem. Some writing guides also refer to form as being similar to voice—meaning a somewhat amorphous element that conveys a liminal overlay of meaning in a story. What is most probably meant in this latter case is simply that all of the elements of the story have worked so perfectly in tandem, and matched so perfectly the vision in the writer's head, that the effect on the reader seems miraculous and cathartic.

THE COMPLEX RELATIONSHIP
BETWEEN STORY ELEMENTS

Imagine that you're hiking along the beach, the ocean spread out to your right and a tropical rain forest to your left. At a certain point you encounter a unique and beautiful organism in a tidal pool—presented to you in a perfect synergy of motion and form. Then imagine that you were to capture and cut apart that animal so you could eat it. You might notice with interest how the heart muscle is connected to the arteries and veins. Later, as you took a bite of it, cooked in some thick sauce, you might remark on the rich taste. But what relationship would either observation have to that initial glimpse of a lightness of movement, that moment of epiphany?

If a story or novel can be imagined as a fantastical creature, so, too, can the elements of narrative be viewed as living systems that work together in complex ways to create a series of effects for the reader. You can say that in general one element—including the Greater and Lesser Mysteries—performs a series of functions within the body.

A Message About Messages
by Ursula K. Le Guin

Ursula K. Le Guin has received the Hugo, Nebula, Endeavor, Locus, Tiptree, Sturgeon, PEN-Malamud, and National Book awards, among others. Among her most iconic creations are the Earthsea books and the novels The Dispossessed *and* The Left Hand of Darkness. *Recent works include* Lavinia *and* Wild Girls. *She lives in Portland, Oregon.*

I MADE A NOTE to myself a while ago: "Whenever they tell me *children want this sort of book* and *children need this sort of writing,* I am going to smile politely and shut my earlids. I am a writer, not a caterer. There are plenty of caterers. But what children most want and need is what we and they don't know they want and don't think they need, and only writers can offer it to them."

My fiction, especially for kids and young adults, is often reviewed as if it existed in order to deliver a useful little sermon ("Growing up is tough, but you can make it," that sort of thing). Does it ever occur to such reviewers that the meaning of the story might lie in the language itself, in the movement of the story as read, in an inexpressible sense of discovery, rather than a tidy bit of advice?

Readers—kids and adults—ask me about *the message* of one story or another. I want to say to them, "Your question isn't in the right language."

As a fiction writer, I don't speak message. I speak story. Sure, my story means something, but if you want to know what it means, you have to ask the question in terms appropriate to storytelling. Terms such as *message* are appropriate to expository writing, didactic writing, and sermons—different languages from fiction.

The notion that a story *has a message* assumes that it can be reduced to a few abstract words, neatly summarized in a school or college examination paper or a brisk critical review.

If that were true, why would writers go to the trouble of making up characters and relationships and plots and scenery and all that? Why not just deliver the message? Is the story a box to hide an idea in, a fancy dress to make a naked idea look pretty, a candy coating to make a bitter idea easier to swallow? (Open your mouth, dear, it's good for you.) Is fiction decorative wordage concealing a rational thought, a message, which is its ultimate reality and reason for being?

A lot of teachers teach fiction, a lot of reviewers (particularly of children's books) review it, and so a lot of people read it, in that belief. The trouble is, it's wrong.

I'm not saying fiction is meaningless or useless. Far from it. I believe storytelling is one of the most useful tools we have for achieving meaning: It serves to keep our communities together by asking and saying *who we are,* and it's one of the best tools an individual has to find out *who I am,* what life may ask of me and how I can respond.

But that's not the same as having a message. The complex meanings of a serious story or novel can be understood only by participation in the language of the story itself. To translate them into a message or reduce them to a sermon distorts, betrays, and destroys them.

This is because a work of art is understood not by the mind only, but by the emotions and by the body itself.

It's easier to accept this about the other arts. A dance, a landscape painting—we're less likely to talk about *its message* than simply about the feelings it rouses in us. Or music: We know there's no way to say all a song may mean to us, because the meaning is not so much rational as deeply felt, felt by our

emotions and our whole body, and the language of the intellect can't fully express those understandings.

In fact, art itself is our language for expressing the understandings of the heart, the body, and the spirit.

Any reduction of that language into intellectual messages is radically, destructively incomplete.

This is as true of literature as it is of dance or music or painting. But because fiction is an art made of words, we tend to think it can be translated into other words without losing anything. So people think a story is just a way of delivering a message.

And so kids ask me, in all good faith, "When you have your message, how do you make up a story to fit it?" All I can answer is, "It doesn't work that way! I'm not an answering machine—I don't have a message for you! What I have for you is a story."

What you get out of that story, in the way of understanding or perception or emotion, is partly up to me—because, of course, the story is passionately meaningful to me (even if I only find out what it's about after I've told it). But it's also up to you, the reader. Reading is a passionate act. If you read a story not just with your head, but also with your body and feelings and soul, the way you dance or listen to music, then it becomes your story. And it can mean infinitely more than any message. It can offer beauty. It can take you through pain. It can signify freedom. And it can mean something different every time you reread it.

I am grieved and affronted when reviewers treat my novels and other serious books for kids as candy-coated sermons. Of course there's a lot of moralistic and didactic stuff written for young people, which can be discussed as such without loss. But with genuine works of literature for children, with *The Elephant's Child* or *The Hobbit*, it is a grave error to teach or review them as mere vehicles for ideas, not seeing them as works of art. Art frees us, and the art of words can take us beyond anything we can say in words.

I wish our teaching, our reviews, our reading would celebrate that freedom, that liberation. I wish, instead of looking for a message when we read a story, we could think, "Here's a door opening on a new world: What will I find there?" ❧

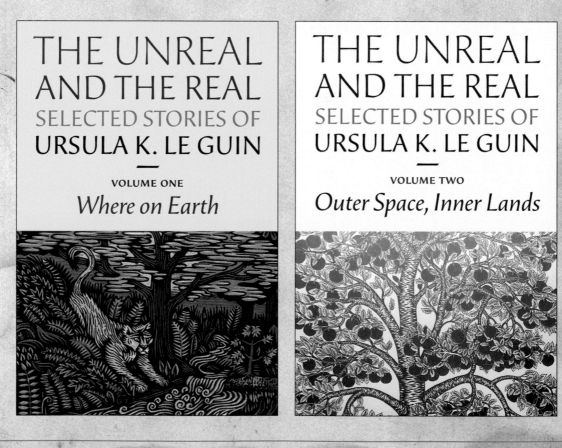

THE UNREAL AND THE REAL
SELECTED STORIES OF
URSULA K. LE GUIN
—
VOLUME ONE
Where on Earth

THE UNREAL AND THE REAL
SELECTED STORIES OF
URSULA K. LE GUIN
—
VOLUME TWO
Outer Space, Inner Lands

Because of the interdependence of these elements, examining each separately results in only a partial understanding of their influence and effects. In isolation, each element of story is a kind of incomplete narrative, disconnected from those other elements with which it naturally forms a synergy and which render its effects complex.

Take dialogue, for example. Dialogue is an element that occurs against the backdrop of a setting, spoken by characters who are usually meant to stand out in sharp relief from the setting—characters who, from their point of view, in a sense create setting, and who exist for us through description, which, technically, includes dialogue . . . which itself is affected more generally by geographical location (setting), quirks of character, and description. To say nothing of "plot," which is usually but not always generated by character interactions and which is often expressed through dialogue. We can say that characterization trumps dialogue in the hierarchy of story elements, but what is characterization without dialogue?

Then, too, there is a **situational quality** dependent on the attributes of a particular story. Where on the hierarchy does dialogue fall in a tale told *all* in dialogue, like Robertson Davies's novel *The Manticore*? What about a story set during a famous historical battle? Depending on the type of story and the emphasis, along with innumerable other factors, any of these elements can, to some extent, mimic aspects of, or effects of, any other. To take it to an extreme: elements may be so changed in their purpose and context that they match up only awkwardly against their standard definitions in a creative writing manual.

Anti-Story: An Anthology of Experimental Fiction (1971), edited by Philip Stevick, provides some wonderful examples of pushing against traditional ideas about the elements of narrative.

THE ROLES OF TYPES OF IMAGINATION

On top of having a good sense of the elements of story and the Greater and Lesser Mysteries, you should also have an understanding of the relationship between your creative imagination and your technical imagination. What do I mean by these terms?

- Your **creative imagination** is what you use to write a rough draft. To your creative imagination, conscious self-editing and commentary on what is being written is poison and leads to a writer becoming frozen or superficial. Your creative imagination needs to let flow whatever comes into your mind while writing, and let it all fall out as it may.
- Your **technical imagination** then comes along to find the pattern or structure to establish balance, to draw out aspects of character or situation suggested by the rough draft, to make the elements of narrative work together in synergistic ways to generate hundreds, even thousands, of effects at the micro and macro levels.

As you might expect, the creative and technical imaginations engage at different times and stages for different writers and perform different functions, depending on the complexity and completeness of the initial vision of the story. For example, if you are the kind of writer who spends a great deal of time perfecting your beginning before moving on, then you are engaging your creative and technical imaginations

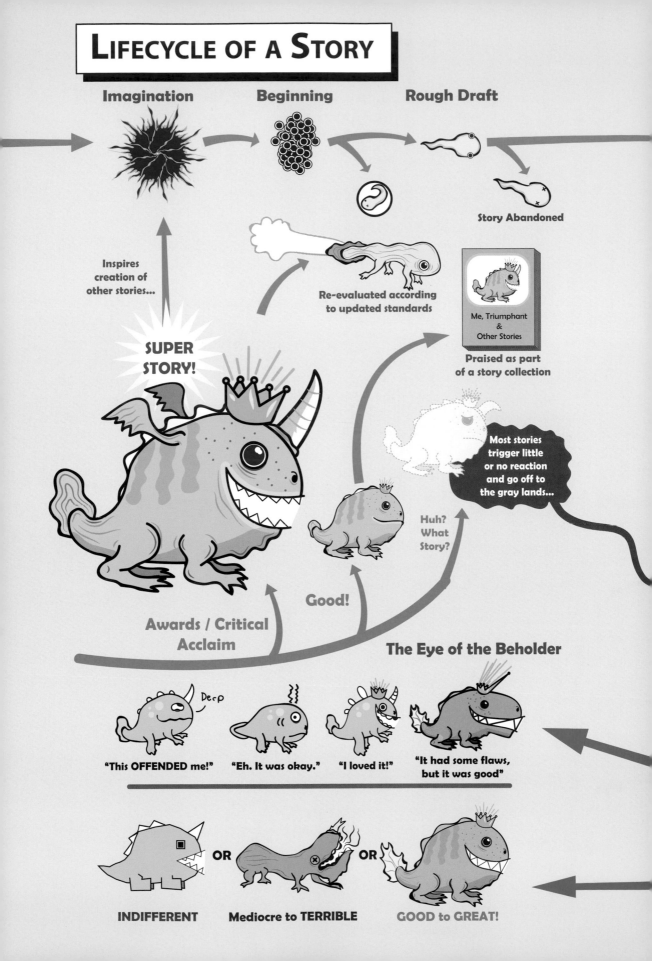

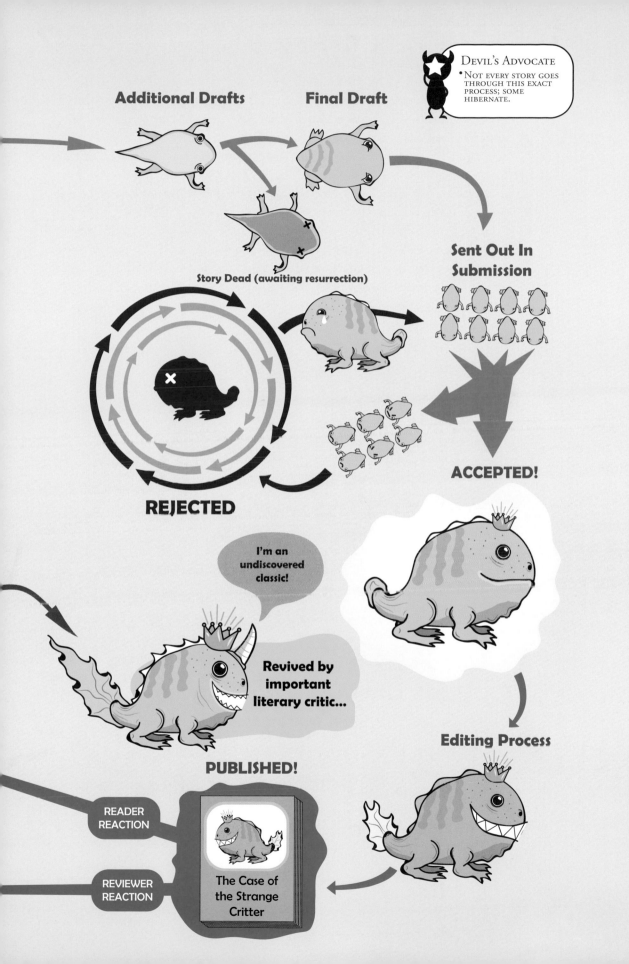

at the same time during that process. If you then relax into writing a rough draft of the middle and ending, you are primarily engaging your creative imagination.

Over time, because of practice, your technical imagination automatically shares information with your creative imagination—a transference similar to the idea of muscle memory. As a result, you will eventually find that some aspects of correction you used to have to impose on your narrative during revision already exist in some form in the rough draft. Like most things in creative writing, this process is not mathematically precise. Because it often happens by imperceptible degrees, you may not even notice the progress at first. This idea of "progress" also varies, depending on what you're writing. If you are working on a type of story you haven't written before—or, for example, using third person when you often use first person—your lack of experience in that mode may create problems in your rough draft that you thought you had long ago gotten past. As ever, you will lurch forward and step back, regroup, and lurch forward again. Eventually, you'll get used to your particular rhythm of internalizing and using what you learn.

ᔕ   ᔕ   ᔕ

The artificial construct of providing discrete definitions and functions for individual elements of a story helps to hasten the process of transference in your writing method. At the same time, respecting the organic nature of the best narrative—creature not machine, redwood not log cabin—will help you to nurture, draw out, and perfect your own unique strengths.

You should approach an understanding of story elements not as if you were approaching a puzzle that, once solved, will never need to be solved again, but so you can create something wonderful or deadly or harrowing or tragic or melancholy.

A story-creature that only you could have brought to life—one that when it's out in the world, readers will respond to, revel in, perhaps even treasure.

You came to this place expecting writing advice, but as soon as you stepped inside, everything changed. Who is that woman in the corner with the gun? Why is someone or some thing hiding behind the potted plant? What right does that penguin have to talk to you in that tone of voice? And, more important, have you stumbled in at the beginning, middle, or end of the story? (Wait. The penguin can talk?)

CHAPTER 3:
BEGINNINGS AND ENDINGS

HOW AND WHERE you start your story is critical to the reader's reaction, the effects you can achieve, and how successfully you reach that vision in your head. Story beginnings also affect elements initially informed by your subconscious, like theme and subtext. Clues to your ending should be embedded in your opening, too, so that when the reader finishes your story—even if it's a surprise ending—they can return to the beginning and think, *Ah—I see, it was all set up from the start.* That talking penguin knows the woman with the gun from way back, and *you* are actually the intruder. This approach creates a pleasurable sense of discovery and, ultimately, closure for the reader—sometimes known as structural or thematic unity, even though it usually expresses itself through reader appreciation of the characters.

Understanding the difference between the flush of initial inspiration and the ways in which your technical imagination then begins to organize the elements of the story is the key to effective beginnings. That first step, however, *is* letting words spill out during the rough draft stage—and having a sense of how you work best helps later. The order and nature of the creative sparks and connections that eventually reveal the story to you—bring the story fully into view, into focus—are part of your unique process as a writer and are sometimes specific to a particular story. For example, I cannot start a story until I have a good idea of the character wedded to

THE WIDENING CONTEXT

- What are we looking at?
- Is it interesting?
- Do we want to know more?

- How does our impression of the subject change now that we have more information?
- Are we still interested?

- What details are becoming clear that weren't before?
- What has the creator decided to reveal second, third, fourth?

- Now that we have the full context, is it what we expected?
- What other part of this scene could have been emphasized first and how would that have mattered?

WITH EACH SENTENCE, WE CREATE OUR WORLDS, OUR CHARACTERS, AND A MORE COMPLETE AND COMPLEX SERIES OF IMAGES APPEARS IN THE READER'S MIND.

some problem; a character in a more casual relationship with a problem isn't ready for my commitment to the story. I also have to have some rough approximation of an ending, even if it changes by the time I get there, or I never finish the story. For me, a strong, *charged image* is usually associated with the story as well. Not understanding the unique conditions through which you tend to produce your best work may make everything else much harder.

However, while such self-examination is important to *you*, the reader doesn't care about your process of inspiration or in what order you discovered parts of the story. The reader only cares about what he or she experiences on the page. That's why you must not mistake the progress of your inspiration for the actual progression of the story. The scene that sparked your desire to create fiction may not be the starting point of the story, and the story itself may not even be about what you thought it was about when you wrote the opening. That talking penguin might just need to be moved to another tale entirely. That woman with the gun might be holding flowers instead (which might be hiding the gun).

A good piece of fiction teaches the reader how to read the narrative from the first paragraph. Think of a beginning as a kind of beneficial restriction or constraint. At the start, more than anywhere else, the reader stares through a telescope focused close in on some particular object, person, setting, or other element. What he or she sees within the range of the lens is a translation of your words into an image or images, possibly with all five senses involved in the interpretation. By the very nature of how words work, the reader cannot receive all of the possible information at once. The limited field of vision means that what is visible—and invisible—defines the story and, sometimes, the *type* of story. And the more your story diverges from reality, the more important it is to get those words right, because you are reimagining The Real in the reader's head.

As the story opens up, as the telescope pulls back, and the reader gains an understanding of the basic context, "rules," and characters, words continue to function in this way— but, especially in a good story, the reader becomes more and more immersed in the fictive dream. The level of immersion as the story progresses depends in part on the skill with which you have handled the entry point for your readers, allowing them to relax into the story. What does "relaxation" mean? It means the reader's ability to enjoy whatever mood, mode, or intellectual response you want to evoke, including anxiety, fear, or disgust. Put another way, readers want to trust you, the author, but if you give them a reason not to, you may never regain that trust.

What the reader encounters second, third, and fourth is also important—both in terms of the order, relative significance, and, again, what we are not shown. This process of acclimation/introduction of information may receive a "reboot" later in the story, when readers realize that what they thought they knew needs to be radically reinterpreted because of new information, without seeming like the writer cheated. However, the process is still most critical at the beginning of a story.

But where should you start your story—and when—given that it makes such a difference in the story's success or failure? For example, right now you're in a room with a talking penguin, a woman with a gun, and someone hiding behind a potted plant. From your perspective, you might want to rewind events to a point where you

A "charged image" is an image that has some psychological or symbolic resonance; it has a life beyond its presence as part of the setting or part of the character's possessions.

1 Myster ODD is unusual and therefore interesting, yes? No.

2 What about this scene is ususual? What is . . . normal? Where's the balance?

3 How does the treatment of color affect how you interpret what is happening?

4 Which character is more unusual and why?

BEGINNINGS WITH MYSTER ODD

1 This image may form an eccentric and interesting composition—it's not every day you meet a bird-skull-headed person in a tweed jacket. However, only for a small subset of stories, including Herman Melville's forgotten classic "Bartlebird the Scribner," will it be enough to meet a weird character in his room doing weird things. A great and uneven burden will be placed on the rhetorical flourishes of any story about Myster Odd simply hanging out where he lives. So what might make this scenario more interesting?

2 In a different scenario, we meet Myster Odd as he takes off his own foot (!?) and brandishes it at a pink mischievous blob I'm going to call Pinky. That's a much more active opening—Myster Odd is doing something—and inasmuch as we've all had the experience of finding something flying around our home that we desperately wanted to swat, we've also given Myster Odd an initial action that a reader can relate to, mitigating the strangeness of Myster Odd and his detachable leg. We've also immediately introduced in Pinky a second character that, for all of its cute bubble-gum pinkness, may be the antagonist. Character motivation and emotion immediately come into play with the introduction of this opposing force. Myster Odd clearly dislikes Pinky if he's willing to take off his own leg to shoo Pinky away. If Myster Odd means to kill Pinky with so personal an implement as his own leg, that's a different order of dislike and a different kind of story.

3 Another option is the introduction of suspense through inference. Here, Myster Odd holds a gun in a primed-and-ready position. Something is rolling across the floor, possibly broken. Not only is impending action seemingly certain, but some action has also occurred just before we got here. Although no second character is depicted, that second character—that opposing force—is still present. This opening requires the reader to supply missing information or to anticipate that the writer will soon supply that information. In this scenario, reader "satisfaction" can take many forms. In one scenario, the writer might reveal that Myster Odd works for the secret service. In another, that Myster Odd is practicing for a part as a spy in a play. Depending on the distribution of elements in the opening, and the tone or mood, either of these outcomes may be seen as a disappointment or as a triumph. Drama and generated interest do not intrinsically emanate from any particular inert element; the theatrics of a drama group can be as fascinating as the inner machinations of the CIA. Everything depends on the writer's approach, and the entry point for the reader.

4 A more direct approach is to start with two characters already in conversation, perhaps in an unusual situation. Both characters depicted here are somewhat surreal or fantastical. Given the possible scenarios inherent to fantasy and science fiction, it's not improbable that your opening might feature two strange characters in an odd context. However, this scenario also demonstrates the dangers of too abrupt an opening: Now you have to quickly explain not just one oddity but two, in addition to the setting. One solution might be to add a normal head to one of the two characters. Another would be to normalize their context. Perhaps they are brothers fighting over family matters. Perhaps the one in pink is a door-to-door salesperson who just sold Myster Odd a book to replace his head. Perhaps Myster Odd is now demanding his money back. Or, perhaps, you will decide that trying to dress up odd in normal's clothing is pointless, and you're going to make the reader do more work by creating an even stranger scenario for the two weird characters. A talented writer can make just about anything work . . . but make sure you know why you're doing what you're doing . . .

"Tentacle Latitudes" (2012)
by John Coulthart.

Even if your novel starts with a scene as intense as a giant squid attacking a ship, you still have decisions to make about what to emphasize and not emphasize.

Using this image by artist John Coulthart, plan the opening of a novel entitled "Krakens Attack at Dawn." You'll need to know who your main characters are and the context for the scene pictured—when and where does it occur, and why does the beast attack? Then list possible ways to begin the scene that change the emphasis. For example, do you begin with the beast being sighted, the attack underway, a few minutes before an attack, or . . . ? What do we see first, second, and third? Provide an explanation for why each opening might be effective. Then come back to your list after you've finished reading this chapter. Has your perspective about what might work changed? If so, how?

can make more sense of it all. However, many writing instructors suggest starting the story *as late* as possible. What does "late" mean? It often means that moment at which maximum dramatic tension occurs without the loss of so much context about character, setting, and other elements that the drama is meaningless or confusing.

Since starting a piece of fiction too soon is such a common error, it's useful to keep searching in your rough draft manuscript for later and later points where the story could actually begin; try to choose the latest possible starting point. Sometimes, this will lead to the unfortunate situation in which all that remains is an ending, but better to know you have no story as early as possible. Many a writer has been shipwrecked on the rocks of No-Story without ever realizing it and wandered desolate coasts confused about why they don't have an audience except for that stalker of a penguin.

Even if you determine that you have begun exactly where you need to, you may learn something valuable about the rest of your narrative through analyzing your point of departure. And if you do change your starting point, just remember that the new beginning now takes on a lot more weight and may need to be reconceptualized and rebuilt to support that weight. At the very least, some information cut along with those opening pages may need to be reinstated at the new start point or soon after.

Wondering about endings? We're a long way from endings, but we'll get there.

THE LURE OF THE HOOK

Because of the need to start in an interesting and immediate way, writers are often told they must begin with a "hook." The idea is that something exciting must be happening to draw in the reader. I have even heard the advice to start with an actual explosion, which is usually a bad idea. Whether literal or metaphorical, too spectacular an opening event may leave you with little room for later drama that doesn't seem like an anticlimax.

Still, *something* must be happening, even if it is as mundane an action as someone clipping their toenails. A skilled writer can suggest political and social significance through even a seemingly insignificant act—and create tension by dwelling on the gleam of the cruel, sharp blades of the nail clipper.

The fact is, anything at all can be made interesting, so you should think less about explosions and more about where in a particular situation or scene the interest lies, and from what perspective. A hook cannot be just a hook, either—it must be a lure and alluring, and it must also be an anchor. You are inviting the reader to some sort of enjoyment or challenge or (perhaps) harrowing experience. Spending too much time on trying to hook the reader may well rob the opening of your book of its allure. In this case, of course, the lure is part of an anglerfish, and it's the reader who wants to be fooled—who wants to be devoured. (Don't think too hard about where the reader eventually ends up; think more about the dangers of extended metaphors.)

The question of what is interesting is perhaps less urgent for novels, where the reader expects to settle in for the long haul, but it still has relevance. There is also the issue, across genres, of what the majority of readers will find fascinating as opposed to difficult to digest. *New York Times* best seller Mary Doria Russell thought about this issue extensively when writing her science-fiction novel *The Sparrow*. Her solution? She decided to remove from the first fifty to seventy-five pages those references to her future Earth that might have confused readers unfamiliar with science fiction's

"The Prologue Fish" by Jeremy Zerfoss.

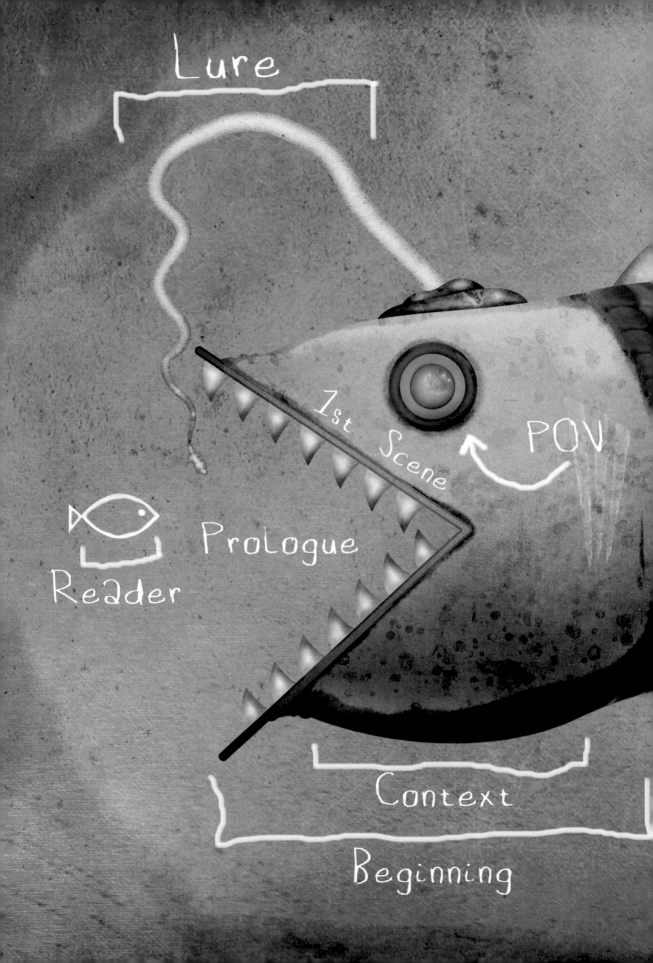

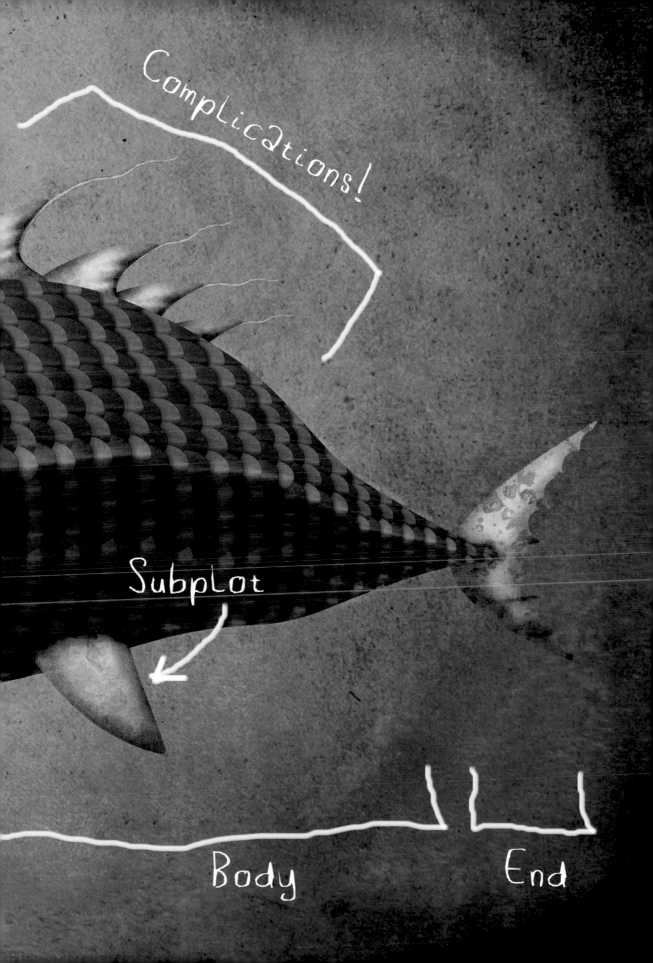

shorthand. This may have gained her general readers—and the book is still powerful—but in terms of the novel's structure and the expectations set, you might argue that Russell destabilized the beginning of *The Sparrow,* and it is not as faithful to its structure and intent as a result. (The opposing argument is that by luring in more readers this way, she actually made the book more accessible, and thus any other arguments are moot.)

A different issue arises when writing books in a series, a fairly common occurrence in science fiction and fantasy: How much information do you pack into the beginning chapters of book two and book three that readers of book one already know? The most elegant solution is probably the one used by David Anthony Durham for his Other Lands fantasy trilogy. Rather than try to add unnecessary recent plot/history to the opening chapters of his second and third books, Durham simply included a preamble at the beginning of each that summarizes the plots of the prior books. This solution provides much-needed context while not destabilizing or unbalancing the openings of books two and three. Many a perfectly good novel in a series has been ruined by the mistaken assumption that crucial prior knowledge must be embedded in the first chapters.

With all of this in mind, what elements do you need for a good beginning? Besides a talking penguin or someone with a gun, that is.

ELEMENTS OF A GOOD BEGINNING

Figuring out the best starting point should be followed up by making sure you've included the right material in your beginning, in the right amounts, and with the right emphasis for the story you want to tell. Most stories require some or all of the following basic elements to be present at the beginning:

- A main character or characters, presented from a consistent point of view
- A conflict or problem
- An antagonist (The source of conflict or the problem—a person or, depending on the theme, nature or society, to name just two possibilities; whomever or whatever the main characters are pushing up against, which, put crassly, could be called the "villain" of the piece.)
- A hint or suggestion of a secondary conflict or problem that may form a subplot or additional complication (This is optional, since it may come into focus later in the narrative.)
- A sense of action or motion, no matter how static the opening scene
- A general or specific idea of the setting
- A consistent tone and mood to the language

The economy and sophistication with which you provide these elements, and the style in which you present them, may depend on whether you are writing a short story or a novel. It's also important to note that an invisible or an ornate style can convey economy and sophistication, while a lush style can be concise. The issue of the *number of words* required to convey an idea, a character sketch, or other element is less important in fiction than that sentences *do more than one thing*. For example, you should be able to write a sentence that advances not just characterization but also setting and conflict, everything in motion at once. Being able to accomplish this is especially important at the beginning of your story, where you often have to convey more information—more context—than in most other places in the narrative.

The type of story or novel also influences the level of precision and immediacy. Some tales allow for a more leisurely introduction of elements; there is nothing particularly nail-biting about the beginning of *The Fellowship of the Ring,* because Mr. Tolkien is playing an extremely long game. Neither does conciseness mean rushing through, shoving too many elements into such a small space that you, or the reader, lose the necessary clarity. If we start off on a journey toward Mordor without our bearings, tagging along with people we know nothing about and care nothing about, we might decide to go AWOL.

A "problem," meanwhile, can begin as small as a hole in someone's sock that leads to something more significant or can metastasize immediately as a looming threat to the survival of God, Country, or Talking Penguin. The idea of a "sense of motion or action" relates to the suggestion of a "problem," with the motion or action a possible expression of the problem, although it can also just be the main character *physically moving.* The point is that motion of any kind draws the eye to look in a particular direction, and the reader assigns some measure of agency or importance to whatever is moving.

The idea of a consistent tone or mood at the opening of a story or novel may seem too abstract, but many a piece of fiction has been ruined by being written in the wrong register. For example, if you start with breathless, emotional words, you run the risk of having nowhere to go in later dramatic scenes. But if you start too un-emotionally—or, alternatively, are too frivolous when you mean to be serious—you may not properly convey aspects of the story or the main character's personality.

Although the number of elements you have to work with to craft your beginning may be finite, they can be combined and expressed in a multitude of ways. Asking yourself a variety of questions can help you to better understand your approach and how it may be interpreted by the reader. Once you have settled on the best possible opening, you should always think about adjusting the balance—like fiddling with the treble, bass, and other settings of a car stereo system to achieve the highest-quality sound. Here are just a few of the possible questions:

- Is the main character, or at least one character, introduced in the very first line? If not, why not, and what is emphasized in the first line in place of character?
- Is the main character fully integrated with other elements: Can we begin to see the character's opinions about his or her environment and about other characters?
- Are the relationships between characters clearly set out in the opening paragraphs so that there is no potential confusion for the reader? (For example, the character the reader thinks is someone's son but turns out to be the cousin instead.)

EXAMPLES OF
MOTION IN A
STATIC SCENE

1998

"When you're Dead," Samantha says, "you don't have to brush your teeth . . ."

– KELLY LINK, "The Specialist's Hat"

2005

We all went down to the tar-pit, with mats to spread our weight.

– MARGO LANAGAN, "Singing My Sister Down"

1930

A man who is about to die is not likely to be very elegant in his last words: being in a hurry to sum up his whole life, he tends to make them rigorously concise.

– JEAN RAY, "The *Mainz Psalter*"

1977

Now I will try to keep awake. The fog. They must have come for me before morning.

– ERIC BASSO, "The Beak Doctor"

1941

The time has come that I must tell the events which began in 40 Pest Street.

– LEONORA CARRINGTON, "White Rabbits"

2010

Children are cruel. No one who has lived in the world need ask for proof of that.

– K. J. BISHOP, "Saving the Gleeful Horse"

1930

On a foggy night in November, Mr. Corbett, having guessed the murderer by the third chapter of his detective story, arose in disappointment from his bed and went downstairs in search of something more satisfactory to send him to sleep.

– MARGARET IRWIN, "The Book"

1971

"Don't look now," John said to his wife, "but there are a couple of old girls two tables away who are trying to hypnotise me."

– DAPHNE DU MAURIER, "Don't Look Now"

1939

With a roar and a howl the thing was upon us, out of total darkness.

– ROBERT BARBOUR JOHNSON, "Far Below"

1989

Our heart stops.

– ELIZABETH HAND, "The Boy in the Tree"

MYSTER ODD PRESENTS:
MEMORABLE
FIRST LINES

What might a good opening line offer the reader?

- A sense of mystery or atmosphere
- An interesting initial situation
- Immediate tension and excitement
- An intriguing statement
- An unusual or interesting description
- A unique point of view

- Have you chosen the right viewpoint character(s)? (Would someone else have more at stake or be more interesting?)
- Have you chosen the right approach to point of view, whether first person, third person, or second person? What happens when you try writing the same opening from, for example, third person instead of first person?
- Is the starting location or general setting appropriate for the story? Will the location or general setting appear again in the story? If not, have you invested words to describe the setting that might be better spent on other elements? (If the location won't be used again, is it the right location?)
- Is the issue or problem or dilemma facing the main character clear to the reader, to the degree required by this particular story? Have you been either too subtle or too obvious?
- In relation to the context of the scene, does the problem faced by the main character seem unintentionally trivial? (If so, both the penguin and I hope you meant to write comedy.)
- Is the tone of the opening consistent, and does it carry through the rest of the story?
- Does the style fit the characters, setting, and purpose of the story?
- Does the emotional content of the words you have used create the correct context and the correct bond or pact with the reader as to the type of story?
- Does the opening support the ending?

When you add the overlay of the requirements intrinsic to most fantastical fiction (including science fiction), certain other questions come to mind. These questions relate to special constraints or responsibilities, some akin to the challenges faced by writers of historical fiction.

- Do we know *where* we are? (Earth Prime, Past Earth, Earth, Earth 2.0, not-Earth, Another Planet, Spaceship, Miniaturized-Inside-a-Weiner-Dog, etc.)
- Do we know *when* we are? (Future, Past, Now, Now-Plus-5-Seconds, etc.)
- If *where* and *when* are implied rather than stated, is the implication providing enough information? Is the implication providing the *right* kind of information?
- If you have stated *where* and *when*, have you been too obvious or uneconomical in your approach? Is there a more elegant way to convey this information?
- Do we know if the protagonist is human or not?
- If the protagonist isn't human, do we already have clues as to how differently this protagonist understands and processes the world from a human protagonist?
- In conveying context, have you provided *too much* information up front, clogging the narrative?
- Do we have a general idea from the word choice and other contextual clues as to whether we are reading science fiction or fantasy? (There are different, more rigid protocols for science fiction. For example, "hyperdrive" figures prominently in most science-fiction worlds that include spaceships.)
- Does your word choice help convey the differences between your setting and Earth Prime in a seamless fashion?

- Have you included too many made-up or unusual words to try to convey your unique setting, reducing the clarity of your opening? (For example: "Space Captain Talking Penguin quarked the 4G switch on his barkolater with his ghost malanges, and on came the entire starbird system, including the psi-beaker app" might give even a dedicated science-fiction fan pause.)

In most kinds of contemporary fiction set in the real world, the reader will make certain assumptions based on their own experience. These assumptions decrease the burden on the writer to render certain elements explicit in the text. Even the historical novelist exploring, for example, Venice in the 1600s, will have some expectation that many readers will know **at least something** about the city. But with most kinds of science fiction and fantasy, you may have to expend more time and energy convincing your readers to "suspend disbelief"—to trick themselves into believing what is on the page is real.

Readers will also probably have some received ideas about Italy, a sense of it, even if those ideas are based on clichés or stereotypes.

When Not to Commit

I've emphasized, to some extent, needing to know what kind of story you're telling and what you need to put onto the page at the beginning to support that story and the characters that inhabit it. But what about those times when your story demands that you not be clear, or when you're not riffing off of the protocols of a particular genre or subgenre? Especially if you want to tell a story that is doing many things, the most effective technique may seem almost like indecision: It requires not committing immediately to any one set of protocols, with the danger that the reader may find your story at first unfocused, even if the individual scenes are quite effective. The dilemma is that there still has to be a compelling reason to read, even if the reader isn't quite sure what kind of story they're enjoying.

One of the best, most successful examples I've seen recently is Kim Stanley Robinson's *2312*. It is an epic science-fiction novel of interplanetary intrigue, but also a character study of a person named Swan and an examination of a plausible future Earth as well as a love story—between Swan and a man named Waltham. In his opening chapters, Robinson could have decided to commit to one of these stories or ideas. To emphasize the love story, he could have started with Waltham meeting Swan. Or he could have started with the first disastrous attack that sets off the intrigue. But he doesn't. Instead, we start with Swan by herself, engaged in an interesting activity. From there, we are gradually clued in to the various elements of story and how they will work in combination. This serves the useful and obvious purpose, too, since it is a science-fiction novel, of acclimating the reader to Robinson's vision of the future.

Cover art by Kirk Benshoff.

THE BEGINNING OF "AMERICAN GODS" BY NEIL GAIMAN

Neil Gaiman is one of the world's most famous fantasy writers, known for novels such as American Gods, Stardust, *and* Neverwhere *as well as the comic book* The Sandman. *He has won the Hugo Award, Newbery Medal, and the Carnegie Medal for Literature, among others.*

THE FIRST THING I knew when I started *American Gods*—even before I started it—was that I was finished with C. S. Lewis's dictum that to write about how odd things affect odd people was an oddity too much, and that *Gulliver's Travels* worked because Gulliver was normal, just as *Alice in Wonderland* would not have worked if Alice had been an extraordinary girl (which, now that I come to think of it, is an odd thing to say, because if there's one strange character in literature, it's Alice). In *Sandman* I'd enjoyed writing about people who belonged in places on the other side of the looking glass, from the Dreamlord himself to such skewed luminaries as the Emperor of the United States.

Not, I should say, that I had much say in what *American Gods* was going to be. It had its own opinions.

Novels accrete.

American Gods began long before I knew I was going to be writing a novel called *American Gods*. It began in May 1997, with an idea that I couldn't get out of my head. I'd find myself thinking about it at night in bed before I'd go to sleep, as if I were watching a movie clip in my head. Each night I'd see another couple of minutes of the story.

In June 1997, I wrote the following on my battered Atari palmtop: "A guy winds up as a bodyguard for a magician. The magician is an over-the-top type. He offers the guy the job meeting him on a plane—sitting next to him."

Chain of events to get there involving missed flights, cancellations, unexpected bounce up to first class, and the guy sitting next to him introduces himself and offers him a job.

His life has just fallen apart anyway. He says "yes."

Which is pretty much the beginning of the book. And all I knew at the time was it was the beginning of something. I hadn't a clue what kind of something. Movie? TV series? Short story?

I don't know any creators of fictions who start writing with nothing but a blank page. (They may exist. I just haven't met any.) Mostly you have something. An image, or a character. And mostly you also have either a beginning, a middle, or an end. Middles are good to have, because by the time you reach the middle, you have a pretty good head of steam up; and ends are great. If you know how it ends, you can just start somewhere, aim, and begin to write (and, if you're lucky, it may even end where you were hoping to go).

There may be writers who have beginnings, middles, and ends before they sit down to write. I am rarely of their number.

So there I was, four years ago, with only a beginning. And you need more than a beginning if you're going to start a book. If all you have is a beginning, then once you've written that beginning, you have nowhere to go.

A year later, I had a story in my head about these people. I tried writing it: The character I'd thought of as a magician (although, I had already decided, he wasn't a magician at all) now seemed to be called Wednesday. I wasn't sure what the other guy's name was, the bodyguard, so I called him Ryder, but that wasn't quite right. I had a short story in mind about those two and some murders that occur in a small Midwestern town called Silverside. I wrote a page and gave up, mainly because they really didn't seem to come to town together.

There was a dream I woke up from, somewhere back then, sweating and confused, about a dead wife. It seemed to belong to the story, and I filed it away.

Some months later, in September 1998, I tried writing that story again, as a first-person narrative, sending the guy I'd called Ryder (who I tried calling Ben Kobold this time, but that sent out quite the wrong set of signals) to the town (which I'd called Shelby, because Silverside seemed too exotic) on his own. I covered about ten pages, and then stopped. I still wasn't comfortable with it.

By that point, I was coming to the conclusion that the story I wanted to tell in that particular little lakeside town . . . hmm, I thought somewhere in there, Lakeside, that's what it's called, a solid, generic name for a town . . . was too much a part of the novel to be written in isolation from it. And I had a novel by then. I'd had it for several months.

Back in July 1998, I had gone to Iceland, on the way to Norway and Finland. It may have been the distance from America, or it may have been the lack of sleep involved in a trip to the Land of the Midnight Sun, but suddenly, somewhere in Reykjavik, the novel came into focus. Not the story of it—I still had nothing more than the meeting on the plane and a fragment of plot in a town by a lake—but

for the first time I knew what it was about. I had a direction. I wrote a letter to my publisher telling them that my next book wouldn't be a historical fantasy set in restoration London after all, but a contemporary American phantasmagoria. Tentatively, I suggested *American Gods* as a working title for it.

I kept naming my protagonist: There's a magic to names, after all. I knew his name was descriptive. I tried calling him Lazy, but he didn't seem to like that, and I called him Jack, and he didn't like that any better. I took to trying every name I ran into on him for size, and he looked back at me from somewhere in my head unimpressed every time. It was like trying to name Rumpelstiltskin.

He finally got his name from an Elvis Costello song (it's on *Bespoke Songs, Lost Dogs, Detours and Rendezvous*). It's performed by Was (Not Was) and is the story of two men named Shadow and Jimmy. I thought about it, tried it on for size . . .

. . . and Shadow stretched uncomfortably on his prison cot, and glanced across at the Wild Birds of North America wall calendar, with the days he'd been inside crossed off, and he counted the days until he got out.

And once I had a name, I was ready to begin.

I wrote Chapter One around December 1998. I was still trying to write it in the first person, and it wasn't comfortable with that. Shadow was too damn private a person, and he didn't let much out, which is hard enough in a third-person narrative and really hard in a first-person narrative. I began chapter two in June 1999, on the train home from the San Diego comics convention. (It's a three-day train journey. You can get a lot of writing done there.)

The book had begun. I wasn't sure what I was going to call it, but then the publishers started sending me mock-ups of the book's cover, and it said "American Gods" in big letters at the top, and I realized that my working title had become the title. I kept writing, fascinated. I felt, on the good days, more like the first reader than the writer, something I'd rarely felt since *The Sandman* days. ❧

This decision not to choose a position, so to speak, to place in the foreground neither love story nor intrigue allows Robinson the space to privilege both strands, to make the novel somehow deeper and more real and less like fiction. The risk, however, is that some readers may be confused as to the point of the story for a few chapters. In fact, some reviewers wrote about the interplanetary plot and mentioned the relationships not at all, even though close to half the plot of the book could be said to be about Waltham and Swan. Some readers on Amazon.com and elsewhere seemed almost indignant about Robinson's approach—summarized, perhaps, as "putting romance in our science fiction slowed this book down!" But the truth is that you will always alienate some readers, and it's better that you do so in the service of being true to your vision; *2312* is a much better novel because of Robinson's refusal to commit too early.

This subject also pertains to the ways in which writers sometimes edit their fiction to provide a more comfortable entrypoint for the reader. To another writer reading such material, the destabilizations can read like deformities of structure or character; to many readers, it's invisible, and all they notice is that the launchpoint into story is easy. Some would thus argue that the deformity is actually an enhancement, and I'm not going to take issue with that here because I think it also marks an ideological difference of opinion on what the beginning of a story is supposed to do. Some writers will argue that distortion is worth it if it provides a more efficient and readable delivery system for weirder/less conventional material embedded later on. I personally find it irritating and disappointing more often than not. The reason I bring up the subject is that the commercial underpinnings of science fiction and fantasy can mean that if you write in those modes, you may encounter more pressure to conform to genre expectations . . . sometimes for the worse.

BAD BEGINNINGS?

Which brings us to another question: What usually doesn't work at the beginning of a story or novel? It's always hard to generalize, but here are a few things that rarely work to start:

- A flashback
- A dream sequence
- Dialogue
- The viewpoint of a minor character

The general reason these entry points fail is that they waste the reader's time. For example, a flashback at the beginning or close to the beginning of a novel doesn't allow enough time for the reader to become invested in the foreground, the present day, of the fiction. Provided too soon, a flashback carries less of the right weight or relevance—because the reader has nothing to compare it to in terms of the characters' lives. Thus, instead of adding depth or understanding, the flashback undermines the entire opening of the story.

Dream sequences pose a different kind of problem. Because they aren't conveying anything real, they usually seem like a cheat to the reader—"Surprise! It was all a dream!" gives the reader a good reason to throw a book across the room and takes up space at the beginning that could be spent fleshing out the character and the world. In surreal, Kafkaesque fiction, a dream sequence also tends to seem stylistically and tonally the same as the scenes set in the awake world, and since the surface of the story is already dreamlike, using actual dreams may both bore and confuse the reader.

Starting a story or novel with dialogue is less of a crime—Elmore Leonard and some others can get away with it—but it usually leaves the reader floating and adrift, without an anchor. Where are we? When are we? Who is the viewpoint character? Not only is this confusing, but it's human nature to start filling in the gaps. By the time the first description kicks in, you may find yourself in a room with a talking penguin and a woman holding a gun, although your readers have already formed a very different mental picture.

The prologue or opening that focuses on a minor character can work in a novel because there is more space to develop the main characters, but it almost never works in the more cramped quarters of a short story. Regardless, the focus on a "disposable"—who dies during the opening or is for some other reason never heard from again—can create a frustrating bait-and-switch situation. The reader thinks they are reading about the viewpoint character, and then they learn the viewpoint character you've presented to them isn't part of the main story at all. If, however, you are writing long novels with multiple viewpoint characters, then it is easier to profitably include such throwaway viewpoints early in the novel. For example, in George R. R. Martin's A Song of Ice and Fire series, they tend to serve to enhance atmosphere or give the viewpoint of a lower social class.

Novel Approaches: "Finch"

Now that you have an idea of what to include in your beginning, what kinds of questions to ask, and what approaches usually fail, the next step is to take apart a beginning and see how it works. A demonstration from a published piece of fiction is more effective than an abstract example. So let's take an in-depth look at the opening of my novel *Finch*, to demonstrate the search for the right entry point into narrative, and the implications of each discarded approach.

Finch is set in the fantastical city of Ambergris. The city is a kind of echo or reflection of certain aspects of Earth, but clearly a secondary world setting. In *Finch,* mysterious underground inhabitants known as the gray caps have reconquered the fantastical city of Ambergris and put it under martial law. They have disbanded the political entity House Hoegbotton and are controlling the human inhabitants with strange addictive drugs, internment in camps, and random acts of terror. The rebel resistance is scattered, and the gray caps are using human labor to build two strange towers. Against this backdrop, the reluctant detective John Finch, a conscripted recruit

A "secondary world" is a setting that is not Earth or some alternative version of Earth. Examples include C. S. Lewis's Narnia, J. R. R. Tolkien's Middle Earth, and Ursula K. Le Guin's Earthsea.

in the police force, must attempt to solve a strange double murder of a human being and a gray cap found in an abandoned apartment. If he doesn't, his terrifying gray cap boss, Heretic, will probably kill him.

Not only did the particulars of Finch's personality, history, and job carry a certain weight and bias that affect the story, but each mode of fiction I used carries with it a whole history of tropes, archetypes, and expected entry points for the reader. Therefore, I had several decisions to make regarding the beginning of the novel, each of which would affect other decisions at both the sentence and scene level, as well as how readers decided to classify both the novel and my main character. The one question I didn't have to worry about was point of view: I knew I wanted the novel to be from Finch's perspective, in the third person.

What was the novel's central nervous system, then? What did I want to emphasize? How did I want to blend these influences so that the result was a chemical rather than a physical reaction? Perhaps most important in terms of the fantasy element: how did I want to introduce readers to the city of Ambergris? And how would that decision position Finch in the eyes of readers?

Two early, abandoned approaches are instructive. In one draft, Finch woke up, fed his cat, and received a message from his boss. In another, I had Finch on the road to the crime scene after receiving the message.

Is there anything potentially wrong with either one, keeping in mind the list of bad beginnings?

EXAMPLE A teeters on the edge of the classic mistake made by many beginning writers: because most people start the day by getting out of bed and making coffee, it seems natural to have the protagonist begin a novel by doing the same thing. The approach almost never works and usually results in significant redrafting to find

EXAMPLE A: WAKING UP

John Finch woke that morning to a pinched nerve in his back, the distant smell of gunpowder and spores, and a message slipped under the door.

He made some coffee, fed his cat Feral, gave a nod to the anonymous lizard that lived on the windowsill, and read the note over weak coffee, even as it got smaller and smaller in his hand. The gray cap administrator responsible for his sector of Ambergris had sent it. Finch had never learned the gray cap's name. It was just a series of clicks and whistles that sounded a little like 'hecleretical' so Finch called him Heretic.

"FINCH" PARTICULARS

THE NOVEL IS A HYBRID OF THESE GENRES:

- Fantasy (urban fantasy, new weird, secondary world fantasy)
- Horror
- Spy novels and political thrillers
- Noir and hard-boiled mysteries
- Visionary science fiction

IMPORTANT ELEMENTS OF
THE SETTING AND STORY:

- An inhuman race called "gray caps" has risen from the underground to conquer the city.
- The city is in ruins from the conflict, and spies and rebels operate in areas of lawlessness.
- The gray caps provide a semblance of normalcy by installing a token police force and other institutions.
- The gray caps have recruited a security force called Partials, human traitors who have allowed their eyes to be replaced by living cameras, part of the gray caps' terrifying fungal-based technology.
- Aspects of the gray caps' rule resemble real-world situations, such as France under Nazi rule.

FINCH IS:

- A former member of a rebel militia.
- A man with a secret, hidden past.
- Pragmatic but also nostalgic about better times.
- Compromised because of working for the gray caps.
- Willing to do whatever it takes to live in a broken city.
- Loyal to his friends.

the novel's real start point. Not only is there little tension in this entry point, unless something about the character's home or daily routine has critical significance to the story, it's a waste of the reader's time.

EXAMPLE B contains no real tension, and the scene functions as a kind of travelogue showing off the city without serving any other purpose. The travelogue also, curiously enough, began to lock me into decisions about the setting that I didn't want to make yet—I needed more time, as the novel unfolded, to further visualize the city. In a real-world novel, we might not even need to know how a character gets somewhere, but in a fantasy novel the reader not told or shown such things may begin to see the omissions as mistakes in worldbuilding by the writer.

Neither example supports the idea of starting a story as close to the end as possible; in a novel, this translates to starting at a point of dramatic possibility or potential relevant to the protagonist or other major focus of the narrative.

Some other points to think about regarding these two failed openings:

- The normal events of a character's day can be a useful contrast to the "emergency situations" or "special events" usually documented by a novel, but foregrounding those normal events or settings may work against dramatic appeal and tension.
- Both the normal-event approach and waking-up fallacy fall into the category of dramatizing "connective tissue." The former is literal and the latter implied; if positioned later in the novel, waking up is a transition rather than a beginning. Such scenes can be dispensed with in the span of a phrase or sentence without anyone noticing the absence of further detail.
- The physical setting you choose to start with may carry more weight than you intend; or, rather, the reader may "imprint" on your first setting and expect it to figure significantly in the narrative. (Some novels, such as the aforementioned George R. R. Martin series or Angela Carter's surreal quest novel *The Infernal Desire Machines of Doctor Hoffman*, contain such a wealth of settings that this doesn't hold true.)
- Transitional text, some of it "travel description"—getting your characters from one point to another—may or may not be useful for your story or novel. Especially with regard to fantasy, writers sometimes mistake descriptions of a setting for narrative, and unless that description is hardwired into decisions about characterization, the reader often suffers as a result. A lot of walking around in your narrative may indicate a general aimlessness. Less likely: You are a genius who has discovered a new way of creating tension through perambulation.
- The wrong specific information conveyed up front can be as bad as not conveying enough specific information. In the case of Example A, the details about Finch's message and his boss exist in such a lack of context that the very precision of the description works to confuse the reader, who has no wider world in which to place this information.
- The wrong kind of introduction to a setting can create the wrong note or tone for the reader. In Example B, the fact that Finch drives a car pushed me toward writer's block. Something about Finch being able to drive seemed not in character, and something about a car being foregrounded as an example of

EXAMPLE B: TRAVELING TO THE CRIME SCENE

Since no one else had claimed it for more important
duty, Finch had the rare privilege of leaving the police
station in the force's only motored vehicle, a ten-year-
old Aventor from Stockton, one of the newest cars in the
city. There was a kid down the street from his apartment
who sold them the gasoline sometimes, in return for food
vouchers. Finch had no idea where he got it.
  The Aventor lurched and scraped down the street as
Finch clung to the wheel, white smoke trailing out
behind him. Something was wrong with the Aventor and
someday it would just stop working. Until then, it felt
like a luxury to drive it and watch the way people
walking on the sidewalks would stop and
turn as if he were the vanguard of
some amazing carnival.

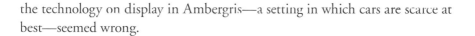

the technology on display in Ambergris—a setting in which cars are scarce at
best—seemed wrong.

How and when you convey information is often the key to success. Considering the
fantasy setting, wasn't there a better entry point to both the novel and the city of
Ambergris? Whom should we meet first, second, third? What *should* be emphasized?
What don't we know that we need to know? In thinking about these questions, I
found my way to four more serious choices—all of which I tried out before selecting
one as the best for my purposes.

  If you've read the novel, you know which one I chose. If you haven't, which do
you think I selected—and why?

- John Finch standing over the dead bodies at the crime scene. Beside him, his
  boss, Heretic, and a Partial (a human traitor).
- Finch at the police station, receiving the call from his boss about the murders,
  telling Finch to come to the apartment.
- Finch poised at the door to the apartment, about to enter the crime scene.
- Finch, staring out over the skyline of Ambergris from the balcony of the crime
  scene.

Consider all of the information I've given you above about the novel before reaching a conclusion. Then turn the page, and we'll start with the options I ultimately
discarded . . . .

OTHER APPROACHES

#1--JOHN FINCH STANDING OVER THE DEAD BODIES AT THE CRIME SCENE. BESIDE HIM, HIS BOSS, HERETIC, AND A PARTIAL (A HUMAN TRAITOR).

In a standard noir or hard-boiled mystery novel, approach #1 would be the writer's choice more often than not. Why? This opening:

- Has a sense of immediacy, of *being in the moment*
- Introduces the case, or central problem, facing the main character, and thus the main story arc
- Creates automatic interest and tension
- Defines the novel to some degree as about solving the murders (even if the novel then subverts this expectation)
- Introduces several characters important to the novel, and sets in motion initial characterization
- Establishes a setting important to the novel: the crime scene

However, the clarity of this opening is a drawback if you want to create a hybrid—a true cross-pollination of genres—as I wanted to do for *Finch*. It sets up an expectation of the solution to the case being the conclusion of the novel. This opening also gets to the point too quickly for my purposes, given that I have the obligation to describe the wider *not-our-reality* setting. There are also these points to consider:

- Introducing the reader to the main character in the context of interactions with other characters creates a different effect than the main character by himself or herself. You can convey a lot about a person through his or her interactions with other people, but sometimes you may wish to show the character in solitude, for contrast.
- Your conception of space and the way in which the characters inhabit space in a setting will determine how readers view them. For example, in terms of hierarchy, can you tell who is the person with the most authority in the scene of several characters looking down at the body?
- The amount of time or space you allow to surround a character or characters affects the reader's view of them because it affects the rate at which you can provide information about them, and the type of information (that won't seem extraneous to the scene).

Noir fiction is a type of whodunnit allied with hard-boiled fiction, but in noir the protagonist doesn't have to be a detective per se. The protagonist may also have self-destructive traits, and the mystery may not be solved.

This issue of how and when to convey necessary exposition is central to one way in which speculative fiction often differs from contemporary mainstream fiction. I touched on this issue in the list of questions you should ask about your beginnings, but it bears amplification here.

A **noir mystery** set in, say, Chicago, in the present day creates a minimum expectation for the writer to, in the first scene, note that location and provide a few details. But a fantasy novelist writing a mystery set in an imaginary place has a greater obligation: to begin to differentiate that location from reality. The ways in which you accomplish this will differ from story to story, but your method should involve careful consideration of what I would call the *rate of strangeness* calculated in proportion to the ordinariness of the situation. You can easily argue that any writer has an equal responsibility, if you want to create something genuine, to render Chicago as intricately as Middle Earth. But the minimum threshold at which the reader will still believe in a shoddily rendered Chicago is lower than that for a shoddily rendered Middle Earth . . . one would hope.

So, for example, in *Finch* I have provided readers with a familiar setup—a murder mystery—and a very odd, surreal city that includes a race of people who use a form of technology fairly alien to anyone other than an expert on mushrooms. That *specific* juxtaposition of the familiar and the strange suggests the possible angles at which the reader can enter the narrative—and which will allow the reader to enjoy my story to a greater or lesser extent. If I had both a strange situation and a strange setting, the burden of picking the right information to convey up front would increase exponentially.

But these strategies cannot be used in combination with approach #1. I abandoned this approach not just because I wasn't writing a noir mystery, but for the practical reason that I would have had to pack too much information into too small a space. The details of the case would overwhelm the details about the fantastical city—which would clash with the character details.

> #2--FINCH AT THE POLICE STATION, RECEIVING THE CALL FROM HIS BOSS ABOUT THE MURDERS, TELLING FINCH TO COME TO THE APARTMENT.

In a **police procedural**, the writer surrounds the protagonist with colleagues who have their own stories to tell—an ensemble cast—and the story is created by weaving these different strands together. If *Finch* were a police procedural, there might be good reasons to start at the station where Our Hero spends most of his day. The station in such novels—like the office or theater or prison or apartment complex in other ensemble fictions—can serve as the nexus, anchor, or focal point for the narrative: a default main stage, with the rest of the settings more or less revolving around it. The attraction of an approach like this one is that a location like the station can appear to contain the seeds for immediate drama because of the possibility of interaction among multiple characters. It's certainly an improvement over Finch waking up in the morning by himself.

This idea of a nexus can take many other forms, however. For George R. R. Martin's *A Song of Ice and Fire* fantasy series, the best way to understand the large cast of characters is to physically locate them in proximity to one another. Thus, many of the opening sequences of Martin's first book, *A Game of Thrones*, occur at a place called Winterfell, where many of the main characters have gathered for the visit of

A police procedural attempts to accurately depict the actions of the police in trying to solve a crime or several different crimes.

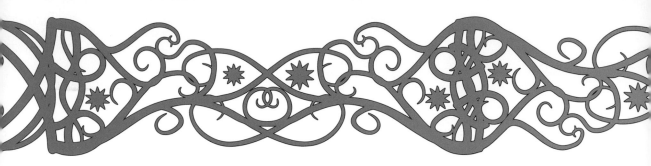

a king. From these scenes, the reader gains a much more complete understanding of character relationships, histories, and motivations than if Martin instead had shown them separately in their far-flung homes. Martin's solution may slow the action of the first third of the novel considerably, but the trade-off is that the reader gains a much greater *clarity* that lasts across the first three installments in the series. The fateful decisions from those early chapters have repercussions across the series, too.

Still, it can be a risky approach, for three reasons:

- Introducing the reader to multiple characters at once may make it harder to flesh out any of them for the reader and create an expectation that they will all be an important part of the story.
- Ensemble casts lend themselves to novels with chapters from multiple viewpoints, which locks you into a certain structure.
- Describing the interactions of several characters up front leaves less space for context about the setting, even though some aspects of setting are embedded in a character's point of view.

As you might expect, this issue of introducing *too many* characters in an opening scene can become very confusing for the reader. How do you handle not just a woman with a gun and a talking penguin, but six penguins, three women with guns, and a pelican in a palm tree? Such scenes require a mastery of staging to properly emphasize or deemphasize particular details, while also making sure minor players don't just stand around watching the scene unfold. If you add the need to introduce key elements of the setting—expressed through your viewpoint character's experience—you begin to see how a novelist can easily lose control of this kind of opening scene.

More important, *Finch* is not a multiple-point-of-view novel; nor is it an example of using an ensemble cast. In the novel as I had envisioned it, I saw Finch's colleagues as secondary characters, with only four or five scenes set in the police station. Opening at the station is also far too early for the kind of novel *Finch* wants to be, almost akin to starting with one of the abandoned approaches mentioned earlier, with regard to dramatic tension. Further, starting at the station would have created an additional requirement: getting John Finch to the murder site, similar to the discarded approach involving Finch driving in a car.

Although I did ultimately write a scene set in the station, it occurs after Finch has met with his boss and examined the murder victims. This decision allowed me to describe the station while Finch types up the details of the case and interacts with his fellow detectives, without my needing to simultaneously introduce Heretic and

the Partial or the wider setting of Ambergris. This placement meant I could also use the scene to bring greater complexity and layering to Finch's character.

#3--FINCH, STARING OUT OVER THE SKYLINE OF AMBERGRIS FROM THE BALCONY OF THE CRIME SCENE (OR SOME OTHER LOCATION).

Epic fantasy novels and sprawling multigenerational depictions of contemporary life alike sometimes provide a prologue or an opening chapter containing a panoramic view of the main setting, usually a city. Such novels tend to be expansive, with large casts of viewpoint characters, so that the scope allows for near-omniscient, sweeping descriptions. A novel like China Miéville's *Perdido Street Station* signals its intent by beginning in just this way, following the course of the ancient river that flows past the city of New Crobuzon. The landscape itself becomes a character, defining and setting geographical limits, imposing itself on the lives of the people who inhabit the novel. In a sense, starting with the setting allows Miéville to stake out closer and more distant vantage points throughout the novel, because of the precedent set. On a smaller scale, landscape descriptions in the hands of miniaturists like Jorge Luis Borges also can become the stuff of amazing stories: whole worlds conjured up in mere sentences.

Questions to ask that may help you decide if you want to use this approach:

- To what extent do you consider the setting of your story to be a character, in terms of its influence on your protagonist and antagonist, for example?
- How intensely do the specific details of the setting impact the characters, and thus the plot?
- When you think about your novel's perspective: Is it a bird's-eye view, swooping down to inhabit the characters, a handheld camera resting on a character's shoulder, or somewhere in between?
- Where do you intend to end the novel in terms of distance from the main character's point of view?

You should also consider **the dangers** in using such an approach. Privileging locations over characters can create a landscape not invested with emotion or point of view, description that is largely inert, lifeless. It may satisfy the epic fantasy reader who enjoys such descriptions, but their affection for travelogue can and should be satisfied in other ways when possible. It may be true that in writing fantasy set in a

You can find an extended discussion of this issue in Chapter 6.

Cover painting by Ben Templesmith (2008) for *Shriek: An Afterword*, the prequel to *Finch*. This approach perfectly visualizes how environment and character influence each other in the novels.

place not-Earth, I have an obligation to describe that place and make it believable on some level. However, I have an equally important charge not to lard the narrative and the characters with excessive description or description *not truly related to the viewpoint character.*

I abandoned the landscape-rich approach after a couple of attempts because I had other challenges with regard to setting (which, in Ambergris, comes with the baggage of history). What were these challenges?

- Striking the right balance so that readers of prior books in the series wouldn't feel as if they were being told things they already knew, but new readers would have the necessary context to enjoy the novel.
- Allowing for a moment of frisson and acclimation for readers, because *Finch* is set a century after the events dramatized in the prior book in the series, *Shriek: An Afterword* (which changed the city in fundamental ways).

I then did write a draft foregrounding a full-on description of Ambergris, but this description lacked the emotional resonance alluded to earlier. It also seemed to signal that, yes, this was indeed a fantasy novel, rather than a hybrid, and set up expectations just as unhelpfully clear as starting with the bodies would have set up expectations of a noir mystery.

How did I know this approach worked best for me? Ultimately, I knew that the focus of the novel was John Finch, and so I decided to choose an opening with him alone at the door to the apartment, about to go inside. On the other side of the door he will encounter not just his gray cap boss Heretic, but also a Partial, a human traitor. Because of Finch's particular background, these things scare and stress him much more than encountering bodies. Ambergris is a war-torn landscape; dead bodies are an occupational hazard of daily life. A couple more dead people, even under mysterious circumstances, won't faze Finch, especially since he has served as a soldier in militias. Therefore, the moment before he must face the Partial and Heretic is the moment of maximum tension for him, not the scene where he sees the dead bodies.

In discussing the novel on my blog, the writer Marc Laidlaw gave his experience of the opening as a reader, and why it worked for him: "It's a threshold moment, and just right—a moment later would be too late, a moment earlier, too early. The room is about to take shape for the first time for Finch, as for the reader. Finch's hesitation at the threshold tells the reader much about Finch and his situation. That's the moment of equipoise, of everything about to change, the balance about to shift . . . it's an in-gathering, a zero-gravity point, and just right for you to shift the weight of the novel onto the reader's shoulders without them really noticing."

> Finch, at the apartment door, breathing heavy from five flights of stairs, taken fast. The message that'd brought him from the station was already dying in his hand. Red smear on a limp circle of green fungal paper that had minutes before squirmed clammy. Now he had only the door to pass through, marked with the gray caps' symbol.

The blogger Matt Denault correctly noted that "in the opening you chose, Finch begins alone, which helps define an arc in the novel when set against where he ends up. There's the theme of doors as portals, yes; also in going through the door Finch takes the reader with him, we and he seeing the situation in the room for the first time, which requires him to set the scene for us. Choice is another theme of the book, and going through a door is an active choice, not passive, so generally a good way to begin a novel and especially so in this case: Finch's reluctant acquiescence helps establish his character, the larger setting, and hits the right thematic note that

DOORS TO NARRATIVE

A DOOR YOU HAVE TO GO THROUGH…WILL YOU?

A DOOR THAT LEADS TO THE OLD FAMILY HOUSE…AND MEMORY.

A DOOR TO THE ABSOLUTE UNKNOWN… AND ANOTHER WORLD.

A DOOR TO YOUR WORKPLACE YOU KNOW TOO WELL…

A DOOR THROUGH WHICH THINGS COME TO YOU…

A DOOR THAT DOESN'T APPEAR TO BE A DOOR.

THE FINAL DOOR BEHIND WHICH YOU WILL FIND… THE END.

A DOOR THAT YOU HAVE BEEN WARNED NOT TO OPEN…

those in control have not outright enslaved the populace, but rather control through surveillance, terror, and co-options." In general, doors provide opportunities in fiction to underscore decisions by characters.

The door to the apartment is also the first of many doors Finch will walk through, and that initial moment of tension repeats throughout the novel in various guises. Doors do represent choices for Finch—sometimes even small acts of defiance—and each time he can decide to face what's beyond them or to turn back. Thus, each time Finch encounters a door, especially in a dangerous context, the reader learns something more about his character.

Now, just as Finch goes through doors in the novel, there are doors the reader will need to open to enjoy the novel—in a sense, a series of *progressions*. I didn't want the reader to get the bends entering what I knew would already register, for some, as a strange setting with strange antagonists/secondary characters. The opening *situation*—a man under pressure—would create that needed bond of familiarity for readers, but I felt further *normalization* would be necessary to integrate the reader's perspective with the world of the novel. I did not want that world to distract from the core and crux: John Finch. I also wanted the strangeness later in the novel to seem ordinary by the time readers encountered those scenes.

So starting off with Finch at the door also granted me the *space*, the *time*, to introduce the necessary strange elements one by one. In doing so, it meant I didn't have to compromise on that strangeness, merely allow each element room to breathe so that my descriptions didn't trip over one another.

The progressions are very simple but important:

- Finch enters the apartment.
- Finch sees the Partial.
- Finch encounters Heretic (stranger than the Partial, so introduced second).
- Finch is confronted with the dead bodies (almost simultaneous with encountering Heretic).
- Heretic leaves Finch alone with dead bodies and the Partial.
- Partial leaves and Finch, on the balcony, looks out over the city.

This time line is supported by the physical space: hallway leading to doorway, leading to living room/kitchen, leading to the balcony, each space performing a different purpose. And, in fact, that floor plan also functions as a telescopic lens or view expanding outward over time and space.

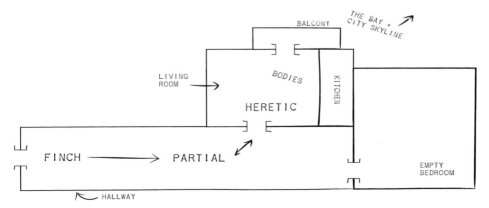

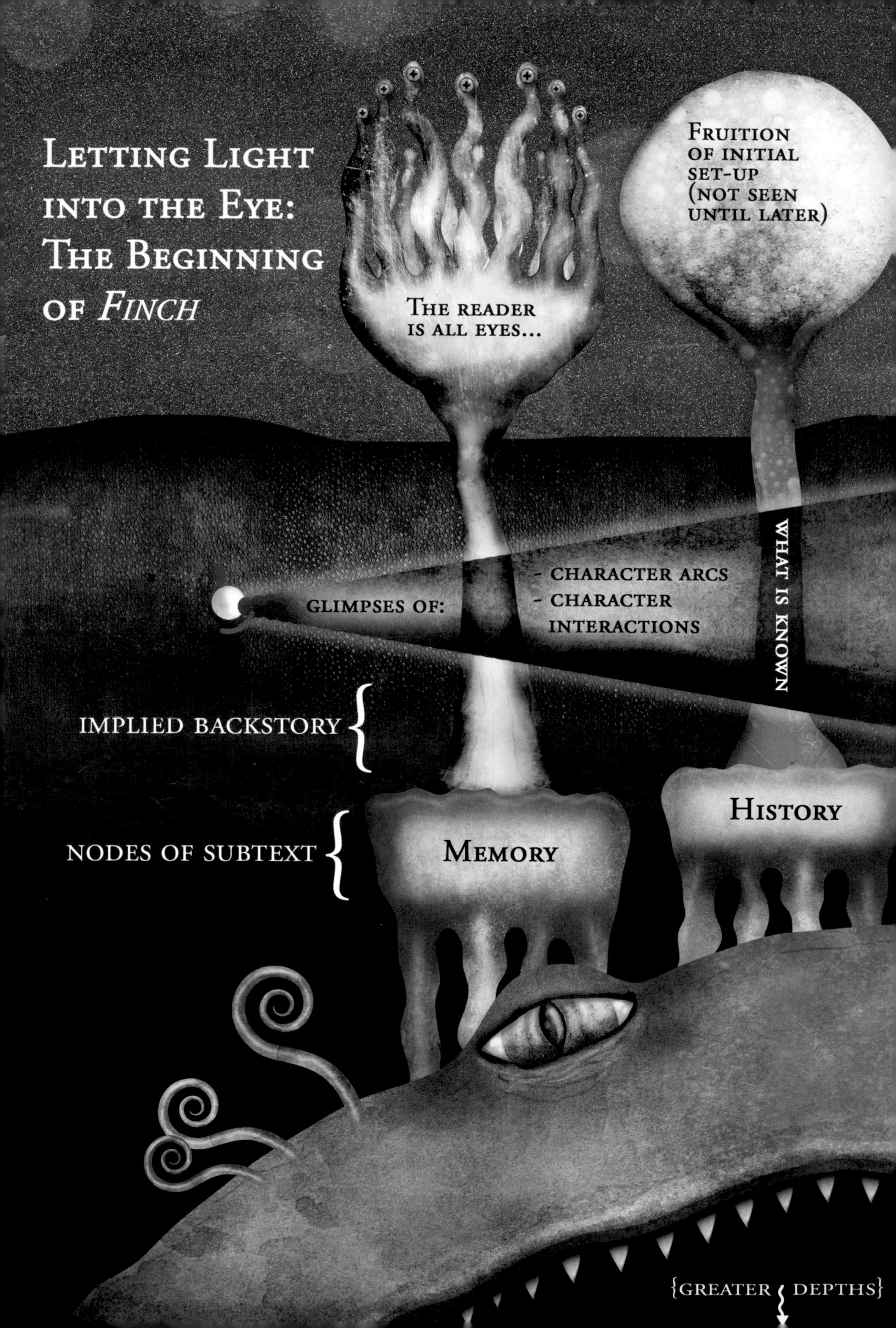

LETTING LIGHT INTO THE EYE: THE BEGINNING OF *FINCH*

THE READER IS ALL EYES...

FRUITION OF INITIAL SET-UP (NOT SEEN UNTIL LATER)

GLIMPSES OF:

- CHARACTER ARCS
- CHARACTER INTERACTIONS

WHAT IS KNOWN

IMPLIED BACKSTORY {

NODES OF SUBTEXT {

MEMORY

HISTORY

{GREATER { DEPTHS}

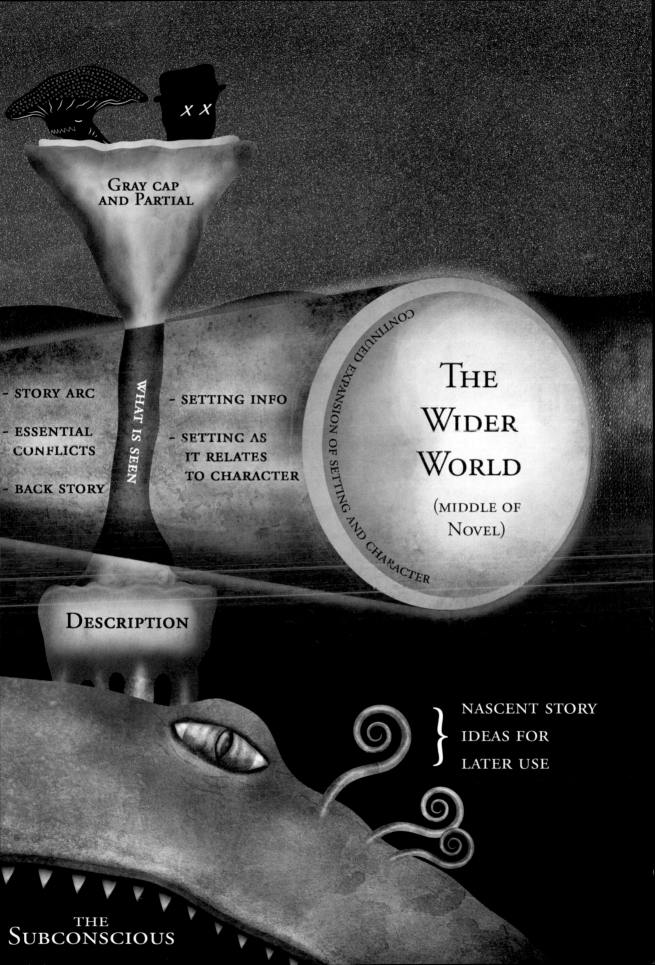

GRAY CAP
AND PARTIAL

- STORY ARC

- ESSENTIAL
  CONFLICTS

- BACK STORY

WHAT IS SEEN

- SETTING INFO

- SETTING AS
  IT RELATES
  TO CHARACTER

CONTINUED EXPANSION OF SETTING AND CHARACTER

THE
WIDER
WORLD
(MIDDLE OF
NOVEL)

DESCRIPTION

NASCENT STORY
IDEAS FOR
LATER USE

THE
SUBCONSCIOUS

The progression also represents the transformation from human to nonhuman: from Finch to Partial to Heretic. It's useful to put space between the Partial and Heretic as emblematic of future conflict between them. The Partial as guard in the hallway also exemplifies his role and status, while Heretic as the gatekeeper to what will be the source of Finch's problems accurately conveys Heretic's role as Finch's boss.

The point of these progressions?

- Acclimate the reader to a strange place
- Create the space to let the oddness of the Partial sink in before getting to the oddness of Heretic, and then the peculiarities of the case facing Finch
- Add further depth of character (When we see Finch with the bodies, the care and thoroughness with which he examines them tells the reader something. He may be a reluctant detective, but if he's given a job, he is going to try to do it as well as he is able. Another person might just go through the motions, but Finch is a man who will try to do the right thing, even when operating from a compromised position.)
- Show Finch in different states of *action* and *reaction*, which speak to aspects of his character

This last point in the list above is very important, since it establishes the framework for a whole host of relationships in the novel. In this very first series of encounters and interactions, the reader receives some fairly complex information about Finch and his world. For example:

- Finch's reaction to the Partial is largely contemptuous, but the reader would not see this so clearly if Finch had encountered the Partial and Heretic at the same time—nor seen so sharply the contrast in Finch's reaction created by then having Heretic leave the room.
- The Partial is fairly scary and has considerable potential power over Finch, so Finch's reaction to the Partial conveys a sense of Finch's bravery or backbone, and further establishes Heretic's primacy.
- Heretic frightens Finch in a way the Partial doesn't, making Heretic much scarier to the reader than if I had just used description to create that sensation. (This also increases the tension in the scene.)

Further, seeing Finch interact with the Partial both before and after Heretic has left is important for a few reasons:

- To show Finch *acting in the same exact way* toward the Partial despite being rattled by Heretic, which demonstrates a certain amount of resilience. He gets rattled but doesn't stay rattled.
- It is useful for events later in the novel to dramatize the range and limits of the Partial's disdain and hatred toward Finch, with Finch's behavior perhaps reinforcing the Partial's attitude.
- The Partial is a recurring character, but he isn't present in many scenes. This

Reader sees the Partial, Heretic, and two corpses, with cityscape in background.

scene is an opportunity to insert him into the narrative, one that also makes sense from the perspective of characterization. (Otherwise, he could have simply gone away with Heretic, leaving Finch alone with the bodies and the city.)

Finally, Finch *does* stare out at the city skyline—abandoned approach #3, but shifted to end the scene, rather than to begin it. By this time, Finch has run the gauntlet of the Partial, Heretic, and the bodies. He's in a different emotional space than when the scene started: more stressed on the one hand, given the unknowns about the case, but also more relaxed because both Heretic and the Partial are gone. In a sense, Finch can now stop playing a role. So when he looks out over the city, it's with a sense of sadness and loss at how Ambergris has changed since the gray caps took control, compounded by his recent encounters—and thus he imbues the landscape with the essential quality of emotion that animates a setting, taking the reader with him.

Yes, Finch *might* have had some of these same feelings if I had begun with him looking out over the skyline, but his thoughts would not have been moored to, connected to, his relationships with the other characters introduced in the scene. The reader might have understood on an intellectual level, but the inversion of the order makes the final moments of the opening scene *personal*. This allows the reader to share in a sense of Finch's life and to invest emotionally in not just the character but also the setting. *Landscape not invested with emotion or point of view is inert, lifeless.*

On the level of "stage business," the description shows the reader every place that Finch visits during the course of the novel. Many of these areas are associated with particular characters, meaning that by the end of this opening scene the reader has, in a sense, "met" almost every major character. In addition, by describing these places in the first chapter, I have freed up space and room for the scenes set in those places later on—I have already provided an initial description and do not need to repeat it.

STYLE, TONE, AND VOICE

Whether you are writing cross-genre fiction, within one particular genre, or something sui generis—and whether using an invisible style or a richer, more ornate style—the foundations of your fiction must strive to attain the kind of *clarity* required for your particular approach to be successful.

One element of my novel that changed drastically from early drafts was the style. Often, the style of a piece of fiction arrives at the same time as the impulse to start writing it down. But, sometimes, as with *Finch*, the style suggests itself after a final decision has been made about where to begin the novel. This makes sense, because deciding on where the novel starts is also a decision concerning the focus of the novel. In this case, the focus is on John Finch.

Once I understood this fact, I realized that I had the opportunity to create a highly form-fitted style for Finch, a style that was meant to:

- Convey a continual, underlying sense of tension or menace, even during times in the novel when Finch feels safer than at other points
- Be tight in on Finch's point of view, be inside of his mind and "on his shoulder" visually
- Allow for a tactile, gritty, street-level experience of the city

Given that *Finch* partakes of noir, the noirish convention of pithy sentences or sentence fragments appealed to me, especially because they would read in places almost like stream-of-consciousness, Finch's thoughts mixed in with description of the surface reality of Ambergris. And while the tone would be consistent throughout, I could experiment with more versus fewer fragments, depending on context—often in the novel, the fragments occur most frequently when Finch feels under greatest threat.

Style is incredibly important to characterization and setting. It determines emphasis, the ability to convey the character's thoughts and opinions, and the context and ways in which the reader encounters or interprets a character.

"Finch" as Short Story

Novels and short stories are very different creatures, and the solutions to the issues discussed if *Finch* were a story rather than a novel would also be different . . . and yet familiar. If the opening chapter of *Finch* helped to define the arc of a short story, time would pass more swiftly, space would be compressed, and our starting point would reflect that. Here are some possible approaches to *Finch* as short story . . .

- The story would have to begin with Finch standing over the bodies with Heretic.
- The character of the Partial, and what he brings to the story, might be compressed into the character of Heretic. The Partial would then either be gone entirely or relegated to the role of a very minor "minion."
- Mentions of characters in the novel who appear later might be stripped out.
- The tight-in approach to Finch's point of view would become even more important as an economical way of imparting information and establishing characterization.
- The story would open up into a series of scenes of Finch investigating the case very quickly, with the scene over the body being pared down as much as possible.
- The story might end with the murder's resolution or non-resolution in the next few days.
- The final scene in the story might be the final scene of the first chapter in the novel—of Finch looking out over the skyline of the city. However, what he sees would be relegated to a couple key "landmarks," connected to the case in some way. There being no room or reason to fully explore the setting, the ending on the balcony now creates an emotional sense of closure, rather than functioning as the setup for something longer.
- The underlying themes might be simplified to focus on whatever resonance is created by the solution to the case and underscore the idea of "another day in the city" in terms of Finch hanging on in such a dysfunctional place.

But *Finch* is not a short story, and in reaching the final decisions that hopefully make it successful as a novel, I have altered the perspective irrevocably. To fully understand how it might have become a short story instead, I would have to start with a blank slate, and begin with a different vision. ❧

Protagonist, foregrounded in a sentence that exemplifies the terse style

Finch, at the apartment door, breathing heavy from five flights of stairs, taken fast. The message that'd brought him from the station was already dying in his hand. Red smear on a limp circle of green fungal paper that had minutes before squirmed clammy. Now he had only the door to pass through, marked with the gray caps' symbol.

Anchor: tangible physical location, a setting that will be returned to and thus made specific

239 Manzikert Avenue, apartment 525.

An act of will, crossing that divide. Always. Reached for his gun, then changed his mind. Some days were worse than others.

A sudden flash of his partner Wyte, telling him he was compromised, him replying, "I don't have an opinion on that." Written on a wall at a crime scene: *Everyone's a collaborator. Everyone's a rebel.* The truth in the weight of each.

Intentional Dissonance: "cold" things often associated with "smooth"

The doorknob cold but grainy. The left side rough with light green fungus.

Sweating under his jacket, through his shirt. Boots heavy on his feet.

Always a point of no return, and yet he kept returning.

Denial infers someone thinks he is

I am not a detective. I am not a detective.

Note that there is no need to show Finch turning the knob and opening the door.

Inside, a tall, pale man dressed in black stood halfway down the hall, staring into a doorway. Beyond him, a dark room. A worn bed. White sheets dull in the shadow. Didn't look like anyone had slept there in months. Dusty floor. Even before he'd started seeing Sintra, his place hadn't looked this bad.

Introduction of another major character—in all, 5 major characters already referenced by first page/ninth paragraph

The Partial turned and saw Finch. "Nothing in that room, Finch. It's all in here." He pointed into the doorway. Light shone out, caught the dark glitter of the Partial's skin where tiny fruiting bodies had taken hold. Uncanny left eye in a gaunt face. Always twitching.

Partial color theme: muted, leeches color from scene: "black," "pale," "dusty," "white," "dull."

- Economy of language without sacrificing meaningful description
- Use of sentence fragments to reduce distance from protagonist's point of view and to increase tension

Came in a hurry—urgency—and told where he came from

Strange message—this is not Contemporary Earth Prime

Gray caps introduced in paragraph 1

Close-in on Finch's POV

Introduction of Finch's partner by paragraph 4, and use of
very short flashback to provide history, texture

Suggestion of factions within the city, and of consequences ("crime scene")

Supports strangeness of setting

Further evidence of Finch's stress, meant to make the reader
feel it; "heavy" to also support "weight of each" above

This has happened before; Finch has endured this before,
more than once

Intentional banality of room to allow focus on characters and
and their strangeness

Introduction of Finch's girlfriend on
Page 1—but not over-emphasized so the
focus remains on the tension of the main
situation

By now multiple fungal references mean
this descriptor should seem less strange
to the reader

In a sense, I didn't really feel as if Finch had a voice, a true point of view, until the prose took on an urgency, which carried through from the beginning and allowed me to work my way into the rest of the novel. The importance of voice and style made me drop the scenes that didn't support those elements. Even events I had written in a more "normal" style changed drastically at times due to the change in the novel's overall style. This was in essence as close as I could get to Finch without being in first person.

MODULATIONS OF TONE AND STYLE: MEMORY HOLE EXAMPLE FROM "FINCH"

#1. Direct, less tactile:

The gray caps didn't communicate with the detectives in a normal way. No, they used a system that Finch and his comrades called "memory holes." They were what seemed like living pneumatic tubes coming up from underground, lined with lamprey-like teeth. Finch found the memory holes disconcerting. They seemed to breathe as they pushed up the message in the form of a slimy black pod. He hated touching the pod, always washed his hands afterwards.

From examples 1 to 3, the prose becomes more fragmented and more in-the-moment, with less immediate context.

Finch exhaled and peered around the desk, glanced down at the glistening hole that the gray caps used to communicate with him. The hole, which seemed to breathe, was about twice the size of a man's fist and lined with lamprey-like teeth, fluid leaking out. The green tendrils lining the gullet had pushed up the dirty black spherical pod until it lay atop the mouth, fluid leaking out. The gray caps called them "message tubes," but the term "memory hole" had stuck. Finch had no idea if the memory holes were living creatures or only seemed alive.

The reader is seeing everything tightly from Finch's point of view, and as a result the horror of this way of communicating is clear—and the reader better understands the tension of even an ordinary day for Finch.

#3. Fragmented, much more tactile:

By example 3, the published version, the sense of dread has increased and the idea that John Finch never gets used to the "memory holes" comes across clearly.

Exhaled sharply. Peered around the left edge of the desk. Glanced down at the glistening hole. It was about twice the size of a man's fist. Lamprey-like teeth. Gasping, pink-tinged maw. Foul. Green tendrils lining the gullet had pushed forward the dirty black spherical pod until it lay atop the mouth. Finch sat up. Couldn't see it. Just hear its breathing. Which was worse. The gray caps always called them "message tubes," but the term "memory hole" had stuck. Memory holes allowed the detectives to communicate with their gray cap superiors. Were they living creatures or did they only seem alive? Fluid leaked out of them sometimes.

THE END OF BEGINNINGS

Not every piece of fiction requires that you explore a range of options as I did with *Finch*, and not every writer thinks about these issues in such an organized way after writing the rough draft. But because a novel is a marathon, not a sprint, it is much more likely you will want to spend time perfecting the entry point for readers rather than forge ahead blind, as you might when writing a short story. Nothing discourages even the most optimistic potential novelist more than realizing halfway in that the walls just erected must be taken down and the floorboards ripped up to get at the source of the rot.

Often, too, the most complex effects depend on the simplest of decisions. Without putting enough thought and effort into these decisions, the foundations of your novel will be flawed, and nothing you build on that foundation will be truly sound. Some of what I've described is working out what an actor or playwright might call "business," including the **blocking** of scenes and stage directions, which can seem like a too-mechanical approach to fiction . . . but as I have demonstrated, these elements are tied to character portrayals and the meaning of your story. The fact is, it's important to get that business right if you want to make sure the middle and ending work in harmony with your opening—and to achieve more complex effects layered on top of what's "simple." Especially since what's simple can be hard to separate out from what's complex. To some extent, when characters are introduced and where they exist in spatial and emotional relationships to other characters define them as people. These decisions support the larger decisions involving scenes, chapters, and the overall story arc.

Figuring out my opening through inhabiting and discarding approaches, working through the options in a logical way, helped me immerse myself more deeply in the life and thoughts of my main characters. It also gave me more ideas for entry points into future books.

Now that we've covered beginnings, you may be wondering about endings.

But the talking penguin has just given me an important reminder.

Isn't there something that comes between the beginning and the end?

Something that often has writers pulling their hair out?

"Blocking" refers to the positioning of the characters in relationship to one another and objects on the stage.

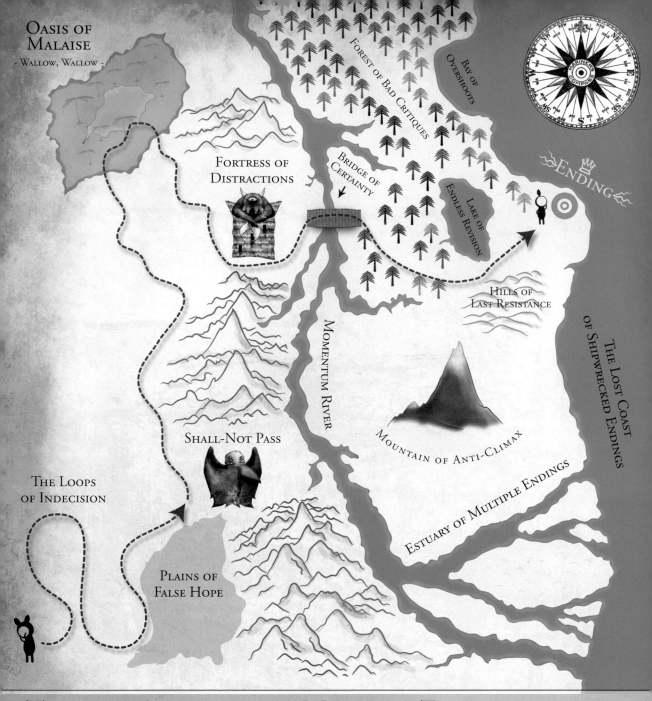

TRUTHS ABOUT THE MIDDLE ZONES ...

- When readers say an ending was satisfying, or moved them, they are really saying the writer did a good job with the journey to get there.
- It is okay to get lost in the middle for a while; it's normal.
- Sometimes if you reach the end too soon, the story suffers.
- Over time, with experience, the long slog gets easier.
- You can lose your way if you do not fully inhabit the viewpoint of your main character.

Middles do, eventually, end, for both writers and readers ...

The Beginning of Endings

The truth is that it's harder to talk about endings than beginnings, and most writing books do not delve too deeply into them. Perhaps this is because we'd like to think that endings write themselves, at least in the best of all possible worlds. You shoot the arrow and, depending on how well you judged the trajectory, distance, and wind, the arrow lands where you wanted it to land. Regardless, the arrow lands where the bow that launched it sent it—that end point becomes the bull's-eye whether you like it or not. The particulars of the arrow's journey fall away in the reader's mind—it doesn't matter if it sped across the vista of a golf course or a rotting industrial park or a pristine forest. (Expect reader complaints if the arrow lands in a pile of cow flop.) All of that lovely tension, pressure, and precision in the drawing back of the bow string, of focusing your eye on the target, the release as the arrow left the bow, the sound it made, the arching progress through the air . . . it must all mean something in the end.

What do we mean by the ending? Although the exact outlines of what differentiates "ending" from "middle" can vary, let's say it consists of:

- The climactic scene or scenes
- The "dying fall" of what comes after
- Any epilogue or grace note

But there's another way of looking at endings that might be of use; it also has to do with the idea of zeroing in on a target. As you progress toward the ending—as you (and thus the reader) begin to get a sense of its silhouette, out in a mist beginning to dissipate—there is often the feeling of things *closing down*. This occurs even in cases where the ending is a form of opening up. While revelations may occur, those revelations must, usually, have something to do with the context and approach set up at the beginning. You can reveal that the talking penguin is actually an angel come down from Heaven to stop the woman with the gun from killing someone . . . but you may find it harder to convince the reader that the talking penguin encountered in act one is actually a colonist on Venus.

In many stories this act of *closing down*, or ending, can be seen as that part of the story during which no new characters, settings, or facts are introduced, but where the ultimate *meaning* or *understanding* of characters, settings, and facts is highly volatile. This can be true of middles to some extent, but it is not an intrinsic property of middles. Withheld motivation, hidden connections, and the sheer inevitability of the consequences of actions set in motion many pages before all factor into the endings of these kinds of narratives. Even in stories where new characters, settings, and facts may indeed be introduced during the closing act—the missing brother turns up, or the characters flee to another country—these elements are by necessity still enveloped by what has gone before, part of a *closing down or resolution,* and can require masterful forethought to avoid seeming arbitrary. In science fiction and fantasy texts, the unreal elements are also up for reinterpretation during endings. However,

WRITE YOUR
OWN ENDING

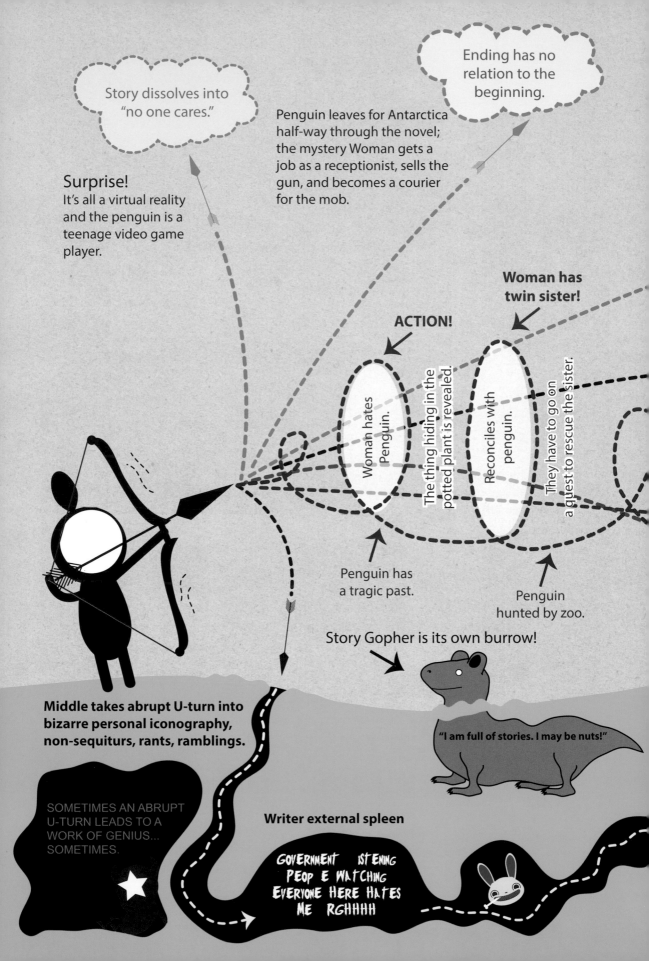

Arrows and Targets
"The Penguin and the Mysterious Woman"

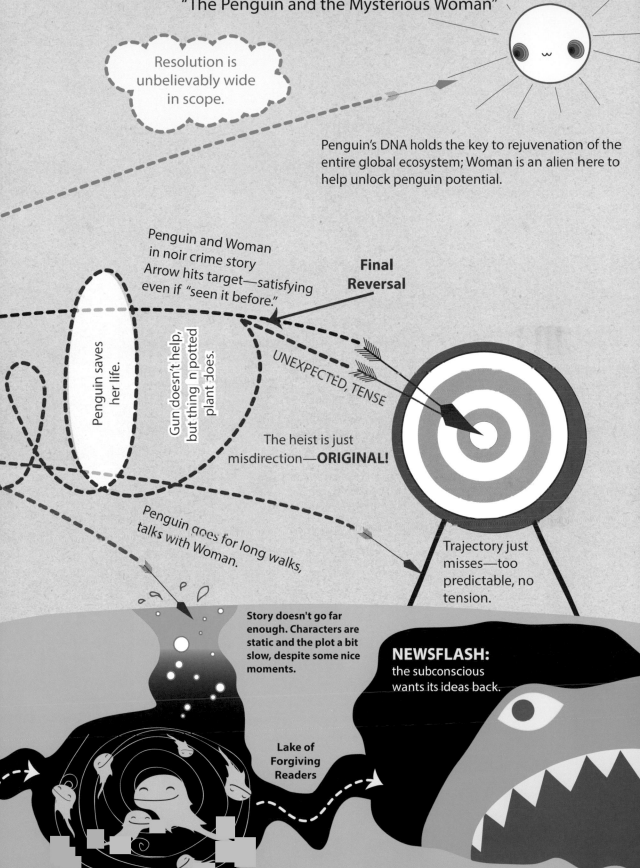

it is rare indeed that the parts of the story that have caused the label of "fantasy" to be applied will function any differently than in a more realistic story. Just because something is part of a make-believe world doesn't mean you have license to pile on new attributes as you're winding down the story.

EXPECTATIONS AND ELEMENTS

The particular details of endings vary dramatically, but do tend to follow certain patterns and provide certain kinds of resolution. In relation to the beginning of a piece of fiction, typical endings can:

- Return to the setting/situation/character dramatized at the start
- Push past the opening setting/situation/character—in essence, travel beyond where a traditional ending might stop
- Reveal the opening as a kind of façade or sham, and present a new and different scenario as the true reality
- End up at a place quite different than the opening, but with some return to a common theme or character

Embedded in endings, too, is a very simple subtext in terms of where the characters are left in relation to the opening:

- Status quo, or the character's view of reality, is revealed as false—the situation at the beginning cannot be returned to because it is intolerable, a lie, a sham.
- Status quo is returned to, either because status quo is perceived as a good thing, or as an ironic thing, with the character possibly unaware he or she is returning to a kind of purgatory or hell.
- Status quo no longer exists to return to or to reject, and the characters, along with the reader, are left out in the unknown.

During the course of the story, the rate of change within the characters or situations can be nonexistent, small, or exponential, creating yet another variable that affects the ending—and the choices made by the main character. Lack of change can itself be a kind of statement.

Whether a particular approach works may depend on the quality of execution, but it is more likely that your ending will stand or fall based on explanation and resolution. *Explanation* refers to the number of unknowns at the story's opening that are known by story's end. *Resolution* refers to the disposition of the central and secondary conflicts or problems in your story. These two elements work in tandem to provide a sense of *closure* for the reader—a sense that the story has a satisfying structure or has achieved a pleasing effect.

How much explanation and resolution the end of your narrative requires depends on the type of story, the kinds of effects you intend, and how much resolution or explanation has occurred during the middle of the story. The possibilities are finite, however, since most endings can only do one of five things:

- Resolve the central question (conflict/problem) posed by the narrative, but leave open-ended other, secondary questions
- Resolve all questions posed by the narrative (which may indicate the narrative didn't pose enough questions)
- Reinvent or recontextualize the questions posed by the novel
- Leave nothing resolved overtly, except by inference or implication, asking the reader to provide the answers from the clues provided
- Reveal that the central question was a false or deceptive one (a trick ending)

Depending on the type of story, the ending may provide the answer to a major external question (who shot the talking penguin?) while leaving unresolved an internal question (will the woman with the gun be able to live with her guilt?). Or, the story may leave the external question unanswered but in some way address the emotional lives of the characters.

A satisfying ending does not need to be a steel trap—it can be as porous as a colander. *You do not need to explain everything*; some questions left in a reader's mind can germinate in entertaining ways. You may find that providing some resolution to the character's inner life is more important than answering questions related to an external event or situation, like a mystery. It all depends on what kind of story you are trying to tell—and what you are emphasizing and what is less important to you, and thus to the reader.

Because the marketing of a book should be separate from the issues related to its creation, I don't like to talk about the audience. But questions of emphasis do speak to a potential audience. Certain types of emphasis may render a text invisible to certain types of readers. Take, for example, Colson Whitehead's amazing zombie novel *Zone One*. It is a literary triumph that embeds classic zombie scenarios within a superlative study of the main character. However, the foregrounding of the character's story in a way that places the zombie scenarios in the background appears to have alienated zombie-fiction aficionados. This aggressive rejection probably reaches critical mass as the novel begins the slow disintegration that signals the last act, and it becomes clear that Whitehead's interests lie at a tangent to those of some of his potential readers. (Although he probably picked up readers who never read zombie fiction.)

When you begin a work of fiction, you are embarking on a journey that seems to admit every possibility; by the end, you inevitably, sometimes without realizing it, take positions and make decisions that are all about constraint, focus, and finding the perfect finale.

MYSTER ODD PRESENTS:

FINAL LINES

1918

After scores of years, wind and rain have worn down the small tombstone, and moss has covered the barrow, erasing all trace of his grave.

— Ryūnosuke Akutagawa, "The Hell Screen"

1953

Next day it snowed, and killed off half the crops – but it was a good day.

— Jerome Bixby, "It's a *Good* Life"

2002

You will understand. You will know joy. You will be nothing. You will be me.

— Michael Cisco, "The Genius of Assassins"

1992

He saw the woman reach out and pull the creature away from the glass, back into the warm, lighted room with her, and the curtain fell again, shutting him out.

— Lisa Tuttle, "Replacements"

1990

The treasures and the pleasures of the grave? They are his hands, his lips, his tongue.

— Poppy Z. Brite, "His Mouth Will Taste of Wormwood"

1913

And the dead man quivered in happiness on his white death table, while the iron chisels in the hands of the doctors broke up the bones of his temple.

— George Heym, "The Dissection"

1950

And then, while the lightning flashed outside, and the radio faded and sputtered, the two old people huddled together in their summer cottage and waited.

— **Shirley Jackson,** "The Summer People"

1983

Telenapota, discovered for one brief moment, will be lost again in the timeless dark of the night.

— **Premendra Mitra,** "The Discovery of Telenapota"

1945

Our minds are permeable to forgetfulness; I myself am distorting and losing, through the tragic erosion of the years, the features of Beatriz.

— **Jorge Luis Borges,** "The Aleph"

1926

Search in a world atlas discloses no town of Xebico. Whatever it was that killed John Morgan will forever remain a mystery.

— **H.F. Arnold,** "The Night Wire"

1912

Silently and with invisible pinions the gigantic ebon birds of terror streaked through the hall of the fête.

—**Gustav Meyrink,** "The Man in the Bottle"

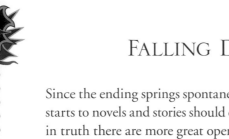

FALLING DOWN AT THE END

Since the ending springs spontaneously from what came before, all those promising starts to novels and stories should end well and be satisfying for the reader, right? But in truth there are more great openings to stories and novels than great endings. All that trust, that excitement, at the beginning is to some extent just writer promises mixed with reader anticipation. An ending has to actually deliver on those promises, or it risks looking like the writer cheated or fell down on the job.

So how does an ending become subpar? The most common reasons are:

- We promise too much.
- We promise the wrong thing.
- We deliver the wrong thing, misunderstanding the narrative we have written.
- We cannot follow through because we cannot, after the initial burst of inspiration, fulfill the implications of our story setup. This may constitute an abandonment of a character or abandonment of a concept.
- We rush the ending, and the accelerated pacing ruins the payoff.
- We bend to perceived audience expectations and manipulate the ending to provide a received idea of what is satisfying.
- We don't trust our main character's story arc and deviate from it, separating plot from character.
- We deliver too much, explaining so much (or in such excruciating detail) that there is no room for the reader's imagination.
- We deliver too little, even though our promises were reasonable. (The stakes are much smaller than we were led to believe.)

This last reason may be the most common cause of reader dissatisfaction. If you offer the moon, you must deliver the moon—or a comparable substitute. If you offer up a woman with a gun and a talking penguin but deliver a conclusion in which we discover the gun is a plastic water pistol and the penguin is actually a man in a penguin suit delivering a singing telegram . . . well, you may not be able to escape the angry mobs. Angry mobs that form because you stayed true to a good idea, even if it's difficult or doesn't have wide appeal, should be welcomed as indicating you've been successful!

For writers of fiction with speculative elements, endings—across any number of possible reasons for disappointment—are often even more perilous. The very thing that readers love about fantasy, for example, can backfire; ask Philip Pullman how some readers felt when he brought characters back from the dead in the third of his The Dark Materials series. They didn't like it. Then contrast that with how J. K. Rowling handled showing glimpses of Harry Potter's parents as ghosts to create an interesting emotional resonance. Fantasy writers may also feel some pressure to "get out of jail free" by using the fantasy element to create closure when it hasn't been earned by the characters or events in the story. *Because everything is possible, nothing has any tension . . . or any weight.* The bit of magic that resolves things too easily or the

The Challenges of Endings by Desirina Boskovich

Desirina Boskovich is a 2007 graduate of the Clarion Writers Workshop. Her fiction has appeared in Realms of Fantasy, Clarkesworld Magazine, Fantasy Magazine, Nightmare Magazine, *and* Lightspeed Magazine.

BEGINNINGS ARE EASIER to talk about than endings; we all start from the same place. Our favorite beginnings are eminently quotable, easy to share. But divorced from their stories, endings are meaningless. A good ending is like a secret that demands to be kept; no one wants to know the ending to your favorite story until they've read it themselves. It's a funny predicament . . . endings are essential, so we're not allowed to ruin them. And thus, we're not allowed to talk about them. But for the next couple pages, I'm going to ignore that rule. There will be spoilers. Consider yourself duly warned.

∞ ∞ ∞

Now I can finally do what I've been dying to do for years: discuss the ending to Stephen King's The Dark Tower series. Through seven doorstopper novels, King describes the gunslinger's epic quest to reach the tower. Along the way, the gunslinger and his friends save the universe. But when he reaches the tower . . . he finds no answers at all. He finds only his destiny, and it brings him back to where he started. I was floored, and not in a good way. This was the cheapest trick, the worst gimmick, the silliest cop-out. But I'd spent months reading that series, so I kept tussling with it. What did it mean? Months passed, then years, and I saw how that ending stuck with me. The right ending isn't always the ending the reader wants.

It took courage to write that ending, I think. It took nerve to carry the story through to its inevitable conclusion. The top of the tower was always meant to be empty. There is no god, there are no final answers; there is only us, and our endless quest. But our search for answers —it's how we save ourselves. It's how we save the world.

Still, that sense of perpetual striving, it haunts me. It's the human story, where there are no true endings; there is just trying and failing, trying and failing, trying some more. Many of my favorite novels illustrate this futility in masterstrokes. In David Mitchell's *Cloud Atlas*, the novel's seven stories unfold inside one another like a set of Russian dolls. The novel's final pages are penned by its earliest narrator, a nineteenth-century sailor. He vows to devote his life to fighting the predatory political systems that oppress the weak. We already know his world's bleak future; we already know he's failed. But we also know there will always be others to fight for justice.

Walter Miller's *A Canticle for Leibowitz* begins after the world as we know it is destroyed in a nuclear holocaust. The novel traces the growth of a new civilization: its dark ages and its renaissance, until it reaches a time much like ours, a time of nuclear energy and space flights and global war. The ending is inevitable. The world is destroyed again, but not before a few humans can escape into space to enact the whole sordid story once again. There's no real conclusion to the story of human struggle.

Which means there's never a happy ending, but there's always hope for one.

Jeanette Winterson's *The Stone Gods* is a brilliant contemporary companion to *Canticle*. Like *Canticle*, it explores humanity's tendency to repeat our mistakes on the scale of history. Like The Dark Tower, the structure is circular; the end is the beginning, the beginning is the end. What remains is the affirmation that life goes on . . . and love. "Everything is imprinted forever with what it once was." I dare you to read this novel's closing scenes and not be moved. I've read the book twice, and I know it works. But I still can't quite figure out how.

In general, endings are tricky, elusive beasts. From Stephen King, I learned: Don't be afraid to take the story to its inevitable conclusion. But Karen Joy Fowler taught me the opposite: Don't be afraid not to. Because it also takes courage to let the reader draw her own conclusions. It takes nerve to exit the moment right before the bomb drops, the train derails, the shots ring out. At the Clarion Writers Workshop, a kind of boot camp for aspiring science fiction and fantasy writers, Fowler had some interesting advice for writers struggling with how to close. In a lecture I'll never forget, she said: "Write your ending. Then delete the last paragraph. If you can, delete the next one, too." What's left? It's often the moment of greatest power. So resist the urge to explain yourself. Abandon that last loose end.

A novel may require a bit more resolution, but in a short story, I like some questions to remain unresolved. My favorite endings leave me leaning forward, mouth open, pulse pounding, longing for just a little more.

Some stories suggest that whatever we've read so far, the real story is yet to come. Like Kelly Link's "Stone Animals": the horrifying tale of a family slowly overcome by a haunting. Their new house is just a little . . . wrong. Until it's all wrong. The change is almost imperceptible; there is no bloody climax. It ends like this:

All around him, the others are sitting on their rabbits, waiting patiently, quietly. They've been waiting for a long time, but the waiting is almost over. In a little while, the dinner party will be over and the war will begin.

The promise of violence is more chilling than violence itself; The End comes right at the moment of unbearable dread.

I admire stories that end with a revelation that undermines the story before it—what you might call a twist. Lisa Tuttle's "Closet Dreams" begins: "Something terrible happened to me when I was a little girl." Years ago, she was kidnapped and imprisoned in a closet. But she escaped. One day, years later, she encounters her kidnapper on the street. She follows him home, determined to finally report him to the police. Then something happens. She wakes up.

. . . I began to tremble as I heard the sound of his key in the lock and woke from the dream that was my only freedom, and remembered. Something terrible happened to me when I was a little girl. It's still happening.

It's a haunting ending, but it's also a beginning: an invitation to read the story again with fresh understanding.

In my own work, I strive for that kind of ending. When I hit on the right note, I know immediately; the moment of awareness evokes an emotional sensation so strong, it's physical. Sometimes I write the story so I can write the ending; sometimes I have to write the story first.

For example, with my story "Thirteen Incantations," I always knew what ending I was writing toward. The story emerged from a charged image that came to me from nowhere in particular: two girls sitting side by side at the edge of something, legs swinging above open air, one girl's hair blowing in the breeze to tickle the bare shoulder of the other. It's a moment of casual intimacy between friends, yet full of unrequited longing. I built the story around this scene, which appears toward the beginning of the narrative, and again at the end, when it takes on a different meaning. Instead of a beginning, it's an ending. Instead of possibility, it's closure.

Like many of the stories I love, my own often end with some degree of ambiguity. In "Sand Castles," my narrator meets a girl who claims to come from a civilization under the sea. The narrator accompanies this modern-day mermaid on her journey to an isolated beach, where she hopes to make her way back home. Throughout the story, his struggle is a lack of purpose. But in the final scene, he overcomes his inertia. He dives into the ocean, following the girl out to sea. Does he hope to join her in her underwater world? Or is he determined to rescue her from her delusions? To me, it doesn't matter. He makes a decision, and acts with courage. That's emotional resolution, and it's enough. The central question of the story—is there an aquatic kingdom, or isn't there?—I prefer to leave unanswered. I'm a fantasy writer, but a cynical one.

Some endings take longer. My early story "Violets for Lee" is a surreal account of a woman wandering her neighborhood, seeking to borrow a cup of sugar on the anniversary of her sister's death. She discovers a vast, disembodied heart, dropped into the rural landscape. So she does what anyone would do; she climbs in and tunnels through. Eventually she reaches the center, where she finds two doors and must decide which door to take.

This was a difficult story to write; weird and slippery, it all seemed like part of some forgotten dream, with the challenge of making dream-logic into story-logic. I wrote the first draft sitting on my kitchen floor, scribbling in a yellow notepad: the only way the right words would come. The ending was no easier. In early drafts, the story ends like this:

The truth is you never know where the door will lead.

But I still know which door to take.

Naked I emerged from this door and naked I return. I take the left side. Right hand on the spherical glass knob, slippery in my grasp. I turn. I push. The door swings open and I step forward, into the blinding light.

The light burns away the past and I taste sweetness. Everything I know falls away.

And only the sweetness follows.

I was writing a lot of endings like this, back then: bringing my characters into higher dimensions, parallel worlds, levels of consciousness that eluded my grasp. In retrospect, I was working out my own conflict; daring myself to surface from my own dream, to try the unknown door. So I reached for the closest ending, and that's the one I found. But it wasn't right. It represented death and reincarnation. It read like my character giving in to grief and renouncing her current life. That wasn't the story I wanted to tell.

I talked this through with my own sister, my ever dependable and insightful first reader. Afterward, a new ending took shape.

Naked I emerged from this door, and naked I return. The glass knob is slippery in my grasp. The door swings open and I step forward, into the blinding light.

Another step, and the light fades into the cool brilliance and blue skies of a beautiful spring day. The breeze on my forehead cools the sweat and dries the tears. I breathe deeply of fresh air that smells like heaven.

Another step. I take the winding path, rocky as ever but lush with violets. I don't look back until I reach the edge of the old lady's backyard. Behind me, on the horizon, the wounded heart grows smaller and smaller. Dark and vague as a bird in flight, it flaps its wings and flies away.

I didn't realize it until much later, but that final image did not come from a dream, as I'd thought; it appears in the opening lines of my favorite poem, Jim Carroll's "While She's Gone," which describes a gull above a castle turret that's actually a heart.

I had committed this image to my subconscious, and it had remained lodged there for years, waiting for just the right moment to appear. Like so much of writing, the right ending always seems to come from pieces like these: charged images and universal symbols, things I know without knowing. Finding the right ending takes thinking and scheming but dreaming, too—intuition's blind and brilliant fumbling in the dark. When an ending works on an intellectual level and on an emotional level, that's a story with staying power. ✦

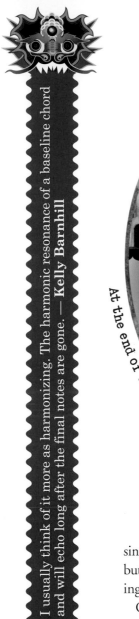

At the end of the novel, Finch and his friend are in a boat looking out across the city of Ambergris.

singular invention or the sudden rescue—there are parallels in contemporary realism, but they don't stand out quite so much. There's nothing like a sudden dragon blasting across the page to signal an unintentional celebration of spectacular coincidence.

Common questions to help test your ending include:

- Have I stopped too soon?
- Have I gone too far?
- Have I tried too hard to provide closure?
- Have I provided too little closure?
- Have I tried too hard to explain the fantastical element?
- Have I tried to make the fantasy element carry too much of the weight of the ending?
- Does my beginning not support my ending?
- Does my ending not support my beginning?
- Do I provide the right kind of closure?
- Have I made things too easy for my characters?

In answering these questions, be aware that you may find the problem lies not with the ending or the setup in the beginning, but something that has gone awry in the middle.

THE END OF "FINCH"

Because I spent so much time getting *Finch*'s opening right, I must admit I didn't have that much trouble with the ending. For me, the solving of the mystery wasn't as important as what happened after, so even though Finch solves the murders, that is not the end of the novel—even though the details of the solution do provide a very personal and, hopefully, satisfying penultimate emotional resonance for the reader. In terms of subplots, as the ending plays out, the reader has some side stories resolved, but at least one related to a secret agent named Bliss was left open-ended. This lack of resolution—of not explaining exactly who he worked for and why— represented a risk. However, a resolution posed a greater risk, for two reasons: (1) the information would have been impossible for Finch to know; and (2) an attempt at a forced resolution in the middle of other threads—ones that definitely required closure—would have shifted the focus. This shift probably would have provided an ending too fragmented, with the reader's eye drawn in too many different directions.

When Finch pushes beyond solving the case, he reaches a point at which certain truths can be revealed about the major characters in his life, and the novel ends at the place where Finch in a sense passes out of the history of the city. The element of the beginning that recurs at the end is Finch's view of the city, in a context where it has completely changed again. A return to basically the same scene that ended the opening chapter of *Finch* signals not a return to status quo—it is a strong sign that nothing will ever be the same again.

The very last moments of the last scene also bring the occupiers' plans to fruition in a complex way that allows for a full-on fantastical spectacle, once again allied to Finch's emotional state. I get to have the extravagant fire-breathing dragon, in a sense, but not in a deus ex machina way. The revelation doesn't make life easier for the main characters, or solve any of their problems. Instead, the spectacle is fraught with ambiguity and a sense of greater mysteries and urgencies, suggesting events that will occur beyond the end of the novel. As a kind of "object" embedded in the text, it is a signpost for *closure* on the one hand and yet signals an *opening up* on the other. Since this opening up occurs beyond Finch's ken, after he is no longer part of a story staunchly from his perspective, the reader shouldn't feel cheated. Instead, hopefully, the reader will feel as if the novel has ended but that the life of the fantastical city of Ambergris continues—that the city exists beyond the last page.

Imbuing fiction with a life that extends beyond the last word is in some ways the goal: the ending that goes beyond the ending in the reader's mind, so invested are they in the story.

THE END OF ENDINGS

In getting to the end of endings, what have we learned? At least a few things. A story will be more or less successful depending on how faithful it is to its own setup, or even to an intentional violation of its setup. This doesn't mean there must be a sense of inevitability, which can kill surprise, but that the arc of the story should not seem arbitrary, broken, or interrupted (interrupted = unintentional; open-ended = intentional).

A good story will reward readers' general expectations—allowing them to complete the story's shape in their heads—while telling an interesting tale with surprises within scenes and even sentences. A *great* story might reward those general expectations to some extent, but thwarts expectations in the particulars of some matter important to the narrative. A great story provides to the reader something unexpected that when *considering the beginning of the story,* still makes sense and does not make the reader feel cheated by the writer—it completes a structure more complex or simply *different* from that expected by the reader.

∞ ∞ ∞

A chapter discussing beginnings and endings is about much more than how to start or end a story. In the beginning the placement, layering, and context of story elements affect the reader from the first word. As you write the ending, you may focus on different questions, but you are still juggling a variety of elements.

Already, then, this chapter has absorbed information and lessons that could have been placed in the chapters on narrative design, characterization, and worldbuilding. I have let this happen to underscore a point: *Writing is organic.* You are creating an animal, not a machine. As you will discover throughout your creative life, processes, approaches, and inspirations bleed into one another, accrete at different rates and levels, depending on what kind of creature your story is to become. To deny this is to deny a story's true potential.

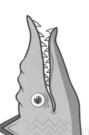

If you've made it this far, congratulations! You've encountered a giant prologue fish, mountainous monsters, a huge subterranean telescope, the life cycle of a story, and many other strange things—and lived to tell about it. But now that you've reached the middle, it's time to turn to serious subjects . . . like story lizards, danger ducks, and the way you organize your fiction. Hold on tight—this is where everything you've encountered thus far goes on a roller coaster ride . . . .

CHAPTER 4: NARRATIVE DESIGN

B Y THEIR VERY nature, all stories conform to some notion of narrative design. Even a story that doesn't seem to be *designed* in the traditional sense forms some kind of pattern. This sense of organization—intentional disorganization counts—distinguishes a work of fiction from, say, an unedited court transcript of a witness's testimony. Within this context, the often instinctual process through which you decide what to emphasize and not emphasize, dramatize and not dramatize builds the story's structure paragraph by paragraph.

Further, one of the fundamental traits of design in fiction is that it requires the writer to know the difference between the *daily existence* of a character and a context in which some situation arises that requires the character to grapple with an issue or problem, whether internal or imposed by the world. In most cases, a normal day in the life of a spy, dragon hunter, or skydiver is not automatically a story, any more than is a normal day in the life of a toll booth operator.

Even if you write primarily by feel, having a better sense of narrative design can help you figure out how the pieces of your story should fit together. The two main ways in which a work of fiction appears to have a pattern or to be organized are through **plot** and **structure**, which most often manifest through use of **scenes**. You may also encounter the term "form," which just refers to the shape created by the structure. How should we define plot and structure? Here are the traditional definitions:

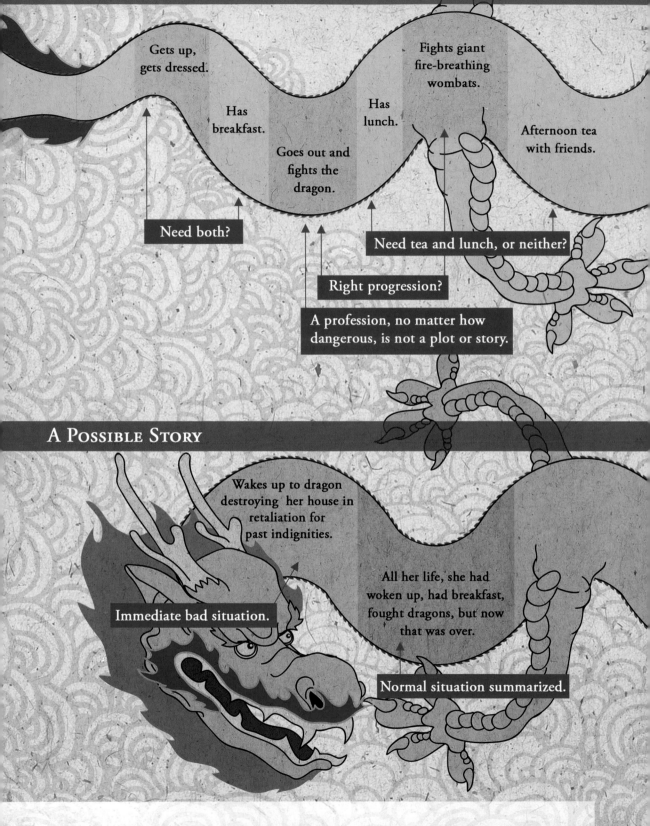

A CHARACTER'S DAY (WHAT DO YOU INCLUDE AND WHEN?)

Gets up, gets dressed.

Has breakfast.

Goes out and fights the dragon.

Has lunch.

Fights giant fire-breathing wombats.

Afternoon tea with friends.

Need both?

Need tea and lunch, or neither?

Right progression?

A profession, no matter how dangerous, is not a plot or story.

A POSSIBLE STORY

Wakes up to dragon destroying her house in retaliation for past indignities.

Immediate bad situation.

All her life, she had woken up, had breakfast, fought dragons, but now that was over.

Normal situation summarized.

NATURAL AND DRAMATIC SCENES — STORY VERSUS SITUATION

Resharpens sword.

Need at all?

Has dinner with her boyfriend.

Showers and shaves.

Fights swarms of militant winged hamsters.

Better placed elsewhere?

How different from dragon?

Sharpens swords, has lunch, gets wombats' pledge to stay out of the widening conflict.

Spends day dodging dragon and making peace with wombats and winged hamsters.

Goes off in afternoon on quest with new allies the hamsters to defeat the evil dragon (dragon fries them, down to the lowliest hamster).

Driven to action/reaction.

COMPLICATIONS MUST OCCUR TO CREATE READER INTEREST.

KNOWING WHAT KIND OF STORY YOU WANT TO TELL HELPS DETERMINE WHAT TO FOCUS ON AND THE SEQUENCING OF SCENES.

THE SECOND DRAGON SHOWS HOW INERT ELEMENTS WITH POSSIBLE, BUT NOT EXPRESSED, DRAMATIC POTENTIAL BECOME A DYNAMIC PART OF A STORY.

- *Plot* consists of a series of events, usually related through cause and effect, that holds the reader's interest or in some way provokes a reaction. (What happens.)
- *Structure* is the organization of the story to form a pleasing shape and one that does not seem random or arbitrary. (How it happens.)

Yet, are these traditional definitions adequate? Because ironically, narrative design, which might seem to be the most "scientific" part of the complex beast we call fiction, is actually the trickiest, most shape-shifty part. After reading other writing books, you'd be forgiven for thinking that defining the terms is as difficult as trying to catch a slippery fish with your bare hands. For example, the great Samuel R. Delany champions structure and claims that plot is an illusion, "distrusts" it because it seems a reader's rather than a writer's perspective. John Gardner, in his classic book *The Art of Fiction*, never gives a satisfactory explanation of the difference between plot, structure, and form. Even novelist Madison Smartt Bell in the brilliant *Narrative Design* has difficulties with the terms. Bell defines plot as "what happens in the story," with form encompassing the pattern of a story's "assembly, its arrangement, structure, and design." First of all, the use of "design" confuses because that term should encompass *all* of the organizing principles he sets forth, including arrangement and structure. Second, what is the difference between plot and "arrangement," arrangement and "structure"? Bell then also proceeds to use the terms structure and form somewhat interchangeably . . . .

Clearly, something is amiss—or even horribly wrong!

Or is it?

Perhaps it just comes down to the way your particular writer brain is wired, and each of you will have slightly different definitions—and struggle with them on your own terms—because the truth resides in your unique vision and thus your unique perception of **narrative design**. For example, I realize my own personal problem with defining plot versus structure is that I never really think in terms of plot. Instead, I think of characters that more or less inhabit a structure, which they may well build, and most of the structure consists of scenes, in a certain order. It's through the confluence of the structure and those progressions that I arrive at what might be called plot. The structure provides the design or the directions, and the scene progressions provide effects like a climactic event.

To me, then, *plot* diagrams are just crude representations of *structures* that emphasize only certain elements of the structure, like rising tension and a climactic event. In a sense, they chart those elements that are most visible to the reader—pressure points that trigger the most noticeable response, or, put another way, what the reader might relate if summarizing the story to a friend. Although valuable, such diagrams do not take into consideration other elements that you as the writer must think about when engaged in the act of creation and revision.

Since so many of my betters have been devoured by this beast that is narrative design, I wouldn't presume not to follow them—although I hope that I can keep the jaws from snapping shut long enough for you to receive the information you need. When writing an earlier draft of this chapter, I came up with the following

Never discount how your process affects how you view elements of narrative design.

description: "Structure is the body of the beast as defined by the bones and organs inside; plot is what the beast looks like in motion, from the outside, *going somewhere*, and scenes are high-level organic systems: the way the blood flows within the story-creature, the way it breathes." Take these metaphors for what they are worth—while I provide you with as much tangible, concrete information as possible. Hopefully, the plot-and-structure beasts won't feast on my bones until I'm done. At least, that's the shape of the story I hope to tell.

"Secretary" by Sam Van Olffen (2012). Sometimes thinking about plot can seem like using a complex machine. But it's important not to let the machinery over-whelm the human element.

PLOT

In what we call a traditionally plotted story, the events of the plot relate to each other by being either necessary or probable, and they lead to a cumulative effect. The traditional plot includes the following elements:

REVERSALS. Characters should experience setbacks that serve to stimulate dramatic interest. At some point, this element may take the form of a *catastrophe*, which is simply a reversal on steroids. A major reversal can happen anywhere in the story so long as its positioning does not create a sense of anticlimax in the reader's mind. (Catastrophe usually occurs close to the end of the story. For example, the monster trying to fit into society is involved in an "incident," one that makes the creature reexamine whether it has chosen the right life.)

DISCOVERIES. Characters should find out things about themselves, other people, or the world in general. These discoveries can pertain to the central external or

internal problem posed by the story, but may also simply add depth and complexity to character while only tangentially pertaining to plot. If tangential, the most successful examples usually have some kind of thematic resonance in place of being anchored to the central problem. An example might be a sympathetic character who turns out to have committed murder in the past, and the repercussions of that discovery on his friends.

COMPLICATIONS. Characters should find that, at least initially, the central problem each confronts has no easy solution. Indeed, as the story progresses, the central problem may grow more complicated and the solution seem murkier for a time. A character's own actions may create further issues rather than making the situation easier. For example, in attempting to use a fiancé's connections to stifle public news of a scandal, a woman ties herself more closely to the fiancé even though she loves someone else.

RESOLUTION. The story should reach a conclusion that satisfies the reader's interest in the characters and the problems posed. Usually, the resolution occurs following a climactic event that may take on the attributes of a major reversal or catastrophe, as described above. As we have seen in Chapter 3, classic resolution does not introduce a new element; it derives its effects from elements already in play. The murderer is set free because continued investigation shows the act was justified; the woman breaks off her engagement because she is no longer beholden to the man; the monster eats both the murderer and the woman because it can no longer deny its true destiny (or appetites).

The resolution may take several forms, depending on the type of story. Instead of showing the end of a conflict between two sides, it might reveal something previously hidden, focus on a difficult decision made by a character, give the solution to a mystery, or solve a puzzle of some kind. Types of stories include The Exploration (of an unfamiliar place), The Discovery (an investigation of an actual mystery or perhaps life's mysteries), The Transformation (charting character changes), and The Event (some happening poses a threat and must be combatted).

Several classic diagrams describe the typical or "median" template for a plot. Here are just a few. Note that because traditional plots tend to focus on outward expressions of action, they do not help map introspective narratives quite as well.

TYPES OF STORIES

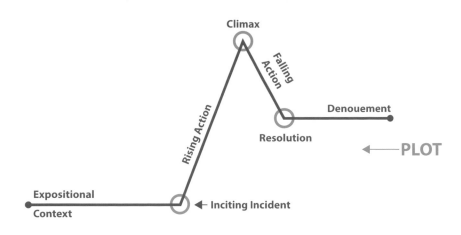

FREYTAG PYRAMID (TRADITIONAL). Character and setting context are established. Once these elements are in place, the day-to-day existence of the character is challenged by some unusual issue or incident (or flare-up of some prior situation), necessitating action by the character, or resulting in the character being acted upon, but in either event leading to further crisis, probably precipitated by the character's actions. This builds to a turning point (climax), after which the repercussions affect the character and possibly others and some resolution presents itself either through the character's actions or some other event that occurs to affect the situation. The full implications of what has taken place are fleshed out in the ending of the story.

Gustav Freytag was a German novelist and playwright who developed his famous pyramid in 1863. We have all labored under the burden of its shadow ever since. At times dutifully, at times with a snarling defiance.

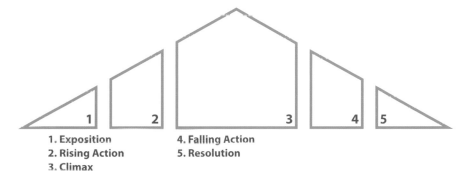

1. Exposition
2. Rising Action
3. Climax
4. Falling Action
5. Resolution

FREYTAG PYRAMID (BELL REMIX). This variation on Freytag's plot diagram used by Madison Smartt Bell attempts to divide the action into shapes of corresponding size and weight: which is to say, to show that the opening of the average story is of necessity shorter than the area corresponding to its climactic events.

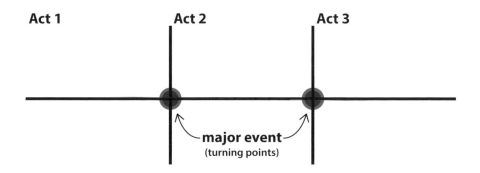

THREE ACTS. In Act 1, characters and context are introduced, along with a disruption in daily life; character motivation is established; and disruption won't go away without

action. In Act 2, the character takes action concerning the disruption (or doesn't), and the disruption takes center stage, with challenges and possible reversals for the character; finally, a clear path emerges. In Act 3, the character's fortunes brighten or darken, and the disruption is defeated or partially defeated or is victorious. After that point, the wrapping up of loose ends can occur quickly or take longer depending on the desired effect.

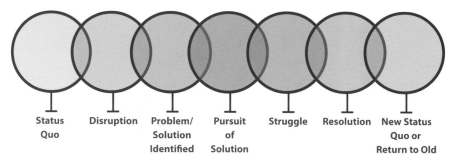

| Status Quo | Disruption | Problem/ Solution Identified | Pursuit of Solution | Struggle | Resolution | New Status Quo or Return to Old |

INTERCONNECTED COMPLICATIONS. This film-school visualization of the average plot eschews showing the dramatic peaks and valleys of Freytag's pyramid or the flat compartmentalization of story as a series of acts in a play. Instead, it focuses on two main issues common to effective storytelling: progressions and transitions. This diagram acknowledges the overlap between parts of the plot, suggesting more *joins* and connections than the other diagrams.

Variations on the standard plot include:

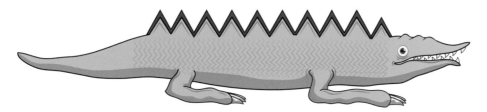

The *picaresque* or *"and now* that *happened,"* wherein a series of adventures featuring the same characters is strung together to form a novel. Cervantes's *Don Quixote* and Angela Carter's *The Infernal Desire Machines of Doctor Hoffman* are examples of the picaresque. The sense of rising action may still occur—there may be some quest or end goal—but the difference between the climactic spike of action or revelation and what went before is usually much smaller: Miniature versions of rising action occur through self-contained set pieces throughout the narrative.

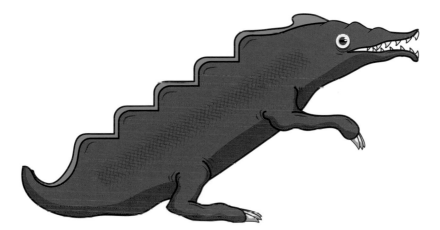

The *staircase is its own risk-reward*, wherein tension continues to build at a steady rate, like climbing stairs that get progressively hotter, until the heat is ultimately relieved or the characters burn up. In such stories, there is little falling action or resolution; the narrative ends soon after the climax.

It's worth noting that if you're a writer similar to Thomas Ligotti, Bruno Schulz, or Leonora Carrington, these diagrams may be as useful to you as shoving grilled cheese sandwiches into your car's gas tank.

The *roller coaster is a roller coaster*, wherein rising action is replaced with two major dips in fortune, forming a "W" with the hero usually winding up on top at the end. Many commercial novels and movies follow this model.

What were the origins
of your story and how does that
affect or not affect the narrative?

Rising Action / Complications

Beginning

What happened immediately
before your story started?

What possibly
uncomfortable or odd
things are you either
hiding or not sharing in
the story?

What is happening in the world
outside of the scope of the story?

How might it more accurately
affect the events in your story?

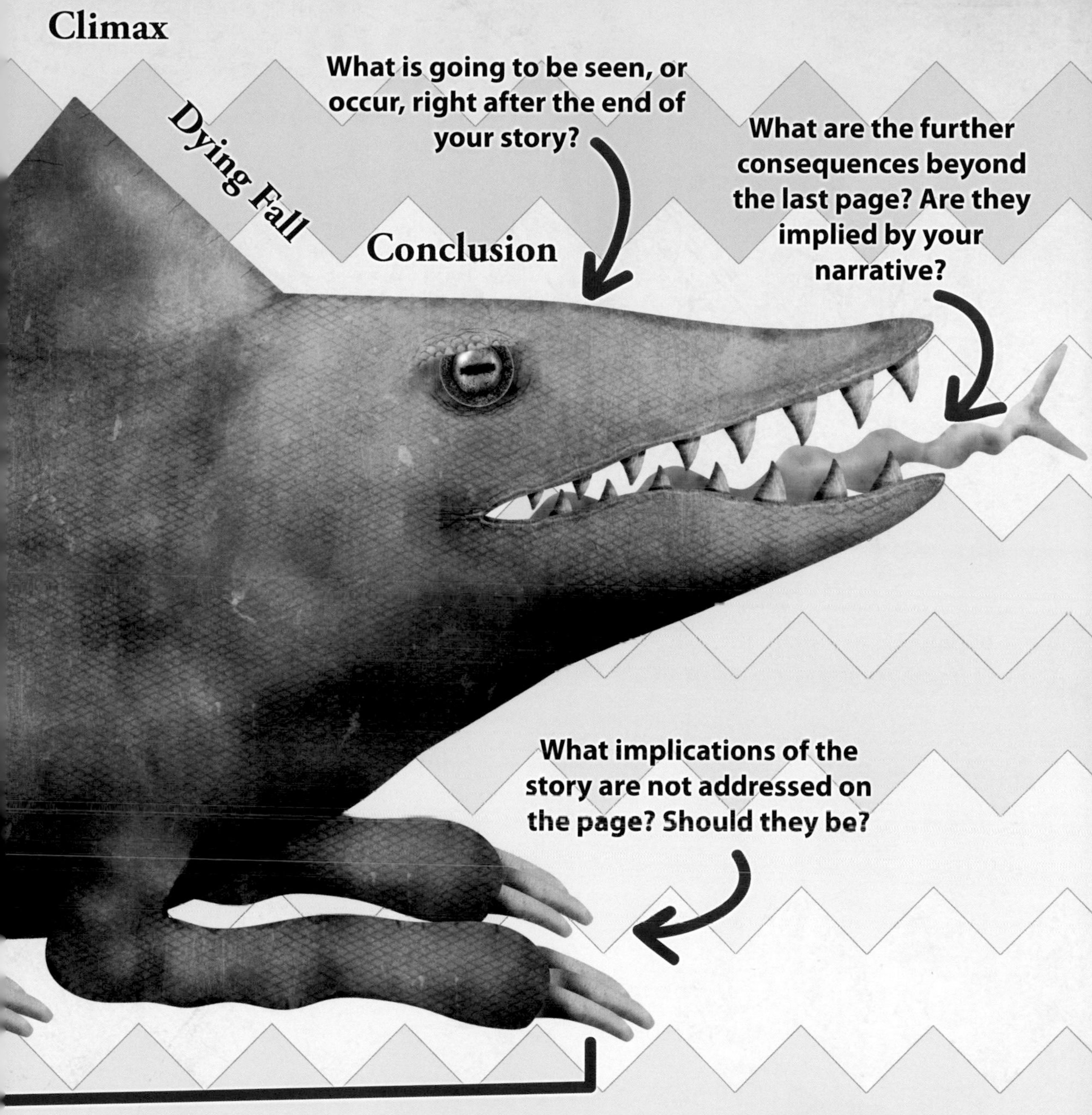

Climax

Dying Fall

What is going to be seen, or occur, right after the end of your story?

Conclusion

What are the further consequences beyond the last page? Are they implied by your narrative?

What implications of the story are not addressed on the page? Should they be?

Life is Not a Plot

— No line is ever ended

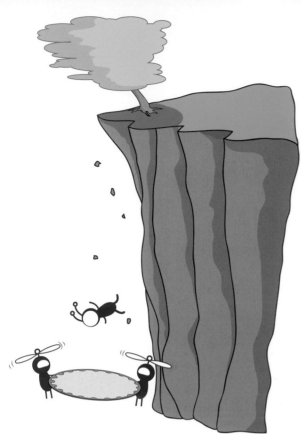

Not a deus ex machina if they are
kidnapping him after they save him.

If it's a story about the stupidity of
obsession, maybe this will work.

In a story about red herrings,
a cat head is a red herring.

Plot Devices

Plot devices are often rightly maligned for creating false drama or making things too easy. They are presented here as a warning. But, in a certain context, plot devices can be used profitably in your fiction. The rules of humor, for example, are often different, and in humor coincidence can be very funny. In mysteries, the idea of a red herring, properly deployed, is an element expected by a reader. Still, be wary—most of the time plot devices hurt your fiction. Readers hate feeling as if the writer has had to turn to a plot device to solve a problem rather than finding a more organic solution.

DEUS EX MACHINA—The term means "God from the machine." It refers to when a character in an impossible position is suddenly extricated from it by introducing a new event, character, or object that seems coincidental. In such cases, the reader feels the writer has violated their own rules or approach to logic.

MACGUFFIN—A goal that can manifest as an object pursued by a character. However, the writer never properly explains the character's motivation. The reader is expected to continue to read simply because the character is shown to strongly want the MacGuffin. Desire for something without some explanation usually means the reader doesn't understand the stakes and loses interest in the story.

RED HERRING—A seeming answer or clue that turns out to be unimportant or outright misleading. A red herring's disruption of a story is directly related to what question it purports to answer. If the question is central to the story and the writer spends a lot of time exploring the red herring, irritation will soon overtake the reader.

These diagrams describe more or less the same thing from slightly different perspectives and, taken together, provide you with a basic understanding of typical plots. However, in addition to their abstract nature, such diagrams do not really acknowledge that characterization drives story, even while they acknowledge that characters, for example, ride the narrative up-escalator that is rising action. Thus, to some degree, plot diagrams privilege event over character. When stories are seen as too mechanical, too *paint-by-numbers*, it is usually for this reason: The writer has taken to heart the basic ingredients in plot and applied them without consideration for how narrative might emerge in a more organic fashion. In bad stories, a mechanical approach often manifests in the form of too much coincidence helping the character. Coincidence should be limited, or always make the main character's situation worse, not better.

Since such diagrams also emphasize climax and conflict, they imply that stories have a central goal or goals . . . whereas *every aspect* of the journey is important to the writer during the writing of fiction. You must attend to exposition, rising action, and the dying fall as urgently as you grapple with the climactic scenes.

Perhaps what's needed, then, to make narrative design concrete is a full-on story lizard, not a story diagram. As much as you need a sense of what goes into story, you also need a sense of an otherwise unmentioned but weighty *presence*: everything that *doesn't* go into story, or could have gone into a different story. Freytag's rising mountain peak, implying a rapid and often tumultuous descent, doesn't exist in a vacuum, surrounded by empty space. It's surrounded by lives and events and an entire world raised up by your imagination. Perhaps those spikes of complications along the story lizard's back could as easily have been part of its spiraling tail. Maybe the story even started at the snout and worked its way back along the spine. Further, how do you "plot" a story of illumination, in which the focus is so intensely about the inner life of a character—or stories about the aftermath of a climactic event, like Jo Walton's Hugo Award–winning novel *Among Others*?

Thus the Freytag pyramid and its doppelgängers are perhaps most useful as a barometer or *baseline*—to gauge, for example, the effect of where you place the climax and how steep you make the rising action (if you have rising action). Such diagrams present a kind of *average* approach that can help make the lines of your own story come into clearer view. But you may also discover that in thinking about narrative design, some of the best stories are most usefully seen not through pondering their plots at all but instead through mulling their *structure*.

STRUCTURE

If you used a diagram similar to Freytag's pyramid to map someone's irregular heartbeat over time, or the spikes and depths of a musical composition, the abstraction would be at merely one remove—indeed, there would be a direct correlation between each spike and the subject matter. But a story is neither a medical condition nor a musical score.

The author of Who Fears Death *(World Fantasy Award winner),* Akata Witch, Zahrah the Windseeker *(Soyinka Prize winner), and* The Shadow Speaker *explains how an image can encompass a novel . . .*

"This drawing is my novel. No, really, it literally is the novel. It's called *Remote Control* (Ghanaian slang for 'juju') and I haven't finished writing the prose version of it yet. The story, every element of it (except the human characters), is in this drawing. At the forefront, I drew those themes, plot elements, and events that are most central to the novel. The story takes place in the city of Accra, thus the cityscape at the bottom. Accra is the foundation of the story. On the right is a representation of the Independence Gate in Accra, Ghana (also called the Black Star Gate), a national monument where some key things take place.

"The point of view that one looks into the image is also part of the story. The perspective is that of someone entering the city; this is precisely what one of the main characters does at the beginning of the novel. The combined sun and moon on the right signifies the fact that the entire novel takes place over twenty-four hours. Lastly, the spider (the details on its body are part of the story, too), the chaotic approaching deluge of scallop-y squiggles and the blastula-looking thing floating above the spider . . . well, you'll have to read the book to find who and what all of those are.

"I write mainly linear stories, but my writing process is very nonlinear. I may write a scene from its middle, then skip to the end, then jump back to the beginning. I'll write portions by hand in a notebook, on napkins, scraps of paper, the sides of shoeboxes. These days, I write sections using a non-electric antique typewriter. When I finish, I type all the pieces into my computer and put them in a linear order. Thus, representing within one image an entire novel that takes place over twenty-four hours appeals to me. I generally believe that the past, present, and future are intertwined and cannot be separated. So showing multiple layers of time in one image appeals to me, as well.

"I drew my novel because at that juncture I didn't have the time to write it. I'm a full-time tenure-track professor and the novel came to me right at the beginning of the semester. I needed a way to write the novel without writing it. I needed to channel the weight, emotion, aura, essence, soul of the novel better than mere notes. It needed to be in the form of art.

"It took me two weeks, and then I set it aside for six months. When I returned to the novel last month, I merely had to look at the image and I knew exactly where I needed to go. I knew the *feeling* of the story. I knew the smell of the story's world. It was all right there in that black-and-white picture of the story that I'd drawn using several thick pungent-smelling black Sharpies. They say a picture is worth a thousand words. This one is worth closer to 100,000." ✏

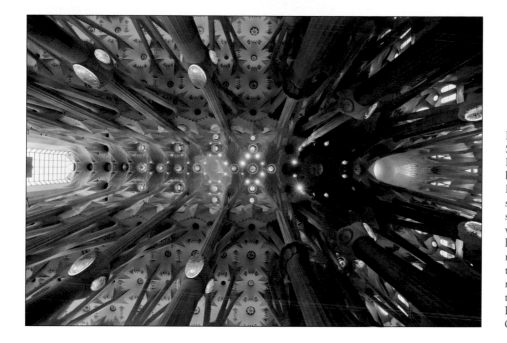

Interior of the Sagrada Família, Barcelona, designed by Antoni Gaudí. Fiction has a similar underlying structure, both at wider architectural level and at the micro level, through the textures and materials you use to build your story. Photo by Ihsan Gerçelman.

Although there may be several classic plots and variations, each story can have a unique structure. Structure appeals as much to the technical imagination as that initial adrenaline rush of inspiration appeals to the creative imagination—perhaps because structure feels as if it can be infinite in its variations, whereas plot does not. And because structure is so individual, an unusual structure isn't necessarily experimentation for its own sake, but more often just a healthy exploration of the perfect way to tell a certain kind of story.

Three examples help to illustrate how a unique structure can further good storytelling. Iain M. Banks's novel *Use of Weapons*, Vladimir Nabokov's "The Leonardo," and Angela Carter's "The Fall River Axe Murders" all gain emotional resonance and additional depth through their approaches to structure, which shouldn't trump character but better express it. The stories' structures may have contributed more to their literary longevity than their plots.

A classic of British space opera, *Use of Weapons* is part of Banks's Culture series. The Culture novels postulate a far future in which humankind has spread out across the galaxy, artificial intelligence has led to the creation of fully sentient spaceship minds, and we have become integrated into a galaxy-wide megacivilization composed of many thousands of different intelligent species.

Banks uses two narrative streams to tell his story of the life of a man named Cheradenine Zakalwe, an agent working for the Culture who intervenes in less advanced civilizations, usually in the context of war or insurgencies of some kind. The nature of his relationship with his controller and the horrible event in his distant past become clear by novel's end. Several of Zakalwe's engagements with other civilizations are documented. One thread in the novel moves forward in time while the other moves back through time, giving readers both a start and an end at the beginning of *Use of Weapons*. There is also a prologue and an epilogue set after everything that occurs in the main text. Potentially complicating the structure, the individual chapters also employ flashbacks. However,

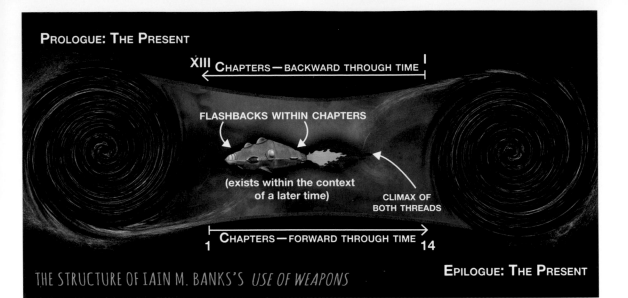

PROLOGUE: THE PRESENT

XIII CHAPTERS—BACKWARD THROUGH TIME I

FLASHBACKS WITHIN CHAPTERS

(exists within the context of a later time)

CLIMAX OF BOTH THREADS

1 CHAPTERS—FORWARD THROUGH TIME 14

THE STRUCTURE OF IAIN M. BANKS'S *USE OF WEAPONS*

EPILOGUE: THE PRESENT

Does envisioning the structure of Iain M. Banks's Use of Weapons help you to better understand the novel? What alterations to this structure would produce radically different effects for the reader?

the flashbacks simply mimic on a smaller scale the wormholing nature of the larger-scale structure of the novel. Thus, this time frame "complication" feels completely natural.

Banks says that telling *Use of Weapons* in a more conventional way "never occurred to me." Although the structure may take getting used to, it does seem organic. What the structure accomplishes is sixfold:

- It reflects the wandering and disconnected nature of the character.
- It demonstrates how a past event has changed the character.
- It allows the reader to see the character in his or her normal post-trauma baseline reality/existence and to think that he was always this way.
- It makes the revelations set out at the end more powerful.
- It acknowledges that this is a story in which the climax occurs at the chronological beginning and that this climax is best understood in the context of first encountering the character later in life.
- It allows the reader to more fully experience a major theme of the novel—the futility of war—as the baseline of the character's existence.

Banks could have written a novel about the events leading up to, during, and just after the horrible event, and a story along those lines may have been just as powerful. But this more conventional approach would not have shown the devastating aftereffects of the event. Nor would starting with the event and proceeding in a chronological way have achieved an organic resonance. In short, Banks was faced with either telling a kind of oddly provincial story—a series of actions on one planet, leading to one terrible event—or using an unusual structure to create a more universal effect, quite literally by expanding the scope to cover many different planets and a longer period of time. In the process, Banks is able to make powerful statements about the nature of memory, guilt, redemption, and history.

Borden was accused of murdering her father and stepmother in 1892. She was eventually acquitted.

By contrast, in "The Fall River Axe Murders," Angela Carter had a much different (smaller-scale) problem to solve: how to write about the **Lizzie Borden murders**, when almost everyone knows how the story ends. Her solution is a brilliant idea expressed

The slow burn ignites.

Day and night before murders, from Lizzie Borden's Perspective

Hot coals of prior incidents (not shown)

Result of rising tension (not depicted in story)

Rising Tension

ANGELA CARTER'S STORY "THE FALL RIVER AXE MURDERS"

through structure: to depict the events leading up to the murders but not to show the murders themselves. Instead, the story leaves the reader right at the threshold. In a very real sense, Carter shows the reader, using careful detail, the preamble to a horrible act—only to deny us the climactic scene or the dying fall. And yet she knows readers will provide that climactic scene themselves simply because the Borden murders constitute a form of common knowledge. Carter's chosen structure is a way of acknowledging that what would normally be the resolution or surprise (the murders) cannot play that role in her narrative. Despite this constraint, her story is an absolute masterpiece of rising tension and unease.

The more general point exemplified by Angela Carter's short story is that with the right approach you can sometimes remove part of a narrative structure from the page, and yet a powerful ghostly outline of what's missing still manifests in the reader's mind. That, sometimes, if you show everything *but* the climactic action, that action will still continue as an inexorable forward movement. It cannot help but be imagined no matter what the state of its presence on the page. A narrative structure that's about absence as well as presence also speaks to the creative dialogue between writer and reader and demonstrates that *creating space* in your fiction for the reader to participate is not always about *accessibility* but can be about generating opportunities for readers to engage in storytelling, which is crucial for the writer's success.

Structure can also intrigue and reward by playing off of readers' expectations. Vladimir Nabokov's "The Leonardo" masterfully manipulates structure to create forward narrative momentum and hold the reader's interest. In the story, residents of a lower-class tenement building in an unnamed European city encounter a mysterious man named Romantovski. Gustav, his brother Anton, and his girlfriend Anna, try

The structure of Angela Carter's "The Fall River Axe Murders" makes explicit the reader's role in the complex contract with the writer. Some elements of story will always be generated by the reader's imagination.

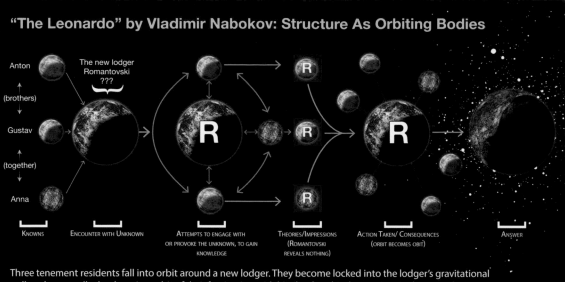

"The Leonardo" by Vladimir Nabokov: Structure As Orbiting Bodies

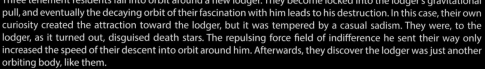

Anton

(brothers)

Gustav

(together)

Anna

The new lodger
Romantovski
???

| KNOWNS | ENCOUNTER WITH UNKNOWN | ATTEMPTS TO ENGAGE WITH OR PROVOKE THE UNKNOWN, TO GAIN KNOWLEDGE | THEORIES/IMPRESSIONS (ROMANTOVSKI REVEALS NOTHING) | ACTION TAKEN/ CONSEQUENCES (ORBIT BECOMES OBIT) | ANSWER |

Three tenement residents fall into orbit around a new lodger. They become locked into the lodger's gravitational pull, and eventually the decaying orbit of their fascination with him leads to his destruction. In this case, their own curiosity created the attraction toward the lodger, but it was tempered by a casual sadism. They were, to the lodger, as it turned out, disguised death stars. The repulsing force field of indifference he sent their way only increased the speed of their descent into orbit around him. Afterwards, they discover the lodger was just another orbiting body, like them.

Thinking of a story structure like Vladimir Nabokov's "The Leonardo" as a series of orbiting bodies, with strong attractions and decaying orbits, reminds us that some stories are entirely reliant upon the character relationships for their effects.

OPPOSITE
Plate 85:
"Ascidiacea" from Ernst Haeckel's *Kunstformen der Natur* (1904). Haeckel's robust representations of marine life remind us of the structural interest to be found in the world around us. Studying the lives of these creatures might result in further ideas for narrative.

without success to learn Romantovski's occupation and other details, with ever more conflict arising between the three and Romantovski. Gustav and Anton are petty thieves who also do odd jobs, but they believe Romantovski thinks himself above them. Eventually, their testing and prodding leads to Gustav getting Anna to flirt with Romantovski, which he then uses as a pretext to stab the new lodger to death. When they then enter his room, they discover that Romantovski was a forger, no better than them. That he was, in fact, *one of them.*

The story allows for every element of Freytag's pyramid of rising tension, with complications and a dying fall of action, but structurally the tale takes the form of three individuals entering the orbit of a mystery (Romantovski) and their reactions to that mystery in aggregate and separately—culminating in a death and a "reveal." The structure allows for the emphasis to be on the three characters, and how they change or do not change as a result of encountering Romantovski, while Romantovski remains a blank slate but for one central mystery about him that makes him equally fascinating to readers and to the other characters.

These three examples suggest the fun and usefulness of playing with structure—they suggest, in fact, that some very entertaining stories are best served by unconventional structures. So long as the results feel organic and wedded to character and situation, they do not have to call attention to themselves; in cases where they do, you are most likely entering the realms of postmodernism or experimental fiction. These are wonderful realms to explore, as long as you intended to do so. But you may want to keep in mind these wise words from Catherynne M. Valente, bestselling author of *The Girl Who Circumnavigated Fairyland in a Ship of Her Own Making* and the non-bestselling author of the structurally and stylistically challenging *The Labyrinth*:

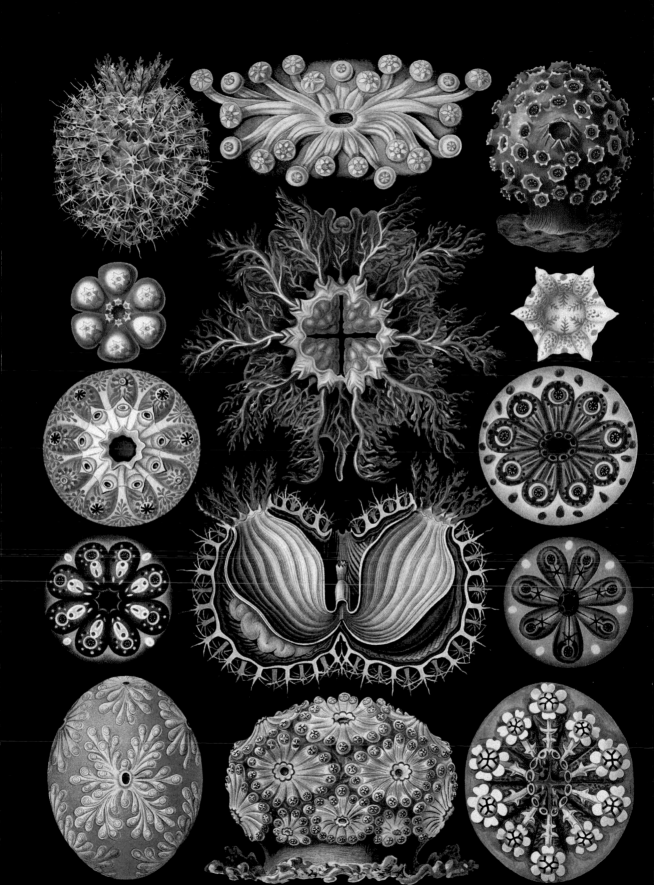

MYSTER ODD PRESENTS
STRUCTURE

The world around you isn't just the place you live, or a repository of possible characters and tactile experiences that can help your writing. You might also find inspiration for story structure there. Even a splash of water, captured on camera, can reveal a hidden structure. Architecture, the symmetry of fungi, or the lines on a gecko's toes can spark inspiration. What might you be missing around you every day that suggests story structure?

My rule of thumb is that given Plot, Structure, and Style, one of them has to tap out and play for Team Mundane. The reader needs something to hold on to while the author experiments with something that excites them: a linear, straightforward structure, unvarnished, solid prose, a plot that lines up with their cultural expectations of narrative. Most really good books pick one of those things to go wild with. Books that pick two are called avant-garde, and those that don't call any quarter for readers without obscure degrees are more often than not called remaindered. Look at Mark Danielewski's *House of Leaves*, which has a structure like "good grief, Charlie Pomo," but the sentence-level prose style is pretty workaday in two-thirds of the book . . . [while] the plot is a pretty standard haunted house story, with a literary fetch quest stapled onto it.

Regardless, you don't have to restrict yourself to seeking out unique structures in existing fiction or using the "average" models of generic structures. On the previous pages, Myster Odd presented some possible inspirations for fictional structures or forms. What would stories with these structures be like? What would these structures in the right context give to readers? Can anything at all suggest a story structure?

CREATING SCENES

Constructed from the various elements of narrative, the *scene* is the principal architectural unit that expresses plot and therefore structure. David Trottier's *Screenwriter's Bible* defines a scene in these strict terms: "A scene is a dramatic unit consisting of the camera placement, a location, and a time. When one of these three elements changes, the scene changes as well." Because fiction deals with words, not moving images, a scene in fiction is perhaps a little more mutable, but Trottier's definition does lock the basics into place.

A scene usually dramatizes interactions between characters, but it can also feature a character alone. A scene almost always dramatizes at least one character *in the moment*, even if the events are part of a flashback to a time prior to the main action in the novel. If you describe a man crossing the street in the rain, who meets and says hello to a passing story lizard, then these events function as a scene, whether or not you convey the man's interior thoughts. The composition of a scene exists along a shifting scale involving the ratio of dialogue and actions unfolding in the present moment balanced against exposition, flashback, and description or summary that does not exist in the present moment. Almost any ratio can be successful as long as the reader has the *impression* of being shown, not told, the story.

A *half scene*, meanwhile, is a mini scene that consists of a few lines or a couple of paragraphs of dialogue and description in tandem that are embedded into what is otherwise summary, or a different scene, as a way of deepening or providing more drama to a section of the narrative. If the man who crossed the street in the rain is sitting in a coffee shop talking to someone, and during the conversation something sparks his memory of meeting the story lizard, and you open up the current scene to include a few lines of dialogue and description from that meeting, then you have created a half scene.

MORE EXAMPLES OF SCENE, HALF-SCENE, SUMMARY

Summary describes action or thought without dramatizing it—a form of "telling" rather than "showing." "After he'd crossed the street to avoid the story lizard (who wants an unexpected story?), he visited the baker, the barber, and the blacksmith before returning home" is summary, not a scene or half scene.

Most fiction consists of scenes with intermittent or linking summary, although both stories and novels are deep and wide enough to allow for or even *require* much larger blocks of pure exposition or summary, and may also use half scenes frequently. *The Birth of the People's Republic of Antarctica* by **John Calvin Batchelor** provides an excellent example of an extended use of summary with half scenes. It works because Batchelor's narrator has a compelling voice that overcomes the ways in which summary can seem less interesting than scene. The collection *Siege 13* by Tamas Dobozy delves deeply into history to explain the present. His stories must, of necessity, often reverse the ratio, so that years may pass in pages of events told to us through summary and half scene, punctuated by short scenes. In this case, the most common unit of the story becomes the exposition.

Batchelor frequently uses this approach. Another notable example is Vladimir Nabokov's *Ada*.

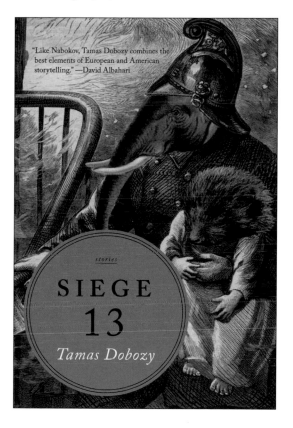

"Like Nabokov, Tamas Dobozy combines the best elements of European and American storytelling." —David Albahari

stories

SIEGE 13

Tamas Dobozy

PACING: BEATS AND PROGRESSIONS

To control effects across scenes and learn how to create and edit scenes, you will need to understand some basic terms, the foremost of which is *pacing*.

Pacing refers to how quickly or slowly a scene and, over the span of a story or novel, a series of scenes seems to play out in the reader's mind. Through any number of affects you can extend or contract the reader's perception of the passage of time. In this context, "time" exists *separate* from the chronology of the narrative or the actual minutes or hours an event or encounter takes in the real world.

Siege 13 jacket art by Allan Kausch (2012). Dobozy's collection uses summary in interesting ways.

Scene time blossoms within the reader, triggered by your level of control over your material. A fistfight (wingfight?) between our friend the talking penguin (let's call him Fred) and his nemesis Danger Duck might play out in seconds in real, objective time but seem to take long, fascinating minutes in the context of your story, as you draw out every detail of every slapping blow and every bead of feather-sweat knocked off in the process. You might slow things down even further by opening up the fight scene to show us a glimpse of Fred's first wingfight as a chick. Or, sped up, the scene might be dismissed in a couple of lines, depending on your purpose in telling us about the fight. Perhaps it's the aftermath you need the reader to fully understand. The important thing is that, in going back over your first draft, *you* know what you wanted to accomplish.

Inherent in the idea of pacing and the way that readers experience your scenes is the idea of *beats* and *progressions*. *Beats* are micro cycles of ebb and flow, progress and setback playing out within a scene—action/reaction, cause and effect, stimulus and response. They operate almost like an insurgency of cells that support the scene's health. You can also think of a "beat" as a "heartbeat" or even "pulse" if that's helpful—and you can regulate that pulse, even skip a **beat or two**.

"A beat is a moment and I think of it as an active, living thing," says Kate Maruyama, author of the novel *Harrowgate*. "'We need another beat here,' is a common note in screenplays, and I use it all the time in fiction. If you look at that progression and you feel it hasn't done all of its dramatic work, it is usually because that moment is missing. Because of my theater geekiness from college, I always imagine a choreographer calling out, '5, 6, 7, 8 and STEP' and beating the back of his hand on the palm of another and making sure the scene has the right rhythm. You can 'take another beat' before a scene comes to a climax, or, *so* importantly, take a beat when coming down from a climactic scene, allowing us and the character to process what happened. Or that beat in dialogue or in a scene where the character has to process the information before saying that devastating line he or she is coming to. The beat is sometimes a pause, sometimes a line, sometimes a look (on film), sometimes a punch in the head, depending on what the scene needs."

A *progression* describes the individual ordering of events and deployment of information in scenes or across different scenes. At the most tactical level, progressions are created through using beats. Your progressions are the key to managing intensity, revelation, and a sense of rising action throughout your narrative. In a story with good progressions, there is a sense of events building upon one another, and there is a cumulative effect that feels natural yet at the same time has dramatic appeal. For example, in a good series of progressions we probably know something about Danger Duck's long-standing enmity for Fred before they fight. As the story continues after the fight, the consequences of the fight continue to play out across the story, across scenes.

Bad progressions can confuse the reader, and they can also be anticlimactic. Certain beats could make perfect sense in relation to one another but seem out of order

A good rule of thumb for fight scenes is to cut every third action-reaction (or beat) to speed up the pacing. You will probably find the scene still makes sense.

BEATS EXAMINED

After years of research, avant-garde Finnish biofictionologist Ninni Aalto has isolated story beats under the microscope. These tiny creatures constitute individual cells of narrative, moments that can take the form of action, expressed emotion, or even just essential pauses. Whole communities of beats combine to form chains of cause-and-effect or less causal strings, depending on the type of tale in which they are found. Here are just a few examples.

ACTION BEAT. This beat, discovered in Chuck Wendig's novel *Blackbirds*, performed the necessary purpose of ending a scene, at a point of high tension.

if used in the wrong progression. Remember in Chapter 3 when I advised you not to start with an explosion in your fiction? In part that advice was about the idea of progressions—and needing to make sure that your progressions ramp up to something more exciting than what came before. If you have been too mechanical in planning scenes, expecting that certain things will occur—this and then this and this—you may find that your beats and your progressions are saying "not this *that* not this *that*." Never go against a pulse that seems natural: rearrange all else instead.

Beats and progressions require continuity and exist because of cause and effect. Even in surreal stories, an action usually causes a reaction or an effect (even no reaction is still a response), whether on a small or large scale. For example, "He insulted her. She left." Or, "He insulted her. She left, never spoke to him again, and turned his friends against him." Opportunities for complex, leapfrogging progressions are often neglected by writers who think too tactically and forget to carry through on the wider consequences of an action. Theoretically, if these implications are carried forward, there is an energy and complexity to the ends of individual scenes and across entire scenes in the later stages of a piece of fiction. Doing so can more or less create your story: the intersection and accumulation—or culmination—of a series of the right beats, grouped under the aegis of the right progressions, to achieve a desired effect. Never forget, as well, that all of this is driven by what your characters do and don't do—and every decision they make creates parallel universes with different beats and progressions.

The Beginnings and Endings of Scenes

Although the most interesting dramatic element of your scene—whether it's a fistfight, a curt conversation, or a sarcastic nod of the head—may occur halfway or two-thirds of the way through, the entry and exit points of scenes are just as important, perhaps more so. Even mishandled, the right dramatic element retains a certain rough power. But clumsily handled scene setups and departures may so distract, bore, or irritate the reader—or point in such misleading directions—that by the time the reader reaches the core of the scene, you have already lost their attention.

CONTAMINATION BEAT. Contamination beats attach to the artery walls of story, quietly making their presence known. This beat formed a pause in Sofia Samatar's novel *A Stranger in Olondria.*

EMOTIONAL BEAT. This beat was found in Ekaterina Sedia's novel *A Secret History of Moscow*, where it created a flashback memory that elicited pathos in the reader.

EMOTIONAL & ACTION BEATS. Sometimes action and emotional beats are too intertwined to isolate, creating a single beat with two hearts. This beat was discovered working to create forward motion and empathy in Tamas Dobozy's short story "The Animals of the Budapest Zoo."

At the beginning of a scene, here are some basic questions to ask, at least some of which should be relevant to your particular scene (assuming for now that you have chosen the right starting point):

- Are we at the location where the scene will take place, or are we in transit toward it? If in transit, what purpose does not already being at the location serve?
- If the scene takes place in a new setting, have you provided enough context about place to anchor the reader?
- Do we know, with clarity, where the characters are sitting or standing? In other words, do we have some idea of how the characters occupy space, and where they are in relation to one another?
- If new characters are introduced, do we have a clear initial view of them and know their relationship to other characters in the scene?
- From the first sentence of the scene, do we know whose point of view we are in? If not, why not?
- Is the context firmly wedded to character point of view? Consider, for example, this context from John le Carré's *The Russia House*: "No other city that he knew hid its shame behind so many sweet facades or asked such terrible questions with its smile." This sentence on setting also reveals much about character point of view.
- Does the description *move* with the story or seem to clot the arteries of the narrative? Are the details integrated with the forward progress, or present moment, of the scene? M. John Harrison's science-fiction novel *Light* includes masterful examples of receiving information only when we need it; elements that are introduced but remain mysterious until explained don't affect our comprehension of the preceding scenes.
- If the scene takes place in a setting already used in the story or novel, have you repeated information already known to the reader and thus unnecessary? Can you provide a new detail about the setting without slowing down the scene?
- Does the general context, irrespective of the setting, take into consideration prior scenes? Is there general repetition of information? Is it necessary—to remind the reader of something important—or should it be cut?
- Do we progress fairly far into the foreground of the scene before flashbacks or other time manipulations occur? In other words, has the baseline reality and the context of the scene's present moment had time to settle into the reader's awareness before shifts occur?

In terms of pacing, you may find that if the scene starts out tense, the scene's middle can be slower and more prolonged as that initial urgency bleeds across the remainder of the scene. But if you start slow, the beats need to begin to quicken as you head into the middle of the scene.

As for scene endings, there are more possibilities, since the need to provide context through exposition is usually much reduced. The scene can keep expanding or it can end in any number of ways—on any particular beat—depending on what you want to express or emphasize. Consider, for example, the differences if you end a

Art by Ninni Aalto

hypothetical Fred the Penguin/Danger Duck scene in any one of these places: in mid-punch; with Fred bloodied on the floor; with Danger Duck's memory of being beaten by his Mallard father; the police hauling them both off to jail; or the bloodied Fred and Danger Duck sheepishly shaking hands in the police car.

Questions to think about regarding the end of your scene include:

- Has something been implied in the scene that must now be made explicit for emphasis?
- Have you made explicit what could have stayed implicit by ending earlier?
- Have you ended on an *action* or a *reaction,* and how would changing your choice affect the scene?
- Is there something at the beginning or (more typically) in the middle of the scene that should really be moved to the end? This usually refers to dialogue or a character's thoughts. While writing a rough draft, you may place dialogue in an order based on a sense of the natural flow of the conversation—forgetting that all conversations in fiction are staged—rather than another order that will also seem natural but better support the overall point of the scene.
- Have you chosen the best closing line—and is there a better one somewhere else on the last page of your scene?

Much like a pool player who must figure out how to set up the next shot through calculating where the cue ball will stop after the current shot, you will need to think about how to manage transitions between scenes as well as how the ending of one scene affects the entry point into the next one—or even scenes that occur much later in the story. Sometimes, too, in thinking about your scenes, you will come to a horrifying conclusion: "This scene isn't necessary for the story I am trying to tell." But don't stay horrified: Cutting an irrelevant scene will only strengthen the remaining scenes.

REPETITION AND INVISIBILITY

Certain kinds of repetition may support your narrative—for example, repetition of sentence construction can serve a useful purpose. Similarly, certain patterns of presenting dialogue (he said/he told her) become as invisible as the repeated use of articles like "the" and "a." The reader requires this kind of invisibility to enter into an immersive reading experience. However, with regard to scenes, repetition can often lead to an undesirable type of invisibility.

Repetition of scene means more than one thing. It can mean that the exact same actions or types of actions occur within multiple scenes—for example, several consecutive battle scenes. But it can also mean a wolf scene followed by a wolf-in-sheep's-clothing scene: The disguise does not truly hide the outline of the all too familiar. For example, if you have a scene in which an executive gives a presentation to the board of her company, followed by a scene in which that same executive attends

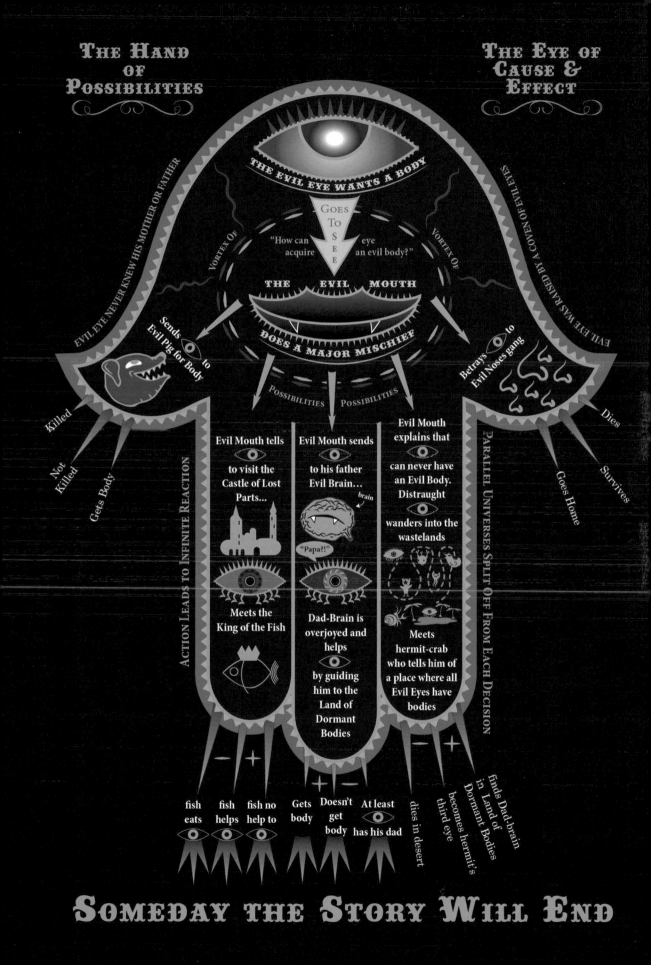

a wedding ceremony and then a seminar . . . then you have, more or less, written the same scene because the basic thrust is the same. Someone is presenting something to an audience; whether the protagonist is on the receiving end or not doesn't matter.

Once you have dramatized a particular type of act or action or scene more than once—sometimes as little as two or three times—it begins to give diminishing returns to the reader, especially if presented back-to-back. Within a very short period of time, this repetition may mean that entire scenes become "invisible" to the reader; they no longer stimulate the reader's interest or excitement.

The only way to recharge the reader's interest is to vary the types of scenes and, through that contrast, rejuvenate the excitement. The more you have depended on the repetition of a type of scene, the more space you will need to put between it and the next use of the same type. For example, if you were to put three battle scenes back-to-back, the reader will usually have reached a point of exhaustion by the middle of the second scene. The action described would become an uninteresting blur. If, on the other hand, you have three battle scenes intercut with two scenes between each that are vastly different, you may keep the reader's interest. The beats and progressions will have a different look and feel. Another solution might be to find different narrative approaches to each potentially similar scene, so that similar events do not seem to have been presented in the same way. For example, have the **second battle** observed from afar, and show the third only through its aftermath. George R. R. Martin successfully uses this approach in his novel *A Game of Thrones*.

Martin discusses his approach to battle scenes in the appendix.

This applies even more crucially to those novels in which one long, central action is broken up into many chapters and scenes. Just because the action is broken up into separate scenes and chapters does not mean that the reader will automatically experience that one long, central action as a series of different actions. Breaking it up into several chapters may just draw attention to the fact that you are basically describing the same act or action over an extended period. Without the context of scenes in sharp contrast to the action, that action becomes largely meaningless.

This brings me to another general rule of repetition of act or action. You must usually begin to *cut* your scenes differently with each new repetition (especially of setting) because, having established a pattern, your reader will then be able to fill in the missing details. The ratio of summary to scene may then also change. Through this shift in the ratio, you will be able to bring out other elements within the scene rather than simply convey certain types of information or basic illuminations of character relationships. In such situations, transitional text that might have served a useful purpose in earlier parts of the novel now becomes dead tissue—it simply underscores in a negative way the repetition that is occurring.

Cutting Scenes

Every scene has a point or points of greatest tension or dramatic potential, and every scene then falls away from that moment, sometimes in interesting ways and sometimes in not-so-interesting ways. The point isn't always to cut away right after

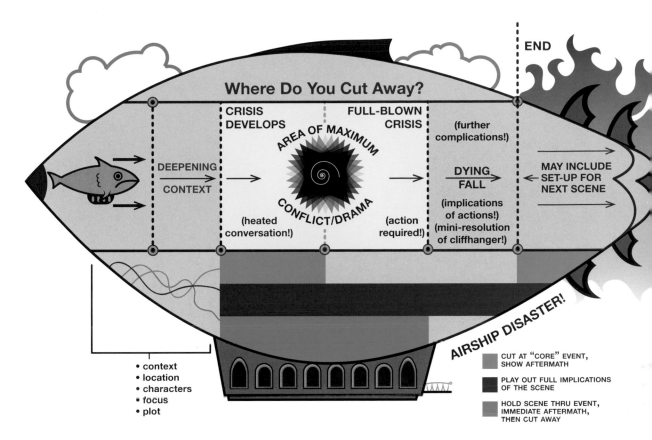

Where Do You Cut Away?

END

DEEPENING
CONTEXT

CRISIS
DEVELOPS

(heated
conversation!)

AREA OF MAXIMUM
CONFLICT/DRAMA

FULL-BLOWN
CRISIS

(action
required!)

(further
complications!)

DYING
FALL

(implications
of actions!)
(mini-resolution
of cliffhanger!)

MAY INCLUDE
SET-UP FOR
NEXT SCENE

AIRSHIP DISASTER!

- context
- location
- characters
- focus
- plot

CUT AT "CORE" EVENT,
SHOW AFTERMATH

PLAY OUT FULL IMPLICATIONS
OF THE SCENE

HOLD SCENE THRU EVENT,
IMMEDIATE AFTERMATH,
THEN CUT AWAY

a dramatic moment, even if this is a common (and overused) way to keep the reader interested in what happens next. In some novels or stories, a long aftermath to a moment of dramatic tension makes perfect sense because the focus is really on how the characters react to a revelation, a new piece of information, or a confrontation. For example, in Tamas Dobozy's memorable short story "The Beautician," the narrator reveals a damning secret to Ilona, the mother of his girlfriend, Eva, that involves Hollo, a person with whom the mother has had conflicts. Although the narrator's motivations are complex, he is basically trying to win over Ilona. Instead of ending after the narrator divulges this information, Dobozy extends the scene so that we see the narrator alone with Eva, and how the divulging of the secret weakens the relationship in unexpected ways. If the story was only about Hollo's past or how his secret is received by the community, Dobozy could have ended the scene earlier. But the story is more about how holding on to and releasing the secret impacts the narrator.

Lingering in a scene takes more skill, generally, than a quick cut—and that skill may need to include excellent characterization. Why? For the simple reason that the material must be interesting over a longer reading time, and during this period the reader has more time to think through the implications (and logic) of what you have presented to them. A more intense commitment to character tends to give you more time because the reader is not just invested in what happens but in observing the character.

Action scenes are no easier to linger in than, for example, dinner conversations.

INTERCUTTING SCENES

Vacationers come to an island with a monster on it, in Chive Muscle's cult classic, *Monster Island Bloody Hellfest.*

APPROACH #1
MULTIPLE POV CHARACTERS ACROSS SCENES, WITH QUICK CUTS AND SHORT CHAPTERS.

1A	1B	1C	1D

Three roughly equal scenes, with brief monster-vision.

2B	2A	2C	2D

Longer sequence of encountering body from point of view (POV) of reporter with three short "reaction shifts" to others, including the watching monster.

3A	3B	3C	3D

Short, intercut scenes of what the characters do when confronted by the monster, followed by the monster's actions.

4A	4B	4C

They flee in different directions; scenes now lengthen to prolong tension of not knowing what happened to B & C. May also privilege one POV over others here in terms of length of chapter to establish which is the main POV character.

Most commercial fiction would deploy some variation on the sequencing above if using multiple characters in this scenario (movies, too, especially in the thriller genre). But you can find this approach across many different kinds of novels. It may just be more obvious in situations where the writer is showing the reader simple, direct actions in a category—like horror—that comes with certain expectations about tropes.

CHARACTERS

A RODNEY THE DENTIST

B CHASTAIN THE REPORTER

C BECCA THE COP

D UGHO THE MONSTER

TO CONSIDER WHEN INTERCUTTING SCENES:

—establish a rhythm
—touch base with each viewpoint character on a regular basis
—figure out which scenes are best shown from which POVs.

APPROACH #2
MULTIPLE POV CHARACTERS, BUT WITH FEWER RAPID CUTS AND LONGER CHAPTERS.

 1A

One long scene to establish Rodney's character, the anchor for the novel, for better or worse.

2B   **2C**

A longer scene from the reporter's point of view to get a hardened journalist's view of the body, followed by the cop, a minor character whose POV on the body is also valuable.

3D   **3A**

A long scene from the monster that allows the reader to gain some understanding of it, as well as its ferocity. This commitment means the monster will figure more prominently than in Approach #1. The sequence ends with Rodney seeing the monster and freaking out, to check back with the main character and give a contrasting viewpoint about the monster.

 4B   **4C**

As they flee the monster, we enter the reporter's POV because she has been in the most extreme situations; thus, she doesn't lose her cool and the writer can more easily convey the details about what's happening. For a similar reason, we check back in with the cop, too. But these more rational POVs occur after seeing Rodney's freak-out. Most likely, the next scene would be from Rodney's POV, the everyman whose reaction is closest to the reader's, after the end of The Fleeing.

You could say that this approach allows for a less frenetic and thus more thoughtful entry point into the novel, which creates a reservoir of interest and sympathy that you can draw on for later scenes that are faster and more action-packed. However, you can imbue any sequence with more or less tension depending on how you use technique within scenes. Whatever approach you use, the goal is to find the perfect synergy of characterization, structure, and story.

UGHO THE YOUNGER'S CAVE-APARTMENT

DEVIL'S ADVOCATE
THE AMOUNT OF TIME YOU SPEND WITH A CHARACTER ON THE PAGE OFTEN DETERMINES THEIR IMPORTANCE IN THE READER'S EYES. SCENES NEED TO MOVE AND SEEM DYNAMIC, BUT YOU CAN SACRIFICE CHARACTER DEPTH IF YOU CUT BACK AND FORTH TOO QUICKLY BETWEEN CHARACTERS. HOW YOU CUT SCENES CAN ALSO DEPEND ON FACTORS LIKE THE DENSITY OF YOUR PROSE AND WHETHER YOU BUILD PLOT IN PART THROUGH SHARING CHARACTER BACKSTORY.

BLOOD BAY INN & SPA

 **ARRIVE BY SHIP**

#1—EXPLORING   #2—ENCOUNTERING THE BODY
#3—DISCOVERING THE MONSTER   #4—RUNNING AWAY

You may also want to employ a general pattern of the same kinds of cuts throughout the story or novel or use different types of cuts for contrast. Each approach will create a different kind of reading experience, and each requires a different level of technical expertise. My novel *Veniss Underground* employs scene cuts entirely differently than my novel *Shriek: An Afterword*. *Veniss* is a surreal, far-future novel that plays out mostly in real time and in which grotesque absurdity is piled atop grotesque absurdity. The pacing of the underground scenes must be fast, with the beats and progressions used to shape each scene creating short, self-contained set pieces that, strung together, form a whole. If I lingered for too long in any one part of the narrative, the reader would have too much time to think about the baseline reality of what they are being shown, and plausibility would deteriorate almost as rapidly as the Boschian world I show them. In contrast, *Shriek* is a sixty-year chronicle of a dysfunctional family that also invokes the history of an imaginary city. The nonlinear narrative includes frequent digressions into the past. The beats and progressions must perform all sorts of localized time travel for the novel to work, and the scenes must be longer and incorporate more types of creative summary. The pace is of necessity slower.

INTERCUTTING SCENES

There are many ways to intercut scenes if you are using multiple-point-of-view characters. The most dramatic way pops up most often in commercial fiction and no doubt takes its cue from the movies: cutting a scene at the moment of a confrontation or right before a confrontation. The need by the reader to find out what happens next means that you can cut to a scene with another character in a situation that is of similar or lesser—even much lesser—urgency before you return to the confrontation. In other words, you are buying or trading time. Cynical manipulations of this approach exist, but it can also be used to create subtle and more passive scenes that add to a novel's complexity without allowing the reader's interest to flag. Done poorly, you may hook readers but create a shoddy novel of artificial cliff-hangers, a common complaint even among fans of, for example, Dan Brown's *The Da Vinci Code*. Done well, and you may create a page-turner with integrity like George R. R. Martin's A Song of Ice and Fire series.

The freedom to use different approaches to climactic moments has many uses. In a novel with accelerated levels of drama, it can ensure that you don't exhaust the reader or obscure your climax with too much side action. Why? Because you can come back to a scene at any point you want—a moment later, a few minutes later, or hours later—and you are under no obligation to always show the actual conflict or confrontation. If you come back a moment later perhaps you've just added a chapter or section break for emphasis or to hold the action frozen for just a beat. A few minutes later and you come back to the confrontation in progress. An hour later and you've cut from the promise of confrontation to showing the reader the aftermath, filling in the details of the encounter with summary. In some cases, a writer will hold the moment of anticipation for much longer. In the Lord of the Rings trilogy, J. R. R. Tolkien

MORE
INTERCUTTING
EXAMPLES

TRANSLATING MOVIE AND TELEVISION TECHNIQUE INTO FICTION

IN A GENERAL way, television and movies often have a bad influence on fiction. Some writers substitute received experience and received ideas from mass media for their own personal vision—or think that the structure of most television shows is perfectly suitable, "untranslated" or analyzed, for novels and stories. There's also the issue of immediacy that an image on the screen can offer versus that less instantaneous *something* provided by fiction. The glut of high-profile fantasy and science-fiction films has intensified this trend. Reading like subpar scripts or in other ways underwhelming, material of this sort appears in editors' slush piles every day.

But there are also specific ways in which other media can positively influence and enhance fiction. One example is the cutaway from scene to scene; you don't get, for example, our hero or heroine driving from point A to point B, just a scene at point A and one at Point B. One reason that J. R. R. Tolkien's Lord of the Rings series feels dated to some is because Tolkien *doesn't* cut away for the most part, leaving in pastoral bits of the quest that slow the pacing and don't always resonate with a modern reader. (The fact that Gandalf's escape from Saruman on eagle back looks so awful on film is a reminder, too, that some things are more convincing on the page.)

Another example of the way in which visual media can be of use to the fiction writer is through leaving out scenes to *imply* or for a particular *emphasis*. Because of a program's time constraint, television has had to become particularly adroit at leaving out scenes that the viewer has to fill in on their own. As a result, some television shows do a brilliant job of *compression* for effect. For example, in the first episode of the HBO series *Homeland*, the wife of a marine missing in Afghanistan for eight years receives the news that her husband has been found, right as she's picking up their son from school. The director and writer had the choice of continuing that scene, to show her telling her son the news. Instead, they cut immediately to the next scene, leaving the viewer with the visual of the mother staring at the son as he walks across the school yard toward her. This cut accomplishes a few important things: (1) you don't have to hear again information you just learned; (2) you don't have to experience a fairly banal scene, which would have to be staged in some unique way to be interesting; (3) the cutaway deemphasizes the son but still emphasizes the mother's concern for her family, which makes sense in terms of the focus of the series; and (4) the resulting acceleration of the pacing better fits a show generally categorized as a "thriller." (For an example of what I consider very lazy pacing and repetitive storytelling, check out the second season of *The Walking Dead*, which is just terrible, with prolonged scenes set around a farmhouse. Better writers would have condensed much of the second season to a couple of episodes.)

These are lessons from visual media that can be directly transferred to fiction. But there are also techniques from movies that you will need to break down and truly *translate* into fiction—opportunities that can yield unique approaches to presenting material to readers. I would, for example, highly advise that you examine in detail the opening to Joss Whedon's science-fiction movie *Serenity*, which contains an excellent example of how to introduce a lot of worldbuilding and character detail in a very short time span. (The director's commentary is a master class about narrative, too.) Of additional use would be studying the opening of *Serenity* compared to the opening scenes of the series that preceded it, *Firefly*—especially the difference in emphasis and the variation in

how the same main characters are introduced. But how would you translate that approach into fiction? Especially since you might not want to use a roving, omniscient point of view?

To give you a small, specific example of studying film technique for its use in fiction, let's return briefly to my novel *Finch*, the opening of which I analyzed in Chapter 3. A noir-fantasy mystery with some science-fiction elements, *Finch* is *meant* to be cinematic—the beats, the structure, the visuals at times mimic similar elements in film.

While writing *Finch*, I found one effect in Ridley Scott's movie *Black Hawk Down* fascinating, because I wasn't at first sure *how* to convert it to a fiction context. Regardless of what you think of Scott's film, the editing is precise and often brilliant. In one scene, attack helicopters are headed into Mogadishu, and at a certain point Scott cuts the sound. The effect on the viewer is a sudden *lurch*. When I saw the film, my stomach seemed to drop when the sound cut off. It was clear that the filmmakers meant for the sudden absence of helicopter noise to put you more directly into the scene—to turn film from a two-dimensional medium into something tactile and immediate.

I liked the effect very much and kept turning over in my mind how it could be used in fiction. The answer came when I was reviewing my structural outline for *Finch*. The novel is broken into sections corresponding to seven extremely important days in the life of John Finch, ones when he's investigating two seemingly impossible murders in the fantastical city of Ambergris.

Each day starts out with a transcript of Finch being interrogated by an unknown person. Where, when, and how the interrogation is taking place doesn't become clear until later in the novel. But the reader comes to expect an interrogation fragment at the start of each new section, so when the last section opens with nothing but a blank page, the effect is equivalent to cutting

the sound in *Black Hawk Down*. It creates a kind of lurch of surprise. At the same time, the blank page where there would be an expectation of the dread associated with interrogation creates a strangely liberating experience. What does it mean for Finch? What does it mean for the chronology of the novel?

Now, this effect will not work for all readers. Some may even have treated the interrogation sequences as little more than epigraphs. But this was still the intent: to suddenly pull the rug out from under the reader. However, unlike the unease caused by the sudden lack of sound in *Black Hawk Down*, it's meant to convey a sense of release, a sense of possible grace, of possible relief . . . although there's always the possibility it just means Finch is dead, the interrogation over. I think there are probably more overt ways to translate this particular technique, but that's how I used it in *Finch*.

Here are just a few questions you can ask while watching films and television to get you started . . .

- How long does the camera linger on a character's face while he or she is talking? If the camera doesn't linger, where does it go?
- At what point are scenes being cut, and how would alternative approaches have created a different effect?
- What is the film doing in terms of nonvisual elements such as sound?
- What kind of movement, or choreography, occurs with scenes, and how are characters placed and/or framed within scenes?
- What scenes aren't on screen that could have been?

If you carry out this "interrogation" of visual media faithfully, you'll soon find that certain techniques you grapple with now as you create your rough drafts will start to work with much less effort. ❧

doesn't let the reader know what happened in Gandalf's fight with the Balrog for what seems a lifetime—and in part we keep reading because we want to find out.

WHAT NOT TO DRAMATIZE

OVERLEAF
"The Hall of Bright Carvings" from Mervyn Peake's *Titus Groan*, as illustrated by Ian Miller.

One other advantage to cutting scenes before or at the point of a confrontation or other significant encounter is that not every such event needs to be dramatized in your story or novel. Sometimes this has everything to do with the point of view of the novelist. China Miéville's decision in *The Scar*, about pirates and a floating city of boats, to cut away before the character's ultimate encounter with a leviathan expressed the author's explicit intent not to cater to the usual expectations about how certain types of fantasy novels end. But other reasons apply—for example, you may not have the skills to convey a particular type of encounter and yet need that event to occur during the time line of the novel. There's no shame in this. If you have no interest in or proclivity for writing battle scenes, you shouldn't necessarily have to write one.

Beyond the eccentricities and skill set of the writer, the decision about what to dramatize concerns emphasis and how "bringing it to life" will either support or destabilize your story. Action scenes with no emotional stakes involved are fairly pointless to commit to the page. A noisy, prolonged fart may be a battle cry in a comedy of errors pitting class against class or just an embarrassing mistake on the part of the writer. Meals may or may not have any more significance or importance when dramatized than if summarized. In *Babbett's Feast* by Isak Dinesen, food is a means of communication and fosters a sense of community central to the core of the novel. Not showing sumptuous banquets would be a mistake. But the same meals pushed into Miéville's *The Scar* would be just as much of a mistake; sometimes a pirate's sandwich is just a sandwich.

Similarly, it's instructional how Daphne Du Maurier handled the sexual relationship between husband and wife in her famous 1950s novella "Don't Look Now" compared to director Nicolas Roeg's approach in the movie version. Because Du Maurier could use words to convey the couple's relationship and Roeg only had images, Roeg's version is forced to be much more explicit in attempting to show the intimacy and love between the two. How would explicit sex have changed the balance of elements and the role of scenes in the novella version?

Some writers almost always take a "less is more" approach to certain subjects. Stephen Graham Jones, known for horror and noir, is a writer who usually lets the sex happen off page. "Not because it is automatically weak writing or undeserving of page time. It's mostly that I've always suspected that people write those pages-long sex scenes for the same reason other writers wax on about unicorns: because, man, they'd sure like to see a **unicorn** someday."

You may or may not have seen a unicorn or two in your day, but try not to be in a hurry to overpopulate your stories with them.

GORMENGHAST: Flay vs. Cook
Blood at Midnight Action Scene

Mervyn Peake's *Titus Groan*, first book of the Gormenghast trilogy, contains one of the great action scenes of all time. Set in a huge castle-like ancestral home, these books follow the often bizarre lives of the inhabitants—including Flay, servant to the lord of Gormenghast, who comes into conflict with Swelter, the Cook. In the chapter "Blood at Midnight," their long-simmering feud comes to a boil. Peake describes Flay (armed with a sword) stalking Cook (armed with a cleaver) up a flight of stairs and watching Cook sneak up on where he thinks Flay is sleeping. Cook "kills" Flay only to find it's a fake-Flay placed there by Flay. In a flash of lightning on this dark night, Cook sees Flay and gives chase. Flay leads Cook on purpose to the Hall of Spiders, which feels like a place where he might have an advantage. Indeed, in a dizzying yet clear sequence, Cook's vision is blinded by spiders and, whirling like a top toward Flay, he embeds his cleaver in a wall and cannot get it free. During this same sequence, however, Cook turns the tables at least once, and it is only after further complications that the chapter ends with Flay having stuck Cook full of holes.

The long scene contradicts most rules about conveying action by using ornate language and complex sentences. Why does the chapter work so well despite this?

- Flay has a very specific plan to lure Cook to the Hall of Spiders.
- Visualizations by Flay anticipating Cook's attack create further tension.
- Peake gives us the POV of both Cook and Flay, for additional interest.
- The scene occurs near the novel's end and it functions as part of the climax. Readers want a climax to have weight and substance.
- The animosity between Flay and Cook has been building for a long time.
- Rain and darkness suggest the need for careful, prolonged description.
- The extreme detail acts like a form of slow-motion so the reader focuses on how, not what. This focus emphasizes character motivation.
- The two combatants are evenly matched, with Flay smarter and Cook stronger.
- Neither party is a professional killer, so there is no expectation of a quick resolution. Indeed, a certain inefficiency is expected.
- Flay's and Cook's prior actions have made both characters fascinating to the reader. A quick ending to their animosity would not satisfy.
- The stakes are high, and will reverberate throughout Gormenghast.
- The details of the confrontation are choreographed brilliantly.

The Uses of Interruption
and Contamination

In a sense, you could say that time itself interrupts and contaminates scenes, sometimes by crushing parts of them into a sedimentary layer of summary, and sometimes by making them porous with dramatized memories. But both interruption and contamination have more formal definitions in the context of scenes. They represent opportunities with regard to pacing, complication, and what I would call the intangible elements of fiction.

Interruption refers to, for example, the suicide note found sooner than intended or the unexpected phone call, or the stranger who starts screaming obscenities at your main character as he or she walks home. A sense of scenes playing out at a steady clip, always in a way useful to your overall plan, may actually mean your scenes are too pat, too lacking in the unexpected richness of life. Since the real world often interrupts us, so, too, should it interrupt scenes, robbing you, the writer, of your careful pacing and attention to narrative detail. Look for opportunities to interrupt your own scenes, sometimes even pushing up events meant to occur later in the novel or story. Things do not have to happen one after the other, and perhaps that lunch conversation really needs to be cut short by the urgent text message you originally meant to arrive in the evening.

Contamination can refer to the ways in which time wormholes through a scene, but also to some other *presence* beginning to infiltrate the edges of the scene, at first undetected by the reader because of the subtle nature of the progressions. This is perhaps a cousin of the interruption, in the way a missionary knocking at your front door is related to the spy sneaking in to take photos of your blasphemous religious texts while you're asleep. For example, in Joyce Carol Oates's novella "The Corn Maiden," the mother of a kidnapped child is questioned by the police. At first, the focus is on the mother and her life, as expressed through her answers to the questions. But over the course of the sequence the police questioning more or less imposes itself on her consciousness and contaminates her point of view and thus the scene. This slow saturation allows Oates to use that slight distance from the mother to then surge outward seamlessly to give us a scene that's really about the police investigation. But any unexpected crosshatching or layering that only registers by degrees, like a creeping shadow, can qualify as contamination.

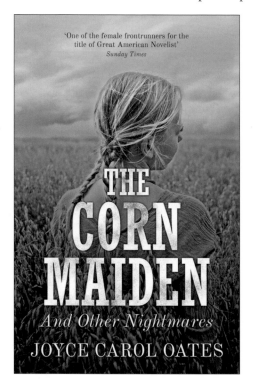

'One of the female frontrunners for the title of Great American Novelist'
Sunday Times

The hardcover jacket of Joyce Carol Oates's *The Corn Maiden & Other Nightmares* (2012). The collection serves as a masterclass of use of point of view and ways to set and frame scenes.

THE ROLE OF TIME

Time figures powerfully if sometimes invisibly in all of this advice about creating scenes. Time in fiction is one of the most liberating, mysterious, and potentially ecstatic powers available to the writer. This expansion and contraction, compression or slow unspooling, is a mighty force working within your story. The supernova of a sun can be contained within a sentence of just three words, while a single line of dialogue can be made to span one hundred years. This, then, is the soul that drives our pacing—an invisible, omnipresent line of force that, drawn back on itself or lunging forward, sometimes simultaneously, forms the visible and invisible hint of both our mortality and our immortality. Writers who understand this and express it in uncanny ways in their fiction can be forgiven much else, because their use of time is often a measure of the uniqueness of their personal view of the world.

A writer who already has mastery in other areas and also understands the uses of time can become iconic. Vladimir Nabokov was such a magician that he could, in the span of one sentence in his novel *Bend Sinister*, begin in the present moment of the scene, only to reach back into the past of the character and then, through some synergy that eludes logic and yet so satisfies the mind in its *rightness,* give us a tactile glimpse of the prehistoric that—without artifice or strain—leads us back again to that trembling current moment teardropping from a branch in the foreground. And something in that sequence reminds us of why we read: to be shown something that, although connected to and a contamination of our humanity, seems larger than ourselves. Often these glimpses, even as they confirm our small and paltry position within this larger something, are somehow comforting. As Thomas Wolfe famously wrote:

> Each of us is all the sums he has not counted: subtract us into nakedness and night again, and you shall see begin in Crete four thousand years ago the love that ended yesterday in Texas. The seed of our destruction will blossom in the desert, the alexin of our cure grows by a mountain rock, and our lives are haunted by a Georgia slattern, because a London cutpurse went unhung. Each moment is the fruit of forty thousand years. The minute-winning days, like flies, buzz home to death, and every moment is a window on all time.

There should be a point to this reverie, but the joy in the uses of time cannot, for me, be separated from the lessons to be learned from examining its use in fiction. With each decision you make about the compression or expansion of time, pocket

The Prague Astronomical Clock, first installed in 1410. This clock tells a complex and intricate story about the uses of time, as it displays not just present-day time but 24-hour time, star time, ancient Czech time, planetary time, the appropriate Zodiac symbol, and many other indicators.

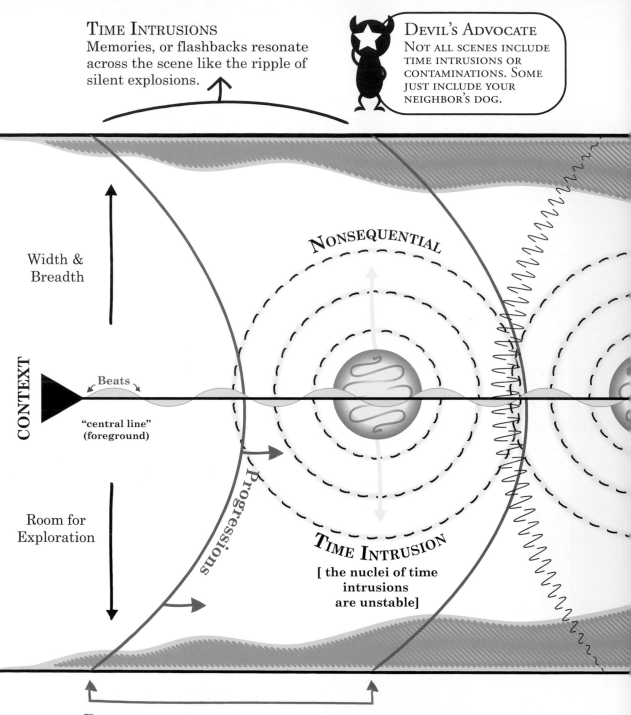

TIME INTRUSIONS
Memories, or flashbacks resonate across the scene like the ripple of silent explosions.

DEVIL'S ADVOCATE
NOT ALL SCENES INCLUDE TIME INTRUSIONS OR CONTAMINATIONS. SOME JUST INCLUDE YOUR NEIGHBOR'S DOG.

Width & Breadth

Room for Exploration

CONTEXT

Beats

"central line" (foreground)

Progressions

NONSEQUENTIAL

TIME INTRUSION

[the nuclei of time intrusions are unstable]

PROGRESSIONS refer to the high-level sequencing for a desired effect, most commonly known to create climax or rising tension in a scene. BEATS are the blood cells of progressions.

THE SCIENCE OF SCENES

INTERRUPTIONS, surging forward from the end, encountering the wave effect of progressions, creating conflict or action. } *life and the world plus other characters do not wait on you ...*

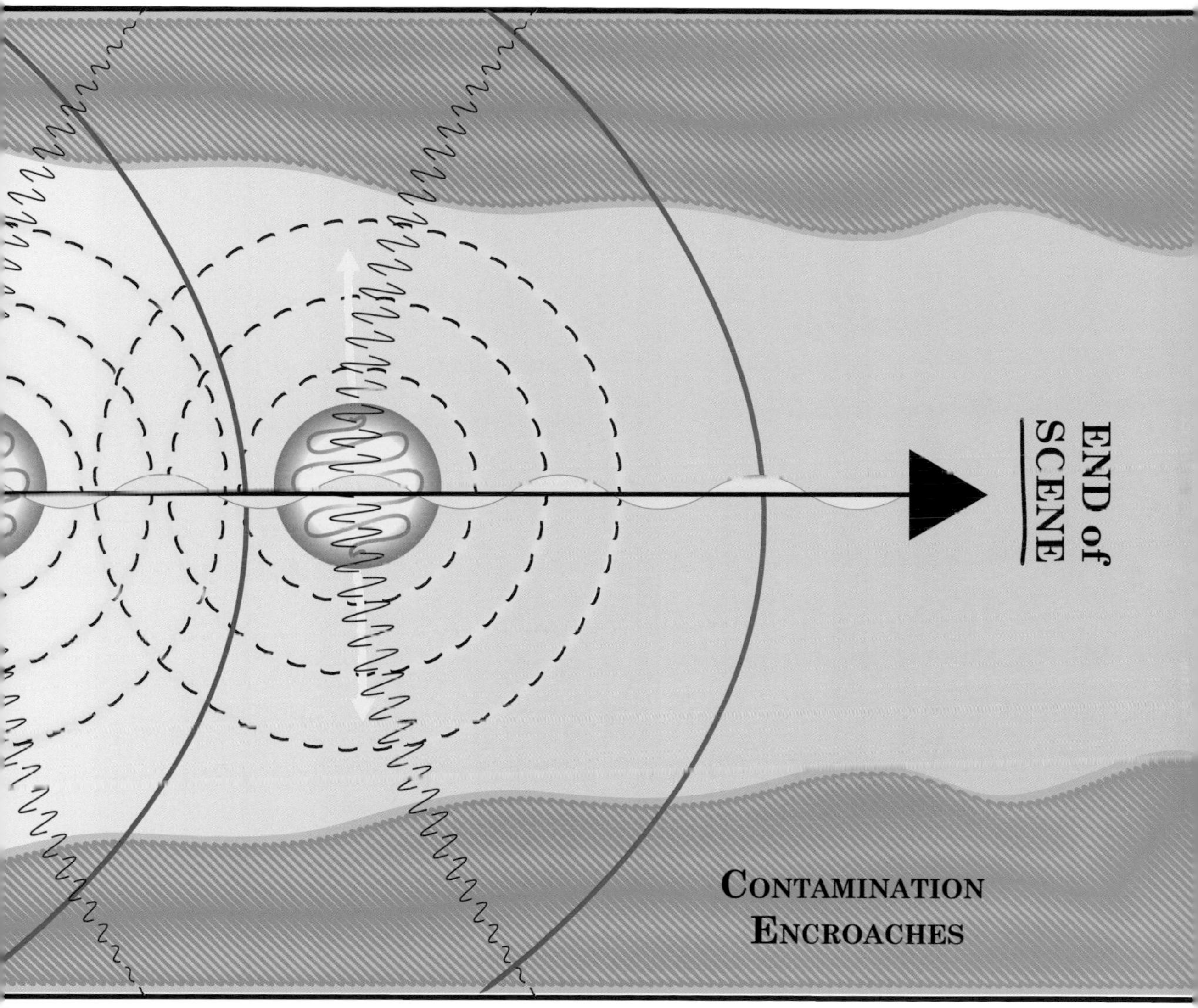

END of
SCENE

CONTAMINATION
ENCROACHES

CONTAMINATIONS suggest a deliberate muddying of the seeming point of the scene, with the accumulated ghosts or detritus of other events or emotions infiltrating the scene. Sometimes a NONSEQUENTIAL TIME INTRUSION will burst and the scene will be entirely enveloped by contamination.

Where contaminations occur in a nexus with time intrusions and interruptions, at a crucial beat in a progression, the writer may have the potential to create a uniquely indelible moment that will live in the reader's imagination forever. But it is in this moment that the writer also faces maximum potential for failure or reader confusion. The numinous lives in the sub-atomic particles of such opportunities.

universes spin off in which your emphasis was different, your focus was different, and your story was thus different. You can simulate the deep dive off a cliff into the sea through learning how to control expressions of time. You can leave a character teetering on the edge of the abyss for so long that you would think your audience would turn away, bored, and yet have them captured there with you. You can eat up the ground with such speed that the character's experience is reduced to a confusion of color and sound and feeling. You can open the door to a family house and be left gasping and naked thirty years before—and fifty pages later. Death can be a tragicomic footnote as in Nabokov's *Lolita*—"(picnic, lightning)"— or a magisterial procession covering an entire novel as in Gabriel Garcia Marquez's *The General in His Labyrinth*.

Pacing is a sometimes mechanical and cold-eyed appraisal of where to cut a scene or extend it—how to extend or lop off crude bits of time. But within those decisions there is this playful ghost of time looping through every scene, its invisible yet tangible presence felt, in sentence and paragraph and page, in ways that are much harder to learn.

As you progress on your own path as a writer, continue to be a time traveler who seeks to master the uses of time along with the more practical and prosaic elements of narrative design.

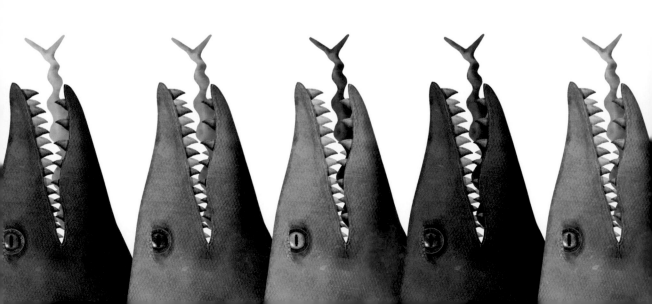

Except in the most experimental instances, stories are about people— or at least feature human beings, aliens, or some organism that you can portray communicating, taking action, living a life. Whether you follow an insurance saleswoman or a king who owns a pet hippo, a talking penguin or an artificial intelligence, you will need to be able to make that person at least plausible, if not believable.

CHAPTER 5: CHARACTERIZATION

FOR MANY WRITERS, all else comes out of characterization: plot, situation, structure, even the reader's perception of setting. However, the ways in which *writers* view characters and characterization can vary greatly. World Fantasy Award winner Jeffrey Ford says "I don't convey things through the characters, they convey things through me. I'm merely a conduit, but they're in charge." But Vladimir Nabokov famously scoffed at the widely repeated idea that characters "leap off the page," especially for the writer. His point? That to the writer this sensation of sudden life can occur with regard to any element of story, and is closely tied to inspiration— that all the components of fiction are equally unreal, words on a page, animated by the writer's imagination.

Brown University Literary Arts Program chair Brian Evenson, an O. Henry Award winner, agrees but also notes that "anything I can say about an actual living person to a friend in life is something I can also say, or that a narrator can say, in a story about a character. I may never have met my second cousin, but my father can tell me stories about him or do things to give me a sense of who he is, and how he thinks about the world. From that I can come to feel like I know him—if I feel that my father is a reliable judge of character and has enough knowledge of my second cousin to convey him. I can tell similar stories about a character and give the reader the similar illusion of 'knowing' someone they have never met," who has never existed except on the page.

Carrie Ann Baade's "Queen Bitch" (2008). What do you think you know about this person from the painting? What don't you know?

This question of the "life" of fictional characters often permeates the writer's own thoughts well after the story has been written. These are people who may be with you for a long time—whose lives may well continue to unspool in your mind long after you have finished writing fiction about them. Vandana Singh, author of the critically acclaimed collection *The Woman Who Thought She Was a Planet*, says that her characters talk to her sometimes, although "most shut up after I've finished the story. But some characters stay on in my head . . . . For a long time, I've been haunted by the character of one story. She's simply there as a presence, a rather comforting one, although I don't know why she's still there." The length of a character's half-life, then, is often not dependent on completion of a story or even what has been expressed on the page. It may even be that this secret storytelling also has a ghostly effect on the reader—that what is not told is still conveyed because of the numinous quality of the imagination.

But do these varying ideas of how writers perceive their characters affect the actual portrayal of character on the page? Not usually—these are just the ideal *constructs*, the ideal entry points, that individual writers create so that they can effectively channel the people they write about. In everything I present about characterization—the core of good fiction—remember that.

TYPES OF CHARACTERIZATION

The extent to which the reader believes that your characters are real while reading, and how long those characters linger (or loiter) afterward, depends on many factors. But we are so used to thinking in terms of some form of three-dimensional, psychologically complete characterization that it's easy to lose sight of the fact that some stories require a different approach, and that this signals not some sort of *lack* but simply different *needs*.

Most novels include examples of full, partial, and flat characterization because secondary characters cannot exist at the same level of detail as main characters.

There are at least **four main approaches** to characterization, with variations that fall somewhere along this spectrum. Few stories are populated by characters written in only one of these modes:

OBSESSIVE IMMERSIVE. Perhaps the only mode truly wedded to a stylistic stance, the *obsessive-immersive* approach includes use of stream of consciousness to get so close to a character's interior that in some sense everything is contained within the character and nothing remains outside. This is not the closeness comparable to a handheld camera on the character's shoulder but the impossible experience of *living inside a*

PROTAG/ANTAG: THE SLIDING SCALE

The protagonist is the hero or main sympathetic character in your fiction. Typically, this is the person with the most to lose or gain: someone that the reader finds interesting to follow. A protagonist can be a proactive instigator or acted upon by outside forces—or struggling with internal conflict.

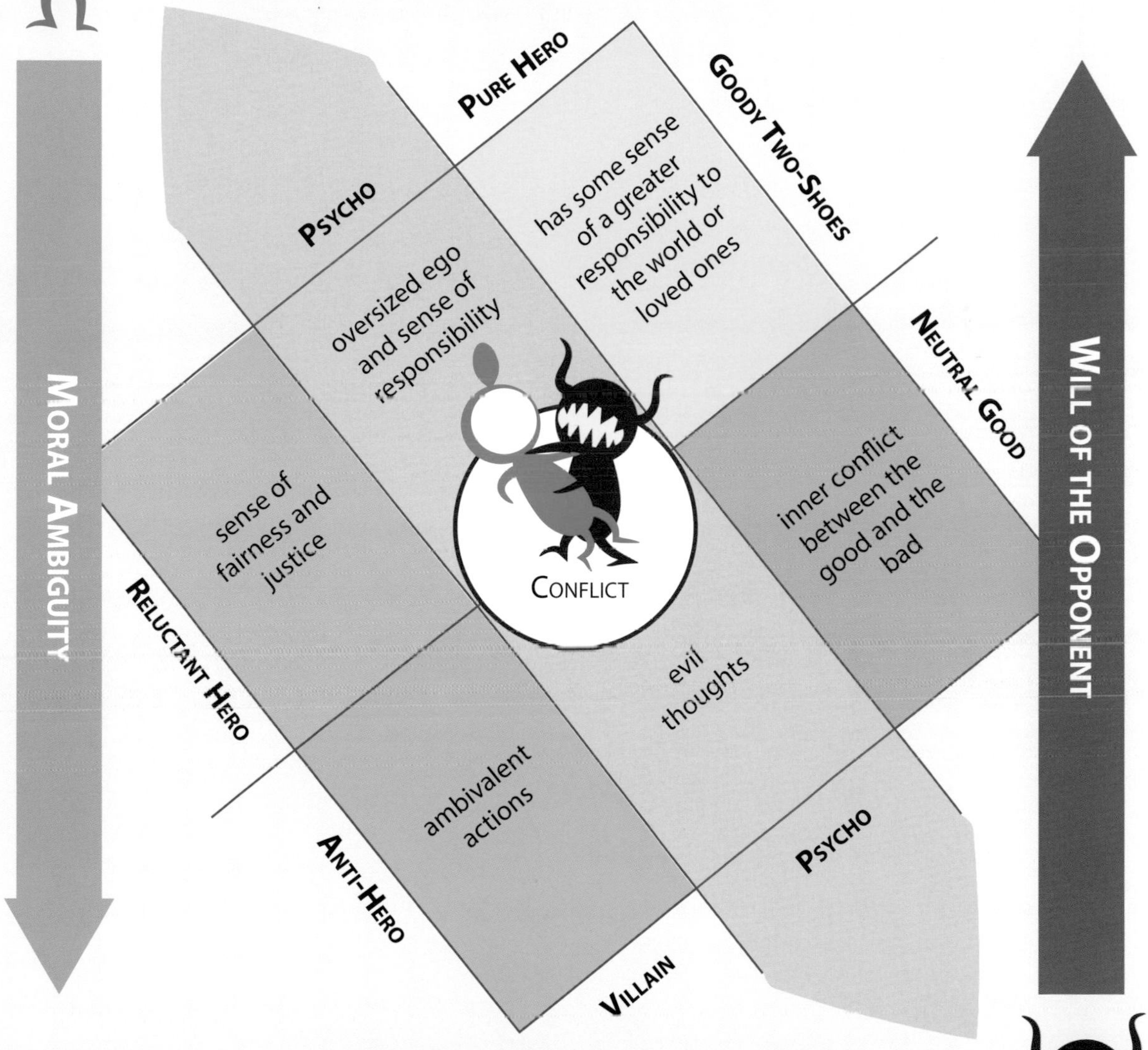

MORAL AMBIGUITY

WILL OF THE OPPONENT

PURE HERO

GOODY TWO-SHOES

PSYCHO

has some sense of a greater responsibility to the world or loved ones

oversized ego and sense of responsibility

NEUTRAL GOOD

sense of fairness and justice

inner conflict between the good and the bad

RELUCTANT HERO

CONFLICT

evil thoughts

ambivalent actions

PSYCHO

ANTI-HERO

VILLAIN

The antagonist opposes the protagonist and, in the most clear-cut cases, may be considered "the villain" of your story. Typically, this is the person who stands in the way of the goals or well-being of the protagonist. Nature or society can also serve in this role. In stories about internal conflict, the antagonist and protagonist may be the same person.

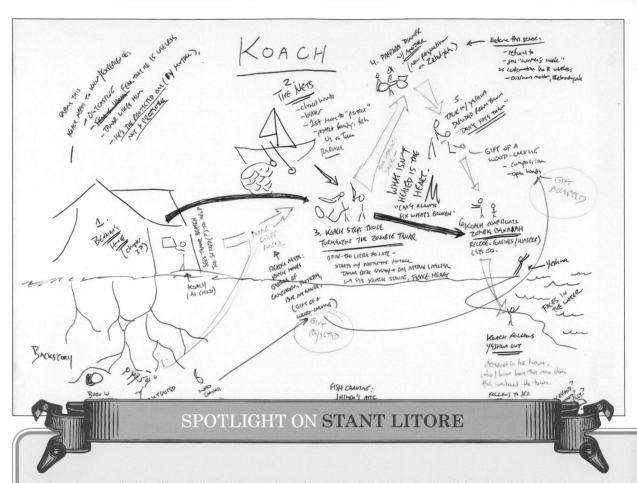

Stant Litore is the bestselling author of the Zombie Bible series, which takes situations and characters from the Bible and posits zombie infestations. The books are very much character-driven and are a unique addition to both historical and horror fiction. The image above shows one way that Litore works plot through character, by mapping the people in his stories, their interactions, and their placement in the landscape of the story. Here are his thoughts on characterization.

"The first thing I do is find out what makes my characters hurt and what makes them happy, find out what they're all doing in this story. I take a very pragmatic approach to backstory: I want to know what moment defined what the character's relationship to their parents, what moment defined their greatest desire, and what moment defined their greatest fear. Those three moments are most of what I need, because those three tell me where the character comes from, what they want, and what holds them back. I write those three scenes. If there's a pivotal relationship in the story that has been going on for some time or that ended prior to the opening of the narrative, I write the couple of scenes that really matter to that relationship: its beginning, its highest point, its first moment of real risk, and where it ended (if applicable).

"Godlike, you as the writer get to set the rules—here are events that have happened in your character's life, here are some obstacles, here is something your character fears, something she desires—but once you have set those parameters, the character executes the story within them, surprising the writer. It's like writing a complex software program, or creating a virtual reality environment, and then running it and seeing what happens. You are creating everything that occurs, yet you are surprised.

"A character can be sympathetic and psychologically nuanced and yet also quite forgettable. Readers need characters they can admire. Even a character—say, a villain—that we dislike, we need to find admirable in some respect. We need to see their moments of strength in meeting some obstacle. Whether we are reading of a soldier carrying his fallen comrade across a field in the midst of battle, or a single mother saying no to her boss so that she can spend the evening with her daughters, or an addict finally picking up the phone and pausing, wrestling with himself before dialing the number to get help—what we are drawn to is that moment of strength, of willpower. The characters we never forget are the characters we admire." ❧

brain or brains. James Joyce's *Ulysses* is an obvious example, but so, too, in a different mode, is Alexander Theroux's *Darconville's Cat*, a sometimes Boschian exploration of misanthropy and misogyny that is simultaneously a phantasmagorical drunken ramble of Golgothian proportions. Thomas Pynchon's *Gravity's Rainbow* also falls into this category by sacrificing natural character context in favor of integrity of character; thus, explanations often occur where they would naturally for *people* but not for *narrative*. Such works may lurk and lurch and create their annihilating effects through the sheer inability to recognize that what they want to achieve is impossible. Practitioners tend to be both the most celebrated and most obscure members of our pantheon of writers.

FULL (sometimes called ROUNDED). *Full* characterization dips into the interiority of the characters, and it often gives the reader a character's thoughts, feelings, personal history, and relationships in a way that conveys a "three-dimensional" sense of a person. But unlike obsessive immersive, full does not seek to erase the world beyond the character. The thoughts of the character do not define everything. Practitioners often fall into the vague category of the "literary mainstream" or "literary fantasy," so defined in part because of this approach to characterization. Margaret Atwood, Philip Roth, Elizabeth Hand, and Toni Morrison are examples of writers who (usually) engage in full characterization.

PARTIAL. Most fiction of any kind—genre or nongenre—uses an approach to characterization that is neither flat nor full but instead *partial*. Character histories, relationships, and opinions may be quite extensive, but true interiority is often more limited than in full, even if we can sympathize or identify with the person as a reader. There are at least two varieties of partial:

- *Idiosyncratic.* The great story writer Kelly Link tends to use partial characterization in many of her stories. The characters aren't flat, as in folktales, but neither do we get a full sense of them; they remain mysterious to some extent yet somehow seem unique.

- *Type driven.* In some kinds of stories featuring partial characterization, unique individuality may be absent and instead *types* are evoked—the plucky airline stewardess, the gruff police detective—to flesh out characterization. As a result, readers may even project onto characters attributes that may not be there because they are adding built-in assumptions about the attributes of certain types. The character will most definitely exert power and influence. However, the writer has more freedom to manipulate the character along a path because fewer character details and thoughts have been given to the reader that would make the reader feel that *this specific person* would not take this action. Usually, type-driven characterization favors external plot over what might be called character-driven narrative. In the best examples, these types transcend their origin, and art is created by the tension between the constraint of the type and the writer's talent.

FLAT. Nonrealistic fiction sometimes uses a form of characterization known as flat (as opposed to full or rounded). Folktales and fairy tales, along with their modern variants, rarely feature rounded characters. **Folktales** are by design highly efficient storytelling engines, packed full of plot. Fleshing out characters would actually be detrimental to the effect of the tale being told (although some writers have played against type by creating fairy tales with partial or full characters). Fairy tales also often deal with archetypes by default and thus exist on a clear symbolic as well as literal level; they are conveying some kind of message or moral or use the vehicle of characters mostly to express some theme or idea. Satirical fiction also comes at characterization from a different stance: that of exaggeration and grotesquery. Take, for example, *Gulliver's Travels* by Jonathan Swift.

All of these approaches are valid, depending on context, and each can achieve interesting artistic effects. Can we really say that obsessive immersive is superior to full or partial, when it is used so rarely? Can we say *full* necessarily works better than *partial* in a hard science fiction novel about an attack on the United States with a new biological weapon? Would partial characterization have been of use to Toni Morrison in writing *Beloved*?

It also helps to understand that the boundaries between these approaches are porous, with variations and cross-pollination that make a mockery of categories. For example, Brian Evenson's brilliant novella *The Brotherhood of Mutilation* provides only brief hints of the main character's thoughts and hardly any character history; it relies almost entirely on the present moment and dialogue to convey character. Yet, we identify with this character due to his perilous situation and gain a deep understanding of him due to the decisions he must make as a result.

Iconic Finnish writer Leena Krohn's nameless narrator in the extraordinary *Tainaron: Mail from Another City* only hints at a past life while chronicling encounters with the titular city's giant talking insects. What we know about Krohn's main character

WEB

Tainaron
EXCERPT

J. J. Grandville illustration from *Gulliver's Travels* (1856).

OPPOSITE
"King and His Hippo" illustrations by Ivica Stevanovic.

The King and His Hippo: Full vs Flat

Although not true in every case, stories featuring flat characterization tend to behave like some ravenous beast feeding a monstrous and insatiable tale-producing stomach. Those details and character interactions that might be drawn out and examined are instead used as fuel for moving on to the next part of the story. By contrast, stories featuring full characterization exist in a space in which the writer clearly feels that deeper exploration of character yields story, too—just in a different way. Take, for example, the case of "The King and His Hippo" . . .

FULL: King Mormeck inherited the hippo from his father, Leppo, when he ascended the throne. Before Leppo's death, Mormeck had been raised by nannies, his mother passing in childbirth. He had seen the old man perhaps five times a year. Mormeck's first memory of Leppo was at court, during a formal event and he had perhaps spent an hour with his father in private during his lifetime. Yet everyone knew that Leppo had long conversations with the hippo, which he had named Leppo the Younger. Mormeck envied the hippo, and hated that he envied the hippo. So when King Mormeck visited the water gardens and first locked eyes with the incredibly ugly beast, he felt many conflicting emotions, chief among them sadness. "What could he have talked to you about, Scourge?" he asked. But Leppo the Younger kept his own counsel.

FLAT: Upon the death of King Leppo, his son Prince Mormeck inherited not just the throne but the royal hippo, which had been quite dear to the old king. But King Mormeck despised the creature and ignored those who said the animal had brought good luck to the kingdom. Soon he forgot the hippo as the empire to the east threatened his borders. At the head of his troops, King Mormeck fought many a skirmish with the Emperor's troops and proved himself worthy of his station. Yet the Infamous Sneed, the court advisor for many years, often spoke in his ear that eventually the Empire would crush their tiny kingdom, that instead they must propose a marriage to the Emperor's daughter. ❧

could be conveyed inside a handful of fortune cookies. However, the observations this person makes about the city's inhabitants—and the things not said—result in a kind of deep characterization. And those things we do know about the character take on added weight because they are our only clues. By the end of *Tainaron*, we feel we know this anonymous, faceless character whose past is mostly opaque to us, and we may also feel that through this character's perspective we have grappled with life's great mysteries.

What category does Evenson and Krohn's approach fall under? What stance do their narratives take? How do we **pin this fictional butterfly** to the killing board? A diagnosis of full, partial, or flat characterization seems somehow inadequate applied to either work.

Another reason to be eclectic in one's approach to character, and generous in thinking about what constitutes good characterization beyond any ridiculously binary idea

of full versus flat, is the fact that literary traditions outside of the United States and United Kingdom can employ vastly different approaches. For example, how would you classify Nigerian writer Amos Tutuola's *The Palm-Wine Drinkard*, one of the finest works of the imagination ever written? In the novel, the narrator encounters forty thousand dead babies that try to beat up him and his wife, before a monster comes along and puts all of them in a bag. After escaping from the monster and also the Deads of dead-town, he encounters a hungry creature that wants to eat them both— and eventually does.

"I said that, rather than leave my wife with him, I would die with him, so I began to fight him, but as he was not a human-being, he swallowed me too and he was still crying "hungry" and going away with us. As I was in his stomach, I commanded my juju which changed the wooden-doll back to my wife, gun, egg, cutlass and loads at once. Then I loaded the gun and fired into his stomach, but he walked for a few yards before he fell down, and I loaded the gun for the second time and shot him again. After that I began to cut his stomach with the cutlass, then we got out from his stomach with our loads, etc. That was how we were freed from the hungry-creature, but I could not describe him fully here, because it was about 4 o'clock A.M. and that time was very dark too. So we left him safely and thanked God for that."

Jeremy Zerfoss's artistic rendering of Amos Tutuola (2012).

TUTUOLA
EXCERPT

Tutuola's imagination often merged with his Yoruba heritage—at the sentence level he is sometimes "translating" Yoruba expressions into English and employing storytelling techniques that come from Yoruba oral traditions. He also created an amazing forward-propelling story engine for characters: one that rescues them from one outrageous situation only to embroil them in an even more outrageous scenario. To stop and reflect, to flesh out character in a normal way, would make no sense at all. Can you imagine how different (and terribly bad) *The Palm-Wine Drinkard* would be rendered if more prosaic three-dimensional characterization had been used? And yet Tutuola's best works are not really folktales, either. They are a hybrid that exists in the spaces between types of story and types of characterization.

WHOM SHOULD YOU WRITE ABOUT?

Characterization, like all else about writing fiction, is a process of exploration and discovery. But there are some basic questions you need to ask to determine if you have chosen the right approach. Asking these sorts of questions is important, whether your character is a clerk in a bookstore in London or a Jell-O–based alien on the planet Blobbo-16 in the Blobbovine galaxy:

- Is the viewpoint character the one with the most to gain or lose?
- Is this the character with the most agency in the narrative, and does agency drive your view of character more than the idea of external constraints on the character?
- Is this the character who most interests you or that you are most passionate about?
- What limitations will you have as a result of using this character?
- If you are using first person, does this character have an interesting way of expressing things?
- Do you want the reader to feel close to this character or more distant?

Cheeky Frawg cover for *Tainaron* (2012). It could be said that the narrator of this novel is merely an observer, and does not have as much to gain or lose as those observed.

Two other basic questions to ask are:

- What does this person need?
- What does this person want?

What a character wants is often far different than what he or she needs. As bestselling author Tobias S. Buckell notes, "Differences between what the characters need and what they want create tension if the character does something to achieve what they want, even if it's not what they need." In extreme situations, the disconnect between what a character wants and what they need is so great that the behavior becomes

Myster Odd in paisley is a different critter than Myster Odd in a business suit.

Giuseppe Arcimboldo's "The Librarian" shows a man made of books. What would such a character look like on the page? How would defining a character by the books they read influence the reader's perception of a story?

Photographing Aleister Crowley, the infamous mystic and occultist, in ceremonial garb reinforces the iconic idea of him as a fringe figure imbued with strange powers. In creating your characters, do you support or undermine their self-made myths?

MYSTER ODD'S CHARACTER CLUB

Every approach to portraying people creates a different impression in the reader's mind.

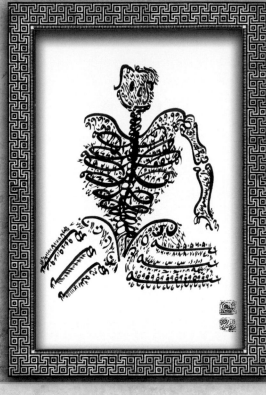

Kristen Alvanson's "Maskh No. 7 (Deathless Spell)" is a skeleton "outlined by movements that shape Arabic and Farsi alphabets and numbers." Close up, the image is revealed as "intricate compositions" of miniature ciphers and alpha-numeric elements. How does this approach compare or contrast with that of Arcimboldo? Is a character depiction of this kind as accurate as a realistic physical description? What is gained or lost?

The title of Carrie Ann Baade's "Explaining Death to a Rabbit" offers intriguing entry points to characterization. The artist writes: "When I was a child, I imagined myself as a rabbit. I collected rabbits and had an eerie obsession with Easter. When I was four, my parents took me to see Watership Down. In the film, the rabbits fight to the death. As you can imagine, this was a traumatic experience."

Henry Söderlund's photograph of Ninni Aalto, a Finnish artist, poses the question "What is staged and what is real?" What is the relationship between the observed and the observer? Is the pufferfish a grace note of humor or something personal to Aalto?

destructive. How far will this person go to get what they want—and how long will they ignore what they need? Too wide of a gap creates crisis, conflict, and thus story.

Explorations of need versus want may well be internal rather than external, or feature an antagonist that isn't another person. "In my own stories, I sometimes feel like the main character is often their own worst enemy," writer Christopher Barzak, author of *One for Sorrow*, points out. "As opposed to having an antagonist outside of themselves in the world. Or the conflict arises from a character whose culture is opposed to their own happiness and freedom; for example, a gay character in a world built for heterosexuals."

Traditionally, too, beginning writers are advised to pick the character with the largest stake in the story and potentially the most ability to take action. As a result, agency has been perhaps overemphasized, even if it remains of real importance in how readers identify or do not identify with characters.

"A peripheral narrator, who mainly serves as a conduit for the reader, can be an effective character," Barzak believes. "So often they're seen as passive, but I think they have a place. In *The Great Gatsby* the resolution happens both outside of the narrator, in the story he's watching play out, as well as within as he makes a final judgment about what he's just watched happen."

Whether your narrator's position in the story makes that person passive or not, the idea of constraint—that, just as in the real world, characters face obstacles and are limited in their ability to act by society, culture, and other factors—also has been used in interesting ways.

To consider whether traditional ideas about agency and constraint make sense for your fiction, ask yourself a few questions:

- *How does the weight of everyday existence affect your character?* Is it a light, almost imperceptible weight that doesn't constrain the character? Or is it a heavier weight that impinges on the character's ability to live, perhaps even to perform basic functions? If you're living in a house in a high-crime area with shootings nearby on a monthly basis, and you have to take the bus to work because you can't afford a car, your environment is pushing back against your hopes and dreams in a very particular way.
- *In what ways does your character create an operational reality that is more or less in line with what one might call "the official story"?* For example, how does it affect point of view and action if a character buys into either one of these two ideas, or into both?
  » The United States guarantees more freedoms for its citizens than any other country in the world, and we must defend those freedoms.
  » All policemen are corrupt, and going to the police should always be a last resort.

Clearly, there are real, concrete elements or facts—dangers and opportunities—that influence a person's operational reality, and this affects their lives. But there is also interpretation of the world, the subjective ways in which a person chooses to analyze, interpret, and internalize, that makes them unique as a character and defines their interaction with their environment.

These issues speak to how environment and perception affect the idea of character agency. Just how much influence does a particular person have within the setting? Agency in fiction has to exist in context to the worldview. Otherwise, agency is not just meaningless or unconvincing, it is often laughable. Unfortunately, agency is often thoughtlessly given to characters who would not have it in reality. Unadulterated, unexamined agency is boring. It can also be potentially deadly in the context of fantastical fiction: Because everything is potentially possible, finding ways to introduce constraint is often an important principle.

Agency is also not a monolithic construct—a character can have lesser or greater agency across a range of possible scenarios. *The high-powered corporate lawyer who, in the context of a family get-together, has no influence due to the presence of a powerful matriarch. The garbageman who is the leader of a community action committee.* Moving past simplistic ideas about character agency is fairly important to creating complex effects.

"Babylon City" (2010) by Ivica Srevanovic's representation of human beings and setting; how heavily does environment affect the character?

OPERATIONAL REALITIES

GETTING TO KNOW YOUR CHARACTER

Beyond the answers to these general questions, you will probably also need to know more specific things about your character, which I've set out in **categories below**. Knowing even some of the answers to the questions posed above will help you understand not just how your character will act or react in certain situations, but help you to make the character more real on the page, regardless of whether you write full or flat characters:

These basic points were fleshed out from a lecture by Canadian writer Karin Lowachee.

Two people stare out of two different windows in two cities in India. How similar are these two people, really? How different are they? What can you tell about them from these photos, and what is hidden from you? (Photographs by Jorge Royan.)

- *Physical appearance.* Extended descriptions of characters have gone out of fashion with many readers, and these details do leave less room for the reader to help create the character in their imagination. But this still remains a potent way to anchor a character, if used well. A description of hairstyle, clothes, and other details also helps to ground a character in a particular time period, society, or social class. You may also experiment with providing no physical descriptions. In my latest novel, I use this technique to force emphasis onto actions and dialogue.

- *Quirks of behavior or thought.* These can be anything from nervous tics or mannerisms to repetition of speech or obsessive thought loops or thought expressed in some other way unique to the individual. Fair warning, though: The average person wastes three years of their life reading generic character mannerisms. Too often writers use "she sighed and crossed her arms" or "he cracked his knuckles" just as placeholders in narrative—a sop to the idea that there must be some description of what the character is doing during a scene. Make sure you know your characters well enough to depict their own specific reactions and mannerisms. (Although *any* herky-jerky collection of tics, smirks, and fidgets, unique or not, can be distracting; sometimes nothing at all is just fine.)

- *Habits.* What a character does on a regular basis helps to define their routine, sometimes at a very specific level. Do they come home every night and make a martini? Or does the character stop at a bar and order a martini there? Making one is a very different habit from going to a bar. Do they always park on the left side of the garage even though there's no car on the right? Do they wake up every morning and put on armor and go fight dragons or go outside and putter around the garden? Even from just the most mundane aspects of daily life, the reader can begin to get a sense of what makes the character happy or satisfied, what helps them relax, or even reveal something deeper. Perhaps there used to be a car parked on the right side of the garage. Perhaps that person is gone now, for any number of reasons.

WRITING CHALLENGE

This image from Shadows *by Charles Henry Bennett (London, 1850s) suggests both the hidden characteristics of a person and, perhaps, a technique: using the attributes of an animal to help in describing your character. Write a paragraph describing someone you know well using only attributes of one particular animal.*

- *Beliefs.* How political is your character? How religious? Are they idealistic about government, or are they cynical? How do they express their beliefs? Are they likely to argue a point of politics or religion with a friend, or are they less confrontational about it? How do their beliefs inform their daily lives? Is there a difference between their beliefs and their actions?

- *Hopes or Dreams.* What a character sees in their future is also important, because it denotes a life beyond the here and now, and it begins to describe what the character wants. Does the character have practical goals, or pipe dreams? Do their hopes revolve around individual aspirations or those of their family?

- *Talents and Abilities.* What a character is able to do and what they excel at provide fertile ground for storytelling and characterization. Is what the character devotes most of their time to in line with their talents? Do the character's hopes and dreams revolve around something for which they have no talent? Are they talented at something they really don't want to do?

- *Insecurities.* We expect characters to be strong on the page, to some degree, but it's their vulnerabilities, their hidden weaknesses, that help to define the limits of their strength and to let the reader know the difficulties in the struggle to be strong. In what areas does the character feel most insecure? How do these insecurities match up with the reality?

- *Secrets and Lies.* What a character keeps hidden reveals a lot about their character. Ask yourself what secrets your character keeps from other people, and why. Many a story has had such a secret at its heart. You should also ask what lies your characters tell, and why. These lies may or may not be related to secrets. Sometimes a person will lie simply to try to make the world consistent with their own view of themselves and their place in it.

What you find out about your character should be placed within a larger context: the continuum of how your character acts in terms of job, relationships, place in society, and other environmental factors. You probably won't use everything you know about a character in your story. You may even decide not to explore your characters in this way unless you are having trouble seeing them clearly. But as Tiptree Award winner Johanna Sinisalo notes, there are good reasons to sketch out your characters at least a little beyond what the reader finds out about them: "I like to know what they eat, how they decorate their homes, their upbringing and childhood, and even what kinds of music they like to listen to, even if I never use this data. This gives me tools to motivate the characters and understand their reactions."

MISTAKES TO AVOID

In my experience, beginning and intermediate writers make some basic mistakes with regard to characterization. These mistakes often pertain to losing perspective because of focusing so hard on the main character and perhaps becoming too "embedded" with the main character and thus too close to your story.

- *Accidentally writing about a sociopath or psychopath.* Because the nature of obsession leads to extremes and because an obsessed character is dramatically interesting, some writers don't realize until too late that they have inadvertently written about a sociopath. I say "inadvertently" because it becomes clear from the context of the story that the writer sees the main character's actions as heroic, even when, if analyzed dispassionately, they are actually the actions of a disturbed individual. Once, a story came to me and my wife about a man who wanted to travel to the moon and spent his entire life focused on that goal to the exclusion of all else. From the writer's comments, it was clear he didn't see the results of his protagonist's actions and single focus. A conclusion written as unabashed sentimental triumph was actually about a monster trampling decent people to achieve his goal.
- *Forgetting to love the evil.* Villains are often the heroes of their own stories, and if you write from their perspective, you should not expect these characters to recognize their actions as evil or morally dubious. Nor should you as the writer editorialize about such a character in most cases. To do so is to destabilize the story you are telling—to be false to viewpoint. This advice does not apply to depictions of certain types of sadists or morally ambiguous, tortured characters who perform evil acts even though they know what they do is wrong.
- *Being too quick to kill—or to revive.* The death of a character should have weight to it. If a story includes the death of a character or characters, the act should be integral to the plot and interaction with other characters. This applies doubly to murder. Conversely, in some fantasy stories writers are too quick to resurrect dead characters through uncanny means. Readers tend to become impatient with any writer who seems cavalier about bestowing either life or death.
- *Ignoring your secondary characters.* Just as your antagonist is a hero in their own mind, so, too, are your secondary characters, who, as in real life, have their

It's also useful to remember to love the evil in your heroes. The impulses towards fear, anger, and jealousy are universal, and make a hero three-dimensional and human. — Nathan Ballingrud

WRITING THE OTHER
BY LAUREN BEUKES

Lauren Beukes is an award-winning novelist who also writes comics, screenplays, TV shows, and occasionally journalism. Her novel Zoo City (2010), *which the* New York Times *described as "an energetic phantasmagorical noir," won the Arthur C. Clarke Award and the Kitschies Red Tentacle. She is also the author of* Moxyland, *a dystopian consumertopia thriller and a nonfiction book,* Maverick: Extraordinary Women From South Africa's Past. *Her current novel,* The Shining Girls, *is about a time-traveling serial killer.*

WRITING THE OTHER is a sensitive topic. It should be. Not least because it's so often been done so very, very badly.

But the truth is that unless you're writing an autobiography, any character you write is going to be The Other.

I am not a serial killer. (Unless my multiple personalities are hiding something from me.) I am also not a '50s housewife, a parking attendant, a car-jacking reality-TV star, a Ugandan e-mail scammer, a Tokyo mecha pilot, or a future-world stubborn-as-heck gay anticorporate activist. And even though my novelist friends Thando Mgqolozana and Zukiswa Wanner like to joke that I'm a black girl trapped in a white girl's skin, I'm not *Zoo City*'s hip, fast-talking, ex-journo, ex-junkie black Joburg girl protagonist, Zinzi.

I don't have a lot of patience for authors who say they'd be too scared to write a character outside their cultural experience. Because we do that all the time. It's called using your imagination.

The other people I don't have a lot of patience for are the ones too lazy to do any research. I heard a radio interview recently with a poet who had written a whole book of verse about the sex workers in Amsterdam's red light district and the incredible empathy she had for these women and how she tried to climb inside their heads to really expose the painful reality of their experiences.

Number of sex workers she interviewed or even tried to engage in a casual chat to get that in-depth insight into the painful reality of their experiences?

Zero.

Sometimes imagination isn't enough on its own. People are people. We love. We hate. We bleed. We itch. We succumb to Maslow's hierarchy of needs, and traffic makes us pissy. But culture and race and sexuality and even language are all lenses that shape our experiences of the world and who we are in it.

The only way to climb into that experience is to research it, through books or blogs or documentaries or journalism or, most important and obvious, through *talking to people*.

I was lucky to have good friends like Lindiwe Nkutha, Nechama Brodie, Verashni Pillay, and Zukiswa Wanner, who were all willing to take me around Johannesburg AND read the manuscript afterward to make sure that I got the cultural details of the people—and the city—right.

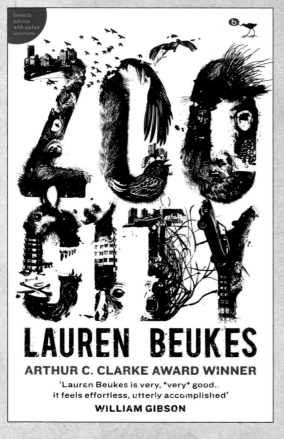

bonsela
edition
with author
interview

b

ZOO CITY

LAUREN BEUKES

ARTHUR C. CLARKE AWARD WINNER

'Lauren Beukes is very, *very* good..
it feels effortless, utterly accomplished'
WILLIAM GIBSON

I read books about Hillbrow, like Kgebetli Moele's *Room 207*, watched documentaries and movies, and turned to Twitter to get expert firsthand info on city details like storm-drain entrances and good places to dump a body (!).

I chatted with music producers and journalists to understand the South African music industry and interviewed refugees like Jamala Safari to get insight into what he'd been through (and referred him to my publisher when he mentioned he'd written a novel about his journey from the Democratic Republic of Congo to Cape Town).

I visited the Central Methodist Church, where 4,000 refugees were sheltering in the worst conditions that were the best possible option for them in that moment; got bounced from the Rand Club; paid for a consultation with a *sangoma* (who diagnosed a dark shadow over my life and recommended I sacrifice a black chicken); and interviewed other traditional healers to make sure

I was on track about the details before I twisted them to my fictional purposes. And I spent a week just walking around Hillbrow and talking to people.

As my official "culture editor," Zukiswa Wanner busted me a couple of times on inaccuracies—almost all of them about inner-city-living details, like Zinzi stopping to buy a single Stuyvesant cigarette from a street vendor. "No ways, dude, I'm sorry, it would be a Remington Gold. That's the cheap generic," or providing the correct slang for the ubiquitous plastic woven rattan suitcases used by refugees: *amashangaan*.

"But is Zinzi black enough?" I asked her, after going through all the notes in Zukiswa's commissioned reader's report, which hadn't addressed the point even once.

She laughed at me. It hadn't occurred to her.

"Oh Zinz is hip and black enough," she said. "Fuck anyone who questions that. What does that even mean? Don't worry about it. I, too, am going to be catching flak. I write purely from the male perspective in *Men of the South*, so you'll have company."

No one (yet) has given me flak for being a white South African writing a black South African. And Zukiswa's *Men of the South* was just short-listed for the Herman Charles Bosman prize. She says she only gets flak from people who assume she's a man and that Zukiswa is a pseudonym.

In the end, I think my question should never have been "Is Zinzi black enough?" It should have been "Is she Zinzi enough?" Because it's not about creating one-trick ponies that reflect some quintessential property of what we think being Other is about. It's about creating complex, deep, rich characters driven by their own motivations and shaped by their experiences.

People are different. There are things we don't get about each other. Usually it's because we haven't asked.

So ask.

And then write. ✎

own goals, emotions, allegiances, and friends. When and where possible, you also should apply some version of the fact-finding set out in this chapter to your secondary characters. The more you know about them, the more they become part of the story, and may well wield influence over your main character in ways you didn't realize—or just react differently than you had expected before you knew them better. For example, in a story by Tamas Dobozy, the main character acquires a visa from a clerk, but when he gets to the border he finds that the clerk vindictively put a piece of blank paper in the envelope. Sometimes if secondary characters make things harder for the main character, you create interesting opportunities for drama or plot.

Are these rogues or heroes, or rogue-heroes? Only the artist Jeremy Zerfoss really knows.

- *"Thick" deployment of character backstory.* As with historical research, exploring the backstory of your characters can create an urgent need to put all of it on the page. But just as with any kind of information, you need to think about how and where you deploy it. Some kinds of stories require a lot of detail up front, and others require doling out the information—a few sentences here or there. Think about how backstory fits the tale you're trying to tell, and what you need, and where. Do not think you have to dump it all on the reader within the first couple of pages. You may be losing some narrative possibilities, too, by not holding back.

- *Disconnect between environment and character point of view.* To some extent, even from within a third-person point of view, you have an obligation not to lard the narrative and the characters with excessive description or description *not truly related to the viewpoint character.* What do I mean by this? I mean that setting is character. Everything your viewpoint character sees or experiences is filtered through that person's perspective. That perspective, which impacts setting, is influenced by heredity/ethnicity, upbringing, education, social and economic standing, and many other factors. One character will notice certain things about their environment, which must be given over to the reader, and *not* notice other things, which should be invisible to the reader or, perhaps, implied by their absence. For example, you might notice the sound of gunfire in any context, but your character might be so used to it that it's as ordinary as the

WRITING CHALLENGE

Imagine your main character is the woman buying lobsters and the man behind the counter is a bit player. Is it clear there can be dramatic potential in knowing what kind of day the man behind the counter is having, and that it could impact your main character's life? Now reverse the situation so the man behind the counter is your main character. How does the customer's demeanor affect your main character's day?

sound of cars on the highway. Failure to account for this is a lost opportunity with regard to characterization.

- *Seeing your characters clearly, without prejudice or stereotyping.* Pulitzer Prize winner Junot Díaz probably put it best when he told me about his own evolution in writing characters: "All the received sexist homophobic patriarchal scripts I internalized certainly didn't help me write good characters and had to be undone or at least confronted before I could begin to write at all. I always say: We boy writers stink at writing women, and it takes a lot of remediation before most of us can write women who approach the human level." All of your characters should be fully human, whatever that means in terms of your approach. Buying in to stereotype and cliché about your characters condemns them to act in ways that are based on false ideas about people in the real world. If you do buy in to stereotype, it should be because you are making some comment about society. For example, a female character objectified by a male character in a story should happen not because you as the writer are oblivious but because your character is clueless—perhaps even as an exploration on your part of "the male gaze."

- *Perpetuating the idea of one story through the characters whose lives you portray.* Although the situation is changing, the dominant story in Western culture still tends to feature middle-class heterosexual white men and women. Putting thought into who you write about and why can help to push back against the idea of there being just one story about a few groups of people. As Díaz says,

Junot Díaz as photographed by Nina Subin; the author's thoughts on the colonization of the body and mind by prejudice are required reading for fiction writers.

"You grow up in the United States long enough as a poor immigrant of color and you learn very quickly that narratives by people of color are not considered universal—but white people stories of course are. You learn that poor people are not as worthy protagonists as non-poor and that immigrant tales are rarely considered as 'American' as, say, a book about non-immigrant Americans. You learn that a book about surviving rape is not considered as 'important' as a book about a sensitive young man surviving one of our imbecilic wars."

CREATING FURTHER DEPTH AND NUANCE

Beyond knowing some of the basics about your characters and thinking about the arc of their progression through the story, certain other considerations may bring additional depth, complexity, and complication. For example, how we receive information about people, which ties in to how we write about them, is reinforced by what Karin Lowachee calls "ways of perception." These ways are best expressed as four questions:

- What do people think of the character? (Let's call her Sarah.)
- What does Sarah think people think about her?
- How does Sarah think about herself?
- What's the actual truth about Sarah? (Is there an actual, objective truth, in your view?)

When I consider these questions, I am reminded of the work of **John le Carré**, a favorite novelist of mine, who often conveys ideas about character perception in his fiction because his spies are seeking insights similar to those sought by a writer. In *The Russia House*, for example, a character says "in certain types of life . . . a player has such grotesque fantasies about another . . . that he winds up by *inventing the enemy he needs*." And in *Smiley's People*, le Carré writes, "Some people transmit . . . Some people—you meet them, and they bring you their whole past as a natural gift. *Some people are intimacy itself.*" (Italics my own.)

John le Carré's novels form an extended master class on a variety of creative-writing topics. Something in the spy-story structure lays bare the mechanisms of his technique just enough for fellow writers to profitably study them, without these mechanisms ever being so apparent that they hinder a reader's enjoyment.

Indeed, depending on what interests you as a writer, there may be an entire tale just in the answers to Lowachee's questions. Joyce Carol Oates's "The Corn Maiden" exemplifies this, in its examination of a teenager's kidnapping by a dysfunctional fellow student and the repercussions. "The Corn Maiden" could be said to be about nothing but the disconnect, contradiction, and conflict between points of view. This becomes explicit in a brilliant scene where Oates interweaves the points of view of the dysfunctional student and the substitute teacher who will be framed for the crime. Oates reveals what the two know about each other and their opinions of each other, side by side with their self-impressions. *"He had a quick engaging ironic laugh. She had a high-pitched nasal-sniggering laugh that surprised her suddenly, like a sneeze."* Because of how it creates proximity, this approach gives the reader a more complete understanding of both characters than if Oates had written two separate scenes. This technique also more perfectly expresses the character's motivations and does more to advance the story.

But there are many other ways to create nuance and depth for your characters. Here are five specific ideas that push beyond the basics:

The effect of environment on characters is covered in Chapter 6.

- Consistent inconsistency
- Action versus thought
- Transfer of energy
- People as symbols
- The secret life of objects

By **consistent inconsistency**, I mean that even the most consistent people . . . really aren't as consistent as you might think. The truth is, we all operate from a kind of floating core of base habits, beliefs, knowledge, and underlying assumptions about the world. This alliance of elements, otherwise known as your mind, fluctuates from day to day depending in part on all kinds of environmental factors—but also because we aren't as logic-based as we'd like to believe. This results in a variety of sometimes contradictory actions and reactions. A man gives money to the Find-a-Penguin-a-Home charity in the morning but kicks a stray penguin on the street at lunch. A woman is polite to her obnoxious neighbor every morning, but on the day she doesn't get her morning coffee she inexplicably kicks over that neighbor's potted plants on the way to her car. Any number of factors beyond our own floating hold on a concentrated consciousness can affect behavior and thought: stress, fatigue, bad news, contrariness. Sometimes a story can simply explore the reasons behind a person's seemingly inexplicable action on a particular day. "There was someone else inside him," says the wife of a spy in le Carré's *A Perfect Spy*. "It wasn't him."

Having a sense of your character's base range of actions, responses, and emotions is important, but so is knowing that the person might not abide by them in every situation. Creating consistent inconsistency can be a powerful way to liberate your character from a preordained path you have set for them—and more interesting for the reader, too.

OPPOSITE
"Transfer of Energy and Emotion" by Ninni Aalto. Actions may have multiple, and far-reaching, consequences.

Action versus thought in some ways mirrors the effects created by Buckell's "need versus want." The fact is, in the real world we may admire the sentiments and ideas

a person expresses, but we tend to assess or judge them by their actions. The more dysfunction between what a character actually does and what they say or think, the less the reader will trust the character. Similarly, if a character is all talk and no action, not only will a reader become suspicious, that reader may also begin to distrust the character. In the crudest example, let's again look at that man who kicked the penguin at lunch. The person who says they love animals but then kicks a penguin is a worse villain in many ways than the one who says "I hate penguins" and then proceeds to kick one. At least the second villain is being **honest** (or not as self-delusional).

Transfer of energy is closely aligned with these other ideas. In the most basic way, positive or negative energy generated by one person tends to affect others. Another crude example: A father shouts at his adopted talking penguin, and the penguin kicks the family cat, who then goes off and needlessly tortures a mouse. Or the woman who compliments the neighborhood mailman, and the mailman comes home in a good mood and suggests unexpectedly to his spouse that they go out to eat.

Transfer of energy can also refer to one event revealing the emotions connected to another event. Some people have trouble confronting their feelings about a traumatic event, especially if there's been no natural opportunity for closure. It may take the next event or encounter similar in structure or emotion to push the issues connected to the prior event out into the open. For example, the man who starts to weep when his wife's father dies—someone he hardly knew—but is really grieving for his grandmother who died the year before. In a wider sense, then, transfer of energy is just one exploration of the emotional lives of your characters.

The concept of *people as symbols or ideas* acknowledges that even a friendship may be more than it seems (and less). For example, the widow who befriends someone who knew her dead husband as a way of holding on to her spouse. Or, the friendship during World War II between two men that begins to have an added element or layer because of political upheaval. A city taken by rebel forces or divided amongst the victors can mean the other person is the only link to a place that no longer exists. People represent more than their selves to other people. A person can be as symbolic as a building or a historical date.

Finally, the *secret life of objects* reverses the idea of people as ideas to consider how objects are the *emissaries* of people—especially in the attachment we have to our possessions. Do not discount the power of objects—or think of things, as opposed to characters, as inert or lifeless in narrative. The general degree to which a character values objects may tell us something important about them, something significant. An object can contain whole worlds, and motivate people to all sorts of actions. *Things* symbolize or epitomize physical wealth or a connection to the past or to a particular person or memory. Because of this, they can bolster and enhance characterization—something even more important, perhaps, in a fantastical setting, where you may need to describe more of the setting anyway. Why not make that description do more than one thing? The photographs someone keeps in their office or on the mantel at home are significant, as are the paintings they choose to hang on the walls.

Sometimes a whole story can result just from these attachments. For example, I recently watched a drama play out when a relative (let's call her Gertrude) gave another relative (let's call her Emily) a family heirloom, an expensive watch, but

The Secret Life of Objects

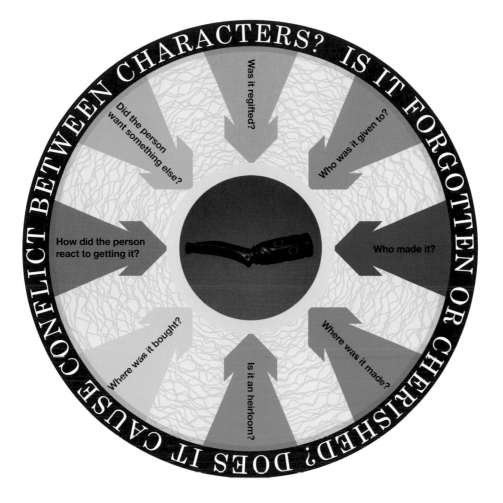

then the giver's husband demanded Gertrude get the watch back because he had originally gifted it to her. This created a lot of tension between Gertrude and Emily and reopened old wounds, old memories. When Emily finally gave Gertrude the watch back, Gertrude felt so guilty that she eventually sent the watch to Emily once more, but then would periodically, halfheartedly, ask for it back. This time Emily refused, creating bad blood with the husband. Out of this situation also came the revelation that Gertrude, an older woman, was experiencing episodes during which her short-term memory was failing her and had forgotten that her husband had given her the watch. Meanwhile, the watch itself requires constant maintenance or it will never work again, and so Emily is constantly reminded of the situation because she has to keep wearing the watch so she can tend to it. And because Emily is not a rich woman and her job takes her to high-crime areas, wearing a very expensive watch makes her nervous . . . . Suddenly, you can see how an event revolving around a single object can have reverberations that spread well beyond the initial situation.

Questions that suggest themselves in contemplating these ideas about creating depth and nuance include:

This cigarette-holder is an heirloom in my family. Inside, through a drilled hole, you can see microfiche showing photographs of a resistance cell from World War I. This object became a vital part of a character's history in one of my novels.

ESSAY ON
HEIRLOOMS

START

Frodo in *Lord of the Rings*, who wins but at great cost.
See also: Henry James's *Turn of the Screw* and J.D. Salinger's *Catcher in the Rye*

The protagonist from *The Palm-Wine Drinkard* by Amos Tutuola, who encounters many strange supernatural obstacles but perseveres.
See also: Neil Gaiman's *American Gods*, and Douglas Adams's *The Hitchhiker's Guide to the Galaxy.*

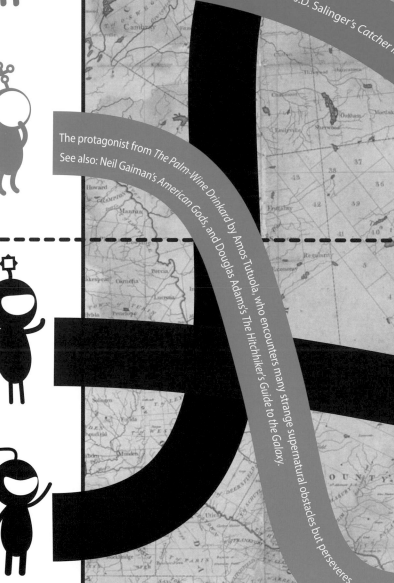

Rock Bottom

What character arcs are
not depicted here?

FINISH

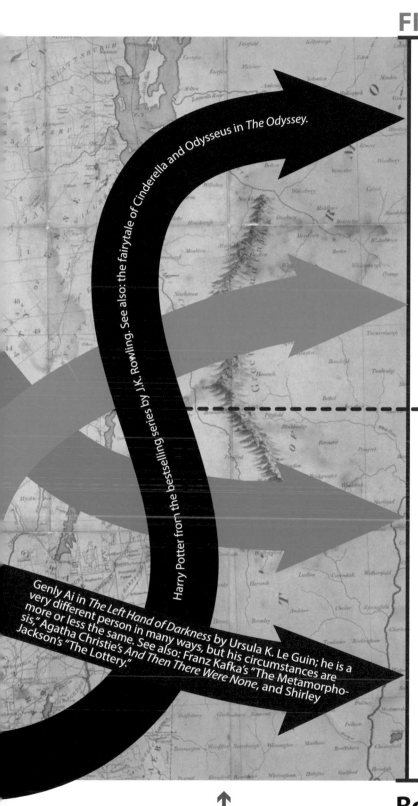

Character starts off in a bad place but winds up winning everything.

Character suffers reversals of fortune but regains previous status.

The Odyssey. the fairytale of Cinderella and Odysseus in *The Odyssey.* See also: the fairytale of Cinderella and Odysseus in *The Odyssey.*

Harry Potter from the bestselling series by J.K. Rowling.

Character may remain somewhat contented, but has lost a measure of happiness or wealth.

Genly Ai in *The Left Hand of Darkness* by Ursula K. Le Guin; he is a very different person in many ways, but his circumstances are more or less the same. See also: Franz Kafka's "The Metamorphosis," Agatha Christie's *And Then There Were None,* and Shirley Jackson's "The Lottery."

Character starts out in a bad place and it only gets worse. (Sometimes this arc isn't about a bad situation but one that remains about the same.)

Rock Bottom?

How different are the character's fortunes at the story's middle compared to the beginning? Could the story you tell end earlier and still form an "arc"?

- How much does another character's view of a given situation differ from the main character's view?
- What kinds of actions do characters take that aren't really about finding a solution to their problems?
- To what extent are characters secretly at odds or in disagreement with other people?
- How much does your character reveal to other people how that character feels about them? How much is held back?
- How does a character use or not use the secrets in their possession?
- How do secrets spread—and to whom? (And why to those particular people?)
- What kinds of information, if known, would give other people power over your character? (How much control would your character then have over their own actions?)
- How quickly, in the right context, can one character's view or opinion of another character change?
- How attached to material possessions is your character, and how does this shape behavior?
- How much does your character want to please others?
- What will your character give up to get something, including approval, from another character?

These are just a few areas in which you can create more nuance and depth for your characters. For certain types of stories, such ideas may in fact be essential. For others, they may simply help you to jump-start characters, scenes, or stories that seem too rote or formulaic.

CHARACTER ARCS

The idea of a character arc refers to the character's journey and also usually has a connection to the plot or *is* the plot. This term can mean something specific and practical or it can mean something mythic and archetypal. In the former instance, I largely mean the position from which your character starts, what happens to them during the story, and where they end up as a result. This may or may not, as the chapter on narrative design should make clear, be the sum total of the story—its point. Charles Dickens wrote at least one, if not several, novels about poor people who either make good or don't make good, for example. In tragedies, a character may start at a high level and be brought low. In more balanced dramas, the character may start lower, and then achieve some kind of permanent success through great struggle and hardship. In comedies, the character may start at a high level, swing very low, and then return to their prior state or some version of it.

These character arcs are not necessarily archetypal, however. An archetypal character journey requires mythic or universal elements that we believe play out again and again across history and may also include moments that we experience on an almost gut or subconscious level as profoundly right. As with theme, writers often access such

Call to Adventure

Freedom to Live

Master of Two Worlds

Refusal of Call

Crossing the
Return Threshold

SEPARATION   RETURN

Rescue from Without

Supernatural Aid

Magic Flight

Crossing the
First Threshold

Refusal of Return

Belly of the Whale
(or, Lost in the Maze)

The Ultimate Boon

Road of Trials

INITIATION

Transcendence

Meeting with the Goddess

Atonement with the Father

Temptation

A Mexican Wrestler Version of
Joseph Campbell's Monomyth?

WHAT MIGHT A Luchadore (Mexican wrestler) version of Joseph Campbell's Hero's Journey look like? First of all, it might eschew the language and symbolism of the standard quest—the journey that resembles the standard heroic fantasy novel—in favor of references to gyms and tournaments. Second, it would reflect the complex role played by the Tecnicos (the good guys) and the Rudos (the bad guys). In the Mexican wrestling world, Tecnicos often become Rudos, and vice versa. Masks are also very important in this tradition.

In such a story, the supernatural aid might come from the ghost of famed wrestler El Santo telling Hector, a humble carpenter, that in another realm the Rudos have thrown off the rule of the Tecnicos. Perhaps Hector must take up his father's legacy to restore the rightful balance—finding the world beyond the real through an odd door in the back of a local gym.

Once there, he must fight his way through a wrestling labyrinth located inside a huge mountain, one of many trials before he meets Rapturous Demise, the Queen of the female wrestlers. Following her wise guidance, the story might open up into a road trip through the unreal world, each step marked by temptations as well as tournaments and wrestling matches—against the Blue Demon, against The Big Death, against Rock Made of Rock. Along the way, Hector, renamed El Topo— "Holy Mountain"—meets his father and, after much conflict, receives the man's blessing, and his wrestler mask. Then would come the final bouts with the Blue Demon and, of course, the main villain, the Man of a Thousand Masks. El Topo, at great cost, might emerge victorious, restoring the rule of the Tecnicos.

El Topo would rule for years in that place before being drawn back to the real world, achieving mastery of both places. Hector/El Topo would live a long life, teaching his children every lesson learned in our world and the next. Sometimes the ghost of El Santo would still visit him, and if he is seen by his grandchildren smiling as he talks to himself, well, they have the grace to grant him some secrets. ⟐

Thanks to Barth Anderson for research.

archetypes by instinct, as part of being embedded in a particular culture or gestalt. Perhaps the most famous of these character arcs is Joseph Campbell's hero's journey, otherwise known as the "monomyth." Many writers swear by this character arc, even though, as writer John Crowley notes, it may be something absorbed without conscious thought.

"It's vital to me," says writer Stephen Graham Jones, author of *Growing Up Dead in Texas*. "It's so deep in my head that I don't even think about it anymore. Without it, I don't know where I'd be, having to figure it all out by trial and error. The way I see it, he mapped it all out for us once and forever, and it's perfect, adaptable, in need of nothing."

The journey Jones's characters typically take "is pretty much Odysseus's ride through Hades. They start out up top, they think they have to go lower, they do, it sucks, and they sometimes make it back to the daylight." For Jones, something about Campbell's approach speaks clearly to his particular interests as a writer—it is personal.

What does the hero's journey consist of? Several key events or moments that map to three phases of the journey: Separation, Initiation, and Return.

- *Separation*. During this initial phase, the hero must receive a call to adventure, initially refuse that call in some way, and then reconsider the quest. Usually, a supernatural element makes itself known to the hero and convinces the hero to accept the quest. The end of the separation phase sees the hero crossing a threshold into the land of adventure: the place where the story mostly takes place. This can be a metaphorical transition, but often it is a literal one, into a fantastical world, for example.
- *Initiation*. During this phase, the hero must first endure a final separation from the world or idea of the world before the adventure began. Then, the hero faces a series of tests. Some tests are physical, some mental. In addition to the tests that naturally occur as a result of the quest, the hero must: "meet the goddess" and thus experience unconditional love; resist various temptations; reconcile with his father, or a father-like figure; experience some sort of death and rebirth, again literal or figurative; and achieve the goal of the journey or quest. At the end of the initiation phase, the hero often refuses to return to the world he knew before he accepted the call to adventure.
- *Return*. During this phase, the hero decides to indeed go back to the world he knew before, but to do so he requires help, sometimes of a magical sort. In successfully returning to his old world, the hero becomes the master of both, achieving a balance between the physical and the spiritual realms. He then is able to lead a peaceful and fulfilling life, while sharing his wisdom with others.

MEXICAN
WRESTLER
MONOMYTH

Although this might seem like a stylized or highly ritualistic approach to storytelling, writers easily disguise the subtext all the time, using this structure for the most realistic and the most surreal of adventures. In this chapter, I've reimagined the hero's journey as the quest of a Mexican wrestler, to show how it can be repurposed across cultures. But I've also included what I consider an "antidote" via Michael Cisco's rendition of what he calls "the zero's relapse."

MICHAEL CISCO PRESENTS: THE ZERO'S RELAPSE

Michael Cisco is the author of novels The Divinity Student, The Tyrant, The San Veneficio Canon, The Traitor, The Narrator, The Great Lover, *and* Celebrant. *His short fiction is collected in* Secret Hours, *and has appeared in* The Thackery T. Lambshead Pocket Guide to Eccentric & Discredited Diseases, Lovecraft Unbound, The Weird, *and elsewhere.*

THE RELAPSE TAKES the form of a series of orbits which are rendered as circles merely for the sake of convenience in representation, as the actual orbits may be entirely shapeless. These orbits do not revolve around a center of gravity, but will always pass through the same point or nodus, which is the World Anus, or point of universal emission, where each orbit, however eccentric or irregular, however distinct in flavor or tenor, is compressed and folded into a single compact mass prior to its rejection. It is the persistent rejective action of the World Anus that drives the series of relaptative orbits.

As each orbit is passed by the World Anus, the acute investigator will observe the secondary expression of an ethereal residue precipitated from the opening on a trajectory tangential to the general oscillative orientation of the relapse. This prolapsed material flees the Aeolian bag of winds while failing to reduce its momentum, although the pressure built up in the World Anus prior to the departure of the afflatal ventura can act as a propellant with respect to the next iteration of the cycle.

PICKING UP SOMEWHERE IN THE MIDDLE

SUDDEN DEATH—The point-of-view figure is either already dead or killed right away, or looks back from death. In any case, the trajectory has no beginning to speak of, but dawns with death.

FORCED TO GO ON—The point-of-view figure is too perverse or stupid to die, and/or qualifies for a job.

STEPPING IN SOMETHING—A proto-person whose background is of little to no importance wanders into a pre-existing set of as yet only partially configured circumstances.

NOT REALLY GETTING IT—The proto-person and the situation begin to shape each other. The proto-person typically doesn't understand this, either thinking that the situation is far more developed than it is, or acting with an inadequate grasp of the extent of his or her ability to influence that situation.

UNABLE TO TELL SYSTEM FROM STORY—Unaccountable events could indicate the operation of an independent supernatural system, or the proto-person is noting the activity of the story itself as it shapes him or her. Since the system or story is no less ignorant and unformed than is the proto-person, it forms him or her as ineptly as he or she forms it.

AMBUSHED BY PLOT—As the proto-person evolves into a protantagonist, or self-opposing tangle, he or she will be attacked by a plot, which endeavors to confine the protantagonist in a character mold, exactly suited to a series of already familiar events that are arranged in the most easily predictable order.

TRANSMOGRIFIC EVASIONS—The protantagonist evades capture by the plot. This is accomplished by means of a series of contortions in behavior and derangements of thinking. The resulting confusion is sufficiently deep to affect the protantagonist, as well, so that,

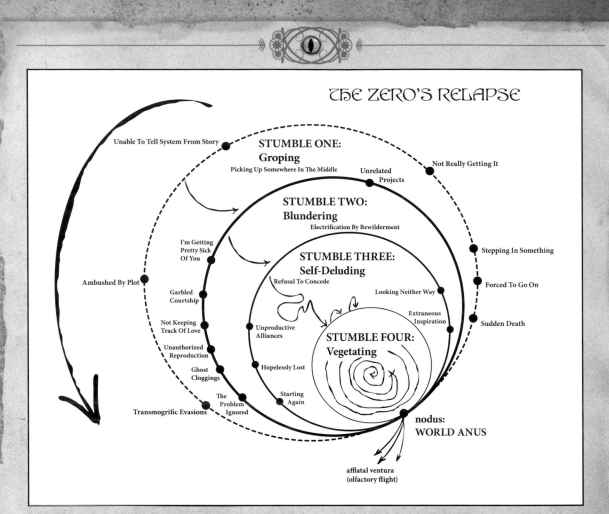

The Zero's Relapse

STUMBLE ONE:
Groping
Picking Up Somewhere In The Middle

Unable To Tell System From Story

Not Really Getting It

Unrelated Projects

STUMBLE TWO:
Blundering
Electrification By Bewilderment

Stepping In Something

I'm Getting Pretty Sick Of You

STUMBLE THREE:
Self-Deluding
Refusal To Concede

Looking Neither Way

Forced To Go On

Ambushed By Plot

Garbled Courtship

Extraneous Inspiration

Sudden Death

Not Keeping Track Of Love

Unproductive Alliances

STUMBLE FOUR:
Vegetating

Unauthorized Reproduction

Ghost Cloggings

Hopelessly Lost

The Problem Ignored

Starting Again

Transmogrific Evasions

nodus:
WORLD ANUS

afflatal ventura
(olfactory flight)

becoming lost, he or she loses the bloodhounds of the plot as well.

ELECTRIFICATION BY BEWILDERMENT

Unrelated Projects—Having escaped the plot, which continues to unfold and to be influenced by the protantagonist negatively by his or her absence, the protantagonist, who has purchased freedom at the cost of multiplying confusions, exuberantly does whatever he or she wants to do instead. This usually involves a vainglorious pursuit that is extremely arduous, highly unusual, dangerous, and expensive.

I'm Getting Pretty Sick of You—The attention of the narrative starts to wander as the protantagonist loses its interest. It will revert to the protantagonist whenever he or she does something especially interesting, but this phase of the cycle often involves the introduction of new, more compelling characters. The narrative appears to become anxious to prove that it can sustain

a well-fashioned traditional-type character, often with a skillfully constructed backstory.

Garbled Courtship—The protantagonist meets another character, making a bad impression. Nevertheless, these meetings are repeated, and an effort is made to establish clearer communications. These efforts consistently result in partial failures, which are usually not noticed, so that both parties are confident they understand each other perfectly. The other character is far more often right about the protantagonist than he or she is about them.

Not Keeping Track of Love—The protantagonist is too busy with the unrelated projects and neglects the other character. Lack of attention causes the other character dissatisfaction and anger, which are also misunderstood and under-recognized by the protantagonist.

Unauthorized Reproduction—The protantagonist

creates other characters, whether they are living beings or technological contrivances or resurrected from the dead, as a consequence of Unrelated Projects. These beings are typically released into the world to wreak havoc at random.

GHOST CLOGGINGS—As the plot continues to unfold incorrectly, malfunctions and structural failures increase. Unable to find outlets in ordinary action, cause-and-effect chains, and scenes, various participants in the plot—characters, objects, settings, even symbols—break halfway back into the protantagonist's circumstances, manifesting as apparitions that interfere with a clear view of events.

THE PROBLEM IGNORED—Since the protantagonist has no idea that he or she has anything to do with the precipitation of these ghostly apparitions, he or she just keeps going as before, ascribing meanings of his or her own to the apparitions and further estranging them from the impacted plot.

REFUSAL TO CONCEDE

EXTRANEOUS INSPIRATION—The protantagonist suddenly believes he understands the true nature of the apparitions and the nature of the story he or she is living. This conception has nothing to do with the nature of the original plot.

LOOKING NEITHER WAY—Having settled on this new conception of the nature of the story, the protantagonist wildly guesses at his or her role in that story, and adopts this role with excessive assurance. This usually involves an additional spate of inventions, the heedless abandoning of his or her former love interest, and a great deal of additional activity.

UNPRODUCTIVE ALLIANCES—At this point, the protantagonist will call on the various ghostly projections and other characters to reassemble in altered juxtapositions in an effort to realize a fantasized destiny.

HOPELESSLY LOST—The plan fails, despite the fact that everything and everyone involved performed their part correctly.

STARTING AGAIN—Armed with the now-proven knowledge that such an approach cannot succeed, the protantagonist self-disintegrates into component elements that collect in an inert mass, steadily sinking into the fundament of existence. ❧

Why would Campbell's hero's journey require antidotes? Well, for one thing we can't all be heroes or write about heroes. So perhaps part of the answer lies in the very title, "The Hero's Journey," and in a writer's suspicion of what has been codified as canon. But there are other reasons, like the gender roles in Campbell's version. An antidote could take the form of depicting a female-specific journey, in which the women encountered by the main (female) character are more diverse and complex in their roles.

Campbell's ideas also derive largely from Western philosophy and religion; their universality may not be as universal as we think. As writer Vandana Singh says, "All distillations of complex phenomena (such as epic stories) that promise to be universal are suspect. Even in physics there are very few truly universal laws. . . . From the Indian epic perspective you might consider the *Ramayana* to be a close fit to the hero's journey, but on the other hand there are various retellings of the *Ramayana*, among them some from the point of view of Sita, the consort of the hero, Ram. Her story doesn't follow the arc. If you consider the *Mahabharata*, you might also find parallels, but the story is so complicated by multiple threads and so populated with characters that there is no true one hero on his lonely quest. Even less of a fit is the *Kathasaritsagara*, with its labyrinthine structure that keeps pulling you into different point-of-view characters."

Whether you tend more toward a practical or archetypal approach, examining the path your characters take may help you to bring out or de-emphasize certain aspects of that journey when you finalize the story. This effort may even solve deficiencies of plot or structure.

If you get stuck, remember what may seem simple: We all have obsessions, and we all have complex emotions. Remember what your characters most desire and how they express that desire. Also remember that no one can, or should, know everything about the characters they create. As the terrifically talented John Crowley says:

"Nadal Baronio" by Óscar Sanmartín (2006). From the book *Leyendario Criaturas de Agua* written by Óscar Sipán and illustrated by Sanmartín.

I really don't know how to create characters. I tend to respond to inner promptings that are like those by which we understand people in dreams. I don't construct them, as some writers do, to do the tasks set for them; nor do I let them go, and follow their adventures. I know where they are going, but not how they'll think about getting there. Those whose hearts I can't (or won't) look into, in the way fiction can, are the most mysterious. I often don't know what they are inside, even if I know their power over characters I can inhabit. Like people in dreams.

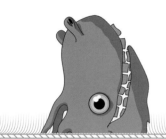

All fiction writers engage in some form of worldbuilding whether they call it that or call it creation of "setting" or "milieu." Even in the most extreme experimental cases, the writer can be said to have taken a position. Plonking down a tree in a desert along with two guys waiting for a third who never arrives still constitutes a setting. A "world" can be as small as a storage closet and as large as an entire universe; indeed, some stories have taken place on the underside of a leaf, within a single droplet of water.

CHAPTER 6: WORLDBUILDING

EVERY SETTING OF every piece of fiction ever written is by definition a product of someone's imagination—and to some extent, therefore, phantasmagorical and, yes, fantastical, because it does not exist in our reality the way it does on the page, no matter how we might try to provide an illusion of a one-to-one ratio. For that matter, your version of, say, Chicago, is vastly different than the talking penguin's version. Indeed, for the reason of *subjective interpretation* alone it is impossible to truly replicate reality.

I make this observation about worldbuilding to point out that even "realistic" fiction is not really all that realistic—any more than fictional dialogue of most sorts is like speech in real life. Instead, realistic fiction favors one particular *stance* or *position* over another and then builds a construct to support the stance. The approaches taken by some writers of nonrealistic fiction just tend to be more noticeable—the irony being that many fantasy writers use realistic techniques to achieve their effects. The location of your stories on the map of fiction does not necessarily determine your stance. For example, Salvador Dalí created extremely surreal, fantastical paintings using intricate, realistic detail at the brushstroke or "sentence" level. The overall effect is nonrealistic but the method is a form of intense devotion to realism. Similarly, in works like his *Books of Blood*, Clive Barker engages in excesses of grotesquerie that only work because they often occur against a backdrop of the mundane.

This idea of "stance" or "position" is important in a wider context because we need to be honest about the term "worldbuilding." Within the closed vessel of a story or novel we may indeed be constructing an ecosystem, each part dependent on and affecting the others. But no matter how complete we might try to be, we cannot truly build a world, as this witty passage from Lewis Carroll's *Sylvie and Bruno Concluded* exemplifies:

> "That's another thing we've learned from *your* Nation," said Mein Herr, "map-making. But we've carried it much further than *you*. What do you consider the *largest* map that would be really useful?"
>
> "About six inches to the mile."
>
> "Only *six inches*!" exclaimed Mein Herr. "We very soon got to six *yards* to the mile. Then we tried a *hundred* yards to the mile. And then came the grandest idea of all! We actually made a map of the country on the scale of *a mile to the mile*."

"Have you used it much?" I enquired.

"It has never been spread out, yet," said Mein Herr: "the farmers objected: they said it would cover the whole country and shut out the sunlight! So we now use the country itself as its own map, and I assure you it does nearly as well. Now let me ask you *another* question. What is the smallest *world* you would care to inhabit?"

You can use Google for about ten minutes and discover a wealth of information about our own world—delving down into details about countries, governments, cities, cultures, history, religions, and ecosystems that convey some idea of Earth's complexity. But consider that even when we are *literally mapping the world*, we make decisions to condense, provide approximations, and in other ways reduce the world to signs, symbols, and approximations.

In fiction, we make the same kinds of decisions about setting as about character; we never include everything, any more than we would be exhaustive about a person's backstory. You are creating a *model* of a world, putting only certain elements of that model into play. Otherwise, you and your reader would get hopelessly lost in the details.

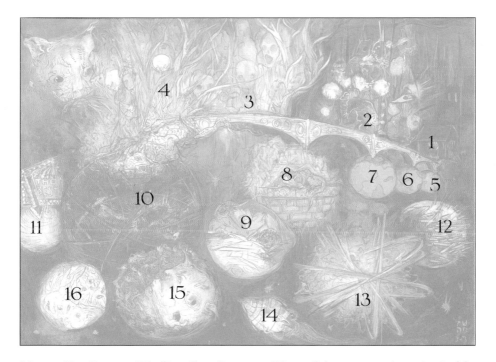

MYRTLE VON DAMITZ III'S "ALL OUR FICTIONAL WORLDS" (see next page) was inspired by "Un Autre Monde" (1844) by J. J. Grandville. The painting catalogues different types of settings, as explained by the artist. 1—*Kafka's Shed*. 2—*The Carnival Masquerade*: the fantastical and the numinous. 3—*The Supernatural Lands Between*. 4—*The Faerie Realms*. 5—*Earth Prime: Our Reality*. 6—*Alternate History Earth: Might-Have-Been* (poles reversed on all maps). 7—*Parallel Earth* (continents different from ours). 8—*Secondary Worlds* (Middle Earth, Narnia, etc.). 9—*Mathematical and Mechanical Worlds* (radically different technology or worlds created from mathematical theory). 10—*Metaphysical Worlds* (Borges, Calvino, infinite libraries and other wonders). 11—*Satirical Worlds* ("Best" meaning "the best of all possible worlds" from *Candide*). 12—*Future Earths* ("human-made, floating barge-pods as large as continents"). 13—*Alien Worlds* (the truly different, beyond our solar system). 14—*Artificial World: Generation Ship*. 15—*Surreal Worlds: Dream Logic*. 16—*Microscopic Worlds* (a paramecium in a petri dish).

WORLDVIEW VERSUS STORYVIEW

So what does a fictional world really need? It depends on how you want your setting to affect the story and characters—and, ultimately, the reader. But regardless of your approach, thinking about the difference between *worldview* and *storyview* may help you in your decisions:

- **Worldview**. What you as the writer know about the world of the story. The worldview establishes a wider context and may contain many more stories than just the one on which you are currently focused.
- **Storyview**. What the characters know and believe about the world.

As Will Hindmarch, a writer and gaming expert, puts it, "Storyview can encompass the point of view of the story's narrator, even if that narrator is not strictly a character in the story. A third-person subjective point of view can be wrong or misinformed about the world at large—it can believe things the writer knows to be incorrect and which may, for example, be revealed as incorrect later on in the story."

Even when the writer merely withholds information about the world, "she is making use of the gap between Worldview and Storyview," according to Hindmarch. "'All the chimera are dead,' a character might say, uncorrected by the third-person narrator, even though the writer knows that in some remote corner of the world . . . a chimera still lives. The difference between Worldview and Storyview is about the information the writer chooses to share—and *when*."

Storyview is impacted not just by the individual characters you choose to write about but also by their larger position within the world. As critically acclaimed writer Ekaterina Sedia notes in these points I've adapted from her lecture on diversity, there are at least three possible vantage points for characters:

- **Native of the Culture**. Unless you are writing about a culture you come from or an approximation of that culture transposed into the fantastical, this is the most difficult vantage point to write from because there's a different cultural default. A common mistake is for the writer to impose their own prejudices and values; in the worst cases this results in an appropriation of another culture on a scale of failure from "seems too simplistic" to "that's offensive." Remember that people who live in a culture do not notice the common things, only deviations from normal order or something unusual. It is also important to know whether the culture the character comes from is dominant or in the minority. For example, if the dominant culture is a violent matriarchy, a member of this culture probably wouldn't comment on how overbearing a woman is, but rather would notice a woman who is

"Atlantis, Beneath the Waves" by Charles Vess (2004). How does the story about a setting change over time? The myth of Atlantis originated in antiquity, with Plato, but was soon discounted and sometimes parodied. Early Christians took the myth seriously and revived it. Since then, it has featured in several mystical traditions, each time with different characteristics.

SEDIA LECTURE

being submissive and weak. And even within minority cultures, there are huge differences in perspective— Zimbabwe not only has various tribal ethnicities and a white minority, but also a significant Chinese minority.

- **Tourist or Visitor.** This position may be easier to write and to relate to, both for the writer and the audience, because of shared cultural values. Many ordinary things for a native will be unusual to the visitor. Depending on the insight of the individual character, they may miss nuances and misinterpret things, which can be useful in creating narrative ambiguity. However, it's generally wise to avoid the kinds of cliché encounters in which the tourist's worldview is perpetuated as unquestioningly superior to that of the people encountered by the tourist. Why? Not only is this approach common but it's boring, and usually false in some way.

- **Conqueror or colonizer.** This position within a worldview provides the greatest potential for conflict and willful misunderstanding. It is also a position all too common in the real world, creating situations that often affect a region for centuries. However, it may be difficult to create reader sympathy for the main character.

Cover art by John Coulthart for *The Epigenesis* (2010), an album by Melechsesh.

All three of these approaches to the worldview, expressed through storyview, can create interesting clashes, contradictions, and insight. The tension between what you know about the world and what the characters know often helps to create narrative.

Beyond where you position your story within a world, you also need to consider your stance on consistency and constraint. According to David Anthony Durham, who has written both the epic fantasy Acacia trilogy and historical fiction, "There's an element of freedom in worldbuilding, but I'd call it a 'responsibility,' as well— to establish the rules of your world and then live by them. I can decide to plop a desert down here and mountain range over there, but then I—and my characters— have to live with the challenges created by that. I don't unmake stuff when it poses problems. Just the opposite. Watching how the characters are bound and challenged by the things I created is what it's all about."

Sometimes, too, the kind of fiction you write may force you to place certain kinds of worldview information within the storyview. Why? Because readers make certain assumptions about the real world that they do not make about fantastical worlds. As a friend said to me once, "Fantasy can be a tougher con job than realism." For example, a character can use a telephone in the real world without the writer needing to provide details about the type of phone and the process of how you make a call.

- Consider for a moment a fantastical city, with two characters in conflict who may have very different experiences of that city. What Myster Odd has revealed is the World Entire, but not the world as these two know it.

- The antagonist is most familiar with the creatures and people in blue. The protagonist is most familiar with those in green. Where green and blue merge, points of common experience surface between the two.

- The antagonist grew up in the under-city beneath the street. The protagonist grew up above. This separates their experiences in another way, even if they each may have designs on the territory of the other. It speaks to what each values and does not value; it might even speak to different cultural backgrounds.

- Yet, it is clear each character has some understanding of the world the other lives in, even if it is not a complete understanding. There is a cross-section of shared perspective.

- The city entire lies before each of them, but do they see it entire? No, they do not.

These characters can affirm or undercut the main characters' view of the world they live in depending on their deeds and words.

But in a fantastical setting clearly deviating in its overall level of technology from Earth Prime, you may have to provide those kinds of details—especially what might be called *the exceptions*, if the setting otherwise adheres to our laws of science and general sense of societal norms.

As you progress along the spectrum of style and approach into the absurdist, surreal, and metaphysical, readers do not expect as much baseline *fact*, even if a story is set in the contemporary United States. At the very least—as in the surrealist fiction of Leonora Carrington or Hunter S. Thompson's nonfiction—the use of metaphor and image would be colonizing and reshaping the reality of the setting. Getting a message to a friend by talking into the maw of a giant squid might seem entirely normal to the reader in that context. Instantaneous galaxy-wide travel that entails being eaten by a giant transdimensional bear and reconstituted on the other side—the messy type of teleportation—might work best with a minimum of explanation or detail.

CHARACTERISTICS OF A WELL-REALIZED SETTING

Regardless of how you approach worldview and storyview, most well-realized settings exhibit a range of particular characteristics. I do not mean to imply that every characteristic below, or even the majority of them, should be present in every scenario. These are options to think about in determining your stance. They range from the basic to the complex:

- The setting exhibits a ***coherent and consistent logic,*** and the various pieces of that world fit together to some extent. Even *Alice in Wonderland*—especially *Alice in Wonderland*—has a kind of perfect if absurd logic to its setting: It adheres to internal rules and doesn't break them. Coherence and clarity should apply to all aspects of the world, whether we are in Bag End, the industrial milieu of Michael Swanwick's *The Iron Dragon's Daughter*, or the more metaphysical locales described by M. John Harrison, Leena Krohn, or Jorge Luis Borges.

- The setting has built-in wider ***cause and effect***. We understand the overall motivations of the institutions and major players because of the historical and societal context. This, perversely, can allow for greater deviation and eccentricity within the characters, because the main thrust of their intent or motivation is clearly defined by the setting. Ursula K. Le Guin's careful study of societies in *The Dispossessed* provides a good example.

- Good and strategic uses of ***specific details*** convince the reader and do not seem jarring or unintentionally contradictory. Further, a dragon in one story should be different from a dragon in another story, and those two should not be confused with the dragon in a third. J. K. Rowling isn't the most descriptive of writers, but she picks the right details. When she shows you a hippogriff flying, you believe

EXTENDED ANALYSIS
OF A SETTING

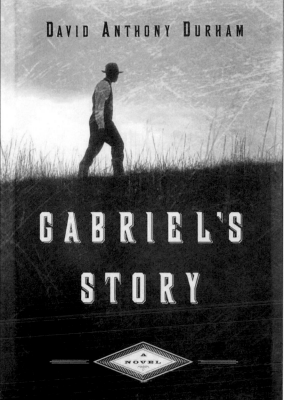

David Anthony Durham is the author of six novels: The Sacred Band, The Other Lands, Acacia, Pride of Carthage, Walk Through Darkness, and Gabriel's Story (New York Times Notable Book, 2002 Legacy Award). His books have been published in the UK and in nine foreign languages.

"For my first novel, I wanted to make readers see, feel, and smell life in a sod house on the Kansas prairie in the 1870s. How could I pull that off, though? I wasn't alive in the 1870s. Nobody I knew was. I'd never lived in a sod house, and I'd only ever driven through Kansas. So where to start? Research, of course. But having a list of materials sod houses were built with and a scattering of black-and-white photos doesn't bring what living in one would be like to life. Reading first-person accounts comes closer. I wanted to provide the intimacy of a first-person account with the large construct of a hopefully compelling narrative.

"So, I put myself —and readers, I hope—on the shoulder of a character like Gabriel, an Easterner newly arrived in the West. We step off the train with him. Ride in the wagon out on to the expanse of grasslands. With him, we climb down from the wagon late that night and see the low, dark mound of a thing he's going to live in. We lie on the cot, listening to insects in the walls and the mice in the roof and the snoring and farting of the other people in the one room. And we look at the old, battered stove that heats the place with dried cow dung. We don't need to know the make and model of the stove because Gabriel doesn't know it either. He sees it, though, and I wanted readers to as well: the shape and look of it, the smell of it, the low light it casts about the room. For me, those details— real ones combined with imagined ones—build the suspension of disbelief." ◆

Take a close look at Aeron Alfrey's flying city (2009). Several questions might occur to you. Is the setting fantastical but realistic—or is it surreal? What kind of cause-and-effect might exist here? What are the creatures lying dead on the ground? Is the city fleeing? Is it in the midst of being destroyed? Construct a reasonable rationale for the setting of this image that might lead to story, even if it uses the logic of dream.

it not because she immerses you in details about hippogriffs, but because she knows that showing how the wing flexes from the torso and how the creature lifts off from the ground will convince the reader. Even a character passing through a marketplace in a fantasy setting may provide an opportunity to position your world in relation to the real world. Thus, writing "the marketplace was full of people and stalls selling clothes and food" might not be your best option.

- The setting ***impacts the characters' lives*** in surprising and interesting ways. The more the **present and past** of a place complicate the lives of characters and make things more difficult, creating obstacles, the more character and setting will seem to exist together rather than apart. Alasdair Gray's *Lanark* would be a vastly different novel if the fantastical life of the titular character were not bound by the constraints of Scottish history and culture, including interference, to put it mildly, by the British.

Good examples include The Jerusalem Quartet by Edward Whittemore and *Mother London* by Michael Moorcock.

- A certain ***depth and width*** is expressed consistently across chapters or stories. Whether you are writing about the real world or an imaginary one, the reader may expect some sense of the setting having dimensions and weight—and that, as a result, actions will have consequences dictated by the particulars of the setting. This sense is sometimes conveyed by what is not on the page. If you write a setting across several stories or novels, the ghosts of what readers *don't see* still

What Everyone Knows by Catherynne M. Valente

Catherynne M. Valente is a New York Times bestselling author of fantasy and science-fiction novels, short stories, and poetry. Her full-length novels include Yume no Hon: The Book of Dreams, The Grass-Cutting Sword, The Orphan's Tales, Palimpsest, *and* The Girl Who Circumnavigated Fairyland in a Ship of Her Own Making.

As a sort of freelance folklorist, I am enormously interested in the stories cultures tell about themselves. In genre fiction, this is called worldbuilding.

Any piece of history or genealogy or backstory that might fill in a fictional world is a story that world tells to itself about itself. It's not necessarily fact. For example, a lot of people love medieval settings *in part* because they got the idea that it was a paradise for strong white men. Women had no power, everyone had the same religion, the West was the prime cultural force in the world, gays were on the Extreme Down Low, and everyone who mattered was a warrior poet. The world was your Ren faire!

This is a story Western post-Renaissance culture tells about itself to itself. It is not fact. Any list of facts about medieval times would have to include Eleanor of Aquitaine, Margery Kempe, Julian of Norwich, Empress Theodora, Anna Comnenus, Joan of Arc, the flowering of Islamic culture, Byzantine culture, China, India, Kievan Rus, and the Great Schism, all of which fly in the face of that picture.

But the reasons for telling a particular story about the medieval world are very revealing and have a lot to do with the Renaissance's Crisis of Needing to Be the Awesomest. They always are. And when I think about my own fictional cultures and worlds, one of the things I consider is who is telling the story of *this* history I am choosing to side with in my narrative, telling it to whom, and why.

There's a shorthand to this. To me, the most interesting question, *whether the answers are true or not*, about a culture is: *What does everyone know?*

For example, in America, everyone "knows" we're the best. Everyone knows childhood is a time of innocence and fun. Everyone knows killing people is bad. Everyone knows the economy will get better. Everyone knows what a real family looks like. Everyone knows motherhood is wonderful. In conservative culture, everyone knows life was better in the fifties. In liberal culture, everyone knows the 1960s were where it was at. Everyone knows what the Dark Ages were like.

A quick way of figuring out whether something falls into the cognitive hole of What Everyone Knows? Ask yourself what statement would get the most outcry within a given (large or small) group. What you cannot say in that group, even if you think it. The things you can say, which would cause only responses of *Agreed!*: That's What Everyone Knows.

The thing about What Everyone Knows is, it's only sometimes factual—I hesitate to say "almost never," but that's probably closer. But it's

true, in the sense that people comport their lives according to their belief in it, teach it to others, and get upset when What Some Other Group Knows comes into conflict with it. Most stories, at their core, involve someone finding out that What Everyone Knows is or is not true, and what they do with that information.

So when writing, it pays to ask yourself What Everyone in This Story Knows. Buggers are the enemy. Winter is coming. The Doctor will save us. There is nothing unusual about our family. Magic is/isn't real. The King/Queen is bad/good. You can/can't fight the Man. They only come out at night.

In fact, when you don't ask this question explicitly, you fall into communicating What You Know as though it's What Everyone Knows.

Women aren't as good as men. There is such a thing as a rightful ruler. Beautiful people are better than ugly people, or vice versa. Technology is always good, or always bad. God is real or God is dead, humanity is especially good or especially crap, people with British or Russian or Arab accents are automatically suspicious, one gender expressing traits of another is gross or funny or punishable, robots will destroy us or robots will save us. And even from this list you can probably tell a little of What I Know, which may or may not jibe with What You Know. We all communicate the stories of our culture—whether that culture is a country, a planet, a family, or a fandom—in most of the things that we say and do. That is why folklore is awesome and necessary for understanding human groups. ❧

can register with the audience. For example, a reader could conceivably enter China Miéville's Bas-Lag fantasy setting at any point in the trilogy and still feel the weight of certain prior events in the reactions and actions of the characters.

- The setting both **mirrors our real world and deviates from it** in interesting ways, with any real influences fully "cooked" and assimilated in the process. By "cooking," I mean that any real-world context has been so recontextualized and rethought that the source material is largely unrecognizable. Once your setting has some built-in complexity, further cooking becomes much easier. There is sufficient existing context to soak up new information or details without the result seeming **derivative**. For example, in my Ambergris novel *Finch*, occupiers of the city demolish existing industrial buildings to build a prison camp; this is a direct transference of the details of Israeli settlements in the West Bank.

Similarly, that dragon should also not be a pale imitation of Smaug from Tolkien's *The Hobbit*, unless such an allusion is your intent.

- The setting *is in some way personal* to you, the writer. Fantasy can become too symbolic or stylized to allow for the creation of a living, breathing story. One way to combat this effect is to focus on what makes setting meaningful to you. A fantasist like Angela Carter, for example, is on record as having avoided stagnation first through integrating into her work the feminist ideals that helped define her sense of self, and by slowly changing from a more stylized approach to worldbuilding to a more realistic one. Another good example is Tamas Dobozy and his collection *Siege 13,* which gains real power from drawing on the autobiographical details of his upbringing as the son of Hungarian immigrants. The world created evokes the events of World War II, but in a deeply personal way.

- The setting has *sufficient mystery and unexplored vistas.* Readers like to know certain facts about a setting, to have an anchor, but to know everything is somehow disappointing. The unknown world provides a sense of adventure and possible discovery. There is also something limiting to you, the writer, in adding too much. Sometimes the writer needs space in a setting to let the imagination work its magic. Sometimes you will regret having filled in too much because your next story or novel set in the same place requires contradicting what you've already set out. More than one heroic fantasy novelist has quietly had a map in an early novel redrawn to accommodate some new inspiration.

- The setting exhibits varying levels of *consistent inconsistency.* Much like the individual people who live there, the real world is layered and complex. In a city like London modern buildings exist next to those from the 1600s, with St. Paul's Cathedral right next to a skyscraper. Similarly, you might in some regions of the world see a farmer using oxen to plow his field while he talks on a cell phone. Places and cultures change over time, and often the past walks side by side with the present. Be careful not to reduce your worldview down to something monolithic that ignores this fact, or you may experience a slow creep toward other generalities (and banalities).

- The setting reflects that *we live in a multicultural world.* Whether you read these words sitting in New York City or Istanbul or Brussels, you encounter people different from you every day. Ethnic, religious, cultural, class, and language diversity exists everywhere, to some extent. You can profitably explore a homogenous culture, but one particular failure of worldbuilding in fantasy

The Casa Batlló, Barcelona, designed by Antoni Gaudí. Real-world places can often be as fantastical or surreal as imaginary ones. Architecture can convey the architect's sense of narrative, suggesting that fantastical tales about setting don't arise from writers alone.

has been an *unthinking* homogeneity that doesn't exist in real life—for example, some watered-down version of a medieval feudal system applied across not just one society but an entire planet. Another good example is an alien society with members who have more or less the same personality and who express at most one or two beliefs. As Sedia notes, "Individuals can be quite different from each other, and can be at odds with dominant cultural values. Try to avoid one of anything: a single religion, a single ethnicity, a single country populated by a single 'race,' etc. Common stereotypes include Holy Simple People, Warlike People, Honor-Obsessed People, Hive Minds, Crazy Arab-Like People, Industrious People, Artsy People, and Amazon Women. Having such stereotypes tends to have a trickle-down effect on other aspects of your worldbuilding; for example, you make up customs that don't make any logical sense for the culture in question."

- Certain objects within the narrative are acting as ***extended, literalized metaphors*** supporting the reality of the setting. These objects function on the surface of story as a physical, real thing, bringing with them the context of the setting's history. But they also bring some resonance from the real world. For example, in my fantasy city of Ambergris fungal bullets are edible when spent, and during times of war starving survivors often dig them out of bodies. The real-world equivalent is the fact that food packets and bombs dropped on Afghanistan by U.S. forces were roughly the same size and color, causing tragic confusions.

SETTING ON METAPHOR

The Role of Maps in Narrative: "The Heroes" by Joe Abercrombie

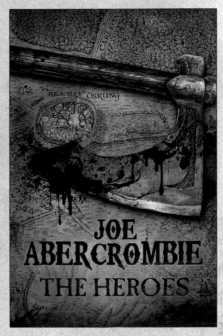

New York Times *bestseller Joe Abercrombie studied psychology at Manchester University and worked as a freelance film editor for a decade. His first book,* The Blade Itself *(2006), was followed by two other books in The First Law trilogy. Several books set in the same world have followed, including* The Heroes *and* Red Country.

The Heroes is unusual for an epic fantasy book, in that it's the story of a single battle, a good ninety percent of it taking place in one valley and in a compressed time period. Landscape is always important, but vitally so in a battle, where wrinkles of terrain are going to have a profound impact on the tactics, the movement, the development of the battle in general, and, as a result, the stories of the characters caught up in it. In a battle, features as innocuous as a hill, a stream, or a ditch can become fearsome weapons or terrifying obstacles. A good map, therefore, was absolutely central to the writing of this book.

The terrain for *The Heroes* developed along with the plotting—the landscape subordinate to what I wanted to do with the armies and the characters, the scenes and scenarios I wanted to cover—but once I knew who my central characters were going to be and had a good idea of how the battle would develop over the course of three days—and the map therefore drawn up—the shape of the ground, the distances, the sight lines, and the physical obstacles started to influence the detail of the way certain scenes would develop. Ground and story twist and flex along with each other during the writing.

I started with a central hill that would dominate the valley—high ground that could change hands several times—and I put some standing stones on top called the Heroes, which tied in nicely with my central theme. I wanted the scale of the battle to steadily build as more units arrived, going from a squad-size skirmish to full engagement, but I also wanted to focus the action so that I could bring my characters together in a few key places for the biggest dramatic payoff (one would hope). So I split the battlefield with a river and gave it three practicable crossings—two bridges and some larger fords overlooked by the central hill.

Conscious that an entire book covering one battle in one unremarkable valley runs the risk of becoming—ahem—monotonous, I was very keen to provide as much variety in the terrain as I possibly could. The goal was to include a rich assortment of settings and types of action to lend the story more texture and interest. So I put in forests and orchards where units could surprise and be surprised, open fields suitable for charges, a town where desperate and confusing urban warfare could happen, inns and villages at key junctions where troops would be staged and the injured nursed, as well as bogs, hedges, and walls. I'd shift or trim the exact shapes and positions according to the way I wanted a scene to develop.

CARLEON →

Bright
Farm

OSRUNG

Lynn

Heron Farm

Rot Gill

Black
Fell

OLLENSAND →

Map for Heroes by Dave Senior.

DS '10

Map sketch by Joe Abercrombie.

One of the key choke points was the Old Bridge, over on the west side of the map, a narrow crossing of the swift-flowing river and the perfect place for a desperate hand-to-hand fight, crushed in and at close quarters. The Union, coming from the south, desperately needs to capture the bridge from the Northmen. Disgraced swordsman Bremer dan Gorst is keen to win glory by involving himself in the fight, and he plays a key role in the midst of the action. Professional coward Prince Calder, on the other side, watches the combat develop from behind the relative safety of Clail's Wall to the north of the bridge. Veteran Curnden Craw is able to see how this engagement fits into the overall development of the battle from a vantage point on top of the Heroes. Positioned beside the overall commander of the Northmen, Craw is frustrated at being unable to take part himself. Other characters, downstream from the bridge, are able to see the corpses from both sides floating past.

The following day, the open fields between the Old Bridge and Clail's Wall become the perfect ground for a vainglorious cavalry charge. Thinking up some way to defeat that charge is the key moment in Prince Calder's development from coward to, if not hero, then not *quite* coward. Terrain creates event, which bears on character.

Maps are something of a staple at the start of epic fantasies, but with *The Heroes* we included four additional maps throughout the book, showing the positions of the opposing armies at the start of each day's fighting—the sort of thing that's perhaps more familiar in military history than in fantasy.

Maps were vitally important to me in making the action feel precise and convincing and the story authentic. Maps also give the reader a quick overview of what is a complicated and potentially confusing situation. But I think the maps in *The Heroes* further add a sense of weight and reality: a sense of the story being an invented history, and one that is concrete and plausible. Generally speaking, I want things to feel *real*. Maps, used carefully, can help you create that sense. ◆◆

- The setting allows for **several different operational realities**, which may clash with one another. An operational reality is often based on a certain idea or ideology and leads to a group or individual having a particular objective. Any time one operational reality does not have enough points of commonality with another, issues arise. For example, any country that has been conquered or reconquered and which contains many ethnicities may display this effect. These rifts between the visions of the past and present automatically create conflict, which often expresses itself through vastly differing stories about the same events. Especially in an urban context, operational realities may also be expressed through physical alterations to a setting. These changes are both literal and figurative—and they often reflect conscious decisions by groups of people that favor their vision of a place over another group's vision; a kind of revision or rewriting of history by which people intend to reclaim the future.

- As a result of this last point, **collective and individual memory** plays an active role. For example, in areas of the world where native tribes have been displaced, the operational reality held on to by those peoples may be largely invisible because, beyond the few markers left in the city that explicitly signify their original claim to the place, their vision exists mostly in their minds. It is kept alive by memory and its expression in ritual and written records, and possibly by the very act of continuing to speak, write, and read in their own languages. Thus, memory can be not just informational or a recollection of events—nor is it just there to add depth to character or to provide inert, character-based exposition. Instead, it is often a very proactive act of defiance or survival.

- Several crucial **miscommunications** and moments of **imperfect comprehension** occur. This point speaks to the way different operational realities are not always compatible because of cultural, religious, or technological differences. For example, in the police station in my novel *Finch*, the new conquerors of the city have supplemented telephones with "memory holes," which are the ends of living pneumatic tubes leading to the underground. The conquerors find this method of communication ordinary, standard, nonthreatening—it is a nonissue. But to the humans who have to use these enhancements, the experience is horrific and alien, causing extreme discomfort. Why are such moments important? When in fiction we match up too perfectly the meeting points between cultures or differing worldviews, we make assumptions that can degrade the quality of our fiction—and we miss opportunities for further complexity. The kind of complexity that organically creates conflict, characterization, and more specificity of detail. Said another way, a seamless landscape and a seamless harmony of ideas intertwined as the backdrop to the events in a novel can be a sign that not enough thought has been put into the elements of the setting/milieu. Surely if there is conflict in the foreground, between characters, then it is possible that elements of the setting may also be in conflict in some way?

The operational reality of oppressed groups is not always kept alive deliberately: it may survive in children's rhymes or a way of cutting cucumbers. These memories exist in the body. They lie in wait, like seeds. — **Sofia Samatar**

"Ice Land" by Sam Van Olffen. A harsh physical environment can affect your story and your characters. It can also normalize what someone else might find extreme.

In considering some of these ideas, it may seem as if research is clearly required. But your ideas and approach may not require it. Rhys Hughes writes fantasy deeply indebted to the Welsh countryside and mythos, interpreted through his own surreal sensibilities, and the results have a wonderful sense of place, without a need for research. If he wasn't Welsh or wrote in a more realistic vein, Hughes might indeed need to look up more than a few things. Conversely, many of my stories are heavily influenced by study of Byzantine, Venetian, Sicilian, British, and Southeast Asian history, along with my own experiences living overseas. Remember, too, that research often reveals that the real world is a very strange place, even if we don't always realize it. Among the facts that have stuck in my mind are a civil war in Byzantium between two rival theater groups and the fact that the Visigoths wove their leaders' cloaks from field mouse pelts.

In addition, the natural emphasis on cities in fantasy and other forms of fiction should not blind you to the fact that ***all settings can be complex.*** Rural and wilderness areas are not simpler places—they may simply exhibit a different kind of richness. "Rural" equals "less sophisticated" is just one of the more unfortunate clichés about setting. As for wilderness, in our world it, too, is shaped by both human hands and the human gaze. Just the data on the transfer of biodiversity caused by Christopher Columbus's trips to the New World proves the truth of this, but so, too, will any chapter in Simon Schama's *Landscape and Memory.* Certainly, this is true in the St. Marks Wildlife Refuge, where I often hike. The trail I take, which inspired my novel *Annihilation*, was once used by early Native Americans, then by the Spanish and other colonizers, and then by Seminole Indians, before becoming part of our modern landscape. That's a lot of history for a pristine wilderness.

Not only can all settings be complex, but the special ability that fantasy and science fiction have to extrapolate shouldn't be squandered on low-concept ideas if you can help

WEB

WILDERNESS
SETTINGS

The hiking trail at the St. Marks National Wildlife Refuge in North Florida. Although this appears to be a "natural" setting, it has a long and complex human history.

it. For example, at a French SF convention, Utopiales, I was on a panel where we discussed the possibility of breaking down a redwood tree's ecosystem into its component parts and using that as a guide for how to build an environmentally friendly city, one that might look from the outside almost exactly like a forest. Something similar should be happening in terms of innovation, where possible. Innovations can be world-spanning or something small that also provides the perfect detail—the key to your setting.

DANGERS AND OPPORTUNITIES

Especially in a fantastical context, your worldbuilding is susceptible to three specific problems, which, ironically enough, can also be strengths in the right context.

- **Setting devours the characters.** If the writer doesn't sufficiently differentiate the characters from the setting, then the setting can devour the characters. The details of the setting can push the characters aside or seem to make the characters and their actions less important. Many real-world **environments** are so harsh or impose such rules or restrictions on people that such a scenario is believable. Or, the point of the story is to explore or report back on a strange place. But in cases where this isn't meant to happen, this situation parallels going to a concert where the sound mix is off and the singer's voice is drowned out by the guitar and drums.

- **Fantastical talismans dominate other details.** This approach puts the focus on some living element of the fantasy setting and elevates it to the level of character,

Frank Herbert's *The Dosadi Experiment* exemplifies this approach, in its story of people trying to survive in a fragile, hostile environment.

OPPOSITE
"A Dream of
Apples" by
Charles Vess (1999).
The Green Man
myth—a face made
of leaves—has
a rich history in
world cultures. The
motif is often used
to mean rebirth,
renaissance, or to
symbolize Nature.
The Green Man
appears in many
fantasy novels.

deemphasizing the rest of the setting. The dragon is described well, and we believe that it might fly, but we're not quite as sure about anything else, including the village the dragon just burned down. The backdrop is all a bit hazy, or a bit too familiar, because, in focusing on the fantastical talisman, the writer has had to fill in the rest hastily. The dragon may be so freighted with all the appropriate and expected tropes of its species that it doesn't really fly in the sense of a creature with enough individuality to make choices for itself, including torching villages, and so the clichéd dragon literally drags down the rest of the story.

Perhaps the writer has some expectation that conjuring up the dragon might be enough, as it takes flight with all of the appropriate dragon tropes both lifting it up and weighing it down. But in extreme cases, the backdrop almost disappears because these talismans usurp the function of setting. For example, China Miéville's *Un Lun Dun* features anthropomorphized trash cans, smog, and other monsters that would normally be used as details of the city setting. Instead, as literalized metaphors that break away from the backdrop, they leave precious little setting in place. As a result, parts of the novel almost seem to be acted out in front of a blank wall.

- ***Detail overwhelms other elements.*** "Worldbuilding" with a capital "W" presents an engorged mass accumulation of detail with enough narrative authority to out-fire-breathe a dragon. This immersive level of detail may be the primary reason why a particular type of reader picks up a novel: They want all of it. But the approach often disguises the fact that the reader is being presented with an encyclopedia of facts rather than being shown the complex ways in which fact is open to interpretation and how point of view has a huge impact on what is visible or invisible in a story. It may also simply reflect a lack of ability on your part to distinguish an important detail from an unimportant detail.

As indicated, each of these approaches can work, as long as they don't represent a failure of control or thought. So much depends on the proper execution of your intent. Leena Krohn's *Tainaron: Mail from Another City* largely defines its setting through descriptions of the giant talking insects that inhabit the titular city, while Tolkien's *The Silmarillion* privileges places over people, and epic fantasist Steve Erickson's Malazan series sometimes uses the encyclopedia approach to worldbuilding.

But as writer and teacher Matthew Cheney notes, "The reader who loves Tom Clancy novels because of their obsessive levels of detail doesn't want Tom Clancy to be a 'better' writer any more than those of us who prefer *Anna Karenina* to *Patriot Games* would have really wanted Tolstoy to cut any of the passages about harvesting. I also hear there are people who like the whaling chapters of *Moby-Dick*. But I'd rather read another hundred pages of Tolstoy on farming—in part because the farming in Tolstoy also builds the character of Levin in my mind, and gives me information about nineteenth-century Russia, which interests me, and that also connects to the overall structure of *Anna Karenina*."

On the Synthesis of Minor but Note-worthy Universes by Charles Yu

Charles Yu is the author of the novel How to Live Safely in a Science Fictional Universe, *as well as the story collections* Third Class Superhero *and* Sorry Please Thank You. *His writing has appeared in* The New York Times Book Review, Slate, *and* Oxford American. *He lives in Santa Monica with his family.*

Step 1: Fabrication

I've only ever made one universe, to date. I hope to make a few more in whatever time I have left, but who knows? There's a lot of luck involved.

The one I did make, called Minor Universe 31, is somewhere between a shoe box and an aquarium, in terms of size. You can go visit it, and the inhabitants there are still in existence, still moving around inside. I don't want to take it apart because, well, I am terrible at anything involving technology. I can barely change the batteries on my remote control without screwing something up. My worst nightmare is that I pop the lid off the back of MU-31 and start pulling wires out to get a better look, and then when I go to put everything back in the box, it doesn't fit anymore . . . and on top of that, I didn't learn anything. I think that's the thing about making a universe: Even if you're the one who built it, you don't necessarily know how it works.

So I don't have a whole lot of useful knowledge in terms of how to build one. Put four walls up. Voilà? Maybe. And then, if you're so inclined, punch out one of the four walls, and leave it open like that.

I can, however, shed some light on how *not* to fabricate a universe. I look around my workshop (which is embarrassingly messy), and what I see are lots of broken prototypes. Partial universes, lots of them, ranging from wire-frame structures, which are nearly complete with texture and even detail, all the way down to mere fragments, little scraps that are not much more than a few toothpicks bound together by some conceptual rubber bands. (If you haven't seen these, they're neat—although working with them can be tricky, since they often snap back in your face, which is quite painful.) These starts all have one thing in common: They're empty shells. Inert. Hollow, brittle, not structurally sound. These are contraptions without any power source. And it goes without saying (although I guess I'm saying it): Even the best-looking chassis is useless without an engine.

I started all of these with the idea of top-down engineering. I could build a universe and then put people in it. I know some people can do this. I can't. Which leads me to…

Step 2: Biochemistry

So now I don't go into that part of the lab much anymore. At least not at the beginning. Okay, maybe I still do. What can I say? Old habits.

But when I am exercising self-control and discipline, I don't go in there. Not until I have something living. The plan: Make something vital, something alive, and then worry about the housing. Grow something, then give it a place to live, not the other way around.

Instead of constructing a shoe-box reality, you can grow one. In a fish tank. Which is what I did

with Minor Universe 31. This is the one time I've ever gotten a novel-size universe working, so I can speak only from my unique experience, but with that disclaimer, here are a few things I learned:

1. Some of the big-box stores (Trauma Depot, Orchard Hardware, and Experiential Supplies) sell gallon jugs (or even big, industrial, five-gallon drums) of homogenized life experience. Don't use that stuff. You have to home brew. Seriously. It's a pain, but you have to do it. It's tempting to go for a premade mix of standardized ingredients, for a couple of reasons: You know people have a taste for it, and, in terms of sheer volume, it's nice not to have to cook up so much of your own raw material. You can just imagine how quick and easy and good it might feel to buy a few gallons, unscrew the caps, and glug the stuff into your universe tank, two bottles at a time, filling it up really fast.

But what goes for pastries goes for universes, too. (Note: I don't know anything about pastries.) What you get out can only be as good as what you put in. So use your own stuff. You'll know it best: its idiosyncrasies, its material properties, the little quirks of how it changes under heat and pressure.

2. While we're on the topic of homogenization, I would like to add: Don't do it. Leave things lumpy. People want to know how the protagonist's father's dress socks looked against his pale white shins. People want to know the titles of the strange and eclectic books lining the walls of his study. People want to know the sounds he made while snoring, how he looked while concentrating, the way his glasses pinched the bridge of his nose, leaving what appeared to be uncomfortable-looking ovals of purple and red discolored skin when he took those glasses off at the end of a long day. Even if those lumps make the mixture less smooth, less pretty, even if you don't quite know what to do with them, even if they don't figure into your chemistry—they don't have a place in the

reaction equations—leave them there. Leave the impurities in there.

3. Volatility is not necessarily a problem. Let stuff explode.

4. Insolubility is not necessarily a problem. Not everything has to mix together well. Sometimes two substances that don't react can still produce some interesting boundary layers.

5. Concentration is key. Reagents, enzymes, catalysts. Not everything goes in at a 1:1 ratio. Some substances should only be introduced in trace quantities. You need just enough to get things going.

6. It's not just chemistry, it's biochemistry. The bio part comes from you. You need primer. Genetic material. DNA to start the polymerase chain reaction. At a minimum, a healthy dose of blood. For good measure, consider wringing out a washcloth full of tears. Preferably tears of sadness, although joy tears will do in a pinch.

And, if you can stomach it, I recommend ripping off a piece of your own flesh and dropping it into the beaker. Smell the vapors, enjoy the fizz. Watch yourself, a piece of your self, disappear in the solvent of your own concoction.

Step 3: Making Sure It's Plugged In

This step is easy to forget. I don't know what this means; I lost track (and control) of this metaphor a couple of pages ago. Basically, the only place you can plug in your universe is into your heart. No, that's not true. Any heart will do. The reader's heart is probably a good idea. Yes, that's it. Plug your universal fish tank, the one with your life material, enzymes, and a piece of your own flesh, take the plug in the back and jam it into someone's heart, and the thing should run. If not, don't despair. Actually, it's okay to despair. As long as you try again. ❧

THE STRANGENESS OF THE WORLD

"Bird-Leaf" by Ivica
Stevanovic, based
on Brian Evenson's
anecdote below.
Sometimes the tricks
the mind plays on a
person contribute to
a more complex view
of the world.

Especially when creating imaginary worlds, it is easy to think strictly in terms of making the unfamiliar familiar. The reader must have an understanding of the setting that allows them to enjoy your story or novel. But in describing your setting, you may want to be careful not to tamper with an essential strangeness or inexplicable quality that we often find in the real world. You control the extent of what you make known and what you keep mysterious. This idea goes beyond the idea of "unexplored vistas."

As Caitlín R. Kiernan wisely notes, "a single mystery is worth innumerable solutions." This idea appeals to many writers; sometimes it's even the point of the writing. Brian Evenson, for example, thinks that his fiction "is partly about the impossibility of knowing anything for certain, about our inability to eliminate doubt from our notion of the world. That's something built into perception in that perception is always about interpretation. What we tend to do is interact less with the world and more with a representation of the world we create in our minds." Within this context, Evenson notes how often "we misperceive things." For example, he remembers once "watching a bird move across a parking lot in what I felt was an exceptionally strange way and wondering if it was injured . . . until I got close enough to realize it was not a bird at all, but a leaf that my mind had decided was a bird and had worked very hard to make a bird, constructing a whole narrative to justify a misperception."

Evenson had a hard time not feeling that "a sort of sleight-of-hand trick had been performed, that there had been a bird out there before and that something, possibly malicious, had substituted a leaf for it."

"I'd like to think that unknowability is the dynamo at the center of it all," Stephen Graham Jones admits. "The improbability engine of whatever that is that generates

OPPOSITE
"Hole" by Ben
Tolman (2009).
The normal rules of
logic and perception
do not apply to
surreal or dreamlike
approaches to
setting.

all the power. I mean, I don't see any other reason to write, other than that you're trying to make the world make sense. . . . But built into that is that the world is fundamentally a mystery. Inexplicable. Even as you try to explain it."

John Crowley also believes it is a "central problem and central opportunity in creating work that has fantasy or the fantastic at its heart":

> The world, this one, *is* inexplicable, and realistic novels can only be great and large-hearted and convincing if that inexplicability is featured: only if—even if there is a fixed and resolved plot—that inexplicability convincingly surrounds the characters and action. That beautiful dialogue at the end of *Ulysses* where Bloom and Stephen are trying to break into Bloom's house, a dialogue that keeps insisting on rational answers to practical questions but in fact stands for the wondrous inexhaustibility of the world.

Further discussion of this topic can be found in Daniel Ableev's unpublished interview with Ligotti. All Ligotti quotes here are from Ableev's interview.

For the great weird writer Thomas Ligotti, meanwhile, "Strangeness is a perspective. It's not immanent in anything. If you read a book in which everything is at odds with the commonplace world you believe you live in, the book has to refer over and over to the things in that commonplace world or everything in the book will begin to seem completely familiar. This is a truism for fantastic writers. First they have to establish the commonplace rules of their stories, and then they can introduce violations of that invented commonplace world." But Ligotti contends that "most fantastic and supernatural horror stories **aren't written to create a sense of the strange**. They're written to introduce a threat to the characters in the story, which soon becomes much like any other threat—a wild animal or a murderer, for instance." It helps, then, "to sustain a sense of strangeness if the story sticks close to the banal, or what we think is the banal."

One great example of strangeness in worldbuilding occurs in Ligotti's story "The Clown Puppet." The story's narrator works the night shift at a pharmacy and has "a

certain perspective on the world that leads him to call everything nonsensical. That perspective lends a bit of strangeness to the story." Ligotti's thoughts about "The Clown Puppet" emphasize that strangeness can be built in fiction through small, mundane details: "The narrator calls the pharmacy where he's working a 'medicine shop,' which is not how such an establishment is usually referred to. Yet this nomenclature is not so unconventional that one can question it. There are no people walking about outside who might serve as customers. There's nothing wholly unusual about that, but it makes the narrator's presence behind the counter of the medicine shop, while the owner of the shop is snoring in his apartment above the shop, seem somewhat questionable. What time is it? Is the narrator working in the middle of the night?"

But Ligotti also contends that it's not just what's included in a story that makes the worldview strange—it's also what's missing. "In 'The Clown Puppet' there are almost no touchstones in the narrative to what the reader knows as 'real life.' So a sort of baseline of strangeness has been established that sets the stage for the title creature of the story, which exists at a higher level of strangeness and thereby takes the story into another realm. But while the narrator does not welcome the visits he receives from the clown puppet, he resents them more than he actually fears them, which is a strange perspective to have and one that makes the meaning and status of the clown puppet entirely mysterious."

As Crowley acknowledges, though, fiction tends to strive toward at least explication of a problem or situation—a quest, a crime, a treasure, a mystery. "So how then can I as a writer draw that inexplicability into my fantastic fiction? In part it's through allegory: the soluble mystery stands for the insoluble. For me, too, it tends to [occur through] characters who feel themselves to be in a world that they can't grasp in its essence, even if readers think *they* can."

ඏ ඏ ඏ

The places and spaces in which story occurs are not inert or merely backdrops to action—they have energy, motion, and create certain effects depending on your approach. Thus, worldbuilding is not just about creating colorful stages for your characters—worldbuilding can be part of what is taking place. In thinking about worldbuilding as an entry point into story, remember these ideas:

OPPOSITE
"R'lyeh" (1999) by John Coulthart, an attempt to present H. P. Lovecraft's world in a photo-realist manner.

OVERLEAF
The Dreamlands of H. P. Lovecraft mapped by Jason Thompson (2011). Thompson says of the piece, ". . . it includes all the place-names mentioned in 'The Dream-Quest of Unknown Kadath,' 'The Doom That Came to Sarnath,' 'The White Ship,' 'The Cats of Ulthar,' 'The Other Gods,' and all of Lovecraft's even marginally dream-based stories and poetry. In addition, it shows regions from the work of Gary Myers, Lord Dunsany, and a few other sources that feel like they would be at home in the collective 'realm of wisdom that many know.'"

- Anchoring your fiction correctly in place, situation, and history enhances the emotional resonance.
- Landscape not invested with emotion or point of view is lifeless.
- The real world and personal experience feed into imaginary settings and are a vital part of worldbuilding.
- Approaches to setting and character should be multidirectional: organic and three-dimensional, with layers and depth.
- Throwaway settings are like throwaway characters: a missed opportunity.

"Mormeck Mountain" by Mo Ali (2011). Where does character end and setting begin? The distinction isn't always so clear-cut. This illustration for my novel-in-progress, *The Journals of Doctor Mormeck*, depicts the main character, Mormeck. He just happens to be a living mountain with a laboratory facility run by angels located on his "head."

One of the main differences between writers who succeed and those who don't is the ability to revise—to be able to step away from the manuscript and see it clearly enough, with fresh eyes, to understand both its strengths and its weaknesses. The more effective you are at expressing your technical imagination through revision, the greater chance you will have of connecting with readers in the way you intended. More importantly, you owe it to the talking ~~pig~~ penguin, the woman with the ~~steamroller~~ gun, and ~~the potato elf~~ the thing hiding behind the potted plant to revise properly.

CHAPTER 7: REVISION

AS SHOULD BE clear by now, the entire writing process is infused with the idea of revision. Even my initial process of scribbling down notes—bits of dialogue, fragments of description—is fraught with revision. First, there are the ideas that I never write down. Then, when I look at my assembled notes before I sit down to write a first draft, I discard or change some of them. This continues as I progress through the rough draft—I'm already changing and discarding what's on the page, and new ideas come along that affect the narrative.

Some of this may be invisible to the conscious mind, because the main propulsive forward motion is the writing of the rough draft. But acts of revision *accrete* around this state. When you emerge from inspiration and cease writing for the day, your mind is still mulling this or that aspect of the story and altering events, characters, and descriptions before you sit down to write the next day. Depending on your writing process, you may even go back and revise the previous day's work before continuing forward.

So, in a sense, after the initial spark for the story or novel, *every* act exists simultaneously in a liminal, interconnected state of writing/revision, revision/writing. The very act of translating the perfect, shining vision in your head into the imperfect vessels of words could be considered the first, most radical revision: ever after you are engaged in a struggle to make those words suffice.

Sometimes that struggle is blissful, sometimes frustrating—and it may require sacrificing a lot of time and many pages. For example, British writer Ian R. MacLeod revises by "trying out beginnings and building on the foundations until they start to feel wobbly, then maybe do something else and come back and take it apart and throw lots away and build a bit more."

Jeffrey Ford doesn't even think in terms of drafts: "I have more of the sense of being like a sculptor, working on a block of stone and revealing more and more of what already exists within the stone. I have always had the feeling that the stories already exist, as if in some alternate universe, and the act of writing is an act of discovering them. . . . For me, it's all one thing, the writing and revising."

John Crowley, on the other hand, writes not rough drafts so much as "draft pages, draft notes, draft scraps, but for the most part I can only write when I know pretty well—very well, actually, most of the time—where I'm going and how I might get there. The idea of writing an entire novel, or even a large part of one, only to basically discard it is dreadful to me."

Everyone's process is different, but when I use the words "revision" or "rewriting" in this chapter, I mean what happens **after you complete** what you consider a rough draft. If you're the kind of writer, like Caitlín R. Kiernan, who perfects each paragraph and each scene before moving on, you can still use the advice in this chapter, but you may apply it in a different way.

> For example, I never wrote down my story idea about a man who tries to dynamite armadillos in his backyard only to find out they are aliens.

WHAT IS REVISION?

In theory, the process of revision is very simple. As David Madden writes in his brilliant book *Revising Fiction,* revision means asking questions about each chapter, each scene, each paragraph, each sentence: "What effect did I want to have on the reader? Have I achieved it? If not, how may I revise to achieve my purpose?" This journey through your draft isn't just an analytical process:

> To paraphrase Socrates, the unimagined, unexpressed life is not worth living. It is a mistake to separate imagination from more intellectual functions. With strict logic, ask yourself: If this happens, what might happen as a consequence? As you ask that logical question, your imagination is stimulated to explore your raw material to produce all kinds of images.

Exactly because revision combines analysis and redeploying your creativity, most things you get wrong in your first draft can be fixed in revision, especially as you gain experience. Usually, however, it is easier if you have *too much* in your first draft rather than *too little*; *mangled* can be altered more readily than *the invisible*. Also, Madden, like me, assumes that the *foundational ideas* of your fiction aren't so incurably clichéd that no act of revision can ever revive your particular **story lizard**.

According to Madden, a beginning writer goes through the following stages with regard to revision:

> If your story is about two people who meet in a bar and—surprise!— one turns out to be a werewolf and the other a vampire, your story is dead on arrival.

• He makes a mistake but fails to see it.

- He makes a mistake, he sees it, but doesn't know how to fix it—or reimagine it. He hasn't learned enough about the techniques of fiction.
- He makes a mistake, he sees it, he has learned how to fix it, because he has learned some of the techniques of fiction, but he just can't do it.
- He makes a mistake, he sees it, he knows how to fix it, he fixes it—and by now he has learned that solving technical problems in the creative process is just as exciting as writing the first draft. (Then book reviewers come along and tell him he only thinks he's fixed the problems.)

Over time, your creative imagination and your technical imagination will begin to work in tandem to create great fiction. Perhaps the most important part of that process is the idea of the act of revision becoming *exciting* to you. The more positive you can be about the revision process, the more likely you are to actually dig into the guts of your fiction in a meaningful way. Simple self-loathing and disgust at the blindingly pathetic horribleness of your own words may not be enough. You have to be willing to sacrifice pages of rough draft and to perhaps radically change or add to what's left. Junot Díaz, for example, thinks of each "version of a chapter one draft as like a compass which will lead me to the next better version, the next compass. So I don't mind all the throwing away if it gets me to where I want to go in the end."

My well-thumbed copy of David Madden's *Revising Fiction* (1988), which I have reread at least a dozen times.

Most of *Revising Fiction* consists of insightful questions with which to interrogate your first draft, along with solutions that include examples of how famous writers fixed their own problems. Chosen from throughout the book, here are just a few of those questions:

- Do passages that reflect your own biases or judgments *intrude*?
- Has your style evolved out of the *point of view* for this story?
- Are any *minor characters underdeveloped*?
- Should the *sequence* of scenes be restructured?
- Have you used too many stock *dialogue and thought tags*?
- Do you open the story with an overlong description of *the setting*?
- Is your use of *flashbacks* crude?
- Have you failed to imagine ways to create *tension*?

Madden's book is one of those rare essential reads for a writer, and it's one that will stay useful as long as you write. As you progress as a writer, *Revising Fiction* evolves with you and never becomes obsolete. I've referred to it for the past twenty-five years.

DRAFTING STRATEGIES

FROM YOUR ENVIRONMENT to timing issues, many factors can help influence the writing of your rough draft—and whether you wind up with a completed manuscript. Here are some questions to ask that may help your process, so that you can get to the point of revising your story or novel. Keep in mind, though, that even experienced writers with long careers often only finish half of the stories and novels they start. The main point is to make sure your process isn't getting in the way of success.

Have you started to write too soon? In other words, have you thought through enough of the implications of character or plot beforehand to be able to express narrative on the page? If not, you may be unable to finish the rough draft. I need to have a clear idea of the main character, some kind of initial situation, and some impression of a possible ending before I start to write. Otherwise, I never finish. What do you need to know before you start?

Can you leave gaps and still get to the end? Sometimes, given the obsessive nature of writers, you will get hung up on a particular sentence, paragraph, or scene. There may be a good reason for stopping and reevaluating what you've written to that point; something may need to be resolved earlier in the story before you continue. However, many times a writer will fixate on a single, tactical problem that doesn't affect the rest of the narrative. In such cases, you can leave a placeholder and move on without harm.

Do you have to write the story from the beginning? You may suffer from the mistaken belief that because a story has a beginning, which is what the reader encounters first (unless there is a squashed bug on the title page), you must start writing at the beginning. But sometimes it is better to start with the part of the story that most interests you, and let the story open up from there. You may even find that this nonlinear focus changes your understanding of the story.

Do you know the kind of story you want to write? "Kind of story" can mean anything from wanting to explore character to wanting to write about a particular situation. It may not mean knowing up front that you want to write about something as abstract as love or death . . . but it might. It could even be a thought in your mind that's entirely frivolous, like "I want a dragon in this story!" Having even a vague idea about the focus of the story or what you want to express in general terms may help carry you forward.

Are you doing all you can to provide your imagination with the appropriate surroundings? A noisy, cluttered, or otherwise distracting environment can make it difficult to concentrate on your work and create an impediment to completing drafts. However, a pristine, silent environment can also sidetrack some people. If you have the option to change your writing environment, you may want to experiment with what works best. Personally, I'd prefer to write in bars, but there is no bar in the world where, if you're scribbling away madly in some far corner, an inebriated person won't come up and ask you what you're doing.

Have you created the right outline? Some writers don't like to outline, but this may stem from a misunderstanding. The outline commercial publishers may require from a writer delineates major characters and plot-points, with some extended outlines describing what will happen chapter by chapter. Its primary purpose is to convince an editor to buy a book either not yet written or only partially written—and to reassure the editor about its contents. Indeed, because this approach is perceived as the industry-standard, many writers equate "outline" with this one template—an unwelcome constraint that snuffs out inspiration. But a smart, personalized approach to outlining can provide structure while also allowing for significant improvisation. For my novel *Finch*, set over

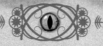

the course of one week, my outline was divided up by day. Within each day, I had a list of expected scenes and who would probably be in those scenes. With this structure in place, I could relax into the actual writing of the scenes. Thus, the process of discovery for me during writing was finding out what the characters would say and do. It was the equivalent of a director of a movie bringing all of the actors into a room to shoot a scene, giving them their motivation and history, and then allowing the actors to create their own dialogue and reactions. For novels on a wider canvas, you can expand this "matrix" to include reminders of the relevant history of a place or even the memories of a character that may come into play during a set of scenes.

You can also map narrative directly through character and let focus and structure evolve from that. This kind of outline shows the accumulated backstory and backstory of each character and how this impacts their relationships. It is probably most useful for novels and stories where the focus is more about the inner lives of individuals than narrative that lets in a wider context. As Stant Litore, creator of The Zombie Bible series, says, outlines are "tools, not a table of contents," and approaches them in an interesting way: He doesn't outline until he is "a third to half" of the way through his rough draft. That's the point at which he has "written enough to start learning who my characters actually are, what crises they have faced and will face, what holds them back, and what drives them forward."

As I wrote *Finch*, my seven-day outline changed on a constant basis. At the end of two or three writing sessions, the improv occurring in certain scenes meant I had to go back through the outline for the rest of the novel and make adjustments, sometimes major. The order of scenes and events changed, and some scenes dropped out entirely. Toward the end, I abandoned the seven-day outline to focus on an outline mapping the

characters, which helped keep track of the various factions represented in the novel and their actions. None of this was cheating because an outline is an artificial construct to begin with; it is there to help, and if it's not helping, then it needs to adapt or be gone. An outline, contrary to myth, is not like the blueprint for a building.

Detail from my outline for *Finch* (2008).

Always remember that an outline should (1) exhibit the structure and contain the information you need to write the novel; (2) not include those elements you don't need to be able to write, or information that may actually impede you or stifle your creativity; (3) be suited to the kind of story you are telling; and (4) be a living, evolving document that can accommodate new inspiration, new discoveries, if necessary. ❧

SPECIFIC QUESTIONS FOR WRITERS OF THE FANTASTICAL

If you are writing in a nonrealistic mode, you may need to ask some variations on the questions in Madden's book, however. With any luck, your use of the fantastical will be so integrated with the characters and plot that yanking it out of its context for dissection won't be necessary. But because a fantastical component can have some of the characteristics of a separate *element* of narrative, you may need to do so.

Here are just a few examples of the kinds of questions you may need to ask. They may have meaning to you as a writer beyond how they apply to revision of a particular novel or story.

What kind of imaginative fiction am I trying to create? In some ways, this is a question about the way you view the world, and may be part of a larger search for an understanding of your voice and perspective. For example, when I first started out, I considered myself more or less a realist . . . until I started getting feedback from first readers. They almost always reported back that my work was "strange" or "surreal." It wasn't until I had this sense of my writing from an audience that I realized I wrote mostly in a Kafkaesque mode, even when nothing fantastical happened in my stories. This in turn affected my revisions—I soon learned that I couldn't afford a dream sequence because the "real" scenes were too dreamlike. I also had to be careful that the surreal aspects of my fiction didn't overwhelm story logic or characterization. To give another example, I once met a writer at a workshop who thought he was writing hard science fiction like Gregory Benford or Justina Robson, but his fellow students all interpreted his work as a mixture of J. G. Ballard and Italo Calvino. Without a sense of how the results of your worldview and voice are interpreted on the page, you cannot effectively revise because certain techniques and approaches don't work as well for certain modes of fiction.

Is the fantastical element wedded to the emotional impact—and does it need to be? One of the biggest mistakes fantasy writers make is to think that the "sense of wonder" or "sense of awe" created by the speculative element is enough to carry the day for the reader. But, as in any other kind of fiction, you usually have to have compelling characters through which readers can appreciate those astounding moments. Otherwise, it's just eye candy. In addition, those characters have their own arcs during the course of the story, the fruition of which may or may not be tied to the fantastical element. Losing sight of the characters' journey in favor of The Spectacle can be a real danger—making the reader ask "Why should I care?"

Have I allowed an infatuation with the fantastical to overwhelm or unbalance my story? In addition to losing sight of the emotional impact, you can privilege the fantastical element to the point that your story begins to stagger under the weight—in a sense, the fantastical element sucks all of the oxygen out of the room, and you're left with some baroque, encrusted monstrosity that moves slowly, weighed down by the awesome excesses of your imagination. While some types of stories require this kind of approach, you need to be sure you intended it—and that it provides some

other reward for the reader. Catherynne M. Valente's short novel *The Labyrinth* is a good example of how an Overwhelm can actually work for the reader: It functions as an extended love song to language and myth; the meaning and the reward are embedded in each sentence.

Have I put too much weight on "solving" or explaining the fantastical element? As discussed in the section of *Wonderbook* on endings in Chapter 3, readers do not necessarily require closure in two areas at once. So, for example, a reader may enjoy a story in which the character arc is resolved—some decision is reached, or some crisis comes to a head—but aspects of the fantastical element remain unresolved. Perhaps we never find out much about the mysterious creature hiding behind the potted plant, but we derive enough closure from Fred the talking penguin's personal growth and how he survives a hit put out by the mob. Further, trying to tie up all loose ends with regard to the fantastical element may force the story along lines that seem predictable or artificial, sacrificing true character actions for the demands of a plot imposed by, say, the overemphasis on magic in a text. One of the most successful fantasy series of all time, George R. R. Martin's A Song of Ice and Fire, actually deploys less magic than you might expect.

Have I written a story in which the fantastical element isn't actually necessary? One consequence of thinking of yourself as a "fantasy writer" as opposed to a "writer" is that you may write some stories in which you introduce a fantastical element for no good reason—just because you are more comfortable with that **element** being

Jeremy Zerfoss expresses his inspirations in collage form. Sometimes you can become paralyzed by your range of options. When your options include the fantastical, it can become even harder to choose the right details.

The Leonardo exercise in the Workshop section of the appendix addresses this issue.

Daniel Abraham—*A Shadow in Summer* (Tor, 2006)—I had serious clarity issues, especially in the first draft. Information I thought was obvious by implication was totally obscure to the readers. I wound up throwing the first draft out entirely and writing the second from scratch.

Tobias S. Buckell—*Ragamuffin* (Tor, 2007)—I couldn't quite get a handle on the book. I wrote the first third four times, each time trying to get the tone and voice right. Once I found the right feel and wasn't forcing it, a first draft came about quickly afterwards. Another thing I struggled with was structure; it has an abrupt transition halfway through to new characters and threads. A draft without that didn't work as well, so I reverted.

Jesse Bullington—*The Folly of the World* (Orbit, 2012)—I intended this novel to address how one's mental state impacts one's perception of reality. My main stumbling block was that in early drafts I had a late-game reveal that the fantastical occurrences were indeed transpiring, as opposed to keeping these elements confined to the POV of a character of dubious mental stability. Once I realized that the novel would be stronger with the potentially fantastical aspects left open to interpretation, I overhauled the first third and rewrote the rest from scratch, to maintain an ambiguity essential to the work.

Richard Kadrey—*Aloha From Hell* (HarperVoyager, 2011)—The first draft laid out the structure, but the text was a lifeless lump. A second draft took care of technical problems with setting, plot points, etc., but still did nothing to give the book the spark of life. In the third draft, I took Candy, a character who was supposed to become romantically involved with my protagonist in a later book, and dropped her in the center of the novel. Her presence changed everything. Ninety percent of the structure remained the same, but with Candy in them the scenes took on new life, and the motivations became stronger, and the tone turned from dour to exciting.

J.M. McDermott—*When We Were Executioners* (Night Shade, 2011)—Working out the beginnings, middles, and ends of a complex tapestry of a novel, balanced with emotional and impressionistic scenes, I had to walk a line between plotless dreamscape and plotted novel. It takes time and effort to find that balance.

Nicole Kornher-Stace—*Desideria* (Prime, 2008)—I wrote 150 pages when I was too inexperienced to do justice to a project as complex as a 17th-century unreliable narrator novel with three parallel storylines and a complete five-act play embedded in it. Luckily, I realized that around the halfway mark and put the book on hold for a couple years. Of course, then the second half read very differently from the first half—not only did I understand the characters' thoughts and motives better, but I'd come to grips with the voice of the book. So while there were few revisions to the second half, I had to go back in and rewrite the first half entirely.

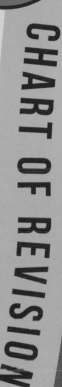

CHART OF REVISION

 # = DRAFTS

These edifying, sometimes horrifying, tales of revision from over twenty contemporary writers should make clear that no one path leads to a finished, publishable manuscript. The eyes of the revision snakes reflect the number of drafts for each novel. The publisher and publication date are included in parentheses.

3

Aliette de Bodard—*Master of the House of Darts* (Angry Robot, 2011)—I changed my mind about the plot several times when writing the first draft, which meant a lot of my rewrites were focused on making the entire book consistent and pruning nonsensical ends. I had also severely downplayed the severity of the threat the narrator faced (a magical, city-wide plague), so scenes were changed to increase the body count and make the disease much more viscerally threatening.

4

Jim Hines—*Libriomancer* (DAW, 2012)—Much of what I worked through was tying plot and character development together, taking my initial outline and character sketches and revising both in order to create a story where the events were natural developments of the characters' choices, desires, and occasional mistakes. I also had to work on the details of my description. For this book, it was really important to capture the feel of Michigan's Upper Peninsula, and the various Michigan settings I used in the story. They had to be real, or else my Michigan readers would skewer me for getting it wrong.

7

Stephen Graham Jones—*Seven Spanish Angels* (Dzanc, 2010)—I gave my editor 350 pages, of which he kept a single solitary one. So I wrote it again, and again, up to a grand total of 2,000 or so pages. The issue was goodness, and absence of badness, and it took me that many pages to come close. By the end, the novel was completely different in tense, voice, POV, content, main character, and, most important for me, ending.

26

Simon Ings—*The Weight of Numbers* (Atlantic, 2006)—This was supposed to be a set of short stories linked by theme, but my inner hack, for whom any consequence-free connection was a Missed Opportunity, would not be silenced. The result: two years of shuffling and rewriting, as I nudged unalike narratives closer and closer together in a way that I hoped wouldn't make the poor reader's brain explode.

Delia Sherman—*The Magic Mirror of the Mermaid Queen* (Viking, 2010)—Pacing and plot are always a struggle. I tend to overcomplicate events at the expense of the plot arc. Most drafts had to do with pruning unnecessary scenes, making sure the plot made sense without them, and that each of the many characters had an emotional arc of his or her own.

Peter Straub—*Mystery* (Dutton, 1989)—I had to realize that the book actually wanted to be about something very different from my original intention. In the end, I had to go right through deleting passages about a mad, savage twin brother and inserting material about a great old detective of the Sherlock Holmes type. Only then could the book get up on its legs.

Jeffrey Thomas—*Health Agent* (RDS Press, 2008)—At the halfway point there is a transition in the protagonist's life after he loses his job. I wrote about a page in which he takes a factory job and then falls in love with a deaf woman. I was afraid these events mirrored from my own life would contaminate the novel, so I wrote another novel instead. When I returned, I took my protagonist down another path, keeping the plot truer to my original vision of a tight detective thriller.

Karin Lowachee—*The Gaslight Dogs* (Orbit, 2010)—I couldn't get the main character's POV right. I wrote about 20 pages then scrapped that entirely. I decided to add another POV character. After the first draft, I needed to include more of the history and bolster the antagonists' roles and beef up the protagonists. The ending changed entirely by the final draft to add more emotional completion.

Carrie Vaughn—*Kitty's House of Horrors* (Grand Central Publishing, 2010)—This was my take on the slasher movie. I had a clear picture of what I wanted: a scary experience, because no matter how competent the main characters, the bad guys were also extremely competent. This required a lot of tweaking of the action scenes, constructing drawn-out, multi-layered sequences in which every action had a counter-action, and a counter-counter action. I wanted it all to be believable and intense, to create the most immediate experience possible.

Lisa Tuttle—*The Mysteries* (Bantam, 2005)—For the first two drafts I struggled with trying to tell the novel through the experiences of two main characters, mother and daughter. I tried alternating POVs, both first and close third, but could not make it work. I then tried a complete change in the next draft, when I let a formerly minor character—a detective investigating the situation—tell their story, along with his own; it was transformed. Did a second ("final") draft and sold it; then a final revision for an editor who felt there were problems with pacing and structure.

Pamela Sargent—*The Shore of Women* (Crown, 1986)—I began by thinking this would be a novella solely from one of the two main characters' point of view. After writing 200 pages, and seeing this story was not a novella, I realized that I could only tell the story by also relating the other point of view as well. I then added, altered, and deepened many details during the rewrites, which added to the complexities of the plot; the last rewrite was devoted to foreshadowing, tying up loose ends, and editing the prose.

# of drafts

6

Nene Ormes—*Särskild* (Styxx Fantasy, 2012)—When I did a synopsis for the second book I still had a few rewrites left to do on the first book. Soon I realized that the difference in tone between what I had written on the second book and what I wanted came from precon-ceptions from the synopsis stage. After that, I got a handle on the character voices. The plot needed revising a few times as well, but ended up very close to the plot from the first synopsis.

11

Sofia Samatar—*A Stranger in Olondria* (Small Beer Press, 2013)—I had a horrible time with a transitional chapter, in which a supernatural event shatters my main character's life. I kept trying and failing to describe this event in the smooth, contemplative style of the earlier chapters, until my editors suggested I try a more urgent, fragmented, present-tense style. That was the answer. Before I got there, I think I rewrote that particular chapter 15 times.

3

Kristine Kathryn Rusch—*Diving series* (Pyr, 2012)—I write out of order, particularly in science fiction. Then I have to assemble the scenes into a novel. Finally, I must make sure the book's information flow works. All my Diving novels have been in this pattern. (The fourth, underway, is proving no different.) The good thing is I also get a lot of novellas out of it. The bad is that I use only about 50 percent of what I write.

3

T.A. Pratt—*Poison Sleep* (Bantam Spectra, 2008)—I wrote 50,000 words that I had to almost entirely throw out due to fundamental structural flaws and a plot that descended into incoherence. I subsequently rewrote from page one with only the same basic premise and main characters. I had altered mental states in a way that was convincing without becoming confusing. I had to work on a key relationship that involved romance and betrayal to create a balance between fore-shadowing, suspense, and surprise.

200+

Patrick Rothfuss—*The Name of the Wind* (DAW, 2007)—Over 14 years, I revised almost everything. I would move, add, or delete chapters. I reworked entire plotlines. I tweaked tone and pacing. I added characters and subplots. I read my manuscript at least 20 times, trimming out words and phrases, making the prose leaner. I looked at every instance of the word "that" in my manuscript, removing the non-es-sential ones. I also had over 100 beta readers. After talking with them, I would change the manuscript based on their feedback.

5

Ian Macleod—*The Light Ages* (Ace Books, 2003)—I tend to build and build into a story from the founda-tions of possible beginnings, which equated to: (1) finding the mood and basic story arc for a big, late-Victorian fairy tale; (2) developing appropriate characters; (3) fitting both into a workable premise; and (4) refining the charac-ters and the setting to fit the premise. The final push was more about plot, and working right through to the end.

present. To give an example, in a workshop run by my wife and me, a writer presented a story that was a poignant examination of the relationship between a father and son. The father had just died, and the estranged son had come to the funeral, opening up a welter of old, painful memories. To this potent mix of past and present, family and community, the writer had also added witches that haunted the father's house. But this element really had nothing to do with the story, and it felt perfunctory and thin—especially juxtaposed against the richness of the character relationships. Later the writer confessed that, after writing a witch-free first draft, he had added the fantastical element because he felt strange about presenting a nonfantastical story to the group.

Have I followed through on the implications of what my imagination has come up with? Just as you want to think through the implications of your plot, your characters, and much else, you need to take a step back and see if you have gone *far enough* and, if not, whether or not you have to push further and harder in terms of the development of the fantastical or surreal aspect. Related questions include: "Have I been sufficiently rigorous in sticking with the rules/constraints of my fantastical element or fantastical/future milieu?" and "Have I made it too easy for the protagonist through my use of fantastical elements?"

But despite my emphasis here on the fantastical element, revision is about testing *all* aspects of story, and doing so in an organized fashion.

How many drafts does it take to get to the perfect story or novel?

As many as needed.

(And no piece of fiction is ever perfect.)

Systematic Testing

Are you a systematic or chaotic revisionist? If you just dive in and start reimagining your story or novel with a minimum of preliminary notes, you may be an agent of chaos. Like some kind of manic badger, you just tunnel in there, in part because that's the best way for the story to stay alive in your mind. But even so, you should consider adapting at least some aspects of a systematic approach to revision. Having some kind of method to your tunneling will make it less likely you miss something important (like a juicy mole).

TESTING EXAMPLES

I've set out a three-step revision process below; follow it to test your rough draft or second draft (or third). Incorporate as many or as few steps as work for you—in the order you prefer—so that you can adopt it as your own and make it as effective as possible. Not all stories or novels will require all steps. Further, step 1 and step 2 exist in symbiosis with each other, and at times they can be condensed.

STEP 1: REVERSE OUTLINING

Many writers hate the idea of using outlines for novels or other writing. The reasoning is that, yes, you need to know where you're going, but if you know too much, it's not interesting to write, and you are too bound by what you've written in the outline. That talking penguin actually becomes stale and blasé before long. Although I do outline some novels—and outlines can take many forms—I came to novel writing through an organic process of writing longer and longer stories. I felt that in order to maintain a natural writing method, an approach I had embraced when writing stories, I should continue to leap off into the unknown. Still, even back then I outlined every novel: I just waited until I'd finished the rough draft. At that point, I created an outline from what I had on the page, and you can do the same. Wherever there's a rib missing, I know I need to perform some reconstructive surgery. Wherever there's a second tail or a fifth leg, I know I've kept something in that might need to be **amputated**. Eventually, through reverse outlining you come to know the true shape of the creature that is your novel.

How exactly do you reverse outline? One way is to examine the structure of your story or novel and do the following:

Sometimes you'll actually keep that second tail because it's necessary to the story.

- List each scene. (With an indication of whose point of view we're in if the novel or story includes more than one point of view.)
- List every action or act that occurs in each scene—do not include anything that occurs "off-stage." ("Fred sticks the fork into Danger Duck's eye." "Fred faints." "Danger Duck runs away." "Fred's pet capybara calls the police.")
- In a summary for each scene, list any necessary information conveyed.
- Ask yourself a series of questions based on your list. These questions would include:
  » Do actions have consequences? (If Danger Duck throws a stone, does it break a window, or do we never find out?)
  » Is there true cause and effect displayed on the page, for every action or act?
  » Is every necessary action or act within a scene dramatized on the page?
  » Are there actions or acts that are unnecessary to the scene, ones that should be airlifted out and included in some other part of the story or novel?
  » What other action(s) could have occurred but didn't?
  » Have I started and ended the scene in the right place for the effect I want to achieve?
  » Is there true cause and effect between scenes? (Another way of putting this is: Are your progressions sound? For example, you might have a flashback scene in the wrong place, or you might jump three weeks forward and realize that's too jolting a gap in the narrative.)
  » Are there unnecessary scenes? (If there are scenes in which nothing happens, is this "nothing" necessary to the characters or narrative?)

SPOTLIGHT ON PETER STRAUB

Straub is perhaps the most influential supernatural fiction writer of his generation, with his work subverting tropes and defying easy classification. He has also been extremely influential as an editor of anthologies and as a member of Conjunctions *magazine's editorial board. The pages reproduced here are from a novel in progress with the working title of* Some Kind of Fire.

"I used to write everything out in longhand first, I suppose because it made me feel so close to the material. I like big bound journals with lined and numbered pages, made by Boorum & Pease. Although I'm just as likely to start writing on the computer now, the journals feel like 'home.' Of course the computer has the advantage of being faster—if you start on it, you eliminate the step of having to type everything out. What I usually do is start in the journals, roll along for about a hundred pages, then either type that up or dictate it to a typist, and begin the fresh material on the computer. In the journals, I write on the right-hand pages, and revise both on those pages and on the blank, facing left-hand pages. The left-hand pages are usually used for material that is to be inserted into the original paragraph. Xs and XXs identify the places where the revised sentences go. When I have gone as far as I can with revision at this stage, I type up a nice clean copy . . . and immediately begin to revise like crazy all over again. The primed-out pages often get turned into wiring diagrams. Then of course I install the new changes on the hard disk and begin the whole process all over again. Every page will go through at least four or five revisions, some of them ten or twelve." ➤➤

1

At 6:45 of the second morning following her husband's cremation and the installation of

his urn in the terrible one-man family crypt, Margot Hayward Mountjoy awakened to the

recognition that she was feeling better than she had in months.

A sober, unavailing, not entirely expected grief attended her, but not somehow

real depression. Grim, airless depression, more an atmosphere than an emotional

condition, she had actively feared. You breathed depression in, you breathed it out,

increasingly overtaken with each cycle. Margot had not anticipated feeling overthrown by

living emotion. Nor had she imagined that Harry's long-delayed demise would result in

Harry-apparitions slipping into view to gaze at her in what very much appeared to be

accusation. Margot was not a monster. Not at all. Not not not, at all. Neither her inner nor

outer life could properly be considered monstrous. The failure of absolute depression to

appear on schedule did not make her a monster, for depression could be lying coiled in

the shadows, waiting to ooze out. The Harry-ghosts seemed to accuse her of monstrosity,

but she knew herself, not some creaky afterlife, to be the source of these frowning

specters. Harry was not on some ghostly mission of revenge. He wandered through the

house and the city of Minneapolis dogging his widow because the widow had set him in

motion.

For that, too, was grief, yesterday's glimpses of her husband leaning against walls

or gazing at her, arm crossed over his chest, from a half-empty sidewalk on the other side

of Mount Curve. She called him up, and far more attentive and obedient than he had been

life, he came. Never in life, however, not once while still devouring Scotch whiskey,

Straub draft page photographs by Kyle Cassidy.

The simplest reason for this kind of testing? To determine whether there is any confusion in your story's surface—places where the reader will have a bumpy reading experience because of lack of clarity on your part. More than once, I've made an assumption or a leap between actions or scenes that I couldn't actually justify after I went back and tested the writing. I've also found opportunities for strengthening elements that appeared sound but could still be made better.

The effectiveness of this process depends in part on the kind of story you're telling, although even a surreal dream of a tale requires a type of logic—perhaps an even more rigid logic than a conventional approach. Performing this exercise should dredge up all kinds of valuable intel in the context of your overall revision process.

Step 2: Interrogating Your Characters

However, stress testing your story's structure will get you only so far. You also need to examine the interactions between characters, because, on some level, characterization is plot. To that end:

- On a piece of paper, write out the names of your characters in a circle.
- Draw lines connecting the characters that have some relationship to one another.
- Write the relationship or relationships between two characters on the line you've drawn between them (whether "mother/son" or "friend" or whatever).
- Take a good look at characters who do not seem that connected to other characters, and make sure that is a strength in the story, not a weakness. Consider whether

there are connections between the characters that you haven't thought of and how those connections might change your narrative.

- With your diagram of character relationships in hand, look again at your list of scenes broken down by action and act.
- Examine the interactions between characters. Ask yourself the following questions:
  - » Why does X act or react this way? Is there another way he or she might have reacted? How would that change in reaction affect the rest of the narrative?
  - » When X fails, does that failure have consequences?
  - » What would happen if people who don't know each other did know each other? (For example, what if the hero knew the villain before the story started? What kind of history do they have? How does that affect the narrative?)
  - » Is there a history or past between these two (or more) characters that you haven't considered, ones that might drive their actions or speech in this scene?
- Write brief summaries of the story from the point of view of all of the nonviewpoint characters. How do these people feel about the events in the story, and how do their opinions differ from those of the viewpoint character(s)? Also, how do they view the main character(s)?

You'll find that this kind of testing helps to create *depth, layering*, and *connectivity*, as well as determining whether you've made things *too easy* or *simple* for the characters in your story.

At one workshop, I applied this form of interrogation to a scene in which the main character acquiesces to a demand by the antagonist. I asked the writer, "What if X says no to Y instead? Isn't that more in keeping with X's character anyway, and how does that change the story?" It turned out the writer hadn't thought about the possibility of X saying no, but that saying no immediately turned scenes that plodded along into totally different scenes with much more subtext and dramatic potential. The initial "yes" had just been the writer's knee-jerk way of moving on to the next scene, and the next.

I then asked a second question. "Are you sure that X doesn't already know Y before this scene?" This possibility also had never occurred to the writer, but creating a past between X and Y opened up additional opportunities for character development. It also fundamentally altered the rest of the story. The writer found that X's mistress had a connection to Y as a result of this testing, and suddenly what had been a simple A-to-B story with little tension had a three-dimensional quality to it.

STEP 3: PARAGRAPH-LEVEL EDITS

Especially when starting out, applying a mechanical approach to paragraph-level edits can be a great way to improve your craft—to begin to see your voice and style appear on the page unencumbered by technical deficiencies. Early in my career, I realized that I had a somewhat lush style and that I was using too many dialogue tags. So, using different-colored pens, I would circle all adjectives and adverbs in my story and circle all "said excitedly"s. Then I would do a revision pass that was just about reducing the number of unnecessary descriptors and tags. Over time, by the

CHARACTER CIRCLE: "THE GHOSTS OF GRANDVILLE CORPORATION"

QUESTIONS: TYPE OF STORY

—If your story is about the mystery behind the Grandville Corp., what is missing in the character connections? What is more or less important?

—If your story is about one person who works at the corporation, what information is backstory and what should be in the foreground?

—Where is clear existing drama in the conflict between character situations or relationships and the wider world?

QUESTIONS: CHARACTERS

—Can any characters be cut without hurting your story? Or combined?

—Do any characters need to be more connected to the others? Should a character be friends with another character they don't know in the current draft?

—Does any of the friction between characters pertain to your story?

—What happens if animosity is eased or intensified? And how does this affect character backstory?

ALSO THINK ABOUT

ABSENT CHARACTERS

Even though Grandville Corp.'s founder Isabel Snerk disappeared mysteriously five years ago, does Snerk's influence still manifest in certain ways?

SUPPORTING CHARACTERS

How do supporting characters affect your main character circle? Do they have information or agency that some of your main characters do not?

DEAD FAMILY

Does Mary-Sue's memory of her father influence her daily life and actions or thoughts?

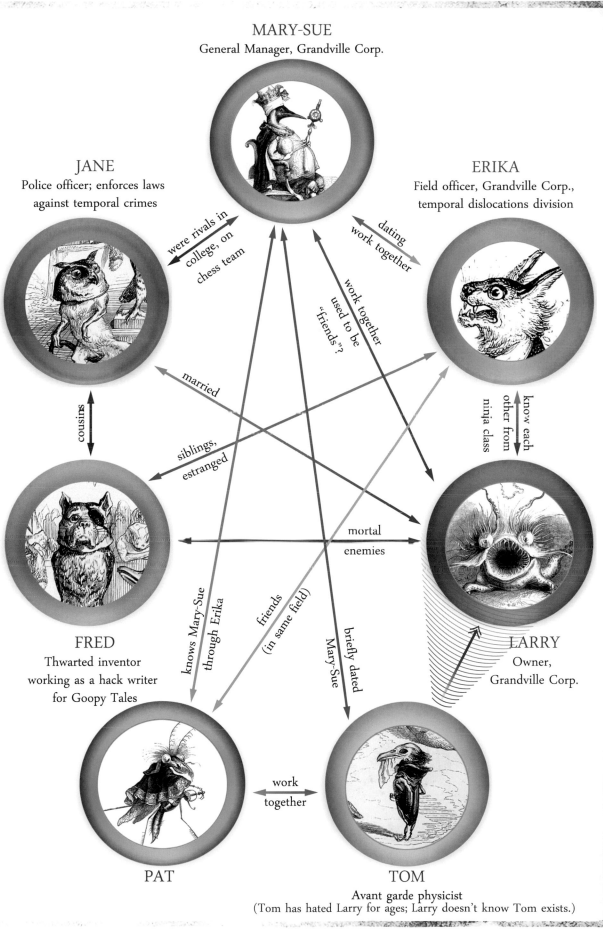

MARY-SUE
General Manager, Grandville Corp.

JANE
Police officer; enforces laws
against temporal crimes

ERIKA
Field officer, Grandville Corp.,
temporal dislocations division

were rivals in college, on chess team

dating
work together

work together
used to be
"friends"?

married

know each
other from
ninja class

cousins

siblings,
estranged

mortal
enemies

knows Mary-Sue
through Erika

friends
(in same field)

briefly dated
Mary-Sue

FRED
Thwarted inventor
working as a hack writer
for Goopy Tales

LARRY
Owner,
Grandville Corp.

work
together

PAT

TOM
Avant garde physicist
(Tom has hated Larry for ages; Larry doesn't know Tom exists.)

mechanical process of pruning these unnecessary words from my drafts, I found that I used fewer of them to begin with, and eventually stopped circling them. I did the same thing with the verbs, nouns, and pronouns in my sentences, to test if I was making strong choices. Sometimes I would also isolate dialogue or exposition in an attempt, again, to isolate issues and deal with them—much as Lev Grossman describes in his essay in this chapter. During some pass-throughs, I would mercilessly examine each paragraph, each sentence, and ask myself questions like:

- Can I express this sentence in some better or more interesting way?
- Am I showing off with this sentence; should it be expressed more directly?
- Have I used specific detail or generalities? (If the latter, is there a reason to not be specific?)
- Should this sentence actually be two sentences?
- If I cut this paragraph, is anything lost?
- Should this descriptive paragraph actually come earlier and be shortened?

Does this process seem too artificial, or too simplistic? Perhaps, and it's just one example of a revision process, but sometimes being mechanical is good because it relieves you of the burden of coming up with a spark during revision. The process jump-starts that spark and helps you to see the story with fresh eyes.

YOUR PROCESS: TO KEEP IN MIND

By now you may have guessed that I believe in applying rigorous discipline to revision. The subconscious often needs your conscious mind working in an organized way so that it can relax into finding a path forward.

Revision is hard, repetitive work, but it teaches you about language and narrative at an immersive, nitty-gritty level. It also requires certain optimal conditions, which may vary for every writer. Some commonly held ideas about revision are indeed true. You do need distance from the manuscript, usually achieved by sticking it in a drawer for a couple of weeks after you've finished the rough draft. You also may need to change the font or the margins, or, in the case of short stories, have a friend read your work to you—all of this so you can see what you've written with fresh eyes.

Another piece of wisdom that works: It is usually best to try to separate out levels of edit; a paragraph-level edit is a vastly different enterprise than one at a chapter level. This is a different phase than *identifying the problems*—this is the phase of enacting solutions. Some examples:

- You might focus on what you view as the biggest problem first, because solving it has far-reaching effects on the rest of the narrative.
- You might reserve one round of revision for making only line edits to your work, while you take care of reimagining problematic scenes during another round of revision.

OTHER WRITERS'
WEAKNESSES

THOUGHTS ON REVISION
BY LEV GROSSMAN

Lev Grossman is the New York Times *bestselling author of* The Magicians *and* The Magician King. *He is also the senior book critic for* Time *magazine.*

I CAN THINK of only one time in twenty years of writing fiction when I wrote a passage of any significant length that I didn't subsequently have to rewrite. The passage involved a character turning into a goose and flying to Antarctica. It was about a thousand words long, it's still one of the best pieces of writing I've ever done, and I'll never know how I did it. It was an ordinary writing day. I wrote in a coffee shop. I sat on a couch. It was hot out. The one thing I know for sure about that day is that unless I start writing novels that are entirely about sentient geese, it's almost certainly never coming back. When I write a first draft, it is, almost invariably, crap.

One of the first tasks of the writer, I have found, and not the easiest, is forgiveness: You must forgive yourself for writing crap first drafts. Perform whatever ritual of absolution you have to, pray to whatever cruel god or gods you have to, but do that for yourself. Only once you've forgiven yourself can you begin the serious work of writing, which isn't writing at all. It's revising.

In fact, not only do I forgive myself for writing bad first drafts, I expect myself to write bad first drafts. That's my baseline assumption. I write my first drafts with the absolute certainty that I'll either throw them away or that future-me, bless his long-suffering heart, will correct their many egregious faults later. Either way, it's not something for present-me to worry about. Filling a blank page is hard enough as it is. I find it helps if you set the expectations very low.

And it helps even more if you keep them low, at least for a while. Part of learning to revise is knowing when *not* to revise. When you're writing fresh copy, it's tempting to stop and go back over your pages right away, while they're still all glittery and new and you're still under the spell of your initial inspiration. I won't tell you not to do it, but just be aware that (a) it's a time suck, and (b) its usefulness is limited. Your job in the first round of composition is completing a draft. It's all about maintaining forward momentum and not bogging down. It's about writing the way people read, fast and fluid. Think of it this way: You're on a Jet Ski, and if you slow down you'll sink into the icy, shark-infested waters you're trying to skim over. The only thing worse than a crap first draft is the first draft you never finished in the first place.

In fact, I find that the longer I wait to revise, the better my revisions are. If it were possible to express the effectiveness of a given set of revisions numerically, you could construct an equation demonstrating that their value is directly proportional to the time elapsed since the first draft was written. In other words, where revising is concerned, procrastination is your friend. The publication of my third novel, *The Magicians,* the one with the geese in it, was pushed back six months at the very last minute over a legal issue. My agent had told me it was done. My editor had told me it was done; so had my editor's boss. Two months into the delay, I came back to the book and reread it. It was an utter mess.

I rewrote the entire thing during those six months, twice, and I shudder to think what would have happened if they'd printed the first version. Zadie Smith once wrote: "It turns out that the perfect state

of mind to edit your own novel is two years after it's published, ten minutes before you go onstage at a literary festival." Very sad, but very true.

The lesson is, stay away from your draft as long as you can—for as long as it takes—until you and your draft no longer recognize each other. The object of the game is to come back to your work the way a stranger would, someone who knows nothing about it and has no vested interest in understanding or even liking it. Someone who can be surprised by it. And the best way to do that is through the application of copious amounts of time.

There are other ways, of course. You can change the font. If you write on a computer, you can print out your draft; if you write on paper, you can type it into the computer. Either way, when you're revising you want to put yourself in the position of a reader, not a writer. It's one of the curious properties of good prose that while hardly anybody can write it, almost everybody can recognize it when they see it. You want to engage those naturally deadly accurate readerly instincts that everybody has—instead of those limp, unreliable writerly ones—and put them to work for you.

That moment, by the way, the moment when you're reunited with your draft for the first time, is the gut-check moment, the one that requires forgiveness. Coming back to your words after they've gone cold and congealed like leftovers from a greasy spoon is never fun. Because you will still have, somewhere in your mind, your original inspiration, the vision that compelled you to sit down and write in the first place, a vision of something raw, radical, hilarious, beautiful, thrilling, and new. Your first draft isn't going to be all those things. It may not be any of those things—not yet. No inspiration survives its first contact with the blank page, and this is the moment when you realize how deeply you have betrayed your vision. Never will the ideal and the reality be so far apart.

But this is also the moment that separates writers from would-be writers. Serious attrition happens at this point, because people misinterpret that disappointment and despair. You have to embrace it and recognize it for what it really means: It means that the spirit of your original inspiration is still alive. It's down there somewhere, in the back of your mind, trapped under the rubble, but it's healthy. Its life signs are good. All you have to do is dig it out.

I tend to make my revisions in several passes, sweeping for different things each time. Sometimes it's as simple as keeping a running tally of which bodily senses are in play. English is a very good tool for describing sights and sounds, and as a result it's very easy to treat your characters as if they have eyes and ears and no other sensory organs. I devote one whole set of revisions to making sure I'm always engaged with the other senses: touch, taste, hot, cold, pain, smell. I like to make sure I know how every scene in a story smells.

Sometimes I sweep the text for what I think of as Unmade Decisions. What season is it? What year is it? What is everybody's age, race, religion, sexual orientation, last name? Where did they go to college? What were their parents like? Lo, the universe in which your characters live is bland and generic until you make decisions about it, and when you don't make your decisions, readers know it. They can smell indecision. Even minor characters require decisions. Their personalities are as big and weird as those of your main characters, even if they only happen to get one or two lines in the final story.

Sometimes—often—I sweep for pacing. One of the things that makes writing novels so exceptionally difficult is the sheer chronological disparity between how they're written and how they're read. Readers read fast, incredibly fast. They'll wolf down 10,000 words at a sitting. Writers write slowly—for a lot of us, 10,000 words is at least a week's work. Which means that even while you're down there covered in ink, under the vehicle, tinkering with semicolons and word order and plugging in any number of near-synonyms one after the other just to see what happens, you have to remember that the reader is going to blow through that sentence you just spent half an hour on in about three seconds.

Because of that, readers are aware of things about your book that you aren't. They see your sentence, but they're equally aware of the structure of the paragraph it's in, and the pace of the chapter it's in, and the shape of the whole book. That old chapter you haven't looked at for six months? It's fresh in their minds. They're making dozens of connections between that chapter and the one you're working on now, connections that you must be in control of. One of the hardest things to do while you're revising, just cognitively, is to think of the entire complex system that is your novel, to hold it in your mind completely, while at the same time focusing on one sentence. It's tricky, but you have to, because your readers will.

Some days it's impossible. But that's why we're writers and not, say, musicians. Nobody's watching. If you have an off day, you can just go back and fix it tomorrow. Nobody has to know.

When I finished the first novel I was really proud of (it was my third overall, but who's counting), I realized that I'd gotten the entire first chapter wrong. When I looked at it as a writer, I thought, fine, good enough, but every time I came at it as a reader I bounced off it. And if I couldn't read it, who the hell could? So even though I'd spent, literally, months of my life writing and reworking it, I selected the whole thing and hit "delete" and started over from a blank page. In the end, the first sentence of the novel was, chronologically, the very last one I wrote.

Faulkner said a smart thing about this: "Don't bother just to be better than your contemporaries or predecessors. Try to be better than yourself." That's what revising is all about, being better than yourself, and you can never stop trying. Because after you learn to forgive yourself for writing bad prose, you also have to learn that other people won't. Authors can be merciful, but readers? They're absolute bastards. They're out for blood. And if you let them down, they will never, ever forgive you. ❧

- You might follow the thread of one character or one subplot through the manuscript, making relevant edits and seeing how they affect other elements of the story.
- You might spend most of your editing time on the story's beginning because you only discovered what you were writing about a third of the way in, and the rest of the draft is much tighter.
- You might focus only on the ending at first because in prior drafts you were always exhausted by the time you got that far.

Without a plan, you can get lost in the bloody mess that your manuscript may resemble after having been marked up as a rough draft, whether with a pen or through revision tracking on a computer.

A less commonly held idea? Revision is work that should not be done on a computer. The talking penguin and I both believe this with almost religious intensity. I believe you need to *physically mark up* your manuscript in hard copy to understand the weight of words. It is too easy to give your fiction a pass if you read it on a screen, and it is too easy to become distracted by the Internet. The ideal way to engage in detailed editing work, for me, is to take a printout to a coffee shop or nature park and, without interruption, immerse myself in the text.

But no matter what your approach, take revision seriously. Johanna Sinisalo likes to tell the story of a colleague who published an article about how he never rewrites a story more than once so as not to "lose the freshness of the text." But in her experience, "The illusion of the 'freshness' of the story is a result of vigorous editing—the literary clichés, worn metaphors, too-obvious solutions and lazy style are exactly the mistakes you commit in the first drafts. . . . Careful rereading and lots and lots of rewriting is, in my opinion, the key to produce text that's flowing beautifully and sounds fresh and original."

As Ian R. MacLeod notes, "Wannabe writers of all ages don't seem to realize just how messy and destructive the process has to be, and they get stuck in line-by-line edits when they should be looking at the bigger picture."

You will also, hopefully, learn not to throw out anything you write—don't hit "delete" on your prior drafts if they contain very different text, and *never* throw out a story you put aside because it isn't working. You have no idea how flotsam and jetsam, scenes or descriptions or characters, may be of use in some other story. The maudlin love scene from "Jack and the Terribly Sentimental Relationship" may be resurrected to good effect in "Jill and the Comedy of Errors" decades later. A turn of phrase, a fragment of dialogue—you never know when you might need it.

Whether you use any of this advice or find another way, the goal should be the same regardless: to not only improve the current story or novel but through repetition to internalize what you learn to make your next story better from the beginning. This process of becoming better isn't an exact science—it's more like a start-stop, with two steps forward followed by a hop to the side, a step back, and then a dizzying, whirling dance of revelation . . . followed by a step sideways. But some parts of revision should become easier over time simply because revision is also a process of better understanding your writer self. With understanding comes the ability to see clearly.

Sample novel
excerpt with
line-edits

Choosing First Readers

Most if not all writers have at least one more step in their revision process, because they share their rough drafts with a writing group or a trusted band of first readers. Thus, your revisions may include the opinions of others. As the depiction of the Forest of Bad Critiques in Chapter 3 may suggest, I think selecting the right people to read your work is very important. Here are a few points to remember, based on my own experience:

- **Diversity.** By "diversity," I mean true gender and multicultural diversity—preferably, in this Internet age, including readers from countries other than your own. The point? Although we all share similarities and literary influence knows no geographical boundaries, having multicultural, international readers may expose you to different ideas about fiction and about life that impact elements of your manuscript. This also applies to male writers writing female characters and vice versa. But I also mean: (1) readers who love all kinds of fiction, not just the kind of fiction you write; (2) readers who are not writers; (3) readers who, when they are writers, have varied levels of experience. You need nonwriter readers because presumably the general public is your audience, not just other writers, and readers who aren't also writers may have a different perspective on what you've written. You also need to be wary of having only peers or writers with less experience than you read your work. You must seek out readers with more writing experience. If you were a tennis player, you would need to keep playing better and better competition to improve, and the same goes for who's critiquing your writing.

- *A Limited Number*. You do not need twenty potentially different takes on the same story. Generally, unless you are strong-willed and ultraconfident, too many voices leads to the creation of "compromise stories" that attempt to incorporate most suggestions, even when these opinions represent very different ideas about the story. A rotating group of about fifteen first readers, from which you choose five to seven for any one story or novel, should give you a sufficient range of opinions, if you pick wisely. For my novel *Shriek* I had too many first readers. The novel was idiosyncratic, with some experimental aspects. Reactions were impossible to reconcile, but if I had it to do over again, I would have left out the first readers who love experimental fiction because to a person they wanted me to ditch any attempt at a traditional narrative and go with a fully experimental approach—which did not match my intent.

- *Analysis and Empathy*. Ideally, you want readers who are good at providing cogent, analytical comments on your work and who don't get hung up on petty details or are unable to sympathize with what you are trying to do. Any reader who continually brings their own agenda to your work and tries to impose their own vision shouldn't be part of your revision process for very long. Sometimes, too, a trusted first reader will prove unsuitable for a particular book because of a particular inability to empathize; in one case, I had to discard a reader's

"Big Fish Eat Little Fish Eat Big Fish" by Molly Crabapple (2012). Make sure that during the process of soliciting comments on your story or novel that you don't confuse things with too many first readers. You want to eat the comments, not have them eat you.

BESTIARY OF FIRST READERS—TO AVOID

The *grammar weasel* will pick apart your sentences for any slight, insignificant offense. These creatures will ignore the fact that you can autocheck grammar and spelling on your computer. The grammar weasel always has six typo-pencils at the ready, ignores any major problems in your fiction, and equates a comma splice with war crimes.

The *smile fish* hates all misery and especially in fiction. God forbid a dog trips on a banana peel and dies in your fictional story. You will hear about it—at length. "Can't you write fun stuff?" The smile fish weeps at imaginary poverty, war, muggings, and wants only the happy happy. If you let it, this creature will expunge anything gritty or unpleasant from your work.

The *me-mirror* will make your fiction all about its experience of the world and want you to make the story better reflect its life. The truth is, to the me-mirror, you and your story don't really exist. This creature faces its own face while reading and even its shoes are eager to discover more about itself. All the while, the me-mirror will claim "It's not about me—it's about improving your work."

The *gloom squid* will do everything within its considerable power to interpret every element of your prose as melancholy and goth-romantic. "I love the rot layered upon the rot in this scene." Just remember to wear black or there will be protests. Also remember that fiction is dead, the world is dying. Why do you even try?! The gloom squid will cry cry cry.

comments because he clearly had a set view of marriage that colored his ability to analyze the atypical relationship in one of my stories.

- **Specialists.** Sometimes you'll write a story or novel where you feel you need a particular point of view or type of experience. This may require you to seek out a new first reader or two just for the work at hand. For example, Karin Lowachee had her novel *Warchild* critiqued by a group that included an ex-military man, because that book dealt with war and posttraumatic stress disorder. Lowachee was able to confirm that *Warchild*'s approach worked through this first reader's analysis: "He told me that he had been convinced that (a) I'd served, and (b) practiced martial arts, not only because of the details I'd gotten right, but through the entire mind-set and nuance."

- **Reject the Continual Ego Boost.** First readers who always love your work aren't useful to you except as an ego boost, especially if they're light on analysis. There's nothing wrong with an ego boost—I've certainly been known to send a manuscript to someone just because I needed a hug . . . but recognize that this is why you are sending your work to this particular person.

- **Turnover.** Inevitably, some first readers you find valuable at first will fade in value. Over time, they will become too familiar with your work and will be unable to provide valid criticism because they no longer have the necessary distance. When you do find a first reader who stays valuable to you over several years, take steps to make sure they remain healthy for a very long time to come. You do not want this person to skydive, bungie jump, or run with the bulls in Pamplona. (I am blessed to have two such first readers, including my wife, Ann.)

Beyond working with individual first readers, you may also belong to a writers group that doubles as a workshop. I have always been and will always remain ambivalent about writing groups that also critique manuscripts. The social aspects of writers groups can provide valuable emotional support and affirmation in a creative field that is tough and forces you to spend a lot of time by yourself. But such groups also can support the idea that writers should continually workshop their fiction, and this idea can be detrimental to your growth as a writer. Selective use of workshops when you are beginning to write, and the occasional masterclass, can be of great value. But at some point you have to take the training wheels off. Most long-term workshops also tend to smooth out a writer's individuality, and a kind of groupthink can set in over time. Worse, workshop participants are preprogrammed to find something wrong with a story, even if nothing is wrong.

The point is not that you should ever stop learning, but that ultimately you and only you can be the arbiter of how you express your own unique vision.

STORY FISH THAT MAY REQUIRE REVISION

Reader sees hook coming; too much scaffolding.

Subplot kicks in to draw attention from main plot deficiencies.

Black smoke from plot having to work too hard to overcome weak characterization. Smoke screen of hurly-burly and artificial twists may fool the reader…or may confuse them.

POV is adequate but too familiar.

Ending has closure but seems a bit hurried and perfunctory.

Opening is in correct proportions but has no life.

Prologue encased in hard glass; too self-contained, it feels less like an entrance than an obstacle.

All the nuts and bolts of the plot are glaringly obvious.

An assortment of bling and moving gears creates action to divert attention from clunky storyline.

SPECIES: MECHA-FISH

- Because of paint-by-numbers approach, author's intent becomes too obvious, throwing the reader out of the story.
- Reader feels manipulated rather than entertained
- Characterization tends to fade after the set-up; motivation is weak and people do things mostly to further the plot or make things easier for the main character.
- Scenes in the latter half of the novel may seem rushed or blur into one another; a sameness sets in due to lack of imagination or the reader not caring about the characters.
- The entire apparatus labors under the flaws of a design in which things that should be invisible and inside the story are on the outside. The story works too hard to perform simple tasks and to move forward.

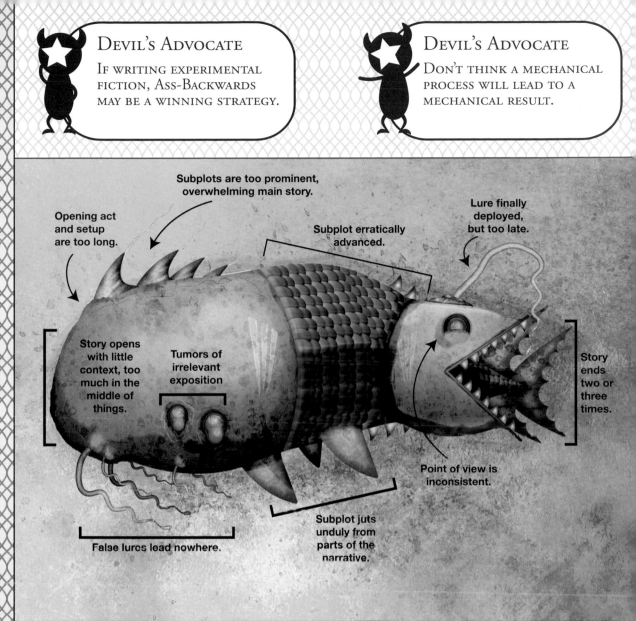

Subplots are too prominent, overwhelming main story.

Opening act and setup are too long.

Subplot erratically advanced.

Lure finally deployed, but too late.

Story opens with little context, too much in the middle of things.

Tumors of irrelevant exposition

Story ends two or three times.

Point of view is inconsistent.

False lures lead nowhere.

Subplot juts unduly from parts of the narrative.

SPECIES: THE ASS-BACKWARDS FISH

- Swims in the wrong direction, unable to see where it is going.
- The opening of the story doesn't provide a specific focus or point of interest.
- Elements of the story are not in harmony or the right length in proportion to one another.
- The overall structure and resulting form are not pleasing to the reader.
- Because the point of view is inconsistent, the reader is close-in on the main character sometimes but more distant other times.
- By story's end, other, irrelevant information and subplots have been shoved into the story fish.

Note: Some novels, like Martin Amis's *Time's Arrow*, start at the end and end at the beginning. This is different than being unintentionally ass-backwards.

RECONCILING FEEDBACK

What do you do with the comments you receive from your first readers or fellow workshop participants? Especially while still developing your voice and your style, consider processing comments in a systematic way. Why? To get the most out of those comments and to better weed out irrelevant or harmful comments without losing valuable information.

Here is an approach that has worked for me.

- Read and absorb all comments, no matter how absurd you find them initially—in short, internalize them all before rejecting any.
- Once you've had a chance to think about each comment, separate out the ones that you think apply across *most or all* of your fiction. After further thought, make a list of the most useful ones that denote *both* strengths and weaknesses. Use that list to improve your writing in general.
- Before continuing further, make sure you know what you want the novel or story to do (what it's about thematically and what you want it to accomplish), perhaps even using the structure/character testing discussed above.
- Make a list of all the specific comments that support your vision.
- Make a list of all the specific comments that don't support that vision.
- Explain to your own satisfaction why you're not using comments that don't support your vision of the story. (For example, "This comment isn't applicable because my novel is not really about the dueling dragons but more about the friendship between the talking penguin and the woman with the gun." Or, "This first reader didn't even understand that the story is set in the future even though I give the date in the first paragraph; therefore, these edits are unusable.")
- Use all remaining comments to improve your story.

This kind of systematic approach will allow you to get the most out of feedback in the same way that an expert butcher wastes not a bit of the meat from a carcass.

FINDING MY WAY BY KAREN JOY FOWLER

Karen Joy Fowler is known for her subtle yet powerful approaches to science fiction and fantasy. Her novels include Sarah Canary, The Sweetheart Season, *and the bestselling* The Jane Austen Book Club. *She won the World Fantasy Award for her collection* What I Didn't See and Other Stories.

I SPENT MANY years writing bad stories. I knew they were bad while I was writing them, but I was surprisingly okay about it. I was learning as I went, and my improvement in terms of prose, of pacing, of dialogue, scene, and character was so evident, even to myself, that I felt quite cheerful about the whole thing. Then I hit an equally long period in which, having fixed the obvious, my stories continued to disappoint, only now no one could explain why. *That* made me grumpy.

The problem generally seemed to manifest at the story's end. All went swimmingly, what with my improved prose, pacing, and dialogue, until the story was over and people realized that, though they had been liking it, now they didn't. *It just needs to be better*, my writing group would tell me, as if this were helpful. *You need to make it better.*

The standoff between me and the ends of my stories resolved quite suddenly in a single afternoon while I was listening to the poet Robert Hass talk about the ends of poems. It was a wide-ranging, brilliant lecture, full of its own fascinating stories. Hass talked about writing endings you believed in. He talked about embracing contradiction—*put some yes in your no*, he said. *Put some no in your yes.* He talked about multiple ways to read a single story. He talked about the human need to find shape and meaning in the world as something very moving, but also, simultaneously, hilarious.

Whatever revelation I had that day didn't come in the form of theory. Instead, while I sat and listened, I thought of two different endings to two of the disappointing stories I'd long been working on. I went home, changed those endings, and thought of a new ending for a third story while working on the other two. Those three stories with their three new

endings became my first professional sales.

Now when I try to say something concrete about what I learned that day, this is the closest I can come. I realized that I don't believe in godlike authors. Or even bossy ones.

I'd been telling readers not only what happened, but also how to understand it, how to feel about it, what it meant. I'd been leaving no room in my stories for my readers' own opinions and reactions. Instead, I'd directed them into narrower and narrower channels. And I'd been doing this because I'd had the unconscious conviction that stories were supposed to be tidy.

A tidy story can be a wonderful thing. It can be loved for its craft, its cleverness, its beauty, its perfection. The reader can admire it as a well-made object. A woman cuts her hair to buy her husband a watch chain, only he's sold his watch to buy her a comb. It's beautiful.

But when a tidy story is not well made, its artificiality ceases to be a strength and becomes a fatal flaw. And most tidy stories are not well made.

Certainly mine weren't.

True stories (whatever that means) are messy, and stories need mess (by which I mean ambiguity, uncertainty, unreliability) to ring true. Every detail can't be seen as neatly serving the writer's purposes. My tidy stories had all had endings I didn't believe in, because what I believe in is mess.

We think of childhood as a time of magical thinking. Children begin, as early as eighteen months, to create imaginary worlds in which they play imaginary roles and have imaginary powers. I myself remember being Davy Crockett, d'Artagnan, Zorro, Annie Oakley,

and Mighty Mouse. I've stitched samplers as Laura in *Little House on the Prairie*, and talked to animals as Fern in *Charlotte's Web*. I've been a dog (a collie) and a horse (a pinto), a spy for the French Resistance, an Indian guide for Lewis and Clark. By the time I was eight, I'd died and come back to life many, many times, pierced with arrows, bullets, blown up by grenades disguised as snowballs.

But the most fantastical of my imaginary worlds turned out to be the one I'd thought was real. As a child, I believed the world was run by competent, sane, and benevolent adults. I believed this for much longer than I believed in Santa Claus.

That belief has since gone down like the *Titanic* (on which I also spent time as a child). The world is run by nitwits and psychopaths. Some of them are stupid, and some of them are psychotic, but all of them are rich. I like the world quite a lot, most of it. I don't like the people who run it much at all.

Less enraging, but more troubling, the whole idea of a real world seems to have dissolved. Reliability, predictability, plausibility—all standard features of my childhood landscape—now gone up like so much smoke.

I was thirteen years old on the day President Kennedy was murdered. At thirteen, the official version of events was good enough for me, though my faith in official versions would soon be destroyed by the Gulf of Tonkin incident. Still, Tonkin was simply a lie, and a lie ultimately reinforces rather than undermines the idea of truth. The Kennedy assassination, on the other hand, became emblematic for me of something far more disconcerting—a story in which no version that has been told or can be imagined seems to cover the reported facts.

Among the things in which we've now learned to put no faith:

1) The impartial observer: Perceptional bias is an inevitable feature of observation. Eyewitness accounts are increasingly understood to be unreliable in the extreme. It's appalling that so many people have been put to death based on them.

2) Memory: The day after that Robert Hass lecture, he told us that the subsequent reports he'd heard of what he'd said had astonished him. So it's entirely possible that my account above contains unconscious fabrication. Wouldn't be the first time. The process of interpretation begins at the very moment of memory formation, so distortion is baked right in. This distortion is amplified if you tell someone what happened, as I, in the case of the Hass lecture, often have.

Plus, it's pathetically easy to implant, revise, or erase a memory. This can be done to someone else but is even easier to do to yourself. You do it all the time without even knowing what you're up to.

3) Identity: We've already discounted your memories. Now is the time to say that there is no you. You are a you-all, not a singular creature, but an assemblage made up of multiple codependent biological beings, including bacteria, worms, and insects. In fact, if you believe in the research of Kevin Lafferty at the University of California, Santa Barbara, your behaviors may be substantially controlled by a parasite you got from your cat. (You are free to disbelieve this, of course. I just note that your disbelief serves your cat-parasite masters well.)

4) Character: Current psychological studies suggest that character plays a surprisingly small role in human behavior. Instead, we are highly responsive to trivial changes in circumstance. We are like horses in that. Only not so gifted.

5) Current psychological studies—

6) In fact, scientific studies of all kinds: In 2005, John Ioannidis of Stanford published a paper entitled "Why Most Published Research Findings are False." In it he addresses selective reporting and lack of replicability in biomedical research. Jonathan Schooler at Santa Barbara has been drawing attention to "the decline effect," a frequent occurrence in which the findings of statistically solid, methodologically sound experiments decline over time as the experiment is repeated.

Some of this can be explained by human fallibility, but some cannot. Instead, it seems likely now that the world is filled with vast amounts of noise, which we often mistake for meaningful results. We think we know a thing just because we've proved it.

All of which is to say that I don't use ambiguity in a story as a literary device or a postmodern trick or to dodge my writerly responsibilities. I use it in an

attempt to acknowledge that the things we think we know are submerged in a vast sea of things we don't know and of things we will never know. I mean to admit to my own impressive lack of comprehension about the world in which we live.

I want also to deal with a paradox—language is an imprecise and inadequate vehicle even for that small subset of things we think we know, but the only way I have of saying that is in that same imprecise and inadequate language.

Plus I want my stories to contain some things I have no words for, things I cannot say.

So now I write messy stories, stories in which people—including myself, including my readers—don't know and can't say everything. I think of these don'ts and can'ts as my negative space. I create this negative space as carefully as I create anything else in my stories. I am looking not just for ambiguity,

but for ambiguity that works. Functional ambiguity. Another paradox.

I have the reader constantly in mind. I think about what I want him or her to now know, but I'm equally attentive to what I don't want known yet, as well as to what the reader will never know. The negative space is where I put the things I have no words for. It's the room I leave in my stories for the reader. I know what I meant to put there, but the reader is free to find something else entirely and often does.

Some readers dislike a lot of room, and my stories won't work for them. To those who do like this way of storytelling, I'm grateful. I know I expect a lot of you. But I swear I don't do this to be cute or evasive or obtuse or difficult or to look smarter than I am.

I do this because we live in a messy, noisy world that we will never understand. That's not a complaint. I'm surprisingly okay about it. ●

DON'T KILL THE SPARK

As with most things related to writing (and, perhaps, life), revision requires balance. Which is to say, you can also revise too much and kill the vitality that makes your story fresh and interesting. If you're just fiddling with things at the paragraph level, without a clear idea of why you're doing so or changing sentences to be more formally perfect, you may have reached the point where additional revision has little or no value.

Over time, you will develop a good idea of when you are done with a piece of fiction—or when it is done with you. But, especially when starting out, you may need to reconcile yourself to an uncomfortable truth. That truth is: It's okay to ruin a story or two. (I can hear the cries of horror and alarm even as I type these words.) If you are meant to be a writer, you have more stories in you. Sometimes to learn you may, indeed, dissect your story-creature, only to put it back together wrong-way up during revision. And it may never come back to life. The fact is, we usually have too much of an obsession in our impatient world with making sure everything we write counts—that we will get an end product we can submit and eventually see published. But if you take the long view—the view that if you are meant to be a writer, you may have a career that spans forty or fifty years—the most important thing in the short term is to steadily improve in the art of writing. You need to

DEAD STORY
UNDEAD STORY

A TALE OF
The Beatification

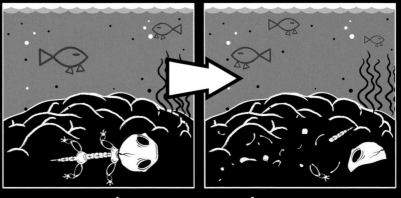

The new story contains the ghost of the old one, is haunted by it in the writer's mind.

The new, successful story flies and does not live in water.

PARTS THAT REMAIN FROM OLD STORY

Hands

USED TO FIX "Blob Story"

Extra Heart

USED TO FIX THE "Heartless Story"

Could have used hands...

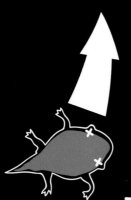

Dead story decomposes, flesh decays, inspiration fades, all is lost.

Story fades to bones in the sediment at the bottom of the writer's brain.

Time passes and the bones drift through the back waters of the writer's brain.

FAILED STORY LIES DEAD. R.I.P.

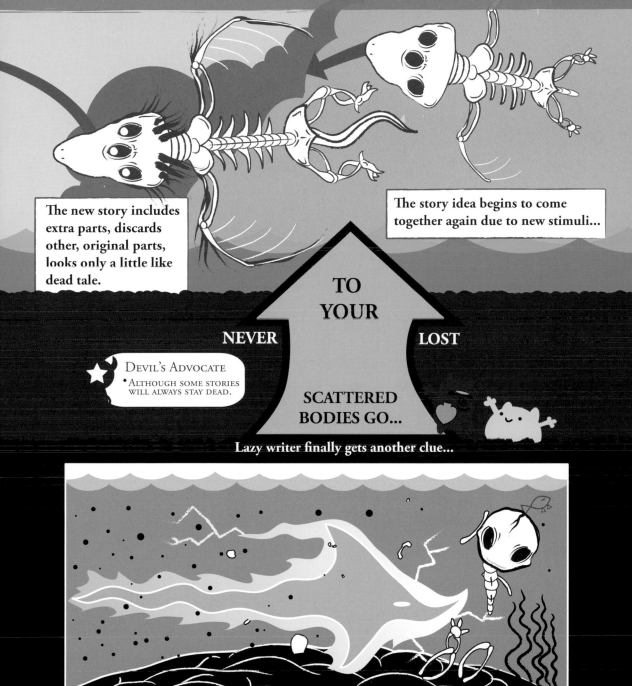

understand sooner rather than later how you achieved the effects that made one story take triumphant wing like a nightingale, while a misbegotten accumulation of mistakes led to another story that burbles incomprehensibly as it lurches its way across the kitchen floor toward you like the experiment from *The Fly*.

Try not to kill the spark, but know that another spark is coming—and another, and another after that.

The ***longipus*** buries any valuable advice in lengthy twenty-page critiques with even more lengthy asides. You must work hard to extract any gems and ignore strong evidence of undue feelings of ownership of your fiction exhibited by the longipus. This creature will never stop until death and believes its essays are a kind of fiction. It remains coiled inside its own brain for long hours.

Do Not Crash   Do Not Burn

WORKSHOP

APPENDIX

LARP & WRITING BY KARIN TIDBECK
GEORGE R. R. MARTIN ON THE CRAFT OF WRITING
GAMES & STORYTELLING BY WILL HINDMARCH
WRITING EXERCISES
DEVELOPMENT OF A WRITER

LARP
& WRITING

KARIN TIDBECK

S *wedish writer Karin Tidbeck is the author of the story collection* Jagannath, *winner of the Crawford Award and a finalist for the James Tiptree Jr. Award. She has published short stories and poetry in Swedish since 2002, and in English since 2010. Her English publication history includes* Weird Tales, Weirdfictionreview.com, NPR.org, Shimmer Magazine, Unstuck Annual, *Tor.com,* Lightspeed Magazine, *and the anthology* Odd?. *Her first novel,* Amatka, *was released by Sweden's largest publisher in 2011.*

Loosely termed, LARP—live-action role-playing, or LARPing as I'll sometimes call it here—is the collaborative, improvised telling of a story where the participants physically act out their parts. This essay is written from the perspective of the LARP tradition native to Sweden, Norway, Denmark, and Finland, also known as Nordic LARP. Also, this sort of role-playing has nothing to do with Dungeons & Dragons or hack 'n' slash and everything to do with character and storytelling.

A LARP can take just as many forms as there are types of story. A common stereotype is "hitting each other with rubber swords in someone's backyard," but it can also mean refurnishing the inside of a World War II submarine to be a spaceship or playing out a forty-eight-hour psychological drama in a "black box" theater with only duct tape on the floor to mark out rooms and furniture. Some LARPs are just for fun; others are artistic experiments or political statements. Some are created for educational purposes, such as an interactive method to teach history to high school students. Others are mixed-arts projects, like an improv version of *Hamlet*, where the audience gets to play the nobles in the royal court, and parts of the play are shown as film sequences.

At some LARPs you can go casually in and out of character; at others, going out of character in front of others is expressly forbidden. No matter what their level of ambition, though, most players spend a lot of energy creating a new reality. Doing so means creating fact and fiction about and within the world.

LARP-related fiction can be created inside or outside the perspective of the game. On the inside is what your character would experience and perform, and these activities contribute to the illusion: writing a letter to another character, telling a story, writing a song, reading a newspaper. This is commonly called "diegetic" information. Likewise, the term for the outside perspective is "nondiegetic," and that's what the players themselves know about the game. Nondiegetic information can be a booklet describing the world and its backstory, a presentation of the characters, or a map of the game area. Nondiegetic fiction can be a short story about your character written in the third person.

Creating diegetic and nondiegetic fiction and art is a great creative exercise that not only contributes to the collaborative work of art that is your LARP. It can also create seeds for other projects, and it even offers ways out of writer's block and other writing problems.

I wrote fiction for LARP for ten years. Some was commercial (stories designed for education or art projects); other tales were for fun, as art, or as storytelling experiments. For me, it all began with tabletop role-playing games. I was so excited after ending a session that I wanted to explore my character further and wrote anecdotes about important points in their lives. Shortly thereafter, I became part of a contemporary-

> "LARPing gives you a 360-degree immersion, and you can really sink into that other person's mind."

fantasy LARP project as a character developer. We wrote character sheets that consisted of ten pages of text and art illustrating the characters' lives: anecdotes, internal monologue, poetry, pictures, even made-up horoscopes.

In another project, loosely based on some of Ursula K. Le Guin's short stories of a civilization living in four-part marriages, characters were developed in family groups through drama exercises and group storytelling. We started out with no characters at all and would then do an exercise like the "statue game": Put two players in front of each other, pose them randomly, and then ask them: what's going on? What's your relationship to one another? Ten minutes later, the players would have figured out they were sister and brother and known what their childhood had been like. More of the family's story would surface when the pairs were switched out and were finally allowed to move and talk as their characters.

A third example is a LARP I organized about a 1970s commune, where the players were given only three lines of character information and had to discover the rest

during the game. We used a "do you remember?" kind of method for establishing relationships and history. A character would ask the other, "Do you remember when we demonstrated in that square, and you . . ." and then trail off, giving the other a chance to either say yes or no to this suggestion. The other might say, "Yes! I do remember! I threw a rock at the police, and they put me in jail." They could also say, "No, I don't. You must be thinking of someone else," but that wouldn't really lead anywhere. Saying yes is always more fun, even if it's "yes, but." With this collective dredging up of memories, the ensemble members established who they were, what their relationships were, and what the game was about.

The funny thing is that I very often suffered from writer's block, but *never* when writing or storytelling for LARPing. My own projects would wilt while I produced characters, game-related fiction, and entire story arcs for LARPs with seemingly little effort. I think this has to do with two things. Being alone with your story can be a huge burden, since all the responsibility of making it a good story lies with you.

Production photos and film stills from *Who Is Arvid Pekon?*, based on a Tidbeck story.

Creating a story with someone else eases that weight. With others along during the creative process, you go to unexpected and eye-opening places.

All forms of role-playing have a number of uses for a writer. If you organize one, you get to create a world and invite others to play. As a player, you train yourself in conquering fiction and making it yours; you learn to be open to your own creative impulses, to accept and incorporate input from others into your own art. Role-playing is also a great way to try on someone else's skin and see the world from a different point of view in a very hands-on manner. You can get to know your characters intimately by pretending to *be* them, not just pretending to *see* them.

LARPing gives you a 360-degree immersion, and you can really sink into that other person's mind. Doing something with your body is different than just going somewhere in your head. Add to that the sensation of physically experiencing the world as someone else, the mental agility that improvising with other people can give you, and the unexpected emotional impact of your character's feelings and state of mind bleeding over into yours. What's even better is that the presence of others will mean you're not completely in control of the story, which will jerk you out of your normal habits, if you're willing let it happen. Put briefly, you hone your storytelling skills in a number of ways.

The storytelling techniques used in role-playing and LARPing are extremely useful for a writer: for getting to know your characters and your world and for relieving writer's block, as well. If you're having trouble because your characters feel uninteresting, or you're not sure what they want, you can grab a friend and do the statue exercise. Or just have your LARPing buddy interview you as your character. You can write diary entries as your character. You can dress up as your character and try out moving or talking like him or her. I can't recommend playing a character from one of your stories for the entire length of a game, just like I'd never recommend playing yourself. Getting inside your character's head is good, but there's a balance between that and becoming too attached to and protective of your characters.

If your story is set in another world, then methods that LARP organizers use to enhance their players' experience can be handy. Does your world have newspapers? Write a news piece. What about literary traditions? You can write a poem or a passage from a book by a famous author. Write someone's shopping list, a bad joke, a list of popular insults.

Role-playing and improvisation are cardio exercises behind the creative process that supports fiction writing. You can participate in LARPs and games, you can join an improv theater group, or you can organize something yourself. You can tell any story in any genre, and it can go in just about any direction. For your brain, these are probably among the most exhilarating exercises ever, and they will reward you by offering a very interesting place to live and create.

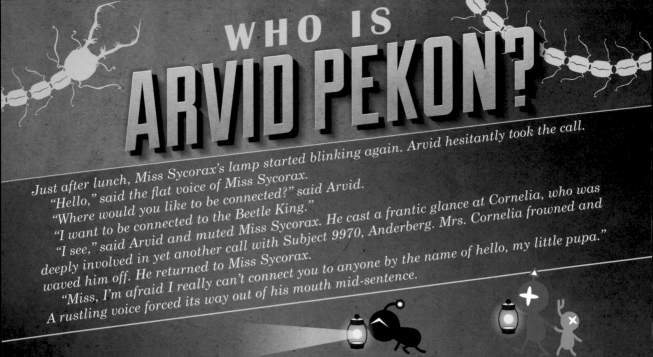

WHO IS ARVID PEKON?

Just after lunch, Miss Sycorax's lamp started blinking again. Arvid hesitantly took the call.

"Hello," said the flat voice of Miss Sycorax.

"Where would you like to be connected?" said Arvid.

"I want to be connected to the Beetle King."

"I see," said Arvid and muted Miss Sycorax. He cast a frantic glance at Cornelia, who was deeply involved in yet another call with Subject 9970, Anderberg. Mrs. Cornelia frowned and waved him off. He returned to Miss Sycorax.

"Miss, I'm afraid I really can't connect you to anyone by the name of hello, my little pupa."

A rustling voice forced its way out of his mouth mid-sentence.

Who Is Arvid Pekon? had its beginnings in a 2002 avant-garde LARP version of *Hamlet* that I took part in. It was set in a bunker under Elsinore castle during the 1930s—a very elaborate and completely immersive game. There were three old field telephones in the game area, from which you could call to a "switchboard" and ask to be connected to characters not in the game. This was a tremendously useful system for feeding plot information to the players, advancing the story (Norway has invaded!), or just giving the players an extra dimension by letting them have a conversation with their mother or a friend. I was a player in the first staging of the game; in the second one, I was at the behind-the-scenes switchboard. We had a great time dialing up players to give them plot information or impersonating the people they wanted to talk to, all the while trying to keep track of who had said what and when. The next day I woke up with the idea of what would happen if such a switchboard existed in real life. The story I wrote has since been turned into a short film starring an acclaimed Polish actor. Stills from the film's shooting are reproduced on the opposite page.

TIDBECK'S LARP EXERCISE: SWITCHING ROLES

This is actually a method more than an exercise. Doing writing exercises as someone else can help with both writer's block and getting out of a rut. It's most fun to do this in a group. It doesn't have to be a full-on role-playing situation, just a chance to step outside of your usual way of thinking.

Write some first names on scraps of paper (some of them must be of another gender than the one you identify as) and put them in a pile. Create another pile of notes, this time with professions. A third pile will have personality traits ("shy," "aggressive," "loves romance"). Draw one first name, one profession, and two personality traits. This is your character. Does it look meager? Don't worry; your brain will fill in the blanks in no time. It's what brains do. Now, do a simple writing exercise: automatic writing is a good place to start or use a prompt. Don't try to imagine what this character would write; just *pretend* you are him or her writing.

If it's hard to get into character, have someone interview you as your character. Again, your brain will fill in the blanks. If you're alone, write an introduction speech or a diary entry.

This method can be made as complex—or simple—as you like, and it can be applied to just about anything. For this to work, there's only one "must": respect what you're doing. Be sincere about your character and his or her work. Irony or sarcasm will kill the experience.

GEORGE R. R. MARTIN ON THE CRAFT OF WRITING

Four-time Hugo Award winner George R. R. Martin is one of the best-known fantasy writers of his generation. He has written for television and has crafted some of the most iconic stories of the past forty years, including "Sandkings" and "The Pear-Shaped Man." However, he is famous for his Song of Ice and Fire heroic fantasy series, which has sold millions of copies and been turned into a drama on the popular HBO television cable channel. Inspired by the War of the Roses, Martin's Song of Ice and Fire novels are known for their addictive nature, in part due to compelling characters and the complex yet page-turning story lines. I interviewed Martin via telephone to talk to him about those aspects of craft that contribute most notably to his success.

What does a typical rough draft of yours look like?
I don't really do drafts in the normal sense. I rewrite a lot as I go along. The first thing I do when I boot up in the morning is reread what I did the day before or the week before. Almost never can I reread something without fiddling with it and polishing it; changing things in what I like, what I don't like. Obviously a lot of of it is just correcting typos and infelicitous phrasing, but sometimes it's more thorough than that; it's structural changes. Rewriting is a constant process for me. I don't plunge through and do a first draft and then go back and do a second draft.

How often do the novels change as you're writing them? Do you often wind up somewhere very different from where you expected?
I wouldn't say very different. It depends on the novel. I think with Song of Ice and Fire I'm pretty well hitting all the beats as I originally envisioned them. I haven't taken too many detours. Although you do discover a lot in the actual process of writing, and that's part of the fun for me—the stuff that I discover along the way. If you go back to some of my earlier books, there were maybe more substantive changes; certainly, I made big changes in my novel *Fevre Dream*.

What changed in *Fevre Dream*?
My original intention for *Fevre Dream* was to end the book with a big steamboat race in which the *Fevre Dream* put out onto the river again and joined the famous race between the *Natchez* and the *Robert E. Lee*. Then I realized that really made no sense. It would've taken the whole world

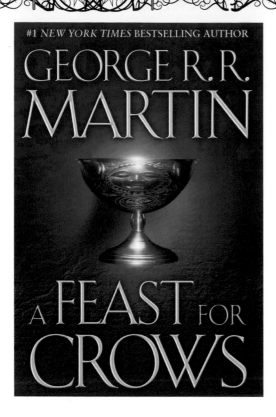

#1 NEW YORK TIMES BESTSELLING AUTHOR

GEORGE R. R. MARTIN

A FEAST FOR CROWS

into an alternate history, since that was such a huge public event, and also, given the actual life spans of steamboats, the steamboat would not have been in a condition to race. So I finally just said, "No, it was a colorful notion when I had it, but . . . no." The idea sort of survives in the actual text of the book as a dream that Abner Marsh has. You could read that and say that a more fully fleshed-out version of that would've been the original ending. But I think the actual ending I chose is much stronger and certainly much more realistic.

You've said your process includes "blind alleys and dead ends." How is that important to a writer?

I think it depends on the writer. I've often talked about there being two types of writers, which I call the Architects and the Gardeners. The Architects do plan everything ahead of time, just as a real architect does, building a house. An architect builds a house, and he knows how many rooms it's going to be, and how many square feet in each room, and where the pipes are, what the roof is going to be made of, the dimensions of everything, even where the plugs are going to be in the walls. He knows everything before a nail is driven, before the foundation is dug, and before all of the blueprints are proofed. There are writers who work that way.

The Gardener just sort of digs a hole and plants a seed, and then he waters it with his blood and sweat before waiting to see what will come up. It's not totally random, because obviously the Gardener knows what he's planted; he knows whether it's an oak tree or a pumpkin. If he's not taken totally by surprise by further inspiration, he has a general idea of what he's doing.

I don't think there are really many pure Architects or pure Gardeners in writing. I think most writers are a combination of the two. But they tend to lean to one side or another, and I lean very much to the side of the Gardener.

As a young writer, did you know you were a Gardener? Did it frustrate you that sometimes you got stuck?

I never really considered doing it any other way, but especially in the early years of my career I had a lot of aborted stories, or stories that I just started, and I had an opening scene, or I had a situation, then I wrote a page or two pages or ten pages, and then somehow I got stuck or it took a wrong direction. I would put that story in the drawer, and I would begin another story. I had a lot of fragments. I think that's what a lot of young writers go through. When Robert Heinlein gave his four rules for writing, the first one was "you must write," but the second one was "you must finish what you write." A lot of young writers somehow get stuck, or it goes awry and they don't finish those stories. Heinlein was right: You have to overcome that. It's a thing I think I have largely overcome, but I wouldn't say I have entirely overcome it.

Let's talk about scenes. You're masterful at being able to cut scenes for maximum tension. From your perspective, is achieving the right effect just a case of shortening or lengthening scenes?

I don't think it's purely a matter of the length of the scene, although certainly that is part of it. One of the things you learn working in television, if you want to keep working in television, is how

to structure your TV shows with act breaks, because you have to factor in where the story is going to stop. You don't want the viewer to click to another channel during that time. There are four-act shows and five-act shows, and four acts with a teaser, or whatever. There may be slightly different structures, but they all have act breaks.

Now, what is an act break? It can be a cliff-hanger. A cliff-hanger is obviously a very good act break, a very powerful act break. But you can't have a cliff-hanger at every chapter. An act break is something that ends the act on a note that hopefully will bring the viewer, or the reader, back into a resolution of something. It could be the introduction of a new element or an interesting new character, a twist or a turn that ends the chapter. Even sometimes just a snappy line of dialogue, something that takes you someplace unexpected or reveals something new about the character, or does a reversal. There are many kinds of act breaks. You want all of your chapters to end with that sort of act break; to end in such a way that, having finished that Tyrion chapter, the reader is anxious for the next Tyrion chapter, but, of course, he doesn't get it right away. He now has to read an Arya chapter or a Daenerys chapter or Jon Snow chapter.

Each of those ends with an act break, too. You read the Daenerys chapter, and then you want the next Daenerys chapter. Again, you can't have that, so there's this constant process going on. But I have to say it's not an easy process. Sometimes it doesn't work right. You reach the end of a chapter, and it just sort of dribbles out, and you have to figure out, well, what kind of act break can you do? Does it involve changing the chronology? Should you change your chronology? You don't want to get too tricky. I do a lot of rewriting and restructuring and rethinking because of this issue. Some of the early drafts have much weaker act breaks than others. This is one of the things I do when revising. It's not easy, but I think it's very much worth doing, and it gives you that page-turning effect you want.

Is there anything dramatized in the Song of Ice and Fire TV series so far that made you want to go back and tinker with something in the books?

I'm pretty happy with the books as they are. I don't know that I would want to tinker too much. The television series has added some great scenes that were not in the books, though. I'm thinking of the scene in the Black Water between Bran and the Hound or the Robert/Cersei scene, during the first season, where they discuss their marriage. Those are powerful scenes that I did not have in the books, probably because I have a very strict viewpoint structure and I don't have the viewpoint character present in any of those scenes. To include them in the books would mean abandoning my viewpoint structure—either that or changing and adding Robert as a viewpoint or adding the Hound as a viewpoint; those are not changes that I want to make. I don't want to just jump into a character for a scene and then never return to them. There's a reason why each viewpoint character is in the book, and I already have an awful lot of them. I don't think I want to add more.

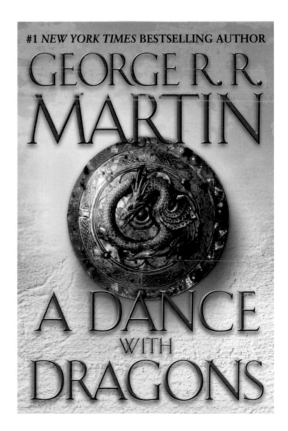

Are there things that you typically have no interest in dramatizing?

I don't think I'd say there's a whole category of things—like, "I don't ever want to dramatize a dancing scene" or something like that. It all depends on the specifics of the scene and the book and what you're talking about. Battle scenes, for example, can get tedious.

In the first book, *Game of Thrones*, I had a situation where I had three battles occurring in fairly close proximity. The question I faced there is, "Well, am I going to dramatize all three of these battles," which would've involved many, many pages of people hitting other people with axes and descriptions of screaming horses and flights of arrows and, you know, "he swung the sword, and the other guy's sword hit his shield" and all that, which is fine and it adds something. But did I really want so much of that written out? So I decided to adopt a different approach there.

The first of those three battles I dramatized in the manner I've described. The second battle I chose to sort of half dramatize. I told it from the viewpoint of a character who was not part of the battle. She was on a hill overlooking the battle, and she couldn't see what was going on, but she could *hear* what was going on. All you got was the sound effects. You didn't actually get any visuals, and you were outside the battle rather than inside of it. For the third battle, I simply had a messenger arrive and tell what had happened.

I could've dramatized all three of those battles, but they were so close to each other that I think I would've been repeating the same sort of thing. Instead, I adopted different approaches. Now, will I always do that? No, not necessarily. Some things are best presented offstage and some things are best dramatized. Those are the kind of calls you have to make. When you come to each scene: Do I want to dramatize it; do I not want to dramatize it?

Another way this comes up is with travel. Especially in fantasy, geography is a big part of what you're doing, and the characters are traveling long distances. Do you just want to cut from one point on the map to the other? Okay, he gets on his horse, he rides up to the castle, and then you cut to four weeks later; he gets off his

horse at the other castle he's going to at the other end of the realm. Or do you want to dramatize day by day what is happening to him and what he's thinking, what he's experiencing? Well, that partly depends on what happens on the journey: who he meets and what he learns and what his thoughts are.

You can have the story line where there's a lot of physical action. You could also have one where there's relatively little physical action, but you're setting a scene, you're showing what the land's kingdom is like, and you're doing some psychological exploration of the character. That's certainly the route I took with Tyrion's journeys in *A Dance with Dragons*. Yes, there are some very important events shown in the Tyrion scenes, but there's also a lot of stuff where he's meeting these other people, we're getting a sense of these other people, and he's going through some huge internal struggles.

Why are setting and description important?

I do think description is an important part of fantasy; at least epic fantasy. I read for vicarious experience. I want the writer to take me out of my skin and take me out of the place I am and bring me somewhere else, whether that place is ancient Rome or contemporary Chicago or some imaginary kingdom—and I want the sensory input. I want to hear the sounds and taste the food and smell the city and all of the things that are going on, so I get the illusion of actually being there. That's what I certainly strive to do as a writer. That's what I look for as a reader.

Setting is a huge part of fantasy. All of the great fantasies not only have great characters in them, they also have great settings. Take *The Dying Earth* by Jack Vance, which I know you love, too. Yes, we love Jack's characters—his various magicians and wizards and all the other clever creations—but a lot of them [read] for the world because the world was so wonderful. Middle Earth, Robert E. Howard's Hyborian Age, my own Westeros—the world is very important. This is something where I think a lot of fantasy falls down. There's nothing memorable about the worlds created. There's nothing unique about them.

It's interesting to me to look at Tolkien, who is always, I think, the model for me. I remember when Tolkien had his first great period of popularity back in the 1960s when I was at college. Everybody was reading Tolkien, and all the college students had "Frodo Lives" buttons and so forth, and they had posters on their dorm-room walls; my roommate had one of them. It was not a poster of a character; it was a map of Middle Earth. That was the big-selling poster, this

You've said that visiting Hadrian's Wall was useful in terms of thinking of the Wall in the North in your series. How important are real world experiences to a fantasy setting?
This was a visit to Hadrian's Wall in 1981, more than a decade before I made use of it. It was a feeling that I always remembered because of the circumstances. I was traveling around England and Scotland with the writer Lisa Tuttle, and we finally reached Hadrian's Wall, which was a place

A view of Hadrian's wall.

map of Middle Earth; it was the land. The place had become a character, had become the soul of the book. Then you look at all the mini-Tolkien calendars that have come out since, and you see imaginary places, like Minas Tirith or the Mines of Moria, or the Woods of Lothlórien. I say those words and images are conjured in your mind. You see a picture of Minas Tirith, you recognize it just the same way you might recognize Paris or New York if either was depicted in a work of art.

we had wanted to visit. It was a late afternoon in October or November, I think, and coming on toward evening, and all of the other tourists were leaving. The sun was starting to set, and it was starting to get cold and dark. The tour buses had all gone.

We climbed up on the wall and had it all to ourselves. With the shadows growing, and the sort of loneliness of standing there, with the winter wind coming up. I stood there and tried

to imagine myself as a Roman legionary from Italy or from Carthage in Africa or from Antioch in the Middle East, and I pretended we'd been assigned there. You're guarding the end of the world, and you're looking at those distant hills and those woods, and you don't know what's going to lurk from them to threaten you and what you're protecting. It gave me a shiver. I held on to that shiver for all those years, and ultimately made use of it when the time finally came to write *Game of Thrones*.

There's a scene in *A Dance with Dragons* that I thought was particularly evocative, where Tyrion is on a boat going down a stretch of haunted river, with ruins to either side and odd events happening. I was wondering if you could talk a little bit about that scene.
I've always been attracted to rivers; there's just something very cool about being on a river and floating down it. You're seeing the banks go by, and you don't know what's around the next bend of the river. There's almost a sense of mystery that is sort of exciting, and I wanted to capture some of that. I also had some material that I wanted to produce there about the history of that place, and backstory that I may pick up in the future—all of which I had hinted at in prior books—and now Tyrion was traveling through the midst of that.

The mists and the history and the curse give that scene its wounded feel. There's a lot of stuff

going on; games within games below the surface. Even as Tyrion is fencing, he's figuring out things and pieces are falling into place. And there are the Stone Men, the victims of greyscale, which is something I wanted to get in . . . this disease.

I read a lot of history and a lot of historical fiction. The things that have impressed me about actual history include the great extent to which our real history was affected by things like the Black Death and rats and fleas and these various plagues that would sweep over Europe or Asia at particular points of time. They have more impact on our history than we recognize, but you seldom see them in fantasy. No one ever seems to get sick in a lot of fantasy novels, despite the fact that the people in the books don't really understand about germs and bacteria and things like that, and their medicine is relatively primitive, which is all part of why these things are a problem. All of that was at play in that chapter.

It's also a very strange scene, something I love about it. I love strangeness in fantasy, but sometimes you're told that you can only have so many strange elements before the reader loses interest. Does this figure into your thoughts ever?
I certainly keep it in mind. It was always my intention to start Song of Ice and Fire with almost no fantasy elements in it, traditional fantasy elements, and then to slowly introduce more, so the amount of magic and strangeness in the books would gradually rise through the series. Even at the end, when I finish the series, it's still going to be low fantasy compared to the very high magic kind of stuff that a lot of fantasy writers out there are doing, where the amount of sorcery and wizardry and spells and such is huge right from the start.

But I just don't find those books as compelling as the ones that are relatively low magic. Again, I go back to Tolkien, even though he had elves and various races and hints of magic in there. I mean, Gandalf being a wizard and all that—you don't really see Gandalf working at his spells. And he doesn't have any super-duper magical weapons. He just fights with his sword like everybody else. The magic swords that various people have, these legendary swords with names, mostly don't have any particular power except they glow blue when orcs are about. I think Tolkien was a pretty smart guy in the way he handled all of that.

Are you saying magic can become a kind of repetitive special effect?

One reason is my own beliefs about magic: If you're going to have magic in your story, you have to keep it magical, so to speak. This is a supernatural element. It doesn't follow the laws of nature. It doesn't follow any laws we understand. There's something frightening about it. This is the unknowable. I think magic should be handled that way. Magic should always remain a little mysterious and a little dangerous. Even though I know there are a lot of fantasy writers out there who devote a lot of time to inventing magical systems: "This is how magic works in my world, and here are the rules of it and so forth."

Magic should not have a system. This essentially reduces magic to fake science, where we have magic rules, and if you put in so much eye of newt and so much virgin's blood into this, you will get something that does that. Well, maybe you will, maybe you won't. I more like the idea that you can't really master some of these things. There are dangers to that and they're not completely understood; make the supernatural dangerous, make the supernatural mysterious. Don't make it just fake science.

You've said that identifying with characters not like yourself is a process of empathy. But what do you need to know about a character to write from a perspective that's different from your own?

It really varies character to character. For some characters you want a lot of backstory; for others, maybe not so much. I don't think there's a hard-and-fast rule about that. Jack Vance is a writer who has always done very well with this, because I always get the feeling when I read a Vance story that all of the characters are people, even the minor characters.

One of Vance's characters checks into an inn, and you know the innkeeper is going to emerge, even if he's only there for two pages, as a definite presence. Whether he's a fool or a rogue, he has his own thing going. He doesn't know that

he's a bit player in a larger story. He thinks he's living in the middle of a story in which the hero is Bill the Innkeeper. I always try to keep that in mind—that each minor character who comes on, even if it's only for one scene, has his own agenda, his own ideas, and he's not just there to serve the leads, so to speak. I don't know if that helps make the characters a little more real, but it seems to work.

But, yes, there are definitely challenges to writing characters unlike you, the writer. There's no doubt about that, and if you're going to write fantasy and science fiction, you're inevitably going to wind up needing to do just that. If I was to write characters exactly like myself, I'd just be writing endless stories about baby-boomer kids born in New Jersey, growing up in the projects in blue-collar families. Which is fine, and I've written about characters like that. But I also want to write about kings and aliens and spaceship captains and all of that—all these things that I've never been.

I think the approach that I take, whoever I'm writing about, is to remember our shared humanity, because the truth is, as much as there are differences between us, we are all basically human; we all have the same fundamental drives. It doesn't matter if I'm writing about a man or a woman, or a giant or a dwarf, or a young person or an old person; they have a certain common humanity. They have far more in common than they have things that separate. If you keep this in mind, I think you'll do pretty well.

Can you give me a specific example where you have gotten stuck because you couldn't figure out something important about a character?

In some cases you have an experience that you're going to write about that you don't actually know about. You have to ask people who might perhaps know about it. I suppose one example that comes to mind is in the first book, when Sansa gets her first period. Obviously this is something, as a male, that I did not go through. It was a crucial scene. Sansa knew she was a captive and that she was supposed to be married to Joffrey, an event postponed because she was still a child. Now suddenly she wasn't a child. In the medieval mindset, there's no kind of concept of adolescence; you go straight from childhood to adulthood—for girls, the start of menstruation, or the "flowering," as they call it. Sansa was now eligible to be married and to be bedded. That's the onset of sexual maturity by their standards.

So I talked to a number of women about the subject, since it's not a subject I often sit around talking about with friends. I said, "Okay, I'm going to ask you a question—it might be a little embarrassing." I had to ask: "What was it like the first time for you? Were you afraid? Did you take it in your stride? What were the physical things? What were your feelings about it?" Yes, not everybody was comfortable talking about it, but some were. I learned a lot about the subject, which I then used in that scene. I think that's what you have to do when you are going to write a scene that involves an experience, an important experience, that you have never had.

What do you think was the weakest part of your writing in the early part of your career?
Working in Hollywood sharpened my dialogue, most notably. When you're writing for television and screen, and particularly if you're on a television show—where what you write is actually going to be made and you're actually going to hear actors rehearsing it and saying it—it rapidly becomes apparent what kind of speeches work and what kind of speeches don't work. When you hear actors saying the lines or a line that's awkward or badly phrased, or admits too many possible readings, that fact jumps out at you.

I think television also improved my sense of structure; that whole act-break thing I talked about before.

How important is it for a writer to be really well-read in the field they're entering?
Actually, there's a certain double-edged sword there. If you're not well-read in the field that you're going into, you run a risk of reinventing the wheel. Of course, you do see this sometimes with mainstream writers who come into science fiction and fantasy. They're using ideas that

"They Weren't Alone" by Charles Vess (*A Storm of Swords* Vol. 1, limited edition, 2002)

always try to encourage the students to read widely in science fiction and fantasy. I remember the first time I taught at Clarion, I circulated a list of fifty great books that every science-fiction writer should read, or maybe not-great books: just fifty books every science-fiction writer should read. Some of them are actually pretty bad books, but they were important books in one way or another in the history of the genre. I did that because in the class it had rapidly become apparent to me that a lot of the participants had never read any of these writers. I was making references to classic stories and novels, and I was getting these blank looks, which I didn't think was good.

Can you remember some of the worst advice about writing you received as a beginning writer?
I remember one editor told me very early in my career when rejecting one of my stories that I should try writing gothics for a while, and I would learn a lot from that.

were old twenty years ago. On the other hand, sometimes people coming in from the outside can bring a different way of looking at things. They're not necessarily so inculcated with the tropes and stereotypes and things, so they're less likely to duplicate them—and sometimes they can do something that's very fresh and original and interesting. You can argue that logic, certainly. Myself, I'm inclined to think it is better to know who went before and what they did.

When I teach at the Clarion Writers' Workshop, or Clarion West or something like that, I

I didn't find that tremendously helpful. But I don't know if I got much bad advice, in general. You get bad advice on specific stories, or, at least, editors or producers or networks will want you to make changes to a story that are not necessarily, you know, good, and you have to resist that. There is sometimes a tendency, particularly for young writers, not to resist, because you want to sell your work and you don't want to get a reputation for being difficult. That's perfectly human. Nobody wants to be difficult. Still, it's your name that's going to be on the book, which is

why prose will always be my first love over television and film, much as I love television and film. It's your book. Editors will make suggestions, but ultimately all they can do is reject a story, and then you can sell it to someone else if you really believe in it. I would say never do anything that you think will make the story worse, because ultimately you will be judged on the quality of the story. You can't plead, "The editor made me do it."

Who was most helpful to you as a beginning writer?

That's an interesting question. I don't know that I really had a mentor. I was kind of off by myself writing my own stories. I read voraciously, and, among other things, I read how-to books. One of the first books about writing science fiction [I read] was L. Sprague de Camp's science-fiction handbook, which I encountered in my public library in Bayonne, New Jersey. I took it out and read it, and then I had to return it. But I took it out again and again and again. Whenever it was due, I would return it, and then I would take it out again. I kept it on my shelf for a year through this ruse. That work had a huge influence on me, but I can't claim that de Camp himself was a mentor. I met him once or twice and talked to him, but I'm not even sure if he knew who I was.

I think the writer and editor Ben Bova was probably the most important editor in my early career. He took over *Analog* magazine in 1971, just as I was starting, and he edited it through most of the 1970s. *Analog* became my main market. It became the market where most of my best stories were published. Then, of course, when Ben went on to *Omni*, he in a sense took me with him, and I published one of my most successful stories, "The Pear-Shaped Man."

What about feedback from your readers? You have a huge audience. I imagine some readers have very definite ideas about what you should and shouldn't write.

I do get a lot of feedback from readers. Most of it is just fan letters; it's very complimentary. But I do get letters from people saying, "please don't kill this character, I love them" or "don't hurt this other character," which I read and certainly

I'm aware of, but I make no promises. Again, I don't think you can let your story be changed by readers. I think that's a mistake.

Art is not a democracy, as I've said many times. The readers don't get to vote on how it will end. There have been periods in history where *Romeo and Juliet* was staged, and they would change the ending because the audience didn't like the fact that Romeo and Juliet both die at the end. They would change the ending so Romeo and Juliet lived happily ever after. That was an audience pleaser during the Victorian era and earlier eras. It was bad. It lessened the power of that work as a piece of art.

Obviously, you've got to please some of the readers, or you're not going to have a career. At the same time, you can't always be running around trying to please them all and taking votes or saying, well, what do you think would be the best way to end this kind of . . . the way that Hollywood does. I think that's a mistake. On my blog I posted, in response to some of these issues, a YouTube video of Ricky Nelson's "Garden Party," which is sort of my anthem, because he sings that you have to please yourself, not everybody else. That's what a writer has to do. In the end, it's your name on it; it's your story. You hope that other people will like it, but it's your story not their story. They can write their own story and end it how they really want.

GAMES & STORYTELLING
WITH WILL HINDMARCH

Will Hindmarch writes games and stories. He has contributed work to acclaimed games, like *Dragon Age*, *Vampire: The Requiem*, *Trail of Cthulhu*, and *Fiasco*. He co-wrote *Things We Think About Games* and edited *The Bones: Us and Our Dice*. His stories appear in anthologies as diverse as *The Thackery T. Lambshead Cabinet of Curiosities* and *The Lion and the Aardvark*.

Games and fiction have different goals that help explain what makes them different. But despite these differences, stories and games can share some common elements, depending on the kind of story and the kind of game. Point of view, characterization, pacing, plotting, and scenes have similar if not always identical applications across story and game genres. Certainly, every game draws on notions of story to different degrees. It's also useful to talk about games in narrative terms, because, for all their differences, stories and games have *us* in common.

Any play-through of a game is a potential story. In tightly plotted video games, the progress through the game levels—from game board to game board, if you will—follows the same course every time, ideally calibrated to deliver a satisfying narrative as part of the play experience. The story is clear, even if the telling of the story may vary in terms of, say, pacing (how long does it take you to fight free of the bad guys?) or characterization (does your secret operative spare the bad guys' lives or not?). The story remains a kind of journey from the first game level to the last even if the details change.

THE RULES FOR
JOURNEY TO
THE WIZARD'S TOWER

THE SETUP: The Prince has been captured by the wicked Wizard and carried off to the Wizard's Tower. It's up to the player's heroine to rescue the Prince. *(For simplicity's sake, we'll assume a single player sitting down to play against the game itself, rather than racing against a competitor. The full version of this game would include additional rules.)*

THE GOAL: At the beginning of play, the default target ending is the successful rescue of the Prince from the Wizard's Tower.

THE STARTING POINT: The player's pawn or "character" begins on the Start space.

PLAYING THE GAME: On each turn, the player rolls a die and moves the character that many spaces forward or back, stopping her character at each Destination space she reaches (such as the Crossroads, the Troll Bridge, or the Ancient Ruins) even if her roll would carry her past it. At forks in the path, the player chooses which direction to travel.

LANDING ON A DESTINATION OR ENCOUNTER SPACE: When landing on such a space, the player draws a card from the deck. Some cards help the character, and some cards challenge the character.

THE NATURE OF THE CARDS: Cards describe treasures the character uncovers, challenges (like monsters and traps) the character must confront or avoid, and trials the character undergoes during her journey. For example, a few cards in the deck change the "win" condition, giving the character a new End space to target, such as the Hidden City or the Tomb of Heroes.

KEEPING OR DISCARDING CARDS: Some cards are held in the hand, and some are placed on the board when they were drawn. A challenge card called the Bandits, for example, blocks the path where it was drawn until that card can be discarded. To overcome certain challenges, the player needs specific cards. The treasure card called the Sword allows the character to discard a challenge card like the Bandits, for example. Some challenge cards are held in the hand, representing things like doubts, hostile pursuers, and other obstacles that move along with the character on her journey.

NARRATING PLAY: As you draw cards and traverse spaces, try weaving a story around the events that transpire. What does it mean for the story if the Bandits appear in the Ancient Ruins or if the Basilisk is encountered in the Hidden City? How do the interactions of the cards unfold in your imagination?

WINNING THE GAME: The player wins by reaching the End space coinciding with the character's current goal while having no challenge cards in her hand. Not all endings are happy for the Prince or the character—one End sees the character rescuing the Prince from the Wizard, while another sees the character interring the Prince in the Tomb of Heroes—but for the player, reaching the appropriate End counts as a win.

To explore how games can provide insight into fiction, I've created a simple board game that we can use as a shared reference. It's called Journey to the Wizard's Tower. It employs some common swords-and-sorcery elements, in part because most readers will be familiar with them. With the board in front of us, we can glean some additional insights.

The Board as Play Space or "Magic Circle"

The game board for Journey to the Wizard's Tower is a play space or playground. Game play happens on these playgrounds, where different rules apply. Playgrounds can be literal, physical spaces, like a tic-tac-toe board or a soccer field—or they can be notional spaces defined by the ritualized thinking of the participants, as in a game like twenty questions. The space where play happens—whether it's a game board or a virtual world—is sometimes also called a magic circle. Within a magic circle, some things are allowed and some things are disallowed, according to the rules of play. Maybe unicorns are "real" within the magic circle, but everyone can speak only in questions?

The setting for any story is also a kind of magic circle. In a fantasy saga's magic circle, magic might be real (an allowance) but unable to heal (a disallowance), for example. Constraints are a part of magic circles just as they are a part of creative play. These constraints become boundaries or obstacles that play can build on or push back against, defining and contextualizing core dramatic conflicts.

CHALLENGE!

THE BANDITS

These Bandits waylay anyone they deem weak or vulnerable, but they respect the appearance of strength.

This card remains in play on the space where it was drawn. No one can move past unless The Bandits are driven off permanently by The Sword or paid off with a Treasure for each passage.

Journey to the Wizard's Tower pits the player's character—a protagonist—against numerous challenges, printed on the cards drawn during play. In game terms, these might all be defined as features of the environment because they come from the cards, and the cards are part of the playground. But if you were to tell a story about the game—narrating as you go, perhaps—you could make the Bandits into characters with ambitions and frailties, just as you might make your own pawn into a conflicted antihero.

Playgrounds yield stories almost automatically, even if most of these stories might be considered mere situations or clichés. But even rote or worn stories can be told well—a writer can control the playground and the pawns so that a good story unfolds. How?

Think of a sports movie in which every circumstance is measured and employed *just so* to cultivate the heightened circumstances that imbue the climactic big game with hefty stakes for the players. Even if we've seen a hundred baseball games and understand the typical structure of a baseball movie, we can still enjoy the story. We might even be carried along to an unexpected ending.

In Journey to the Wizard's Tower, the writer could control the game to produce results that align with her narrative vision. For example:

- Fill the deck with only those cards that suit the theme or motif for one vision of the story.
- Stack the cards in an order that yields a preferred dramatic escalation.
- Instead of rolling the die to move the pawn, decide exactly how far the pawn travels, mapping out a route that best corresponds to the tale in mind.

The writer might attempt to rig every aspect of the resulting story this way. Thus, the game is also the outline for a fantasy story—or, really, several stories, since the board is a play space, not a script, and contains multiple possible journeys and endings. Actual play can imbue and inform this outline:

- The game adds certain fantastical elements as allowances and applies constraints as disallowances. In the game, trolls and basilisks are real.
- The game is played on predefined routes that must be honored, shaping the magic circle and keeping the player from wandering somewhere too dull. No one swims in Gloom Lake, according to the rules.
- Play uses cards that describe how the character interacts with the imaginary world to overcome challenges. Mirrors best basilisks in this world, while only swords drive off bandits. Characters cannot join up with the bandits or parley with the basilisk—It's literally not in the cards.

The play space grants and it limits; in doing so, it potentially provokes and inspires. What we've done is create an environment and load it with potential conflicts and actions that entertain us or enact our vision. We have said what is true and what is possible here. You can rig the game so a specific story (or type of story) unfolds, or you can tell a story that emerges through play. Now ask yourself, as the writer, what story will you tell in this world?

THE EMERGING STORY

If I'm playing games with live players, I don't know which route will be taken through the play space and, therefore, which story will result. Is this a story about the checkmating of the White King? Is this a story about how the ball team won a game they were expected to lose? Is this a story about how the Farmer rescued the Prince from the Wizard's Tower or is this a story about how the Farmer gave her life in pursuit of that goal? The actual play of the game dramatizes the beats of the tale for us. It tells us when the bandits attack.

As a writer, too, I sometimes don't know what's going to happen. Sometimes, even though I'm working alone, I'm surprised by my characters. Writing allows control over the circumstances and facts of the story as it develops, but being able to identify and cultivate an emerging story is a valuable skill. I learned it from playing games.

Now consider the writer who decides what cards are drawn on each suitable space and what numbers the players roll on the dice for each turn. That's controlling the playground and, while it's cheating during play, it is fair game for the writer, whose job is to make sure the story that comes out of the magic circle is worth telling.

But it's a matter of degrees.

Drama sometimes results from inevitability, and the goals of play define the endgame such that any legal outcome may create a satisfying inevitability. *Some* king was going to be checkmated; we knew that when we set out on this tale. Fair play means that the resulting ending feels right—foreseeable even if it was not foreseen.

Yet surprises (and sometimes twists) are valuable in any story. Play allows a writer to surprise herself, to twist the tale by acting on it via the constraints established for the magic circle without succumbing to cold fiat or authorial decree alone. The interaction of agents within the playground—the many pieces of the two armies, the athletes on the teams, the cards and characters on the board—yields unforeseen moments that become rich fodder for storytelling.

When the number of actions available to the players is greater than the choice of *move* or *capture,* surprises abound. For example, what would happen if chess allowed the knight and the bishop to conspire to recruit an enemy rook to their side?

THE ROLE OF INTERSECTIONS AND CHOICE

Drama resides in decisions, and decisions are made at intersections. Decisions are the core component of game play. Every turn, every at-bat, a decision is made, perhaps by rolled dice or the skill of a player's swing or by choice alone. Decisions are also vital components of stories and expressions of character. Consider these decisions and how they affect everything else:

- Will the Farmer's decision to head toward the Nomad Camp rather than the Ancient Ruins make her too late to rescue the Prince?
- What does it say about her when she chooses to reject the marriage proposal of the King of the Hidden City and resumes her quest for the Prince?
- Does the Farmer accept the End she can see, or does she travel until she draws a new End card, prolonging the game to change her fate?

Creative constraints—the limits of play within the magic circle—make intersections clear and appreciable. To stand in an open desert and pick a direction of travel without a map can lead to decision paralysis: too many options with too little information. To stand in a field demarcated with square spaces and populated by enemy chessmen results in many options, but they are more measurable. To stand at a three-way crossroads yields a stark decision: left or right?

A decision isn't worth much without information. Does the character know what awaits him or her down the right-hand path or the left? Does he or she know what's at risk or what may be gained? Suspense can be cultivated whenever we don't know which path a character will take, and that suspense can come from limited information about the path or its consequences. Choosing just how much information to share with the character—and with the reader!—is a matter of craft and artistry.

CHALLENGE!

WIZARD'S AGENTS

Agents of the Wizard pursue you hither and yon, reporting back to him through their nefarious sorcery.

Keep this card in your hand until you can discard it using The Cloak of Shadows. You cannot access the Wizard's City space with this card in your hand; land on any adjacent space instead.

In games, every choice should be *genuine*. Real outcomes with real consequences should result from the player's decision, whether it risks an at-bat or a knight or a perilous card being drawn. The outcome of the game must not just be in doubt—it must be genuinely undetermined until play determines it.

In a story, however, the choices a character makes may be illusory. You may know full well that your protagonist survives any encounters on her way to the Wizard's Tower because you decided in advance that your story is about the Farmer who confronts the Wizard to save the Prince. Every step along that route, then, is meant to generate thrills and suspense and fascination for the reader as audience—to put on a show, to throw the ending into doubt even though it has actually already been determined. In fiction, that's fine. The linear journey can be worth the story.

Consider, though, what happens when you define the magic circle—the fictional world—and the rules by which it operates without predetermining the route or fate of the characters. You may decide that every route at the crossroads takes the character to the River of Woes or in the correct direction of the Wizard's Tower. However, you might not decide which path the character *actually takes* until you get to that part of the story and, as a player in the game you designed, let yourself choose.

Is the choice too easy? Is it obvious? Is it boring? Then you have the power as the writer and the worldbuilder to change that choice to make it more dramatic, to accentuate the doubts or fears or wonderings of your character. You can refine the rules and the world—at that point or in future drafts—to get a good story, told well. Maybe you let your character smell the stink of trolls down one path or recall the warnings of her parents about the rushing waters of the Old Fjord.

Part of making the character's choices work in your story is making the choice right for the character. You may have decided when you outlined your story or mapped your world that your Farmer heroine would venture to the Hidden City, turn down an opportunity for fortune, and continue on her journey to the Wizard's Tower. So what happens if your heroine gets to the Troll Bridge and reveals to you (perhaps while you're writing her dialogue with the troll) that she would prefer to head toward the Ancient Ruins and the Forest of Giants?

More information about the world within the magic circle and the built-in consequences can cause genuinely unexpected outcomes—even unexpected by you, the writer! The ability to move from the aerial view, from which you can see what's over the next mountain or beyond Gloom Lake, and zoom into a character's own perspective to make personal decisions about your world is a vital authorial skill. Your character may have imperfect information, unreasonable expectations, or good sense that outweighs ambition, any of which might require you to act on the character through the rules of play to persuade her to make the decision you wanted. Or your character may persuade you to follow her story wherever it leads.

WRITING THAT ABSORBS

Not every part of every story emerges from the situation and the interactions of play within the magic circle. Sometimes we have to absorb elements and decisions from outside the magic circle into our fiction. This is especially common during rewrites and new drafts, in response to notes from editors or early readers, but it can also happen during early drafts, when you need to shake up your story because you feel it's too tranquil or the flow of consequences seems clunky.

Thinking about games can help you master this element of fiction writing. Unexpected developments are not only common in role-playing and story games—they are often the crux of play and require that new developments be incorporated into the story fabric, letting them build and guide the tale. If a character with secret information is killed, for example, we might decide that his secret was known to someone else, too, or we might play out the consequences of that secret remaining unknown by the surviving characters.

It's not enough for your story to be absorbing; your writing must also absorb the components you put into it for dramaturgical reasons. Here are a few examples:

- You may need a character to survive a perilous encounter that the rules you've established make difficult to survive.
- You may need an arcane artifact to be somehow mysterious, even to an expert in your world's magical traditions.
- You may simply need a character to explain why they make a suboptimal choice.

How do you exert your authority as the writer in such situations? If an early reader says a character's decision is unbelievable, you may want that character to display some thought or take some action that better aligns with the choice you need them to make. Your characters may need to better express *why* they choose what they choose.

To accomplish that goal, you may need the character to absorb a thought or trait that he or she didn't previously possess—like a bout of skepticism or trust, a sudden doubt, or a flight of fancy. If this corrective, applied and smoothed out like clay over a crack, stands out too much, the artifice is revealed, which is why play experience can be so useful in making course corrections. Such experience exercises improvisational skills for keeping players playing, for keeping things in motion

You decide what information reaches the character and the reader. Your reader is a visitor to the magic circle; your characters probably live there. They make decisions for different reasons than you do as the storyteller. You can put an idea into a character's mind just as the idea was put into yours. Just like real people, characters make mistakes, get unlucky, and act on limited information— which makes it easier for you to influence their decision making when you must. If that seems artificial, remember that nothing on the page originates from anywhere other than your own mind.

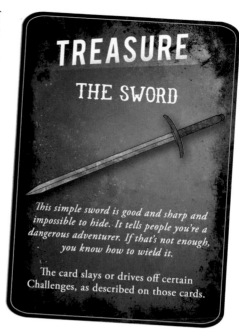

Games and play, especially those aimed at storytelling, help hone improvisational skills and a knack for incorporation (and reincorporation) of unexpected ideas, whether those ideas come from fellow players, the random inputs of dice and cards, or simply unexpected interactions within your own imagination. When creative play gives you an unexpected result that you want to honor—and I hope it does!—relax, listen, and try to incorporate it. You may edit out the idea later, or you might revise the shape and rules of the magic circle to accommodate it, but your story remains yours. Your authority over your tale gives you the power to best cultivate the kind of stories that captivate you. Sometimes that means adding a new path to the Wizard's Tower.

Give your stories and characters enough space to play, and let the surprises emerge.

Turn the page for a writing exercise once you've read this essay and the Wizard's Tower game rules.

THE ROAD NOT TAKEN

Here's an exercise to help you expand your choices and incorporate new ideas while writing. Considering these questions can help you visualize new options and broaden the possibilities within your world. You'll find a lot of questions here, but you don't have to answer them all every time:

1. When you make a meaningful decision for your character—for example, whether or not she puts the sword to her old mentor—hold on to your first idea. Write it down somewhere outside of your story draft.

2. Then write down a second idea and a third. Focus on options that make the decision *harder* for your character, not easier. Tough choices are more dramatic and reveal more about your character once they're made.

You may find it helpful to diagram your ideas. Picture the character standing at an actual crossroads, with each path leading to different consequences.

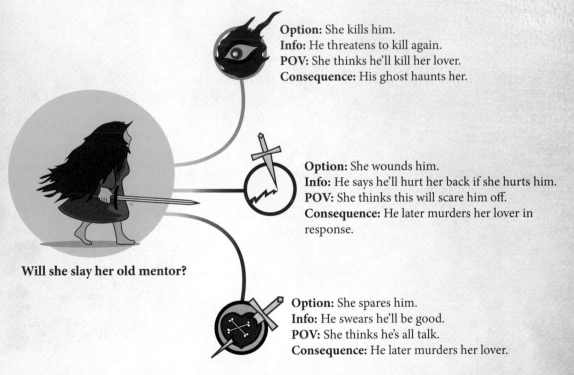

Option: She kills him.
Info: He threatens to kill again.
POV: She thinks he'll kill her lover.
Consequence: His ghost haunts her.

Option: She wounds him.
Info: He says he'll hurt her back if she hurts him.
POV: She thinks this will scare him off.
Consequence: He later murders her lover in response.

Will she slay her old mentor?

Option: She spares him.
Info: He swears he'll be good.
POV: She thinks he's all talk.
Consequence: He later murders her lover.

3. Next, consider how you would communicate each potential option to the character *and* the audience. Does her old mentor promise a compromise or a treasure if she lets him go? Or, for a different major decision, does a talking raven tell your heroine that there's a secret route to the city or does she get the information off a map she buys from a fellow on the side of the road?

Every option is an opportunity to describe how your story's world works and how your character interacts with it. What can we infer about your world if your character trusts the words of a raven? What does it reveal about your character if she gives her now-treacherous old mentor another chance?

4. Consider what happens next for each idea. How would other characters react to your character's choices? What might others—especially the reader!—think about a character who trusts a bird but not her mentor?

Imagine at least one consequence for each action, from your character's perspective. What does *she* imagine will happen if she makes each choice? Does she have enough information for the decision to be difficult for her?

5. Consider what might happen next from an authorial perspective. What actual consequences can result, even if the character doesn't know it? Does the raven's road lead through terrible peril? Does the old mentor honor his promise?
6. Does the reader have more information than the character? Consider the potential of the character's choices to suggest (or threaten) changes to the story, the character, the world (or all of them at once) from the perspective of the reader. Do you want your reader fretting along with the character about the right decision or worrying that the character won't make the choice that might seem clear to the reader?
7. Now, finally, choose which option to incorporate into your story. You might go with your first choice! By exploring a bit down alternate paths, though, you devise details and information that can make your world feel wider than just the path taken by your character. Sometimes, you'll find that your later ideas are the ones that make more sense from your character's perspective. You might decide such options occur to *the character* before they occurred to *you*.

Try this exercise when you're stuck or after you've already done your rough draft writing for the day, so it doesn't interfere with any natural momentum.

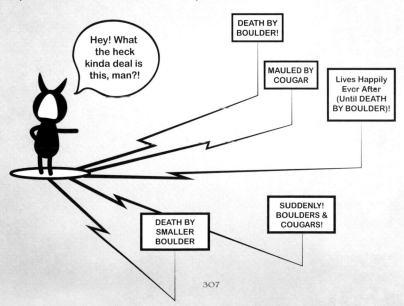

START!

WRITING EXERCISES
(MAYBE YOU WILL FIND THE
ANSWERS YOU WERE LOOKING FOR.)

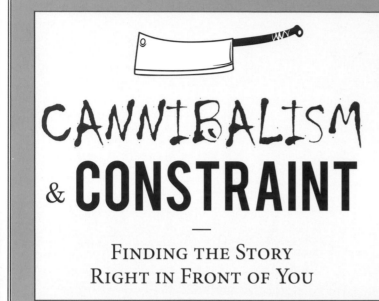

CANNIBALISM & CONSTRAINT

—

FINDING THE STORY
RIGHT IN FRONT OF YOU

Sometimes the best way to start writing is from someone else's inspiration. You can perform the following exercises with any text. The point is to inhabit what you read, to understand it by seeing it in a variety of contexts. You may engage in some cannibalism, but eating your fellow writers isn't against the law, especially if you show some constraint.

Or you could call it a complete meal!

MAKE SEVERAL PHOTOCOPIES OF THE NEXT PAGE BEFORE BEGINNING. READ THE TEXT CAREFULLY. EACH BULLET POINT IS A SEPARATE EXERCISE.

- *Find another story.* Cross out words in the passage, creating a different scene from a different story. Don't worry if you're left with only an opening paragraph to your new story.
- *Find another tone.* Cross out words to create a different mood or texture to the text. Do such deletions for this particular passage change tone in subtle or radical ways? How do you think they might affect the reader?
- *Find another pace.* Cross out phrases and sentences to make the scene move faster while still making sense.
- *Find another voice.* Rewrite the passage in third person. What details from the original did you need to leave out? What new details must be added? How does the rewrite affect our distance from the character?
- *Understand the monster.* Write a version of this passage from the antagonist's point of view that seems sympathetic. (Good luck.)
- *Explore the weight of words.* Rewrite the original passage without using any words that use the letter "e." Do not change the meaning of sentences or their structure. How different is the text now? What changes actually improve the original? (If you curse out loud during this exercise, you can no longer use "i" as well.)
- *Haunt the text.* Retype the passage word for word. What words are you tempted to change? Can you imagine the writer creating the story? What kinds of revisions do you think he made at the sentence and paragraph level to get to his final draft?
- *Make the text your own.* Retype the passage from memory alone. Try to re-create its vividness using your own words. Compare the original to yours. What better choices did you make? What choices seem worse?

For a time the voices of the men in the other rooms were a companionship, and at first I shouted to them now and then, but my voice echoed rather unpleasantly through the long corridors, and had a suggestive way of reverberating around the left wing beside me, and coming out at a broken window at its extremity like the voice of another man. I soon gave up my attempts at conversation, and devoted myself to the task of keeping awake.

It was not easy; why did I eat that lettuce salad at Père Garceau's? I should have known better. It was making me irresistibly sleepy, and wakefulness was absolutely necessary. It was certainly gratifying to know that I could sleep, that my courage was by me to that extent, but in the interests of science I must keep awake. But almost never, it seemed, had sleep looked so desirable. Half a hundred times, nearly, I would doze for an instant, only to awake with a start.

Then I awoke—absolutely. I tried to rise, to cry out. My body was like lead, my tongue was paralyzed. I could hardly move my eyes. And the light was going out. There was no question about that.

Darker and darker yet; little by little the pattern of the paper was swallowed up in the advancing night. A prickling numbness gathered in every nerve, my right arm slipped without feeling from my lap to my side, and I could not raise it—it swung helpless. A thin, keen humming began in my head, like the cicadas on a hillside in September. The darkness was coming fast.

Yes, this was it. Something was subjecting me, body and mind, to slow paralysis. Physically I was already dead. If I could only hold my mind, my consciousness, I might still be safe, but could I? Could I resist the mad horror of this silence, the deepening dark, the creeping numbness?

It had come at last. My body was dead, I could no longer move my eyes. They were fixed in that last look on the place where the door had been, now only a deepening of the dark. Utter night: the last flicker of the lantern was gone. I sat and waited; my mind was still keen, but how long would it last? There was a limit even to the endurance of the utter panic of fear.

Then the end began. In the velvet blackness came two white eyes, milky, opalescent, small, far away—awful eyes, like a dead dream. More beautiful than I can describe, the flakes of white flame moving from the perimeter inward, disappearing in the centre, like a never ending flow of opal water into a circular tunnel. I could not have moved my eyes had I possessed the power: they devoured the fearful, beautiful things that grew slowly, slowly larger, fixed on me, advancing, growing more beautiful, the white flakes of light sweeping more swiftly into the blazing vortices.

Like a hideous and implacable engine of death the eyes of the unknown Horror swelled and expanded until they were close before me, enormous, terrible, and I felt a slow, cold, wet breath propelled with mechanical regularity against my face, enveloping me in its fetid mist, in its charnel-house deadliness.

With ordinary fear goes always a physical terror, but with me in the presence of this unspeakable Thing was only the utter and awful terror of the mind, the mad fear of a prolonged and ghostly nightmare. Again and again I tried to shriek, to make some noise, but physically I was utterly dead. The eyes were close on me—their movement so swift that they seemed to be but palpitating flames, the dead breath was around me like the depths of the deepest sea.

Suddenly a wet, icy mouth, like that of a dead cuttle-fish, fell over mine. The horror began slowly to draw my life from me, but, as enormous and shuddering folds of palpitating jelly swept sinuously around me, my will came back, and I closed with the nameless death that enfolded me.

What was it that I was fighting? My arms sunk through the unresisting mass that was turning me to ice. Moment by moment new folds of cold jelly swept round me, crushing me with the force of Titans. I fought to wrest my mouth from this awful Thing that sealed it, but, if ever I succeeded and caught a single breath, the wet, sucking mass closed over my face again before I could cry out. I think I fought for hours, desperately, insanely, in a silence that was more hideous than any sound—fought until I felt final death at hand, until the memory of all my life rushed over me like a flood, until I no longer had strength to wrench my face from that hellish succubus.

From "No. 252 Rue M. le Prince" by Ralph Adams Cram. Abridged. 1895

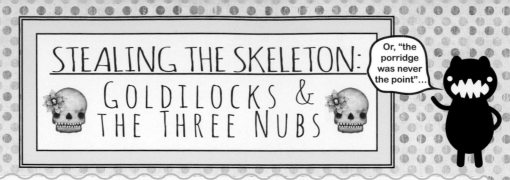

STEALING THE SKELETON: GOLDILOCKS & THE THREE NUBS

Or, "the porridge was never the point"...

Folktales are more diverse than we imagine. Some are powerful story engines that focus on *what happens next*. Others show how the storyteller's cleverness and style are essential to success. Write one of the stories suggested by the three nubs below. Brainstorm more plot twists, as well as other changes. Will your version be humorous or serious? Will the ending be different? Do you need to push beyond the ending given? Compare your version to existing versions by searching for "folktale database" on the Internet.

NUB #1: THE FARMER'S CAT (THE TALE'S IN THE COMPLICATIONS)
After his wife died, a farmer found that trolls came every winter and trashed his house and ate his livestock. One year, a traveling peddler offered the farmer the pick of a "special litter" of cats. Next winter, the trolls noticed that the farmer had a little animal in the house. "What's that? Can we eat it?" the troll leader asked. "It's my cat," the farmer said. "I need it to keep the mice away from the grain that feeds the cattle you eat." So the trolls let him keep the "cat," which was really a bear cub. Every winter the "cat" was bigger and the trolls wanted to eat it. But the farmer found clever ways to stop them. In the fourth year, the bear was big enough to run the trolls off for good.

NUB #2: THE FOX AND THE HEDGEHOG IN THE PIT (THE TALE'S IN THE TELLING)
A fox met a hedgehog the day after raiding a hen house. The hedgehog didn't believe that the fox could eat at his leisure. The smug fox bade the hedgehog come with him to see—and on the way they both fell into a pit dug by the farmer. The hedgehog then pretended he was about to be sick. The fox, disgusted by the vomiting hedgehog, tossed him out of the pit. From the top, the hedgehog admitted it had been a ruse. The fox begged him for help, and the hedgehog said, "You say you're so much smarter—can't you figure it out?" But the hedgehog finally relented and told him to play dead. The farmer would not want anything to do with a stinking corpse and throw him out with the garbage. The fox escaped this way, and ever since, the two have been friends.

NUB #3: THE MÖRKSUGGA AND THE SHEPHERDESS (THE TALE MAY NEED MORE IN THE TELLING) A young shepherdess one summer became haunted by a mörksugga, or ghostly dark sow, who stood in the forest near her fields and watched her. Every night, it stood outside her cottage. When she wished to marry, her youthful suitor was disconcerted by its constant presence. "Only if we can find out why this creature haunts you and make it go away can we marry. Otherwise, what life would our children have with that beast always around?" It took many attempts and much cleverness on the part of the shepherdess, but eventually she rid herself of the creature, and the two were wed and had many children.

CAUSE AND EFFECT:

The Case of the Wheelbarrow Deer, the Severed Finger, and Your Messed-Up Friends

Prior Event → The Present → Aftermath

How Did We Get Here?

Create a believable scenario that gets the reader from deer to finger to friends.

1.

2.

3.

Create a believable scenario that gets the reader from friends to finger to deer.

Where Do We Go From Here?

For each photo, provide at least three paragraphs explaining what led to the scene pictured, what is happening in the image and what happened to all involved (a) immediately after (hours or single day), (b) one month later, (c) one year later. As indicated, also see if you can complete a difficult trifecta by using all three images for past, present, and future, in two different orders. Test your results by showing the images to friends and relating your story. Do they find it plausible? Do they believe the character motivation? Where has your story been more and less successful in terms of cause and effect?

THE SECRET LIFE OF OBJECTS

DEVELOPING A PROFILE

IN A PARAGRAPH OR TWO, BEING SPECIFIC, ANSWER THESE QUESTIONS ABOUT THE OCCUPANT OF THE ROOM. FOLLOW-UP QUESTIONS LIKE "HOW?" OR "WHY?" ARE IMPLIED AND SHOULD BE REFLECTED IN YOUR RESPONSE.

- WHICH OBJECT RELATES TO A PAST TRAUMA?
- WHICH OBJECT IS A RELIC FROM CHILDHOOD?
- WHICH OBJECT IS A GIFT FROM A FRIEND?
- WHY IS THERE A GUN IN THE ROOM?
- WHAT IN THE ROOM SEEMS PARTICULARLY VALUED OR MOST PERSONAL?
- WHAT IS MISSING THAT YOU MIGHT EXPECT TO SEE?
- WHAT SURPRISES YOU THE MOST ABOUT WHAT'S IN THE ROOM?

IMAGE BY GREGORY BOSSERT

LOOKING OVER THE ROOM, WHAT GENERAL OBSERVATIONS WOULD YOU MAKE ABOUT THE OCCUPANT? (FOR EXAMPLE, ARE THEY YOUNG OR OLD? MODERN OR OLD-FASHIONED?)

- THE PERSON RENTING THE ROOM HAS GONE MISSING, AND YOU HAVE BEEN TASKED WITH FINDING THEM. YOUR ONLY CLUES ARE IN THE ROOM. INVESTIGATE AND FILE A REPORT OF AT LEAST 2,000 WORDS. AS PART OF THE REPORT, INCLUDE WHAT THE OBJECTS TELL YOU ABOUT THE EVENTS JUST BEFORE SOMEONE LAST LEFT THE ROOM.

- IMAGINE THAT THREE PEOPLE LIVE IN THIS APARTMENT AND THAT THERE ARE ROOMS YOU CAN'T SEE FROM THIS VANTAGE POINT. WHAT POSSESSIONS BELONG TO EACH OCCUPANT? WHAT IS COMMUNAL PROPERTY? WHAT ITEMS MAY HAVE CAUSED CONFLICTS? IS THERE ANYTHING THAT ONE PERSON REALLY HATES OR LOVES? WRITE AT LEAST 2,000 WORDS ON THE APARTMENT DYNAMIC BASED ON WHAT YOU CAN SEE IN THE ROOM.

VISIT THE ROOM
FOR MORE EXERCISES

SPEAK, DON'T SPEAK: ARE WE THERE YET?

> Shhhh.
> Don't speak.

> Where are we going?

For this nine-part exercise, choose whatever setting you like: crowded or deserted, a city street or a quiet beach. For the first two steps especially there should be no sense of a fictional narrator. Your initial scene for step 1 should be no shorter than 1,500 words and no longer than 3,000 words. Preferably, do not read the next step until you have completed the prior step.

Step 1—Write a scene between two people without dialogue, as if they are being observed from enough of a distance that they can be clearly seen but not heard. Be sure you know beforehand what the two people are talking about and what is happening between them. Be precise in describing their expressions, their physical motions, what they look like, and their environment. Actions and reactions should be shown. Do not rush the description. Remember that you cannot give the reader the characters' thoughts or any direct idea of what they are saying to each other. Use third person only.

Step 2—Write the same scene in dialogue only, with no description or other details. But make sure that the dialogue faithfully synchs with the scene written in step 1. (After you have written this scene, share both versions with readers without telling them you are portraying the same events. Did you successfully convey what you wanted to convey?)

Step 3—Combine your writing from steps 1 and 2, trying not to rewrite your existing text. Do not choose a point of view to inhabit—i.e., do not show either character's thoughts or feelings. Decide what to leave in from the prior steps, and what to take out. When is description needed? When does dialogue replace description? When do the two need to be in balance? Do sections of the scene now need to be cut entirely? Preferably, the result should be not much longer than your version from step 1.

Step 4—Using your step 3 version, separate the dialogue from the description, putting each in a separate document. Do the description and the dialogue make sense to you now without the other element? Ask someone to read the dialogue version who has not read the step 1, 2, or 3 versions. Have them tell you what happens in the scene. Ask someone else to read the description version and do the same thing. Now, go back to your step 3 version and make additional revisions as necessary.

This is a difficult exercise that requires discipline in addition to imagination. If you faithfully followed the instructions, what do you think you learned from this exercise? What do you think you can apply to future stories? Make a list of what you think you learned and compare it to the list online at the Wonderbook website. The website gives you additional, supplementary insight for many of these exercises.

Step 9—Take your favorite version from steps 5 through 8 and again test the scene against your versions in steps 1 through 4. Is there anything you've left out that should be reinstated? Is there any path implied that you veered away from in later drafts? Rewrite the scene from the perspective and with the details that seem to work best.

Step 8—Rewrite the scene from step 7 in first person. How has the change in the motivations of the character changed the way you write the scene now? In variations on step 8, you might introduce a new character who interrupts the conversation, or use a different setting, and learn from how that changes your text.

Step 7—Take your step 4 or 5 version (thinking about what you learned from step 6) and change the scene by changing the attributes of the characters. For example, if one character was honest and not manipulative, make that character the opposite. Or change the overall goals of one character in the scene. This will require changes to the dialogue and the nonverbal cues to reflect the change in character. How does the scene change? Does some of the dialogue get cut entirely?

Step 6—Change the point of view to first person and rewrite the entire scene again. Revisit each decision from step 5 in terms of what you conveyed of thoughts, feelings, and opinions. Think about how the style changes now that the person is directly conveying the scene to a reader. Go back to the results of step 1, step 2, and step 3. Are there sentences or ideas you might need to reinstate because of the switch to first person?

Step 5—Taking your final step 4 version, choose a definite point-of-view and, still in third person, rewrite the scene again. Now you will include one individual's thoughts, feelings, opinions. Do not include flashbacks. Any description of the other person in the scene is from your point-of-view character's perspective, so it will change, too. The result should not be much longer than your version in step 3, so you will face some tough decisions on what to include.

FOUND HISTORY:
Everything's Personal

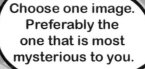

Choose one image. Preferably the one that is most mysterious to you.

A STEP 1 →

Insert the image or an element of it into a story in progress by giving it a new context that fits your story. Write it into your story in a paragraph or two in which it impacts the main character, and then summarize how the presence of this new element might affect the rest of the story.

B STEP 1 →

Write two to four paragraphs on what you think the image portrays, giving a kind of fake history of what is depicted. Treat this as an exercise in straight exposition, not written from a character's viewpoint. It should read more like a piece of nonfiction.

Choose one of two exercises.

Otherwise known as lying a lot.

Transforming something from the real world into fiction is an essential part of how your creativity finds paths into storytelling.

... And Every Thing Is Story

Why, I oughta.

You can jump-start your imagination by making some element of the real world personal or impersonal. If personal elements don't usually enter your fiction, this exercise can help you see how to use them.

STEP 3

Now, take what you've written and apply it to an existing character in one of your stories (not the story from Step 1). Make sure that you alter the context and the nature of the details to be consistent with the character in your story.

A STEP 2

Embed the scene depicted by the image into your own personal history. This image in some way is actually from your past, and part of some moment or event that had importance to you. It may even have impacted your friends and your family, possibly in subtle ways. Write three to five paragraphs with this new part of your history surrounded by real facts about your life. (You may find it useful to test how well you've done by trying out the lie on friends.)

STEP 4 (Optional)

Pull out elements from anything you wrote in steps 1 through 3 and find something you can use as the spark for a new story.

B STEP 2

Think about the complexities of a place, person, or object. Create a more extensive history for this image that showcases it in the context of different time periods. How would things be different decades before or after the photograph was taken? What kinds of layers and contradictions build up and are torn down? Who is forgotten? Who is remembered? Continue to treat this as nonfiction.

No distractions! Work, damn you!

STEP 3

Now, place yourself into the context you've created for the image. Write a first-person entry at a point in the narrative you've created that makes sense. Change details of your life so they fit what you wrote in step 2, but make sure what you come up with is personal. You are you but not you.

Found objects—images or things that you give a new context outside of what they might be in reality—can prove rich fodder for your imagination.

TACTILE EXPERIENCE: GO!
(SIX SEPARATE MINI-EXERCISES)

Taste something nontoxic that is not a food item. Anything. Go lick a pebble if you have to. Then describe that experience in a paragraph.

Walk through a shopping center concentrating on smells. Describe the most unique one in a sentence or two; avoid using the name of the actual smell.

Collect textures by taking a walk and running your hand over whatever you encounter, unless it's dangerous (like a pit bull). Select one or two to use in your latest fiction.

Go to a crowded place. Separate out various conversations. Write down dialogue trying to capture tone, emphasis, etc.

A gecko's sense of touch is incredibly sensitive. Try to imagine how that sensitivity might trump other senses and write a paragraph from a gecko's point of view.

Observe a gecko for a long time. Find and write down one unique behavior that surprises you. Now go run in the rain. Just because you can.

LAST DRINK BIRD HEAD

- Who or what is Last Drink Bird Head?

- Description, anecdote, or story.

- Under 500 words.

- Don't ask—just write.

- Then check your "results" against versions online.

Original paperback design by Matthew Revert

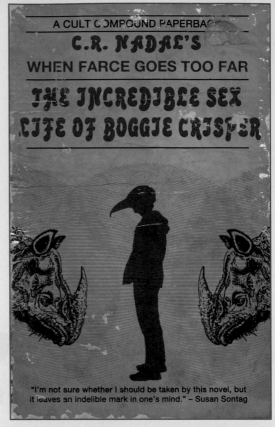

Dome (1968): One of the last in a series of "disaster novels" that shared characteristics with the works of J. G. Ballard but displaying much more warmth and empathy. In the best scenes, Railsea portrayed strong female characters like engineer Sandra Nadal trying to forestall catastrophic environmental damage.

The Incredible Sex Life of Boggie Crisper (1971): Railsea writing a satirical sex romp as "C. R. Nadal." The novel features the erotic theater owner Boggie Crisper, whose outrageous escapades throw into sharp relief both sexist attitudes and new freedoms. Although unflinching, the novel is also very funny and darkly absurd.

DOME Exercise: Write a short summary of the plot of *Dome*. Then write a dramatic scene from the novel as you envision it. Keep in mind any relevant particulars about Railsea, including a style at times clinical but also warm and muscular. Do not revert to your own regular style. Do not write pastiche. Imagine you *are* Railsea. What would she include that you might not? Adding another level of complexity, the character of Sandra Nadal was probably Railsea's alter ego.

SEX LIFE Exercise: Imagine that the novel consists of a series of absurd episodic misadventures, often in bars or at parties. Write a semi-humorous, possibly risqué scene from the novel. Remember that Railsea wrote under a pen name and changed her style—what would *Nadal* focus on? Crisper should be the hero of his own story whether you approve of his behavior or not, but try to provide an undercurrent of detail that pushes against his interpretation of events.

At the liquidation sale for a used bookstore, you spot a paperback from a publisher unknown to you: Cult Compound. Intrigued, you search further and find two others. One is by a Cassandra N. Railsea and two are by a C. R. Nadal. But according to the copyright page, all three are by Railsea. The novels are in terrible shape, missing many pages. Still, you like the writing so you buy them. Later, you search online for information on Railsea/Nadal, without much luck. Ever more curious, you start to read and quickly become mesmerized. One morning, you're sitting at your computer, and some impulse moves you to start writing scenes from the missing pages.

THE FORGOTTEN WORKS OF CASSANDRA N. RAILSEA

ACROSS THE RUBICON OF COMFORT ZONES…

C.B. NADAL'S

The outrageous sequel to The Incredible Sex Life of Boggie Crisperd

A FAMILIAR IN A STRANGE LAND

"Austere where Boggie was boisterous, it's a kind of hymn or dying fall but lovely all the same." - The New York Times Book Review

A Familiar in a Strange Land (1973): Set 15 years after *Sex Life*, this novel has the mournful qualities of a dirge. Lonely and living off the sale of his theater, a much-diminished Boggie has moved into a tiny apartment with his dog. After a mugging he decides to revisit long-abandoned haunts and look up long-lost friends.

FAMILIAR Exercise: Boggie in the second novel has scars, and he's gained experience. The humor in *A Familiar* is more of the wry, self-knowing variety. Write a scene set in the same location as the *Sex Life* exercise, but with only a couple of the same characters. Remember that Boggie may not have seen old friends (ex-friends?) for a while. The actual setting also may have changed quite a bit; certainly, how Boggie interprets it will be different.

RAILSEA Exercise: Write one last scene, from any part of Cassandra N. Railsea's own life. Use your own style. Write it from third person. Include references to her writing based on the details shared here. Make it personal. Search Chapter 1 for additional references of possible use.

Please use third person for the Sex Life *and* Familiar *exercises. First, second, or third person is fine for the* Dome *exercise.*

Cassandra N. Railsea (1944—1989) grew up in rural Minnesota but moved to New York City in 1956 when her parents died in a car crash. Railsea then was raised by her bohemian aunt and uncle, who encouraged her love of writing. "Much of my early writing tried to make sense of my parents' death," she admitted for a 1963 feature on "new talent" for *The Village Voice*. But an equal amount seems to have been devoted to making sense of the world; almost all of her published novels display a keen recognition of the political and cultural underpinnings of society.

The 1960s largely represented Railsea's halcyon years. Despite upheaval, she became a minor celebrity among the literati—a sharp wit with a sharper tongue at parties thrown by editors and more famous writers. Three underrated novels established her reputation: *An Actor Prepares* (1962), *The Rhizome Sphere* (1963), and *Gilgamesh Rises* (1964). She followed these titles with six mid- to late-60s disaster novels that should have catapulted her to stardom. But her publisher, Cult Compound, botched the marketing, and sales entered a downward spiral.

In 1964, Railsea married Charles Tipper, a tall, handsome man who liked her fiction. A structural engineer who came from old money and moved in rarefied circles, Tipper represented a totally different world for Railsea. From the start, Railsea hated "having to go along to fancy parties thrown for politicians and engage in small talk" according to her friend, the author James Sallis. Railsea divorced Tipper after only five years, citing "irreconcilable differences," amid rumors that he had been unfaithful. Many of Railsea's friends believed that the "Boggie Crisper" who starred in her last two novels was an ironic inversion of Tipper.

The literary critic Matthew Cheney may have offered the most cogent analysis of her work. In a personal blog entry, he wrote that "the refined pulpiness of her vision placed her work in between any recognizable marketing niche and led to its obscurity, though today I think we are better positioned to appreciate the soft subversions within her *weltanschauung*. Few people know that the novels she wrote under her own name anticipated the Reagan presidency (*An Actor Prepares*), the rise of the internet (*The Rhizome Sphere*), and the U.S. invasion of Iraq (*Gilgamesh Rises*)." Cheney argues that "her real value, though, wasn't in the perspicacity of her predictions, but rather the way she limned the social forces of her day through the lens of generally entertaining plots without falling into parody or didacticism."

Railsea stopped writing in the 1970s due to depression over both dire sales and criticism from the radical left for not "being outspoken enough," according to Cheney—the latter "a perverse twisting of the facts." The 1980s continued to erase her from the public record. On March 1, 1989, Railsea died of alcohol poisoning, broke and forgotten, in her tiny Brooklyn apartment.

"THE QUICKENING"

For this exercise, you must write a story using the following elements. In any version you write, the rabbit must at some point talk. You may try to explain during the course of the story why the rabbit talks—or you may leave it mysterious. But the rabbit must talk.

Setting: A family-run orange farm in rural Florida during the summer. In addition to the orange groves, an area of forest, and a small lake, the farm includes the following: (1) A Southern-style mansion, sumptuously furnished. This is the owner's house, but he has several properties and does not live there during the summer. (2) The quarters for the migrant workers who pick the oranges. (3) The foreman's bungalow.

Time Period: Any period from the 1940s to the present day.

Length: Between 4,000 and 6,000 words.

Characters: The default viewpoint character is Rachel, who finds Sensio. You can change the viewpoint character to any of the individuals listed below. But whomever you choose as your viewpoint character must be the person who finds the rabbit and feels responsible for it. You are free to make up any additional details about these characters. The story can be written in first, second, or third person.

Sensio—The rabbit, given a name by Rachel. Any other characteristics are up to you. However, Sensio must say, at some point, "I am not a rabbit."

Aunt Etta—She maintains the mansion for the owner while he is away. Aunt Etta has managed to coerce the foreman into reporting directly to her rather than the owner. Originally from Minneapolis, she came south fleeing a bad marriage. She has a strict sense of morality and a mercurial temper, although she can be nice, too. Aunt Etta likes practical solutions to problems.

Art by Ivica Stevanovic.

THE RABBIT MUST SPEAK!

THE FANTASTICAL, YOUR FOCUS, AND MAKING DIFFICULT DECISIONS

Rachel—A twelve-year-old girl in Aunt Etta's charge. Her parents are dead; Rachel's father was Aunt Etta's brother. Rachel's bulky build makes her awkward at this age. At school, she is a bit of a loner. Rachel is not really a tomboy but is often perceived as such. She likes to play with the workers' children, although she isn't close friends with them.

The Foreman—He runs the orange groves but reports to Aunt Etta. He and Aunt Etta may have a physical relationship. The foreman is a tall Mexican originally from Tijuana. He is not named because Rachel doesn't know him very well.

A. C. Pittman—The owner of the farm, absent during the events of the story.

Minor characters: (1) The photographer who takes pictures of Aunt Etta with Sensio. (2) The woman from the Ringling Brothers Circus who comes to see the talking rabbit. (3) Reporters from local newspapers. (4) The orange-grove workers and their children.

Plot: Rachel finds or is given a strange rabbit. She brings the rabbit home, at first hiding it from Aunt Etta. When Aunt Etta finds out, she punishes Rachel by relegating her to her room. But she does not take away the rabbit, and that night Sensio speaks for the first time. Now Rachel is even more determined to keep the rabbit, but she hides the fact that it can talk.

Then one night Aunt Etta hears Sensio talking, and everything gets worse. Aunt Etta sees potential for making money from a talking rabbit. At first she is nice to Sensio. But when the rabbit won't speak in front of reporters, she becomes angry. Nothing comes of a visit by a woman from the Ringling Brothers Circus, either, but Rachel thinks she sees an unspoken message pass between the visitor and the rabbit. Meanwhile, Aunt Etta has ever more sumptuous and bizarre dinners in the mansion, trying to woo Sensio—until one night, frustrated, she serves Sensio rabbit stew. (To decide: How does Sensio react?)

Rachel becomes concerned for Sensio's safety. One day, Aunt Etta hires a photographer—she hopes to send images around to magazines. She ties Sensio to a stake, after dressing him up in a child's clothes. Sensio still won't speak. Aunt Etta flies into a rage after the photographer leaves, and begins kicking Sensio—hard. Rachel believes that Aunt Etta will kill Sensio, and she shoves Aunt Etta into the dirt. When Aunt Etta turns on her, Rachel hits her with a rock.

Does Aunt Etta live or die? Is Rachel blamed? What does the foreman think about all of this? Does Sensio ever talk again? The ending and the order of events in the story are both up to you.

To Think About: How do decisions like which person should be your viewpoint character change the story? How does how you describe the rabbit's personality or its speech change the tone of the story? Visit the Wonderbook website for a detailed discussion once you've completed your version.

THE LEONARDO VARIATIONS

The following notes describe "The Leonardo," a short story by the classic twentieth-century writer Vladimir Nabokov. Writing your own version of this story helps to test various aspects of your writing. For those of you who usually include fantasy or the supernatural in your work, this exercise gives you an additional opportunity: to create fiction without those elements in it. Too often beginning writers use fantasy to "get out of a jam" or to end a story in a fireworks display of sorts—there's the dragon! Here, you have no such crutch. Only read Nabokov's story after you have finished the assignment.

SETTING

A middle-to-lower-class tenement building in a large, unnamed city somewhere in Europe. (You can change the location only.) It's in a bad part of town.

TIME

Anytime from the 1930s to the present day.

CHARACTERS

"Gustav" – a large man who has a furniture-moving job

"Anthony" – Gustav's thin, currently unemployed brother

"Joanna" – Gustav's girlfriend; somewhat gregarious

"Roman" – a new tenant who is not sociable, dresses immaculately (double-breasted jackets, etc.), has the light on in his apartment all night, is lean, and walks with an odd gait.

Both Gustav and Anthony are somewhat thuggish; you get the sense they might be petty criminals. The names here differ from "The Leonardo" slightly to aid you in diverging from the existing version.

NOTE: You can change the gender or ethnicity of the characters (but you can't change the plot).

PLOT

- Roman moves in. The brothers, who largely hang out around the building, cannot stand that Roman keeps to himself.
- They decide to go over as new neighbors, and Gustav more or less forces Roman to buy something worthless from him at a high price, just as a lark.
- But Roman remains closed to them, almost seeming to ignore them, and this continues to irritate the brothers.
- Small escalations occur. Late one night, Anthony, at Gustav's urging, goes up and knocks on Roman's door; the light goes out, but Roman doesn't answer. Another time on the stairs, they jostle him and knock off his hat.
- Nothing phases Roman. So they force him to go to a bar/pub with them and Joanna. Joanna flirts with Roman. Gustav gets Roman drunk. It's a moment where Roman almost seems set to become one of them. But then he retreats into his shell again.
- The brothers are by this time obsessed, especially Gustav. They step up the torments. Roman endures it all.
- At Gustav's urging, Joanna convinces Roman to take her to the movies.
- Afterward, as they're walking down an alley, the brothers confront Roman, and Gustav asks Roman what he's doing with Joanna, his girlfriend.
- Roman's answer is unconvincing to Gustav, and Gustav knifes Roman and leaves him for dead.
- After Roman's death, they finally find out what Roman was doing in his apartment, what his profession was, etc. It's up to you how much you reveal, and the nature of what's revealed.

POV

Limited omniscient, through the two brothers. As if you're a person who witnessed all of this, but always through the two brothers. You can't see into Roman's head, though. You can also choose one of the two brothers if you prefer, or Joanna.

LENGTH

Between 4,000 and 6,000 words.

IMPORTANT POINTS

- Use all five senses to make the setting *real* while simultaneously making the characters and their motivations realistic and immediate.
- NO science fiction or fantasy element is allowed; the one "speculative" element is where and when you set the story.
- You may change any *detail* mentioned in the plot points above. (For example, knocking Roman's hat off is the kind of detail that can and should change. Or, the pub/bar scene can take place somewhere else.) However, the basic plot (mysterious stranger, brothers poking at him, stranger ignores, escalation, escalation, escalation, death, etc.) must remain the same.
- The story should consist of a series of scenes joined by transitional summary.
- The scenes can and should use dialogue, but not out of proportion to the description.
- If you write a story that is all or mostly dialogue, you have failed to complete the assignment. Your story should depend mostly on the narrative storytelling.
- Tone and motivation are up to you. You should make this your story as much as possible.
- After writing your story, visit the Wonderbook website for spoilers about why this exercise is effective. Think about how having a ready-made structure helped and hindered you.

FANTASY

Stages of Writer Development

AWWW. IT'S A MESS!

AWWW. IT'S ADORABLE!

EMBRYONIC

writes fragments

can't finish things

characters fall
off cliffs a lot

has trouble coming
up with ideas

too in love with adverbs
and heroic speeches

feels helpless, but looks
at crapola published and
says "one day I can do better
than *that*"

TRANSITIONAL

tries a little bit
of everything

has no control

can at least finish
a story now

lacks aesthetic
harmony

feels helpless with wild
leaps of ego/confidence

crushed by realizing
stories are often cliched

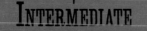

COMFORTABLE WITH MONSTROUS NATURE

BEGINS TO LOOK NORMAL

Intermediate

begins to achieve control
and exhibit unique features

has control but not
always consistent

has better sense of style/voice
and what works better or worse

work more cohesive and focused

hates adverbs and heroic speeches

feels helpless but smugly confident
about future, and no longer happy
with a personal rejection

Advanced

assured and able to
achieve complex effects

has set and productive work habits

more often frozen by multitude
of possible approaches rather
than paucity of them

rarely engages in cliché or
stereotype except for effect

ambivalent about
adverbs and heroic speeches

feels helpless and confident at
same time; realizes quest for
mastery never ends

A composite rendering of
the author and artist, by
Jeremy Zerfoss.

ABOUT THE AUTHOR AND ARTIST

Over a twenty-five-year career, **Jeff VanderMeer** has published hundreds of short stories and dozens of books. He has lectured at MIT and the Library of Congress, in addition to teaching workshops all over the world. Previous nonfiction titles include *The Steampunk Bible* and *Booklife: Strategies & Survival Tips for the Twenty-first Century Writer*. Most recently, he sold his Southern Reach trilogy (*Annihilation*, *Authority*, and *Acceptance*) to Farrar, Straus and Giroux (U.S.), HarperCollins Canada, and The Fourth Estate (U.K.). Paramount Pictures and Scott Rudin Productions have acquired the movie rights. His novels have been translated into more than twenty languages. A three-time winner of the World Fantasy Award, VanderMeer has been a finalist for the Nebula, Hugo, Philip K. Dick, and Shirley Jackson Awards. With his wife, the noted editor Ann VanderMeer, he has edited several iconic fiction anthologies, such as *The Weird: A Compendium of Strange and Dark Stories*. VanderMeer serves as the co-director of Shared Worlds, a unique teen science fiction/fantasy writing camp located at Wofford College in South Carolina. He lives in Tallahassee, Florida.

Jeremy Zerfoss first became interested in art and design at the age of 15 because of an overexposure to manga. There followed an interest in making cute beasties, including murals at local schools. He has for years been involved with Scouting and local design in the Las Vegas area, and first gained exposure through the deviant art community. Zerfoss is heavily influenced by certain strands of pop art, but also superflat, repurposed culture, and his location—specifically, the Mojave Desert. He can be found devouring books when he's not working on his own art projects. He is best known for his innovative and bold line of book covers for Cheeky Frawg Books. His cover for Swedish writer Karin Tidbeck's first English-language short story collection, *Jagannath*, was featured on many national media sites. He has also done art and design work for Symantec, *BullSpec Magazine*, Shared Worlds and RDS Press, as well as various local charities and businesses. Galleries of Zerfoss's art have been featured on a number of sites, including io9.com. He lives in Las Vegas, Nevada, as far away from Jeff as he can get.

ACKNOWLEDGMENTS

First and foremost, thank you to everyone at
Abrams for their faith in this project. Special
thanks to my editor David Cashion, and to everyone there who worked on Wonderbook. Thanks
also to the acquiring editor, Caitlin Kenney, as well
as Howard Morhaim. Thanks beyond measure to Jeremy
Zerfoss for his heroic work on the art; over an almost
two-year span he worked tirelessly on this project. Major
thanks as well to everyone who contributed original artwork;
in particular, Ivica Stevanovic's multiple contributions went beyond
the call of duty. Thanks to my wife, Ann, for managerial, administrative, and
creative support during this time—I couldn't have done it without you. Thanks
to my agent Sally Harding as well as Ron Eckel, Suzanne Brandreth, and everyone at
the Cooke Agency for taking such good care of my career while I finished this book.
Further thanks to Matthew Cheney, who served as the official consultant on the
instructional text, and without whom this book would have been much the poorer.
Others who made significant contributions include: Gregory Bossert, Adam Mills,
Desirina Boskovich, and Teri Goulding. Thanks to my first readers—you know who
you are. Finally, thanks so much to all of the contributors—this book is so
enriched by your presence.

Jeremy Zerfoss would like to thank: my mother, Linda, for her tireless support,
Aunt Georganne, for her help and advice, Jessey, Leah, and Darren for being the
best family ever, as well as my grandmothers and extended family, who gave me
love and books and creepy things over the years. Thanks as well to the Cheeky
Frawg horde, and everyone who offered criticism and advice and wished us
well: Russ, Nate, Angel, Adam for your patience/angst when I disappeared, the
talented people in the texture community and, finally, Jeff and Ann, who showed
me a path through a forest they had never taken and invited me along.
It's been a wonderful journey.

CREDITS

The Povkin, belly full of Wonderbook, sallies forth, unafraid.

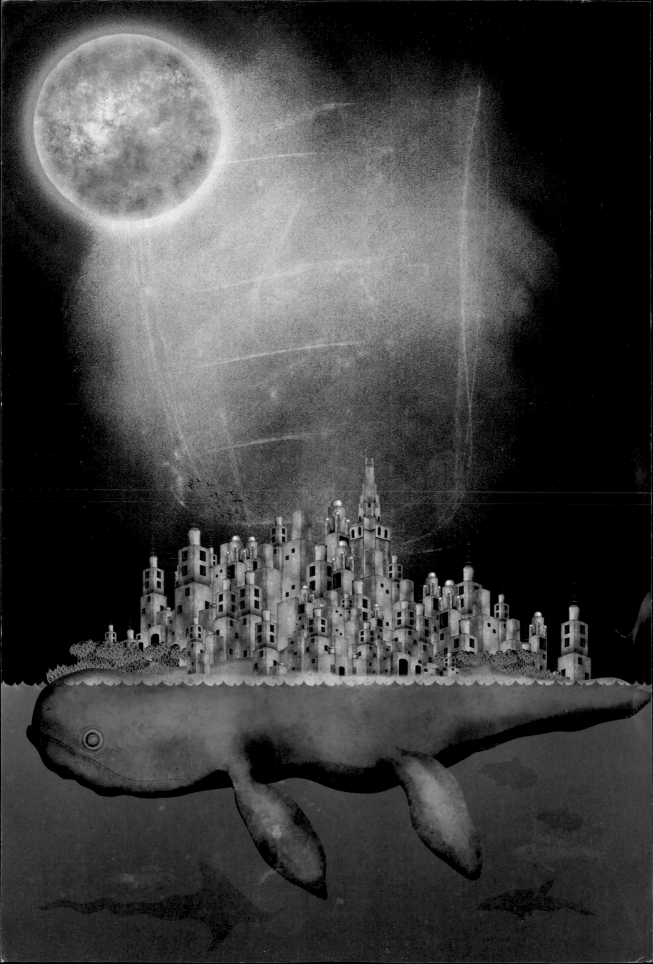